Digital Twin Technology for Solar Concentrators

Scrivener Publishing
100 Cummings Center, Suite 541J
Beverly, MA 01915-6106

Publishers at Scrivener
Martin Scrivener (martin@scrivenerpublishing.com)
Phillip Carmical (pcarmical@scrivenerpublishing.com)

Digital Twin Technology for Solar Concentrators

Edited by

Surajit Mondal

Paramjeet Singh Paliyal

and

Sachin Sharma

Scrivener Publishing

WILEY

This edition first published 2026 by John Wiley & Sons, Inc., 111 River Street, Hoboken, NJ 07030, USA and Scrivener Publishing LLC, 100 Cummings Center, Suite 541J, Beverly, MA 01915, USA

For more information about Scrivener publications please visit www.scrivenerpublishing.com.

Wiley Global Headquarters
111 River Street, Hoboken, NJ 07030, USA

For details of our global editorial offices, customer services, and more information about Wiley products visit us at www.wiley.com.

The manufacturer's authorized representative according to the EU General Product Safety Regulation is Wiley-VCH GmbH, Boschstr. 12, 69469 Weinheim, Germany, e-mail: Product_Safety@wiley.com.

Library of Congress Cataloging-in-Publication Data

ISBN 978-1-394-39017-5

Cover image: Generated with AI using Adobe Firefly
Cover design by Russell Richardson

Set in size of 11pt and Minion Pro by Manila Typesetting Company, Makati, Philippines

Printed in the USA

10 9 8 7 6 5 4 3 2 1

Contents

Preface

The global transition toward sustainable and intelligent energy systems has accelerated the need for advanced technologies capable of improving the efficiency, reliability, and operational flexibility of renewable energy infrastructure. Among the various renewable energy technologies, solar concentrator systems have emerged as a promising solution for large-scale thermal energy harvesting and power generation. Simultaneously, the rapid evolution of Industry 4.0 technologies, particularly Digital Twin (DT) technology, artificial intelligence, Internet of Things (IoT), cloud computing, and advanced analytics, has transformed the way complex engineering systems are monitored, controlled, and optimized. The convergence of these domains has opened new avenues for developing intelligent, adaptive, and highly efficient solar energy systems.

This book, *Digital Twin Technology for Solar Concentrators*, aims to provide a comprehensive and interdisciplinary understanding of how digital twin frameworks can be integrated with solar concentrator technologies to enhance system performance, predictive maintenance, operational control, thermal management, and long-term sustainability. The book brings together contributions from researchers, academicians, and industry professionals working in the fields of renewable energy, digital technologies, artificial intelligence, thermal engineering, and smart energy systems.

The primary objective of this book is to bridge the gap between traditional solar thermal technologies and modern cyber-physical systems. The chapters included in this volume discuss both the theoretical foundations and practical implementations of digital twins in concentrated solar power (CSP) systems and associated renewable energy applications. The content has been carefully organized to provide readers with a gradual progression from the fundamentals of solar thermal systems and solar concentrators to advanced concepts involving digital twin architectures, machine learning integration, real-time monitoring, intelligent optimization, and predictive analytics.

The opening chapters introduce the fundamentals of solar thermal technology and digital twin concepts, establishing the scientific and engineering basis necessary for understanding the subsequent discussions. Detailed coverage is provided on various solar concentrator configurations, including parabolic trough collectors, linear Fresnel systems, heliostat tower systems, parabolic dish concentrators, and Scheffler solar concentrators. The operational principles, design considerations, performance characteristics, and existing technological challenges associated with these systems are critically examined.

A major focus of this book is the integration of IoT-enabled sensing systems, artificial intelligence, and cloud-based computational frameworks with solar concentrators. The contributors demonstrate how digital twins can facilitate real-time synchronization between physical systems and virtual replicas, enabling continuous performance assessment, fault diagnosis, optimization of tracking mechanisms, thermal efficiency enhancement, and intelligent energy management. Several chapters also explore the role of machine learning algorithms, neural networks, predictive maintenance strategies, and advanced data analytics in improving the operational reliability and lifecycle management of renewable energy systems.

In addition to solar concentrator applications, the book includes broader discussions on digital twin applications in renewable energy systems, energy storage technologies, smart monitoring infrastructures, AI-driven optimization frameworks, and intelligent cyber-physical energy networks. These discussions highlight the expanding scope of digital twin technology beyond conventional industrial applications and its growing significance in achieving sustainable and resilient energy systems.

This volume also presents multiple case studies, experimental investigations, simulation methodologies, and real-world implementation strategies related to solar concentrators and digital twin systems. The inclusion of practical examples and analytical models is intended to assist researchers and engineers in understanding the challenges associated with deployment, calibration, interoperability, data acquisition, model fidelity, and cybersecurity within digital twin environments.

The editors sincerely hope that this book will serve as a valuable reference for researchers, postgraduate students, faculty members, industry professionals, and policymakers working in renewable energy systems, smart manufacturing, energy informatics, thermal engineering, and sustainable technology development. It is also expected to inspire future research directions in intelligent solar energy systems, hybrid renewable infrastructures, and AI-assisted energy management platforms.

The successful completion of this book would not have been possible without the dedicated efforts of all contributing authors who shared their expertise and valuable research contributions. We express our heartfelt gratitude to all chapter authors for their commitment, patience, and scholarly support throughout the preparation of this volume. We would also like to extend our sincere appreciation to the publishing team at Scrivener Publishing and Wiley for their continuous guidance, technical assistance, and encouragement during the editorial and production process. Their professional support played a significant role in bringing this work to completion.

Finally, we acknowledge the support provided by our respective institutions, colleagues, research collaborators, and family members whose encouragement and motivation have been invaluable throughout this journey. We hope that this book contributes meaningfully to the advancement of digital twin-enabled renewable energy technologies and supports the global pursuit of sustainable, intelligent, and low-carbon energy solutions.

Dr. Surajit Mondal
Energy Cluster, School of Advanced Engineering, UPES, Dehradun, Uttarakhand, India
Dr. Paramjeet Singh Paliyal
Department of Electrical and Electronics Engineering, College of Engineering, COER University, Roorkee, Uttarakhand, India
Dr. Sachin Sharma
Mechanical Cluster, School of Advanced Engineering and Centre Head-BEST, UPES Dehradun, Uttarakhand, India

1

Solar Thermal Technology – A Brief

Paramjeet Singh Paliyal[1]* and Surajit Mondal[2]

[1]*Department of Electrical and Electronics Engineering, College of Engineering, COER University, Roorkee, Uttarakhand, India*
[2]*Energy Cluster, School of Advanced Engineering, UPES, Dehradun, Uttarakhand, India*

Abstract

Solar thermal technology represents a mature and versatile approach for harnessing solar energy by converting incident solar radiation into usable heat for residential, commercial, industrial, and utility-scale applications. Unlike photovoltaic systems that directly generate electricity, solar thermal systems capture and transfer thermal energy through collectors to a working fluid, enabling applications such as domestic water heating, space heating, industrial process heat, desalination, and electricity generation via thermodynamic cycles. This chapter provides a comprehensive technical overview of solar thermal technology, beginning with its historical evolution and progressing to modern collector configurations including flat-plate collectors, evacuated tube collectors, and advanced concentrating solar power (CSP) systems such as parabolic troughs, solar towers, and dish concentrators.

The discussion emphasizes the thermodynamic principles governing energy absorption, heat transfer, and system efficiency, while highlighting the critical role of thermal energy storage (TES) in enhancing dispatchability and grid reliability. Storage media such as molten salts and phase change materials are examined in the context of extending operational hours beyond solar availability and supporting peak demand management. The chapter further explores multi-sectoral applications of solar thermal systems, from decentralized building-scale solutions to large-scale power generation plants integrated with storage.

Key technical challenges—including capital cost, land use, cooling requirements, and competition from rapidly declining photovoltaic technologies—are critically assessed. Ongoing advancements in absorber coatings, high-temperature materials, nanofluid-based heat transfer media, and hybrid integration with other

**Corresponding author*: paramjeet29895@gmail.com

Surajit Mondal, Paramjeet Singh Paliyal and Sachin Sharma (eds.) Digital Twin Technology for Solar Concentrators, (1–6) © 2026 Scrivener Publishing LLC

renewable systems are discussed as pathways to improved performance and economic viability. Environmental benefits, including reduced greenhouse gas emissions and enhanced energy security, are analyzed within the broader framework of global decarbonization and sustainable development.

By synthesizing technological fundamentals, system architectures, storage integration, and future innovation trajectories, this chapter establishes solar thermal technology as a pivotal component of modern renewable energy systems and a strategic enabler in the transition toward low-carbon energy infrastructure.

Keywords: Solar thermal technology, concentrated solar power (CSP), thermal energy storage (TES), solar collectors, renewable energy systems, solar heat transfer, decarbonization, sustainable energy

Solar thermal technology is one of the most promising and mature approaches to harnessing renewable energy from the sun. Unlike photovoltaic systems that directly convert solar radiation into electricity, solar thermal systems capture sunlight as heat energy and use it for various applications such as water heating, space heating, industrial process heat, and even electricity generation through thermodynamic cycles. The principle of solar thermal technology relies on the absorption of solar radiation by collectors, which transfer the captured heat to a working fluid like water, air, or oil. This heat can then be directly used or stored for later use. Over the years, the technology has evolved from simple flat-plate collectors for domestic water heating to advanced concentrated solar power (CSP) plants capable of generating hundreds of megawatts of electricity [1].

The history of solar thermal technology can be traced back to ancient civilizations, where magnifying glasses and reflective surfaces were used to concentrate sunlight for fire or heating purposes. In the modern era, scientific developments in the 19th and 20th centuries laid the foundation for practical solar thermal devices [2]. The oil crises of the 1970s provided further momentum to research and the commercialization of solar technologies as countries sought alternatives to fossil fuels. Today, solar thermal systems are integral to renewable energy portfolios worldwide, with applications ranging from residential rooftops to utility-scale power plants. Their importance is growing rapidly in the context of climate change and energy security, as they offer a clean, abundant, and sustainable source of energy [3].

At the heart of solar thermal systems are collectors that absorb and transfer solar energy. The most common type is the flat-plate collector, which consists of a dark-colored absorber plate enclosed in a transparent cover to trap heat. These are widely used for domestic water heating and can achieve water temperatures of 60–80°C. For higher temperature applications, evacuated tube collectors are employed, which reduce heat losses by surrounding the absorber tubes with vacuum insulation. Evacuated tube systems can reach temperatures above 100°C and are particularly effective in colder climates. For industrial-scale heat and power generation, concentrating collectors such as parabolic troughs, parabolic dishes, Fresnel reflectors, and solar power towers are used [4]. These systems employ mirrors or lenses to concentrate sunlight onto a receiver, raising the temperature of the working fluid to several hundred degrees Celsius, which can then drive steam turbines or other heat engines for electricity generation.

One of the significant advantages of solar thermal technology is its ability to incorporate thermal energy storage (TES). Unlike photovoltaic systems that require costly batteries to store electricity, thermal energy can be stored relatively inexpensively using materials such as molten salts, phase change materials, or insulated water tanks [5]. This enables solar thermal plants, especially CSP systems, to provide electricity even after sunset or during cloudy periods, thus improving grid reliability and dispatchability. For example, molten salt storage can retain heat at temperatures exceeding 500°C for several hours, allowing CSP plants to generate electricity during peak demand periods when solar radiation is unavailable. This capability provides solar thermal systems with a competitive edge over other intermittent renewable energy sources [6].

Applications of solar thermal technology are diverse and extend across multiple sectors. In residential and commercial buildings, solar water heaters are a cost-effective and environmentally friendly alternative to electric or gas water heaters. In colder regions, solar space heating systems can significantly reduce fuel consumption in buildings. In agriculture, solar thermal systems are employed for crop drying, greenhouse heating, and water desalination [7]. In industrial processes, where a large share of energy demand is in the form of heat, solar thermal systems can replace or supplement conventional boilers, reducing carbon emissions. For electricity generation, CSP plants have been deployed successfully in countries such as Spain, the United States, and India, providing utility-scale renewable power with storage capabilities. Hybrid systems, which combine solar thermal with other renewable or conventional sources, are also being developed to enhance efficiency and reduce costs [8].

Despite its advantages, solar thermal technology faces several challenges that limit its widespread adoption. The initial capital cost of installing solar thermal systems, especially CSP plants, is relatively high compared to other renewable options such as wind and photovoltaics. Land requirements for large solar fields, water consumption for cooling in CSP plants, and site-specific factors such as solar resource availability and climate also pose constraints. Moreover, technological advancements in photovoltaic cells, particularly with the steep decline in PV costs, have intensified competition. However, ongoing research is addressing these issues by developing innovative collector designs, advanced coatings for absorbers, improved storage materials, and hybrid integration with other energy systems. Government policies, subsidies, and international collaborations are also playing an important role in scaling up solar thermal deployment [9].

The environmental benefits of solar thermal technology are substantial. Since it primarily relies on sunlight, a clean and inexhaustible resource, solar thermal systems produce negligible greenhouse gas emissions during operation. Unlike fossil fuel-based systems, they do not release harmful pollutants such as sulfur dioxide or nitrogen oxides, thus contributing to improved air quality. Furthermore, the technology reduces dependence on non-renewable energy resources, contributing to energy security and sustainable development. By integrating solar thermal technology into energy systems, nations can make significant strides toward decarbonization and climate change mitigation targets.

In the future, solar thermal technology is expected to play a crucial role in the global energy transition. Innovations such as high-efficiency collectors, nanofluid-based heat transfer media, and advanced thermal storage systems are being researched to enhance performance and reduce costs. Coupling solar thermal with hydrogen production *via* thermochemical cycles presents an exciting avenue for generating clean fuels. Similarly, integration with district heating networks and smart energy systems can unlock new opportunities for urban sustainability. With supportive policy frameworks, financial incentives, and international collaboration, solar thermal technology can achieve greater market penetration and contribute significantly to global renewable energy capacity.

In conclusion, solar thermal technology represents a mature, versatile, and sustainable solution for harnessing the sun's abundant energy. From simple domestic water heating applications to large-scale electricity generation with storage, it offers a wide spectrum of possibilities to reduce reliance on fossil fuels and mitigate climate change. While challenges such as cost and competition with photovoltaics remain, continuous advancements in materials, design, and hybridization are strengthening the prospects of solar thermal systems. As the world seeks cleaner energy pathways, solar thermal technology is poised to remain a vital component of the renewable energy landscape, bridging the gap between intermittent resources and reliable energy supply.

AI disclosure statement: The author confirms that no artificial intelligence (AI)-generated content or AI-assisted writing tools were used in the preparation of this chapter (including summaries and the abstract). All text, analysis, and conclusions are the result of the author's original work.

References

1. Paliyal, P.S. and Mondal, S., Parabolic Solar Collectors for Sustainable Water Treatment: A Review of Applications, Advancements and Future Directions. *Curr. Opin. Environ. Sci. Health*, 100691, 2025.
2. Paliyal, P.S. and Mondal, S., An analysis of a cross-finned receiver for Scheffler-type solar collectors to optimize solar heating efficiency for direct water heating. *Int. J. Energy Water Resour.*, 1–20, 2025.
3. Paliyal, P.S. and Mondal, S., Optimization of solar energy systems using GSM-based real-time data acquisition in hilly regions. *J. Renew. Sustain. Energy.*, 17, 6, 2025.
4. Paliyal, P.S., Menon, S.K., Mondal, S., Thapa, V., Location Analysis and Environmental Validation for Installation of Hybrid Solar-Wind Energy Generation System in Hilly Areas of Uttarakhand: Study Toward Forecasting. *Forecasting Methods for Renewable Power Generation*, 21–47, 2025.
5. Gairola, M., Paliyal, P.S., Kashyap, M., Bahuguna, N.K., Modeling of Solar Emergency System in Power Station to Mitigate Blackout, in: *Proceedings of Integrated Intelligence Enable Networks and Computing*, K.K. Singh Mer, V.B. Semwal, V. Bijalwan, and R.G. Crespo, (eds.), pp. 19–26, Springer Singapore, Singapore, 2021,
6. Paliyal, P.S., Mondal, S., Layek, S., Kuchhal, P., Pandey, J.K., Automatic solar tracking system: A review pertaining to advancements and challenges in the current scenario. *Clean Energy*, 8, 6, 237–262, 2024.
7. Mondal, A., *et al.*, Analysing solid residential fuel usage patterns in rural and urban slums of Delhi: Implications for pollution reduction and sustainable practices. *Energy Sustain. Dev.*, 80, 101460, 2024.
8. Paliyal, P.S., Mondal, S., Pandey, J.K., An Analysis of Springwater Parameter Status for Different Locations in the Rural Hilly Garhwal Region of Uttarakhand. *Environ. Claims J.*, 1–35, 2024.
9. Kudapa, V.K., Paliyal, P.S., Mondal, A., Mondal, S., A critical review of fabrication strategies, separation techniques, challenges, and future prospects for the hydrogen separation membrane. *Fusion Sci. Technol.*, 80, 7, 803–825, 2024.

2

Introduction to Digital Twin Technology

Sanidhya Sarthak

Department of SoCS, Computer Science and Engineering, University of Petroleum and Energy Studies (UPES), Dehradun, Uttarakhand, India

Abstract

Digital twin (DT) technology enables the creation of dynamic virtual replicas of physical systems to support real-time monitoring, simulation, control, and predictive analytics. A typical DT framework includes sensor networks and IoT devices for data acquisition, high-fidelity physical or data-driven models, computation and communication platforms (cloud or edge), and bidirectional data exchange for continuous synchronization.

In the context of concentrating solar power (CSP) systems—such as parabolic troughs, dishes, linear Fresnel collectors, and heliostat fields—DTs offer significant benefits for system design, control strategy development, performance monitoring, fault diagnosis, and predictive maintenance. Optimization techniques include simulation-driven thermal efficiency enhancement, anomaly detection, AI/ML integration for predictive control, and cost reduction strategies.

This chapter presents case studies highlighting DT implementation in solar energy systems, including a validated DT of a Fresnel collector and a machine learning–based DT for multistage thermal storage. Key performance equations are expressed in SI units, supported by figures showing DT architectures and solar field layouts. The chapter concludes with challenges related to data integration, model fidelity, real-time analytics, and cybersecurity, and outlines future research directions such as standardized DT frameworks, XR and 5G integration, and advanced control algorithms for next-generation solar energy systems.

***Keywords*:** Digital twin, solar concentrator, CSP, parabolic trough, solar tower, fresnel, parabolic dish, optimization

Email: sanidhya.sarthak@gmail.com

Surajit Mondal, Paramjeet Singh Paliyal and Sachin Sharma (eds.) Digital Twin Technology for Solar Concentrators, (7–28) © 2026 Scrivener Publishing LLC

2.1 Introduction to Digital Twin Technology

A digital twin (DT) is a digital copy or virtual representation of a physical system or asset, with bidirectional data flow enabling continuous synchronization between the physical and virtual counterparts. Introduced in the 1960s (e.g. by NASA's Apollo program), DTs have become central to Industry 4.0 and Cyber-Physical Systems (CPS). The DT concept integrates real-time sensor data, historical data, physics models, and analytics to simulate the current and predictive behavior of the physical system. In operation, DTs can be "discovered" and queried within an IoT ecosystem, with abstract information models linking data sources and services. The key capabilities of DTs include condition monitoring, simulation-based testing, predictive analytics, and what-if scenario analysis for maintenance and design.

A formal definition of a digital twin can be expressed as:

$$DT = (P, D, S, AI, I)$$

where:

- P = Physical asset, system, or process
- D = Digital representation of PPP
- S = Sensing and data acquisition layer
- AI = Artificial intelligence and analytics layer
- I = Interaction and visualization interface

2.2 Core Components of Digital Twin Technology

The foundational components of a digital twin can be organized as a cycle of data and modeling stages. First, real-world data acquisition is performed by sensors, IoT devices, and control systems attached to the physical asset. These devices stream telemetry (e.g. position, temperature, pressure) into data platforms. Second, a virtual model (often a software simulation or finite-element model) represents the physical object's geometry and behavior. Third, a simulation/analysis engine uses the model and incoming data to run experiments, assess performance, or predict future states. Finally, a feedback/control loop applies insights or control signals from the virtual space back to the physical asset (e.g. adjusting a controller set point). In practice, this workflow is typically deployed on IT infrastructure (cloud or edge servers) that ensures continuous synchronization. Thus, common DT architectures comprise the following modules:

- **Physical Asset and Sensors:** The physical entity (machine, vehicle, building, etc.) instrumented with sensors/actuators. Sensors capture real-time operational data (*via* IoT connectivity), which is streamed to the twin. Actuators may be triggered based on twin outputs.
- **Communication/Connectivity:** Networks (wired/wireless) and data platforms that transport sensor data to computation systems. This often involves edge devices or gateways, and cloud/IIoT platforms for data ingestion.
- **Virtual Model (Simulation Engine):** A software representation of the asset, including its structural geometry and behavioral model (material properties, dynamics, logic). High-fidelity physics models, CAD models, or reduced-order models form the basis of the DT's logic. These models are purpose-built to integrate data into simulations and are continuously updated as new data arrives.
- **Analytics and Control:** Data analytics, machine learning, or optimization routines run on the model to derive insights. This may include predictive analytics, fault diagnosis algorithms, or control algorithms. The DT can simulate multiple scenarios (what-if analyses) using the current model state.
- **User Interface and Decision Support:** Dashboards, visualization (e.g. 3D graphics, VR/AR views), and APIs through which engineers and operators interact with the twin, monitor status, and receive alerts.

For example, SimuTech Group highlights that "a digital twin has several core components: sensors, data analytics and controls, a communication platform (e.g. cloud platform), and decision-making physics". In other words, sensors feed into analytics engines *via* a communication backbone, and the twin's physical-model "physics" layer drives decision logic. The Dell reference architecture similarly illustrates the DT cycle of input-data → virtual model → virtual simulation → applied feedback. In essence, digital models and simulations form the core of a DT, but what makes it a true twin is that "a digital twin incorporates real-world data and allows the bi-directional exchange of pertinent information". This continuous data coupling is what differentiates a static model from an adaptive digital twin: the twin is constantly refined by live data and can in turn command or predict the physical asset.

2.2.1 Physical Entity and Sensor Integration

At the foundation of every digital twin is a **physical entity**, which can be a **machine, infrastructure, biological system, or industrial process.** To mirror real-world behavior, the digital twin requires **data input from IoT sensors** that capture:

- **Mechanical parameters** (e.g., temperature, pressure, vibration)
- **Electrical properties** (e.g., voltage, current, resistance)
- **Environmental conditions** (e.g., humidity, air quality, radiation levels)
- **Operational status** (e.g., energy consumption, efficiency metrics)

These sensors form a **cyber-physical link** between the real-world system and its virtual twin.

Mathematical Representation of Sensor Data
The data collected from sensors is modeled as a **time-series function**:

$$X(t) = [x_1(t), x_2(t), \ldots, x_n(t)]$$

where X(t) represents a **multi-dimensional dataset** of sensor values over time.

Each sensor measurement is assigned a **weight function** based on its relevance:

$$S = \sum_{i=1}^{n} w_i \cdot x_i(t)$$

where w_i is the weighting coefficient for each sensor input.

2.2.2 Digital Model and Data Representation

Once sensor data is collected, it is processed into a **digital representation** of the physical system. This involves:

- **3D modeling** (e.g., CAD, finite element analysis)
- **Simulation frameworks** (e.g., computational fluid dynamics for aerospace models)
- **Statistical modeling** for predictive analytics

Mathematical Formulation of Digital Twins
A digital twin can be represented as a **state-space model**:

$$\dot{X} = f(X,U,t)$$

where:

- X = system state variables
- U = control inputs
- t = time
- f = function defining system dynamics

This allows the digital twin to **simulate future states** based on real-time input.

2.2.3 IoT and Cloud Computing for Real-Time Synchronization

To achieve real-time responsiveness, digital twins rely on **cloud computing and IoT networks** for:

- **Large-scale data storage and retrieval**
- **Edge computing** for real-time decision-making
- **Remote accessibility** of digital twin simulations Digital twins operate on a **three-tier architecture**:
  1. **Perception Layer** – IoT sensors collect data.
  2. **Network Layer** – Cloud infrastructure transmits and processes data.
  3. **Application Layer** – AI and analytics generate insights.

Mathematically, **data transmission** between layers is modeled as:

$$D_t = \sum_{i=1}^{n} S_i \cdot T_i$$

where:

- D_t = total transmitted data
- S_i = data size from sensor i
- T_i = transmission rate of sensor i

2.2.4 AI, Machine Learning, and Predictive Analytics

Artificial intelligence (AI) enhances digital twins by enabling:

- **Predictive maintenance** using historical data patterns.
- **Anomaly detection** through deep learning models.
- **Self-optimizing processes** with reinforcement learning.

A **predictive failure probability model** using Bayesian Networks is given by:

$$P(F|X) = \frac{P(X|F)P(F)}{P(X)}$$

where:

- P(F|X) = probability of failure given observed data XXX
- P(X|F) = likelihood of observed data under failure conditions
- P(F) = prior probability of failure
- P(X) = overall probability of observed data

2.2.5 User Interface and Visualization Tools

For human interaction, digital twins utilize **graphical interfaces and augmented reality (AR) platforms** for:

- **Real-time system monitoring**
- **Remote operational control**
- **Scenario-based training simulations**

Modern visualization tools employ **immersive VR environments** where engineers can interact with the twin using **gesture-based controls.**

2.3 Solar Concentrator Types

Concentrated Solar Power (CSP) systems focus sunlight to generate heat, which is then converted to electricity or thermal energy. The four main CSP architectures are: central tower (heliostat) systems, parabolic trough collectors, linear Fresnel collectors, and parabolic dish systems. Each type is characterized by different concentrator geometries, tracking degrees of freedom, and a typical operating temperature range.

2.3.1 Tower (Heliostat Field) Systems

A power tower system uses a field of sun-tracking heliostats (movable flat or slightly curved mirrors) to reflect sunlight to a central receiver atop a tower. The receiver contains a heat-transfer fluid (HTF), often molten salt, which is heated to -600°C or more. High operating temperatures allow efficient steam generation and integration with thermal storage. Tower systems can achieve the highest concentration ratios and temperatures among CSP technologies, making them well-suited for large-scale power generation.

In a typical layout, hundreds to thousands of heliostats are arranged around the tower (see Figure 2.1). A dual-axis tracking mechanism allows each heliostat to track the sun and focus on the receiver throughout the day. The optical concentration ratio C can be defined as the ratio of mirror aperture area to receiver area $A_{receiver}$

$$C = \frac{A_{\text{aperture}}}{A_{\text{receiver}}},$$

often exceeding 1000:1 in tower systems. The instantaneous thermal power delivered is

$$\dot{Q}_{\text{in}} = DNI\ A_{\text{aperture}}\ \eta_{\text{optics}},$$

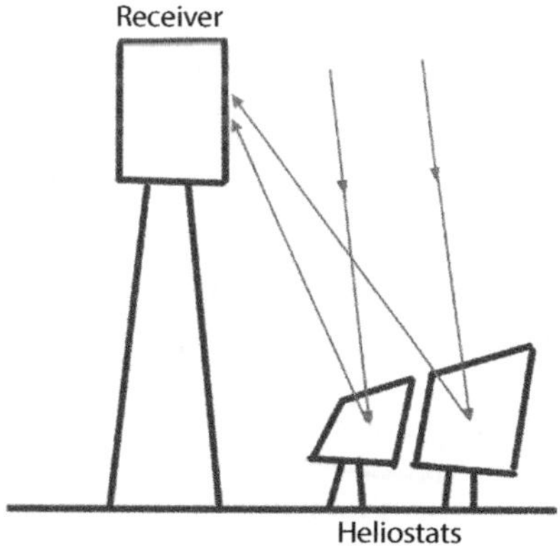

Figure 2.1 Power tower CSP field with heliostat mirrors focusing sunlight onto a central receiver (image source: SolarPACES).

a function of direct normal irradiance, aperture area, and optical efficiency, where the latter accounts for mirror reflectivity and atmospheric losses. The thermal efficiency of the receiver loop then determines net heat output (steam generation). Tower plants (e.g., SEGS, NOOR III) often use molten-salt loop for energy storage, improving dispatchability. Tower fields require substantial land and careful heliostat layout to minimize mutual shading and cosine losses.

2.3.2 Parabolic Trough Collectors

Parabolic troughs use long parabolic mirrors in a linear trough shape to focus sunlight onto a cylindrical receiver tube placed at the focus line (see Figure 2.2). Each trough is mounted on a single-axis (east-west) tracking mechanism, allowing it to follow the sun and maximize insolation on the receiver. Thermal oil typically flows inside the receiver pipe, absorbing the concentrated heat. In commercial plants, the oil inlet temperature (-290°C) is raised to ~390°C.

The instantaneous heat input to each trough is

$$\dot{Q}_{\text{in}} = DNI \times A_{\text{aperture}} \times \eta_{\text{optics}},$$

A function of direct normal irradiance, aperture area, and optical efficiency, with the aperture area being equal to the mirror area of the trough. The optical concentration ratio C is roughly the rim-angle factor and geometry (typically C~50). Parabolic troughs are mature technology with

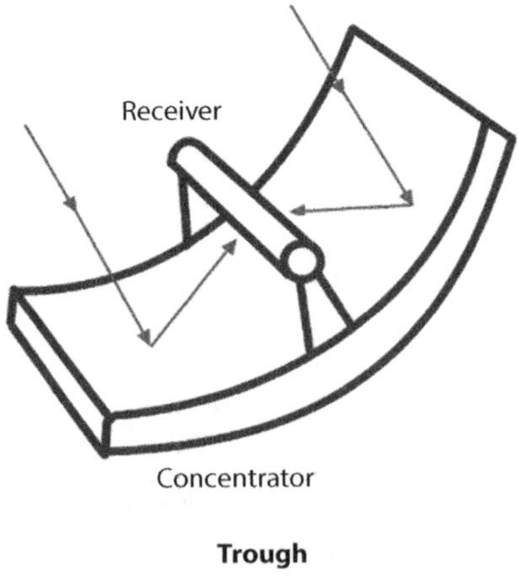

Figure 2.2 Parabolic trough collector array with single-axis tracking (image source: SolarPACES).

extensive commercial deployment. They generally achieve lower peak temperatures (-400°C) than towers, but their modular linear design offers simplicity. Thermal efficiency is somewhat lower than tower CSP, in part due to higher heat losses in long linear receivers.

2.3.3 Linear Fresnel Collectors

Linear Fresnel systems use many flat or slightly curved mirror strips arranged in long parallel rows to focus sunlight onto a fixed elevated receiver tube. The mirror strips can be individually tilted (north-south single-axis tracking) to focus onto the receiver. Because the mirrors are flat (cheaper to manufacture) and installed close to ground, Fresnel fields have lower capital cost per area than troughs, though at slightly reduced optical efficiency.

Figure 2.3 illustrates a linear Fresnel field. The optical concentration ratio C for Fresnel is typically 20-50, lower than troughs. Still, Fresnel systems can reach steam conditions sufficient for turbines. Fresnel plants often use water/steam directly rather than thermal oil, simplifying design. These systems also integrate thermal storage (e.g. molten salt) for dispatchability.

2.3.4 Parabolic Dish Systems

Parabolic dish concentrators consist of individual dish-shaped reflectors that focus sunlight to a point where a receiver/engine is mounted. Each dish is two-axis tracked. Because of the point focus, dishes achieve the highest flux concentration and temperatures (often >1000°C), enabling

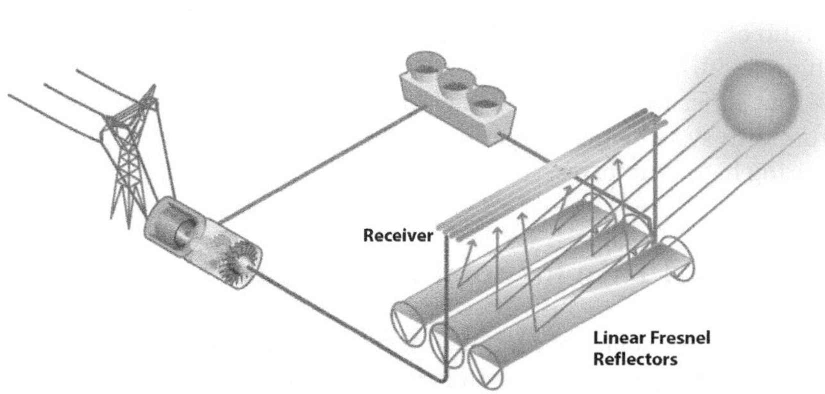

Figure 2.3 Linear Fresnel field (image source: SolarPACES).

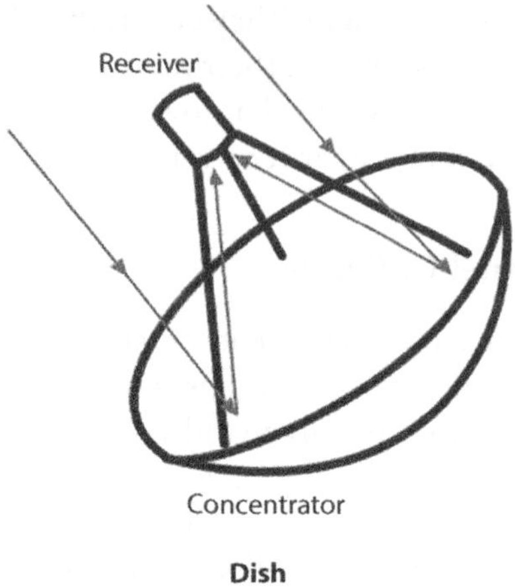

Figure 2.4 Parabolic dish solar concentrator with point-focus receiver (image source: SolarPACES).

high-efficiency Stirling engines or Brayton receivers. However, their high capital cost and mechanical complexity (each dish has its own engine) have limited large-scale deployment.

Figure 2.4 shows a parabolic dish with a central receiver. The optical concentration ratio can exceed 2000 for small dish facets. Thermal efficiency can be defined for a dish-engine unit by

$$\eta = \frac{\dot{W}_{\text{elec}}}{DNI \times A_{\text{aperture}}},$$

the ratio of electric output to the product of direct normal irradiance and dish area. Stirling-engine dishes achieve conversion efficiencies of ~20-30%, but suffer from issues like high maintenance of many moving parts. Future dish systems may target solar fuels (e.g. solar-driven gasification) requiring high heat fluxes.

2.4 Digital Twin for Solar Concentrators

Digital twins for solar concentrators leverage models of the concentrator physics, real-time sensor data, and control algorithms. A DT can include submodels for optical behavior, thermal dynamics, and economic dispatch. Key DT functions in CSP include design optimization (geometry, materials), operational control (tracking algorithms, flow control), condition monitoring, and predictive analytics.

For any concentrator, the DT must simulate its optical performance. Ray-tracing or low-order optical models compute intercepted solar energy on the receiver. For instance, a trough DT computes incident heat as

$$q'' = DNI \cdot \cos(\theta) \cdot \eta_{\text{mirror}},$$

a function of direct normal irradiance, the cosine of the incidence angle, and mirror reflectivity. Similarly, Fresnel DT models treat each mirror segment individually in the focus calculation. These models feed into thermal simulations, such as a nodal heat-balance model for the receiver and HTF:

$$C_{\text{th}} \frac{dT}{dt} = \dot{Q}_{\text{in}} - \dot{Q}_{\text{out}},$$

where the change in thermal energy over time equals the heat input minus the heat output. PDE-based models (e.g. heat conduction in receiver tubes) or simplified lumped models may be used depending on desired fidelity.

The DT must align model outputs with real-time plant data (sunlight, temperatures, flows, power output). This requires data acquisition (IoT sensors, SCADA) and updating of DT state *via* data assimilation or ML fitting. In practice, one employs a digital thread: the DT receives sensor inputs (irradiance, receiver temperature, flow rates, etc.), and outputs predictions or control signals. For example, the DT can estimate unmeasured variables (like mirror misalignment) by comparing expected vs. observed performance, enabling diagnostic insights. The bidirectional nature means the DT can also test operational strategies *in silico* before applying them (closed-loop simulation). Central to many DTs is model calibration and fault adaptation. Data-driven methods (e.g. Kalman filters, adaptive neural networks) can update model parameters (mirror reflectivity degradation, fouling losses) over time. In Section 2.5 we discuss how such approaches facilitate predictive maintenance and fault detection.

In the energy sector, digital twins often integrate with AI/ML: ML models can supplement physics models by capturing complex relationships (e.g. diffuser losses, weather impacts). Kabir *et al.* [11] note that IoT-enabled DTs allow adaptive control in smart energy systems. Recent CSP reviews highlight the synergy of DT with AI/ML: ML models predict exergy or efficiency in PTCs under variable conditions, and neural nets can serve as surrogate simulators in DT loops.

2.5 Digital Twin Applications by Concentrator Type

Below we discuss how DT technology applies to each CSP technology, covering design, control, monitoring, and performance analysis.

2.5.1 Parabolic Trough Systems

Design and Optimization: In early design, a DT enables virtual prototyping. Engineers can parametrize trough geometry (aperture width, rim angle) and receiver tube specs and simulate thermal performance under solar cycles. For example, Zohdi [3, 4] used a genetic-ML DT to optimize Fresnel layouts over multi-season horizons; similar methods apply to trough fields (choosing row spacing to minimize shading, optimizing mirror curvature). Ray-tracing plus heat loss models can compute cycle yield; optimization (e.g. gradient-based or ML) finds geometries maximizing annual output.

Control: Parabolic troughs typically use a simple sun-tracking algorithm (east-west rotation based on hour angle). A DT can refine control: e.g. by correcting for wind-induced deflection or tracking errors. Real-time DT allows supervisory control: if one field underperforms (observed by sensors), the DT can adjust set points for flow rates or include field integration (switching between arrays) to balance output. It can also determine optimal start-up/shutdown sequences, as implemented for Fresnel fields.

Monitoring and Diagnostics: A DT can compare model predictions to actual field performance. Deviations signal faults: e.g. a drop in heat output beyond what the model expects (given DNI data) could indicate mirror soiling, misaligned troughs, or receiver issues. By tracing back the discrepancy through the optical/thermal model, DT can pinpoint likely causes. This digital "shadow" of the field thus provides early fault detection. Anomaly detection algorithms in the DT can flag abnormal thermal gradients in receiver tubes or pump anomalies, prompting maintenance before failures.

Maintenance and Lifespan: Trough receiver tubes and seals degrade over time. A DT can integrate degradation models: e.g. increase in thermal losses or pressure drop as a function of cumulative hours. Predictive maintenance algorithms can schedule tube cleaning or gasket replacement by forecasting when performance will drop below thresholds. The work by Price *et al.* [7] on a field status program could be seen as a basic DT for maintenance data: tracking thousands of identical trough components. Embedding DT enhances this by modeling each component's state and failure probability.

2.5.2 Fresnel Collector Systems

Digital twin implementations have been particularly explored for Fresnel systems due to their complex geometry. Machado *et al.* [12] developed a DT for a commercial linear Fresnel collector used in solar cooling. Their DT encompasses two model types: a physics-based PDE model and a data-driven ANFIS model, both capturing the Fresnel mirror-receiver dynamics across day and night. They showed both approaches achieved accurate modeling of the collector's transient behavior (temperatures 180°C down to ambient). Importantly, the DT was used to optimize startup/shutdown and control reliability. This demonstrates DTs' value in Fresnel design and control: by simulating defocus strategies and flow control *via* the DT, engineers can ensure smooth operation over the whole cycle, even in cooling mode.

Control and Performance: The DT can simulate each mirror segment's aiming; combined with weather forecasts, it can adjust defocus angles to avoid receiver overheating. During rapid DNI changes, the DT can predict receiver temperature evolution (*via* heat balance equations) and command flow rates or defocus accordingly. For example, a control loop might use the DT to compute optimal mirror orientations every few minutes to maximize collected flux while keeping receiver temperature below material limits. This virtual experiment avoids costly on-site trials.

Monitoring and Fault Detection: The Fresnel DT allows fine-grained fault detection. For instance, if one mirror row is out of alignment, the DT (comparing predicted vs. actual flux sensor readings on the receiver) can identify which segment is mispointing. Machado *et al.* [12] even note that their DT is the first to model dynamic "mirror defocus" control for fault diagnosis. Unexpected large errors in predicted vs. measured thermal output signal mirror or pump issues. The DT can then isolate which parameter (mirror angle vs. flow) changed and alert operators.

Optimization: Like for troughs, DTs can optimize Fresnel layout and control. Zohdi [3, 4] used a DT for a Fresnel array to allocate mirrors for customer demand while maximizing efficiency. His ML-DT framework optimized the spatial configuration of mirror fields (choosing mirror heights, spacing) and operating temperatures. Results showed the DT could evaluate hundreds of thousands of configurations rapidly (microseconds), far beyond what direct simulation allows. In practice, such a DT could be used in designing new Fresnel plants or retrofitting existing ones with nanofluid receivers to raise heat capacity (coordinating with Industry 4.0 nanofluid strategies).

2.5.3 Tower (Heliostat) Systems

Design: Digital twins for solar towers must model thousands of heliostats and their optical path to the receiver. This involves 3D geometry and heliostat tracking models. In design phase, a DT can simulate different field layouts (heliostat density, aiming strategies) for a candidate site topology. Genetic or topology optimization can use the DT to find the lowest-cost layout given terrain and sun-path constraints. The DISOPED project, for example, plans a DT for a parabolic trough and thermal storage, but similar principles apply to tower fields. A tower DT can also evaluate different receiver designs (e.g. cavity vs. external receiver) by plugging into the heat balance.

Control: For towers, the DT can optimize the heliostat aiming algorithm. Each heliostat's aiming might incorporate predicted sun movement, tracking errors, and atmospheric attenuation models. The DT can run a virtual simulation of the entire field to compute total receiver flux and adjust aiming coefficients to even out flux distribution on the receiver (preventing hot spots). In operations, the DT might simulate the effect of cloud transients or dust storms on flux and propose preemptive mirror adjustments or reconfiguration of field segments.

Monitoring and Predictive Maintenance: A critical DT application is heliostat fault detection. Mirror assemblies can have drive or calibration failures. By comparing expected (model-predicted) flux based on current mirror aims and weather versus measured receiver output, the DT can identify underperforming heliostats. Emerging AI methods (like CNNs analyzing sky images) could be integrated with the DT for anomaly detection. The Stellio heliostat (benchmark design) is extremely accurate; a DT could model its predicted accuracy envelope and signal if any mirror deviates. Additionally, concrete heliostat prototypes (see Figure 2.1) highlight new materials; a DT could simulate their structural deformation under wind to predict optical offsets.

2.5.4 Parabolic Dish Systems

Design and Optimization: DTs for dishes focus on optimizing dish geometry and receiver performance. For example, parametric studies of dish focal length or rim angle can be done rapidly in simulation. Because each dish is individual, a DT might simulate a network of dishes feeding electric loads. AI/ML enhancements (neural network surrogates) could accelerate optical simulations. Dish DTs can also optimize hybridization: coupling a dish with a Stirling engine or microturbine, using co-simulation to maximize conversion.

Control: Dish tracking is inherently two-axis. A DT control system might refine control laws to counteract wind or mechanical backlash, ensuring the dish stays precisely on target. The DT can simulate dynamic models of the dish structure (even vibration modes) to improve real-time control gains. It can also handle coordinated control if multiple dishes feed into a microgrid, balancing output vs. engine load.

Monitoring: Since dishes are expensive, DTs can monitor each unit's health. Changes in power output versus modeled expectation (given sun position and weather) can flag reflector fatigue or receiver mismatch. If integrated with thermal storage, the DT can manage dish outputs to smooth plant dispatch. In remote demos (like NASA's dish-Stirling experiments), a DT could have been used to validate novel receivers or fuel synthesis processes under concentrated sunlight.

2.6 Optimization Strategies

Digital twins enable a range of optimization strategies across CSP systems:

- **Thermal Efficiency Enhancement:** By simulating heat transfer in real-time, DTs can adjust flow rates, working fluid properties, or mirror orientations to maximize thermal-to-electric efficiency. For example, ML-based DTs can predict optimal flow rates as a function of DNI and receiver temperature to maximize exergy output. Nanofluid DTs can simulate the effect of adding nanoparticles on heat transfer, as in the context of Industry 4.0 and nanofluids.
- **Real-Time Performance Monitoring:** DTs provide continuous comparison of expected vs. actual performance. A dashboard (virtualized by the DT) can track key performance indicators (KPI): efficiency, output, component losses. This enables adaptive control: for instance, if cloud cover suddenly changes, the DT can predict the drop in thermal input and automatically adjust auxiliary heaters or storage dispatch.
- **Predictive Maintenance:** Using historical DT data and ML forecasting, one can predict component failures. For example, tracking the rate of efficiency degradation can signal when receiver tubes need cleaning (soiling buildup), or when pump cavitation begins. ML models (trained on DT-simulated and real failure data) can estimate remaining

useful life of parts. The maintenance scenario from the parabolic trough field [7] can be enhanced by a DT: instead of just logging components, the DT simulates each component's aging.

- **Cost Reduction:** DTs can identify inefficiencies and simulate retrofit options. For example, if the DT shows that current mirror reflectance is low, a cost-benefit analysis can compare mirror cleaning vs. replacement. In design, DT-optimized layouts can reduce material and land costs. A study combining nanofluids and DTs suggests that intelligent control of heat transfer fluids can lower levelized cost of energy (LCOE).
- **Fault Detection and Diagnosis:** DTs inherently support fault diagnostics by model-based reasoning. Common faults in CSP (mirror misalignment, tracking failures, receiver leaks) manifest as deviations between the DT and field. Algorithms can localize faults: e.g., by perturbing one subsystem in the virtual model and comparing the pattern of changes to sensor data. The Fresnel DT cited earlier was used explicitly for fault-adaptive control (mirror defocus).
- **AI Integration:** Modern DTs embed AI/ML for various tasks. ML surrogates (neural nets, ANFIS, Gaussian processes) can emulate high-fidelity physics models for faster simulation. Reinforcement learning or genetic algorithms can be wrapped around the DT for autonomous optimization (as in Zohdi's GA-ML framework). Predictive models for weather or demand can be integrated with the DT to make proactive adjustments. For instance, ensemble learning models have been used to predict trough exergy efficiency from DT outputs.

2.7 Real-World Case Studies

Several implementations of DTs in CSP or solar concentrator contexts have been reported.

- **Fresnel Solar Cooling Plant** [12] – As described above, this study built a DT of a commercial linear Fresnel collector on a rooftop cooling system. Two DT models (PDE vs. ANFIS) were validated with 25 days of high-resolution data. Both models accurately captured dynamic behavior and were used for optimizing start-up/shutdown strategies. This is an industry-relevant application: many plants co-generate heat and cooling, and DTs can improve operational efficiency and reliability.

- **Machine-Learning DT for Solar-Thermal Storage [3, 4]** – This case involved a tower-style Fresnel array feeding a multistage thermal storage system. Zohdi's DT used a reduced-order Maxwell-equation model for optics and a genetic ML optimizer. It simulated years of operation in microseconds, optimizing mirror configurations against customer demand. The DT thus served both as a fast design tool and a potential adaptive controller. The study showcases how a DT can span optical and thermal domains to optimize entire solar-thermal networks.
- **HysolSim for Hybrid Solar Thermal [10]** – A preprint describes HysolSim, a digital twin simulator for a hybrid solar thermal plant (tower, dish, etc.). Although full details are pending, the authors emphasize modeling multiple CSP technologies in a unified DT, presumably for hybrid plant optimization. This indicates industrial interest: e.g., a plant with both dish and tower sections could use a single DT to manage overall power output.
- **Parabolic Trough Field O&M [7]** – While not explicitly called a "digital twin," the field status program for parabolic trough maintenance illustrates DT principles. It tracks each collector's state over time and could feed into a DT that aggregates this data into a virtual field model. Future extensions could integrate this with predictive algorithms for component lifetimes. The paper shows industry moves to digitize O&M for CSP, a trend aligned with DT adoption.
- **SolarPACES and Research Projects:** Programs like DISOPED (EU CSP ERA-NET) explicitly target DT development for CSP (parabolic trough and storage). Although not yet published in detail, they indicate research is being conducted on DT prototypes for CSP. Agencies like NREL and DOE have also funded SmartHelio and HelioCon projects focusing on advanced heliostat and digital technologies, a trend aligned with DT adoption. Industry players (Siemens, ABB, GE) have begun offering "digital twin" platforms for power plants that could extend to CSP, though specific CSP-focused offerings are emerging.

2.8 Mathematical Models and Equations

We summarize key equations used in DT models of solar concentrators:

- **Heat Input:** The incident thermal power on a receiver from concentrated sunlight is

$$Q_{\text{in}} = DNI \cdot A_{\text{aperture}} \cdot \eta_{\text{optics}}(\theta, \varphi),$$

  a function of the direct normal irradiance, the aperture area, and the optical efficiency, which in turn depends on aiming angles. For a dish or heliostat field, optical efficiency also depends on aiming precision and atmospheric attenuation.
- **Concentration Ratio:** This is the ratio of the aperture area to the receiver area. The flux at the receiver is the product of this ratio and the direct normal irradiance (neglecting losses). Higher concentration ratios allow for higher temperatures; towers can reach ratios greater than 1000.
- **Thermal Balance:** For a receiver, the transient energy balance states that the change in thermal energy over time is

$$mc_p \frac{dT}{dt} = \dot{Q}_{\text{in}} - \dot{Q}_{\text{useful}} - \dot{Q}_{\text{loss}},$$

equal to the incident thermal power minus the useful heat carried away and any heat losses. DTs often solve this as ordinary or simplified partial differential equations.

- **Optical Tracking:** Mirror orientation is given by tracking angles. For single-axis (east-west) troughs, the yaw angle is related to solar time. The angle of incidence affects the optical efficiency. Two-axis dishes use altitude-azimuth control: the dish normal is kept collinear with the sun vector, minimizing the incidence angle.
- **Efficiency Metrics:** Overall solar-to-electric efficiency for the system is

$$\eta = \frac{\dot{W}_{\text{elect}}}{DNI \times A_{\text{aperture,total}}},$$

the ratio of the electrical power output to the product of the direct normal irradiance and the total aperture area. CSP systems often quote thermal efficiency (heat out/solar in) and solar efficiency (electric out/solar in).

These models are implemented in DTs *via* numerical solvers or ML approximators. For example, the Fresnel DT by Machado *et al.* [12] solved PDEs for heat transfer and also used ANFIS models trained on data for fast evaluation.

2.9 Future Directions and Challenges

While digital twins offer great promise for CSP, several challenges and research directions remain:

- **Data Integration and Standards:** CSP plants generate diverse data (optical, thermal, electrical). Harmonizing these into a coherent DT requires standardized protocols and data models. Developing open DT frameworks (e.g. based on Industry IoT standards) for solar energy will facilitate broader adoption.
- **Model Fidelity vs. Speed:** High-fidelity models (CFD, ray-tracing) are computationally expensive. Research is needed to balance fidelity with real-time performance. Reduced-order models and ML surrogates (ANNs, Gaussian processes) will be key to fast yet accurate DTs.
- **Cybersecurity and Reliability:** DTs involve sensitive operational data and control links. Ensuring secure, robust DT architectures (especially when involving remote monitoring and cloud computing) is critical. As noted by Rasheed *et al.* [13] (IEEE Access) and others, DT data security must be addressed to prevent sabotage or data breaches in energy systems.
- **AI/ML Integration:** Incorporating AI (e.g. reinforcement learning for control, deep learning for fault recognition) is an ongoing area. Synergies between DT and AI will likely grow, as AI provides adaptive learning and DT provides domain knowledge. Research on explainable AI within DTs will ensure trust in automated decisions.
- **New Materials and Nanofluids:** The next generation of CSP may use advanced materials (nanofluids, advanced receiver coatings). DTs must adapt to simulate these innovations. For example, DTs that model nanofluid-enhanced heat transfer could help optimize fluid formulations and operations.

The chapter by Melesse *et al.* [2] highlights such integrated approaches combining nanofluids with Industry 4.0 optimization.

- **Economic and Grid Integration Models:** Future DTs may incorporate economic dispatch and grid constraints. With solar often co-located with storage, DTs will need to simulate entire plant economics (LCOE, marginal cost) and interactions with smart grids. The Benguerir Morocco case suggests DTs can be applied to urban solar distribution networks; extending this to utility-scale CSP and grid-TCS (thermal energy storage) interaction is an emerging field.
- **Experimental Validation:** More field demonstrations of DTs in CSP plants are needed. Pilot projects where DTs operate in parallel with physical plants would provide data to refine DT models. The reported case studies are few; increasing these real-world implementations will help validate and improve DT methods.

2.10 Conclusion

Digital twin technology is poised to revolutionize the design, operation, and maintenance of solar concentrator systems. By creating live virtual replicas of parabolic troughs, Fresnel arrays, power towers, and dishes, DTs enable continuous performance analysis, model-based control, and predictive optimization. We have reviewed DT architectures and CSP technologies, and shown how DTs address critical needs: enhancing thermal efficiency, enabling real-time monitoring, predicting faults, reducing costs, and leveraging AI. Case studies of Fresnel and hybrid systems demonstrate DT effectiveness in start-up optimization and large-scale simulation. Nevertheless, challenges remain in data integration, cybersecurity, and model fidelity. Future research should focus on scalable DT frameworks (possibly standardized by industry consortia), advanced AI integration, and validation in operational CSP plants. Addressing these will help CSP achieve the efficiency and reliability required for 21st-century energy demands. In summary, the convergence of digital twins with solar concentrator technology offers a powerful pathway to accelerate innovation and deployment of sustainable solar power.

AI dislcosure statement: The author confirms that no artificial intelligence (AI)-generated content or AI-assisted writing tools were used in the preparation of this chapter (including summaries and the abstract). All text, analysis, and conclusions are the result of the author's original work.

Bibliography

1. Digital twin: Data exploration, architecture, implementation and future - PubMed https://pubmed.ncbi.nlm.nih.gov/38444502/.
2. Peer, M.S., Melesse, T.Y., Orrù, P.F., Braggio, M., Petrollese, M., Next-Generation CSP: The Synergy of Nanofluids and Industry 4.0 for Sustainable Solar Energy Management. *Energies*, 18, 8, 2083, 2025.
3. Zohdi, T. I., A machine-learning digital-twin for rapid large-scale solar-thermal energy system design. *Comput. Meth. Appl. Mech. Eng.*, 414, 116177, 2023.
4. Zohdi, T. I., A digital-twin and machine-learning framework for the design of multiobjective agrophotovoltaic solar farms. *Comput. Mech.*, 72, 4, 677–695, 2023.
5. Digital Twin Architecture and Standards https://www.iiconsortium.org/news-pdf/joi-articles/2019-November-JoI-Digital-Twin-Architecture-and-Standards.pdf.
6. A review on digital twin application in photovoltaic energy systems: challenges and opportunities | Request PDF https://www.researchgate.net/publication/ 382426957_A_review_on_digital_twin_application_in_photovoltaic_energy_systems_challenges_and_opportunities.
7. Price, H., Sommers, R., Imponenti, L., Boyle, K., Díaz, M., Integrating Parabolic Trough Solar Fields Into Computerized Maintenance Management Systems. *SolarPACES Conference Proceedings*, 2024.
8. Vision, Disoped, https://www.disoped.com/vision.php.
9. Development of a modular concrete heliostat prototype https://elib.dlr.de/189718/1/Pfahl_forman_SP_22.pdf.
10. Baidya, D., Kannaiyan, S., Bhushan, M., Bhartiya, S., Hysolsim: A Digital Twin (Simulator) for Hybrid Solar Thermal Power Plant. *Preprint*, 2025.
11. Kabir, M.R., Halder, D., Ray, S., Digital Twins for IoT-Driven Energy Systems: A Survey. *IEEE Access*, 12, 177123–177143, 2024.
12. Machado, D.O., Chicaiza, W.D., Escaño, J.M., Gallego, A.J., de Andrade, G.A., Normey-Rico, J.E., Bordons, C., Camacho, E.F., Digital twin of a Fresnel solar collector for solar cooling. *Appl. Energy*, 339, 120967, 2023.
13. Rasheed, A., San, O., Kvamsdal, T., Digital Twin: Values, Challenges and Enablers From a Modeling Perspective. *IEEE Access*, 8, 21980-22012, 2020.

3

Solar Concentrators: A Study Pertaining to Advancements and Challenges in the Current Scenario

Deepak Singh Karki* **and Vinita Sirala**

Department of Electrical Engineering, JBIT, Dehradun, Uttarakhand, India

Abstract

Solar energy has emerged as one of the most viable alternatives to traditional fossil fuels, owing to its sustainability and environmental benefits. Among various technologies, solar concentrators stand out as a crucial component for enhancing solar energy capture and improving the efficiency of solar systems. This chapter focuses on the advancements, challenges, and future directions in the field of solar concentrators, particularly in the context of the evolving landscape of renewable energy. Solar concentrators, designed to focus sunlight onto a smaller, high-efficiency solar cell or heat receiver, have proven to significantly boost energy conversion efficiency. The types of concentrators—parabolic troughs, dish/engine systems, and central receiver systems—have evolved, with each design offering unique advantages depending on geographical and environmental conditions. Recent advancements in materials science have led to the development of highly reflective mirrors, improved tracking systems, and the integration of advanced heat storage solutions, making concentrators more effective and economically viable. However, despite their potential, solar concentrators face several challenges in widespread adoption. The complexity of their design, high initial costs, and the requirement for large land areas in certain configurations hinder their deployment, particularly in regions with limited space. Additionally, the maintenance of concentrator systems, due to the need for precise tracking mechanisms and protection against environmental factors such as dust and high temperatures, presents ongoing challenges. These systems also face limitations in operation under diffuse or cloudy weather conditions, which can significantly reduce their effectiveness. The future of solar concentrators lies in addressing these limitations through innovative

**Corresponding author*: Deepak.karki00@gmail.com

Surajit Mondal, Paramjeet Singh Paliyal and Sachin Sharma (eds.) Digital Twin Technology for Solar Concentrators, (29–42) © 2026 Scrivener Publishing LLC

technologies and materials. Emerging developments in digital twin technology offer promising real-time monitoring and performance optimization solutions, enabling predictive maintenance and fault detection. Integrating artificial intelligence (AI) and machine learning (ML) algorithms can further enhance system efficiency by adapting to varying environmental conditions and improving energy capture. Additionally, hybrid systems that combine solar concentrators with other renewable technologies, such as photovoltaics or thermal storage, could help mitigate intermittency and improve the reliability of solar power generation.

This chapter aims to explore the current advancements in solar concentrator technologies, evaluate the challenges they face, and propose future directions for innovation in this field. Highlighting the integration of digital twins, smart sensors, and AI, it underscores the importance of adopting cutting-edge technologies to enhance the efficiency and scalability of solar concentrators. The development of these systems will not only optimize solar energy capture but also contribute to the global transition towards cleaner, more sustainable energy solutions.

***Keywords*:** Solar concentrators, renewables, energy storage, digital twin, artificial intelligence

3.1 Introduction

The growing demand for sustainable energy solutions has intensified the focus on solar energy as a viable alternative to fossil fuels. Solar power offers an inexhaustible and environmentally friendly source of energy, making it an integral part of the global transition toward clean energy. However, one of the primary challenges associated with solar power is its intermittent nature and the relatively low energy density of sunlight [1]. To overcome these limitations, solar concentrators have emerged as a crucial technology that enhances the efficiency of solar energy collection by focusing sunlight onto a smaller, highly efficient receiver. By increasing the intensity of solar radiation, these systems significantly improve the performance of both solar photovoltaic (PV) and solar thermal applications.

Solar concentrators work on the principle of optical concentration, where mirrors or lenses are used to collect and direct sunlight onto a focal point or focal line. This concentrated solar radiation can either be converted into electricity using high-performance solar cells or used for heating applications in industrial and residential settings [2]. The main advantage of solar concentrators is their ability to maximize solar energy capture while minimizing the amount of expensive photovoltaic material or increasing the efficiency of thermal conversion processes. This makes them particularly beneficial for large-scale solar power plants and concentrated solar power (CSP) systems, where maximizing energy output is a key priority.

Over the years, several types of solar concentrators have been developed, each designed to suit different applications and geographical conditions. Parabolic trough collectors are widely used in CSP plants, where they focus sunlight onto a linear receiver tube containing a heat transfer fluid. Dish/engine systems concentrate sunlight onto a single point, making them highly efficient for localized energy generation. Central receiver systems, or solar power towers, utilize a field of heliostats (large mirrors) to reflect sunlight onto a central receiver at the top of a tower, achieving extremely high temperatures for electricity generation [3]. Additionally, Fresnel lens concentrators have gained attention for their compact design and ability to achieve high levels of solar concentration with relatively lightweight materials.

Despite their potential, solar concentrators face several challenges that hinder widespread adoption. The high initial investment costs, the complexity of design and maintenance, and the requirement for precise solar tracking systems make them more suitable for large-scale applications rather than small residential setups. Moreover, environmental factors such as dust accumulation on mirrors, extreme temperatures, and cloudy conditions can impact their efficiency. However, advancements in materials science, digital twin technology, artificial intelligence (AI), and machine learning (ML) are paving the way for the next generation of solar concentrators [4]. These developments aim to enhance optical efficiency, reduce operational costs, and enable real-time monitoring and predictive maintenance, making solar concentrators more practical and economically viable.

In the context of global energy needs, the adoption of solar concentrators represents a significant step toward improving the efficiency and reliability of solar energy systems. By addressing current limitations and integrating cutting-edge innovations such as hybrid solar technologies and adaptive optics, the role of solar concentrators in the future energy landscape is set to expand. This chapter explores the various types of solar concentrators, recent advancements in the field, key challenges faced in their deployment, and the future prospects of this promising technology. Through a detailed analysis of emerging trends and real-world applications, this study highlights the growing importance of solar concentrators in the global shift towards renewable energy solutions [4].

3.2 Classification of Solar Concentrators

Solar concentrators play a crucial role in enhancing the efficiency of solar energy systems by focusing sunlight onto a smaller, high-intensity receiver. Their design and functionality vary significantly based on the intended application, energy requirements, and environmental conditions. To better understand their capabilities and uses, solar concentrators can be classified into several categories, including optical geometry, concentration ratio, tracking mechanism, application, and structural design.

Category	**Type**	**Examples**
Optical Geometry	Imaging	Parabolic Dish, Parabolic Trough
	Non-Imaging	Compound Parabolic Concentrator (CPC), Fresnel Lens
Concentration Ratio	Low Concentration (C<10	Compound Parabolic Concentrators (CPC)
	Medium Concentration (10<C<100)	Linear Fresnel Reflectors
	High Concentration (C>100)	Parabolic Dishes, Central Receiver Systems
Tracking Mechanism	Fixed	Compound Parabolic Concentrators (CPC), Stationary Fresnel Lens
	Single-Axis	Parabolic Troughs, Linear Fresnel Reflectors
	Dual-Axis	Parabolic Dish Systems, Central Receiver Systems
Application	Solar Thermal	Parabolic Troughs, Central Receiver Systems
	Solar Photovoltaic	Fresnel Lens Concentrators, Concentrated Photovoltaics (CPV)
	Hybrid	Hybrid PV-Thermal Systems (PVT)
Structural Design	Reflector-Based	Parabolic Troughs, Heliostat Fields
	Refractor-Based	Fresnel Lens Concentrators

3.2.1 Classification Based on Optical Geometry

Solar concentrators are primarily divided into imaging and non-imaging types. Imaging concentrators, such as parabolic dishes and parabolic troughs, focus sunlight to a specific focal point or line, maximizing light concentration on a targeted area. These are widely used in applications requiring high-intensity solar energy collection. On the other hand, non-imaging concentrators, such as compound parabolic concentrators (CPCs) and Fresnel lenses, do not create an optical image but enhance energy collection over a broader area. These concentrators are more efficient in diffuse light conditions and are commonly used in photovoltaic and hybrid solar systems [5].

3.2.2 Classification Based on Concentration Ratio

The concentration ratio (C), which is the ratio of the collector's aperture area to the receiver area, defines the intensity of sunlight focused on the receiver.

- Low-Concentration Solar Collectors ($C < 10$): These operate with minimal sunlight amplification and are typically used in stationary setups, such as CPCs.
- Medium-Concentration Solar Collectors ($10 < C < 100$): These require single-axis tracking and are often used in linear Fresnel reflectors.
- High-Concentration Solar Collectors ($C > 100$): These demand dual-axis tracking to precisely align with the sun and are found in parabolic dish and central receiver systems.

3.2.3 Classification Based on Tracking Mechanism

The efficiency of solar concentrators is significantly influenced by their ability to track the sun's movement.

- Fixed (Non-Tracking) Concentrators: These concentrators remain stationary, making them cost-effective but less efficient. Examples include stationary CPCs and Fresnel lens systems.
- Single-Axis Tracking Concentrators: These concentrators adjust their position along one axis, either vertically or horizontally, to follow the sun. Parabolic troughs and linear Fresnel reflectors are common examples.

- Dual-Axis Tracking Concentrators: These continuously adjust in two directions for maximum solar capture, improving efficiency in parabolic dish systems and central receiver heliostats.

3.2.4 Classification Based on Application

Solar concentrators serve different purposes depending on their energy utilization:

- Solar Thermal Concentrators: These concentrators convert solar energy into heat, commonly used in parabolic troughs and central receiver systems for industrial and power generation applications.
- Solar Photovoltaic (PV) Concentrators: Designed to amplify sunlight onto photovoltaic cells, these concentrators improve electricity generation efficiency. Fresnel lens concentrators and concentrated photovoltaics (CPV) are notable examples.
- Hybrid Concentrators: These systems integrate thermal and photovoltaic functions to maximize energy utilization. Hybrid PV-Thermal (PVT) systems are increasingly being explored to enhance solar efficiency.

3.2.5 Classification Based on Structural Design

The structural composition of a solar concentrator determines its optical and thermal performance.

- Reflector-Based Concentrators: These use mirrors or reflective surfaces to direct sunlight. Parabolic troughs and heliostat fields are common reflector-based concentrators.
- Refractor-Based Concentrators: These employ lenses to focus sunlight, such as Fresnel lens concentrators, which are lightweight and capable of achieving high solar concentration levels.

In Figure 3.1 bar chart compares the efficiency (%) of different types of solar concentrators, including Parabolic Trough, Parabolic Dish, Central Receiver, Fresnel Lens, CPC, Hybrid PV-Thermal (PVT), and Floating Solar Concentrators. The efficiency values highlight the performance differences among these technologies, with some advanced designs such as

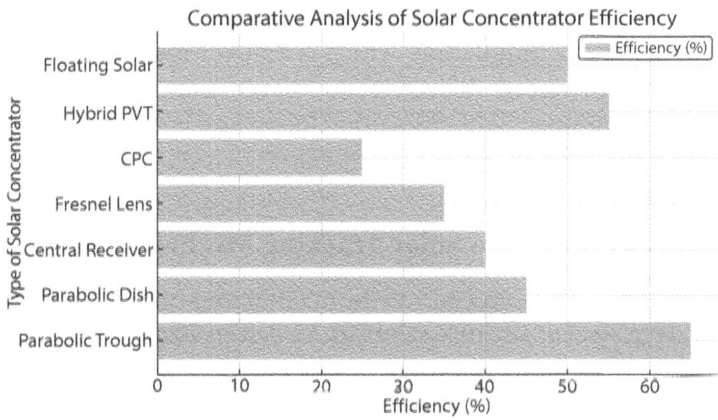

Figure 3.1 Comparative analysis of solar concentrator efficiency.

Hybrid PVT and Floating Solar demonstrating improved overall effectiveness. This analysis helps in identifying the most efficient concentrators for different applications and understanding how technological advancements impact performance.

3.3 Recent Advancements in Solar Concentrator Technology

Solar concentrator technology has seen significant advancements in recent years, driven by the need for higher efficiency, cost reduction, and integration with modern energy systems. Innovations in materials, optical design, tracking systems, heat storage, and smart technologies have contributed to making solar concentrators more reliable and commercially viable. These improvements aim to address the key challenges of traditional concentrator systems, such as high costs, maintenance requirements, and dependence on direct sunlight.

3.3.1 Advanced Materials for Enhanced Optical Efficiency

The efficiency of solar concentrators is highly dependent on the optical properties of the reflective or refractive surfaces. Recent developments in high-reflectivity coatings and nanomaterials have significantly improved light capture and reflection efficiency. New materials, such as silver-based reflectors with protective nano-coatings, offer higher reflectance and longer durability compared to traditional aluminum-based reflectors.

Additionally, the use of anti-soiling and self-cleaning coatings reduces the impact of dust accumulation, which is a major issue in arid and dusty environments. Advanced dielectric multilayer coatings have also been introduced to minimize light absorption losses and enhance the lifespan of concentrator components [6].

3.3.2 Improvements in Solar Tracking Mechanisms

Tracking systems play a crucial role in maintaining optimal sunlight focus on the receiver. Recent advancements in AI-driven solar tracking and high-precision actuators have improved the accuracy and reliability of these systems. Dual-axis tracking systems equipped with machine learning algorithms can now predict and adjust to weather conditions, optimizing energy capture throughout the day. Some modern concentrators use hybrid tracking, where mechanical tracking is supplemented with electro-optical sensors, enhancing efficiency with minimal energy consumption. Moreover, wireless IoT-enabled tracking systems allow remote monitoring and control, reducing maintenance costs and increasing system longevity [6].

3.3.3 Integration of Digital Twin Technology for Performance Optimization

Digital twin technology has revolutionized the monitoring and optimization of solar concentrators. By creating a virtual replica of the concentrator system, operators can perform real-time performance analysis, predictive maintenance, and failure detection. Digital twins use big data analytics and AI algorithms to predict system performance under varying environmental conditions, allowing for preemptive adjustments to maximize efficiency. This approach is particularly useful in large-scale concentrated solar power (CSP) plants, where minor adjustments in mirror alignment and tracking can lead to significant improvements in overall energy output [7].

3.3.4 Advanced Heat Storage Solutions

One of the major challenges in solar concentrators is intermittency, as energy production depends on sunlight availability. Recent innovations in thermal energy storage (TES) systems have helped overcome this limitation. The use of phase change materials (PCMs) and molten salt storage systems allows for efficient heat retention, enabling continuous power generation even after sunset. Advanced graphene-enhanced heat storage solutions are also being explored for their ability to store and release thermal energy more effectively. These advancements in storage technology are crucial for making solar concentrators a reliable alternative to conventional energy sources [7].

3.3.5 Hybridization with Photovoltaics and Other Renewable Technologies

To further enhance efficiency, solar concentrators are now being integrated with photovoltaic (PV) systems, creating hybrid concentrator photovoltaic-thermal (CPVT) systems. These hybrid systems not only generate electricity but also capture and utilize excess heat, making them more efficient than standalone PV or solar thermal systems. Recent research has also explored the combination of solar concentrators with wind and biomass energy systems, ensuring a more stable and diversified energy supply. Additionally, floating solar concentrators are gaining traction for deployment on water bodies, reducing land use concerns while benefiting from natural cooling effects that enhance efficiency [8].

3.3.6 Smart Sensors and AI for Performance Optimization

The integration of smart sensors and artificial intelligence (AI) has improved the operational efficiency of solar concentrators. AI-based optimization algorithms analyze real-time data, including solar irradiance, temperature, wind speed, and shading effects, to adjust concentrator positioning and tracking. Automated fault detection systems powered by machine learning models can identify performance issues in real time, reducing downtime and maintenance costs. Additionally, blockchain-based energy management systems are being developed to enable decentralized energy trading, allowing solar concentrator owners to sell excess energy efficiently.

3.3.7 Self-Healing and Adaptive Optics

A promising area of research in solar concentrator technology is the development of self-healing materials and adaptive optics. Self-healing coatings on concentrator mirrors can repair minor scratches and damage, extending their lifespan and maintaining high optical performance. Adaptive optics, originally developed for astronomy, is now being adapted for solar concentrators to correct optical distortions caused by temperature variations, wind loads, and structural shifts. This technology significantly improves the reliability and durability of solar concentrator systems, making them more practical for long-term deployment in diverse climatic conditions [9].

Table 3.1 provides a detailed comparative analysis of various solar concentrator technologies, including traditional, emerging, and advanced systems. The comparison covers key parameters such as concentration ratio, tracking requirements, efficiency, applications, advantages, and disadvantages.

Table 3.1 Comprehensive comparative analysis of solar concentrators.

Type of Solar concentrator	Concentration ratio	Tracking requirement	Efficiency (%)	Application
Parabolic Trough	30-100	Single-Axis	60-70%	Solar Thermal Power Plants, Industrial Heating
Parabolic Dish	600-2000	Dual-Axis	40-50% (Solar-to-Electric)	Standalone Power Generation, Hybrid Systems
Central Receiver (Heliostat Field)	200-1000	Dual-Axis	35-45% (Overall System)	Utility-Scale Solar Power, Grid Integration
Fresnel Lens	10-500	Single-Axis or Fixed	30-50%	Concentrated Photovoltaics, Small-Scale Thermal Applications
Compound Parabolic Concentrator (CPC)	02-10	Fixed	20-30%	Low-Temperature Solar Heating, Water Heating
Hybrid PV-Thermal (PVT)	10-50	Single-Axis or Fixed	30-60% (Combined PV & Thermal)	Hybrid Power Generation, Residential & Industrial
Floating Solar Concentrators	Varies Based on Design	Dual-Axis or Floating Adjustment	35-50% (Enhanced Cooling)	Water Bodies, Reservoirs, Hydropower Integration
AI-Integrated Solar Concentrators	50-500	AI-Based Automated Tracking	Optimized *via* AI (50-70%)	Smart Solar Plants, Real-Time Optimization
Digital Twin-Enabled Concentrators	50-1000	Real-Time Performance Optimization	Depends on Digital Twin Predictions (Up to 75%)	Predictive Maintenance, Large-Scale Power Plants
Self-Healing and Adaptive Optics Systems	100-2000	Adaptive to Environmental Changes	Improved Optical Efficiency (Up to 80%)	Self-Repairing Solar Mirrors, Space Applications

The table includes conventional concentrators such as Parabolic Troughs, Parabolic Dishes, Central Receiver Systems, Fresnel Lenses, and Compound Parabolic Concentrators (CPCs), which have been widely used in solar thermal and photovoltaic applications. Additionally, it incorporates recent advancements in solar concentrators, including Hybrid PV-Thermal Systems (PVT), Floating Solar Concentrators, AI-Integrated Systems, Digital Twin-Enabled Concentrators, and Self-Healing Optical Systems.

In Figure 3.2 the correlation matrix heatmap visually illustrates the relationships between key parameters influencing the performance of solar concentrators. Each parameter plays a crucial role in determining the efficiency, feasibility, and scalability of concentrator systems. The matrix includes essential factors such as concentration ratio, tracking requirement, efficiency, application scope, technological advancements, initial cost, and maintenance complexity. The color-coded representation highlights the strength of these relationships, where darker red shades indicate strong positive correlations, and blue shades denote negative correlations.

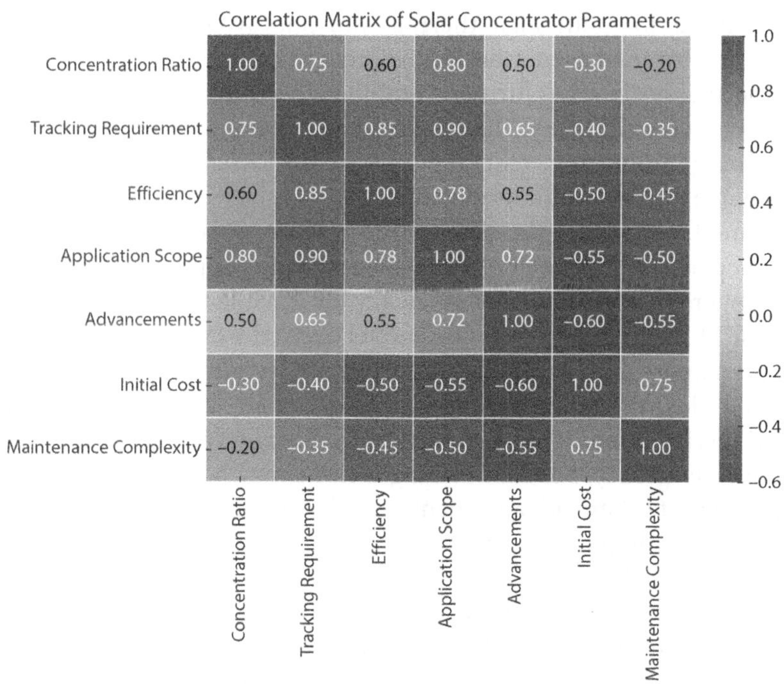

Figure 3.2 Correlation matrix of solar concentrator parameters.

A strong positive correlation is observed between tracking requirement and efficiency (0.85), emphasizing that higher precision in tracking leads to improved solar energy capture and conversion efficiency. Similarly, advancements in solar concentrator technology are positively linked with application scope (0.72), indicating that emerging technologies enable wider usability in diverse environmental and operational conditions. Conversely, negative correlations highlight trade-offs in system design. For instance, initial cost and advancements (-0.60) suggest that while advanced technologies may have high upfront costs, they contribute to long-term cost reduction through enhanced efficiency and durability. Additionally, maintenance complexity and efficiency (-0.45) show that simplified designs and improved system reliability reduce maintenance demands while boosting overall performance.

3.4 Conclusion

Solar concentrator technology has evolved significantly, offering enhanced efficiency, improved tracking mechanisms, and advanced thermal storage solutions for both solar thermal and photovoltaic applications. The integration of AI-based tracking, digital twin monitoring, and hybrid PV-Thermal systems has further strengthened the feasibility and adaptability of solar concentrators. These systems play a crucial role in maximizing solar energy utilization, reducing reliance on fossil fuels, and promoting sustainable energy solutions globally.

Figure 3.3 illustrates the relationship between solar concentration ratio and efficiency (%), using a polynomial curve fitting approach. The blue scatter points represent simulated efficiency data, while the red curve denotes the best-fit polynomial regression model derived from the data. The curve fitting analysis helps in predicting efficiency trends for different concentration ratios, providing insights into how solar concentrators perform under varying conditions. A higher concentration ratio generally leads to improved efficiency, but diminishing returns may be observed at extreme values. Despite these advancements, challenges such as high initial costs, maintenance complexities, and performance variability under diffuse light conditions still hinder widespread adoption. However, emerging materials, smart automation, and adaptive optics are paving the way for next-generation concentrators that are more cost-effective, durable, and efficient. As solar energy continues to be a key component of the global energy transition, concentrator technology will play an indispensable role in scaling up solar power generation and addressing energy demands sustainably.

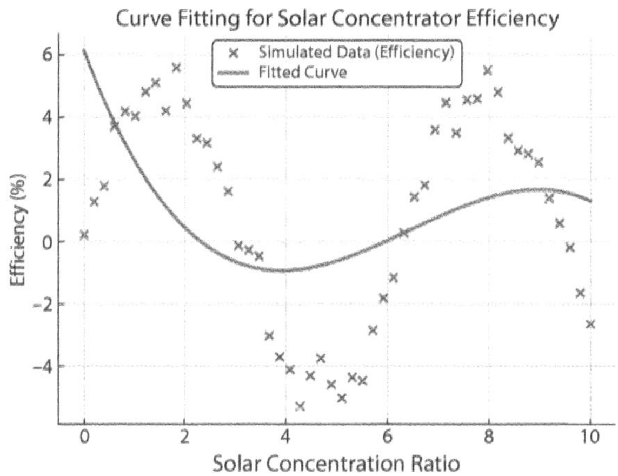

Figure 3.3 Curve fitting for solar concentrator efficiency.

3.5 Future Scope

The future of solar concentrators is set to be driven by technological advancements, material innovations, and enhanced integration with smart energy systems. One of the most promising areas of research is the development of self-healing and adaptive optical materials, which can automatically repair minor surface damage and adjust to environmental conditions to maintain optimal reflectivity and efficiency. Additionally, AI-driven predictive maintenance and optimization will revolutionize solar concentrator operations by enabling real-time tracking, fault detection, and autonomous efficiency adjustments, reducing operational costs and increasing reliability. Another key area of development is the hybridization of solar concentrators with other renewable energy sources such as wind, hydropower, and biomass, creating a more stable and efficient power generation ecosystem. Furthermore, advancements in high-temperature energy storage solutions, including molten salt, phase change materials (PCMs), and graphene-based heat storage, will significantly improve the ability to store and utilize thermal energy for extended periods, making solar concentrators more viable for continuous power generation. The deployment of floating solar concentrators on water bodies offers an innovative solution to land constraints while benefiting from natural cooling effects that enhance efficiency. Additionally, the concept of space-based solar concentrators is gaining traction, as positioning concentrators in space, where solar radiation is uninterrupted, could lead to unprecedented energy capture capabilities for future space missions and terrestrial energy supply. Another transformative advancement is the integration of blockchain technology for decentralized energy management, allowing peer-to-peer energy trading and ensuring widespread accessibility of solar energy, even in remote and off-grid locations. By addressing these research directions, solar concentrators will become more efficient, cost-effective, and scalable, contributing significantly to the global shift toward renewable and sustainable energy solutions.

AI disclosure statement: The author confirms that no artificial intelligence (AI)-generated content or AI-assisted writing tools was used in the preparation of this chapter (including summaries and the abstract). All text, analysis, and conclusions are the result of the author's original work.

References

1. Paliyal, P.S., Mondal, S., Layek, S., Kuchhal, P., Pandey, J.K., Automatic solar tracking system: a review pertaining to advancements and challenges in the current scenario. *Clean Energy*, 8, 6, 237–262, 2024.
2. Paliyal, P.S., Mondal, S., Pandey, J.K., An Analysis of Springwater Parameter Status for Different Locations in the Rural Hilly Garhwal Region of Uttarakhand. *Environ. Claims J.*, 1–35, 2024.
3. Mohammad, N. and Karim, T., Design and implementation of hybrid automatic solar-tracking system. *J. Sol. Energy Eng.*, 135, 1, 11013, 2013.
4. Herrería-Alonso, S., Suárez-González, A., Rodríguez-Pérez, M., Rodríguez-Rubio, R.F., López-García, C., A solar altitude angle model for efficient solar energy predictions. *Sensors*, 20, 5, 1391, 2020.
5. Alhadri, M., *et al.*, Design of a Low-Cost Parabolic Concentrator Solar Tracking System: Tubular Solar Still Application. *J. Sol. Energy Eng.*, 144, 5, 51006, 2022.
6. Racharla, S. and Rajan, K., Solar tracking system–a review. *Int. J. Sustainable Eng.*, 10, 2, 72–81, 2017.
7. Abdelghani-Idrissi, M.A., Khalfallaoui, S., Seguin, D., Vernières-Hassimi, L., Leveneur, S., Solar tracker for enhancement of the thermal efficiency of solar water heating system. *Renewable Energy*, 119, 79–94, 2018, doi: 10.1016/j.renene.2017.11.072.
8. Muhammad, J.Y., Jimoh, M.T., Kyari, I.B., Gele, M.A., Musa, I., A review on solar tracking system: A technique of solar power output enhancement. *Eng. Sci.*, 4, 1, 1–11, 2019.
9. Lorilla, F.M.A. and Barroca, R., Challenges and recent developments in solar tracking strategies for concentrated solar parabolic dish. *Indones. J. Electr. Eng. Comput. Sci.*, 26, 3, 1368–1378, 2022.

4
Basics of Solar Concentrators

Ayushman Srivastav[1]*, Rajesh Maithani[1] and Sachin Sharma[2]

[1]Department of Mechanical Engineering, UPES, Dehradun, Uttarakhand, India
[2]Mechanical Cluster, School of Advanced Engineering and Centre Head-BEST, UPES, Dehradun, Uttarakhand, India

Abstract
As the global demand for sustainable energy grows, solar energy technologies have emerged as vital solutions for mitigating climate change and reducing dependence on fossil fuels. Among these technologies, solar concentrators play a pivotal role in enhancing the efficiency of solar energy systems by focusing sunlight onto a smaller area, thereby increasing the energy density. This chapter explores the fundamental principles, classifications, and applications of solar concentrators, drawing insights from scholarly research and authoritative sources. The chapter also discusses the challenges and future prospects of solar concentrators, emphasizing their importance in advancing renewable energy technologies.

Keywords: Solar concentrators, renewable energy, solar energy efficiency, sustainable energy technologies

4.1 Introduction

Solar concentrators are pivotal in augmenting the efficiency of solar energy systems by focusing sunlight onto a designated area, thereby increasing energy density and optimizing power generation. These systems employ optical devices, such as mirrors or lenses, to concentrate solar radiation onto a receiver, which subsequently transforms the concentrated light into thermal or electrical energy. Functioning as specialized heat exchangers, solar concentrators absorb incoming solar radiation, convert it into heat, and transfer this heat to a working fluid—typically air, water, or

**Corresponding author*: ayushman.107499@stu.upes.ac.in

Surajit Mondal, Paramjeet Singh Paliyal and Sachin Sharma (eds.) Digital Twin Technology for Solar Concentrators, (43–58) © 2026 Scrivener Publishing LLC

oil—circulating through the system. The harvested thermal energy can be directly utilized for applications like water heating and space conditioning or stored in thermal energy storage systems for later use, ensuring continuous availability even during nighttime or overcast conditions.

Advancements in solar technology have led to the development of various concentrator designs aimed at enhancing efficiency and adaptability. Recent research has demonstrated the practical applications and compatibility of solar concentrators with other thermal technologies, significantly improving overall system performance. Notably, the efficiency of thermal systems can be substantially increased by incorporating solar concentrators or reflectors. In addition to concentrators, other techniques such as extended fins, thermal energy storage materials, and hybrid operation modes have been explored to improve thermal system performance. However, solar concentrators are particularly advantageous due to their ability to rapidly achieve the required operating temperatures for thermal systems, a feat that is otherwise challenging without electricity. This capability makes them an attractive solution for enhancing efficiency in various thermal applications.

Another significant advantage of solar concentrators is their ability to facilitate thermal system operations effectively in both indoor and outdoor environments, particularly in applications like solar dish collectors. Numerous studies have experimentally investigated thermal systems utilizing solar concentrators. For instance, Asfaw employed a parabolic concentrator in a household injera baking system with a closed loop water cycle, achieving a maximum plate temperature of approximately 181°C.

This chapter delves into the fundamental principles, classifications, and applications of solar concentrators, drawing insights from scholarly research and authoritative sources.

4.2 Principles of Solar Concentration

Solar concentration is a technique employed to amplify the intensity of solar radiation incident on a receiver, thereby enhancing the energy yield and efficiency of solar energy systems. This process is fundamental to solar power technologies, as it allows the collection of a larger amount of sunlight over a broad area and concentrates it onto a smaller, targeted surface. By increasing the solar flux density, concentrators enable solar systems to achieve higher operational temperatures, making them suitable for a variety of applications, including electricity generation, industrial heating, and solar-powered chemical processes.

4.2.1 Mechanism of Solar Concentration

At its core, solar concentration relies on optical components—typically mirrors, lenses, or combinations of both—to capture and direct sunlight onto a receiver. The major components of concentrators are:

- **Parabolic Reflector:** A parabolic reflector consists of a curved, mirrored surface designed to capture and focus sunlight onto a specific point or line. The parabolic shape is crucial because it ensures that incoming parallel rays of sunlight are reflected toward a common focal point. This concentrated sunlight increases the energy density, making it highly effective for heating applications;
- **Absorber Tube (Receiver):** Positioned at the focal line of the parabolic reflector, the absorber tube plays a critical role in capturing the concentrated solar energy. The tube is often made of a highly conductive material, such as stainless steel or copper, to maximize heat absorption. To minimize energy loss, the tube is usually enclosed in a glass cover with a vacuum layer, reducing convection and radiation losses. A special selective coating is applied to the tube's surface to enhance solar absorption while minimizing thermal radiation. The absorbed energy is transferred to the heat transfer fluid (HTF) flowing through the tube;
- **Supporting Structure:** The supporting structure holds the parabolic reflectors and absorber tube in place. It is designed to withstand environmental forces such as wind and thermal expansion, ensuring stability and durability. The structure is typically made of steel or aluminum for strength and corrosion resistance. Precision in the alignment of the mirrors is essential, as even minor deviations can reduce the system's efficiency. The supporting structure also integrates with the tracking system, allowing the reflector to move smoothly as it follows the sun;
- **Tracking System:** To maximize solar energy capture throughout the day, parabolic trough systems use a single-axis or dual-axis tracking system.
    - **Single-axis tracking:** The trough rotates along one axis, typically aligned north-south, to follow the sun's east-west movement. This is the most common configuration in commercial systems.

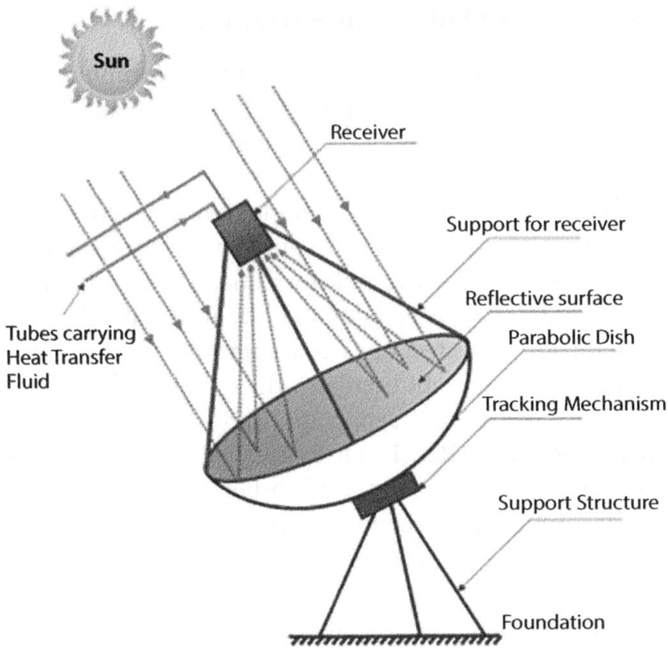

Figure 4.1 Components of parabolic concentrators [1].

  - **Dual-axis tracking:** Less common for trough systems but used in heliostat-based plants, this system adjusts the mirror's position along both horizontal and vertical axes, achieving more precise solar alignment. The tracking system uses motors, gears, and sensors to maintain optimal orientation, ensuring the reflectors continuously focus sunlight onto the absorber tube.
- **Heat Transfer Fluid (HTF) System:** The HTF system carries the thermal energy captured by the absorber tube. The fluid—typically water, thermal oil, or molten salt—circulates through the system, absorbing heat and transferring it to either a power generation unit or a thermal storage system.
  - **Water or steam:** Used in direct steam generation systems, producing steam that drives turbines.
  - **Thermal oil:** Common in commercial plants, with a high boiling point, allowing it to reach temperatures of 300–400°C without high pressure.

- **Molten salt:** Ideal for thermal storage due to its ability to retain heat for extended periods, enabling power generation even when the sun isn't shining. The HTF system plays a vital role in ensuring efficient heat transfer and overall system performance.

Details of parabolic concentrator are illustrated in Figure 4.1:

The effectiveness of the concentration depends on the reflectivity of the parabolic surface and the concentration ratio of the solar concentrator, as well as the alignment and tracking capabilities of the system.

4.2.2 Concentration Ratio and Its Importance

The **concentration ratio (CR)** is a fundamental parameter that defines the performance and efficiency of a solar concentrator. It quantifies the level of sunlight concentration by comparing the area that captures the incoming solar radiation to the area where the light is focused. The concentration ratio is mathematically expressed by the formula:

$$CR = \frac{\text{Aperture Area}}{\text{Receiver Area}}$$

- **Aperture Area:** The surface area of the collector or reflector that intercepts direct sunlight.
- **Receiver Area:** The surface onto which the concentrated sunlight is directed, typically the absorber or heat exchanger.

A higher concentration ratio means that a larger amount of sunlight is focused onto a smaller area, resulting in greater energy density and elevated temperatures at the receiver. This is particularly advantageous for high-temperature applications, such as:

- **Power generation** through steam turbines or Stirling engines, where higher temperatures increase thermodynamic efficiency;
- **Thermochemical processes**, which require extreme heat for chemical reactions;
- **Concentrated photovoltaics (CPV)**, where sunlight intensity boosts electrical output from solar cells.

Concentration Ratios for Different Systems

Various solar concentrator technologies have different CR values, influencing their temperature range and efficiency:

- **Parabolic Troughs:** CR of approximately **30–80**, making them suitable for medium-temperature applications (e.g., steam generation for power plants);
- **Linear Fresnel Reflectors:** CR ranges from **10–40**, offering a cost-effective solution for moderate-temperature solar thermal systems.
- **Solar Power Towers:** CR values of **200–1000+**, capable of reaching extremely high temperatures, making them ideal for large-scale power generation and thermal storage.
- **Parabolic Dish Collectors:** CR of **500–2000**, achieving some of the highest concentration levels, making them suitable for small-scale, high-efficiency power systems.

4.2.3 Impact of Concentration on System Efficiency

The concentration ratio plays a direct role in determining the temperature, efficiency, and overall performance of solar energy systems.

- **Higher Operating Temperatures:** Increasing the CR raises the temperature at the receiver, enhancing the thermodynamic efficiency of heat engines (such as Rankine or Brayton cycles). In solar thermal plants, this results in greater power output for the same amount of captured sunlight. Elevated temperatures also improve the effectiveness of thermal energy storage systems, allowing them to retain more energy for longer periods.
- **Improved Photovoltaic Efficiency:** In Concentrated Photovoltaic (CPV) systems, higher sunlight intensity increases the electrical power output of solar cells. However, excess heat can degrade the cells, requiring efficient cooling mechanisms to prevent overheating and maintain long-term performance.
- **Reduced Material Costs:** By focusing sunlight onto a smaller area, concentrator systems reduce the amount of expensive photovoltaic or heat-absorbing material required.

This lowers material costs while maintaining high energy output, making solar power generation more economically viable.

4.2.4 Optical Efficiency and Losses

The overall efficiency of a solar concentrator is determined not only by the concentration ratio but also by its **optical efficiency**, which accounts for energy losses during the light collection and focusing process. Several factors contribute to optical losses:

- **Reflectivity Losses:** Imperfect reflection from the mirrors or reflective surfaces reduces the amount of sunlight reaching the receiver. Even high-quality mirrors have reflectivity below 100%, causing some energy loss.
- **Absorption and Transmission Losses:** When sunlight passes through lenses, glass covers, or secondary optical components, some energy is absorbed or scattered, reducing the amount of energy reaching the receiver.
- **Misalignment and Tracking Errors:** Solar concentrators rely on precise **sun-tracking mechanisms** to maintain optimal focus throughout the day. Even small tracking inaccuracies or misalignments can significantly reduce the system's effectiveness by lowering the concentration of sunlight on the receiver.
- **Atmospheric Scattering and Dust Accumulation:** In areas with high dust levels, humidity, or atmospheric scattering, sunlight diffusion reduces the effectiveness of the concentrator. Dust accumulation on mirrors or lenses can further diminish optical performance, requiring **regular cleaning and maintenance** to sustain efficiency.

4.3 Types of Solar Concentrators

Solar concentrators are categorized based on their design and focusing mechanisms, each suited for specific applications in solar thermal and photovoltaic energy systems as illustrated in Figure 4.2:

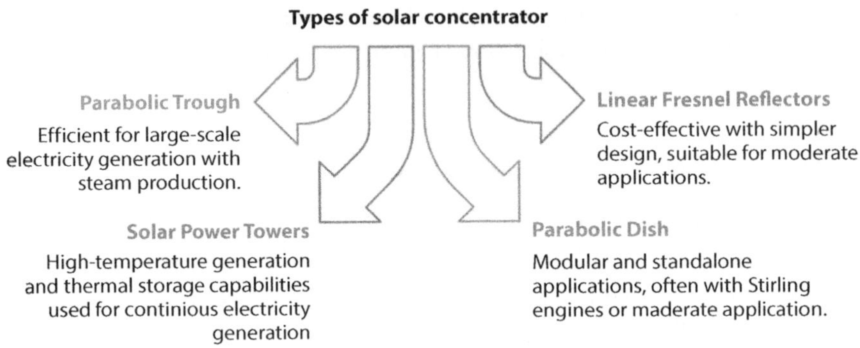

Figure 4.2 Types of solar concentrators.

- **Parabolic Trough Concentrators (PTCs)**, as illustrated in Figure 4.3, are widely used in large-scale solar power plants for electricity generation. They consist of parabolically curved mirrors that focus sunlight onto a linear receiver tube containing a heat-transfer fluid (HTF), such as synthetic oil or molten salt. The heated fluid is used to produce steam, driving turbines to generate electricity. PTCs are ideal for medium-temperature applications (up to ~400°C) and are commonly deployed in concentrated solar power (CSP) plants.
- **Linear Fresnel Reflectors (LFR)** as shown in Figure 4.4, known for their cost-effectiveness and simplicity, are used for industrial process heat and medium-scale power generation.

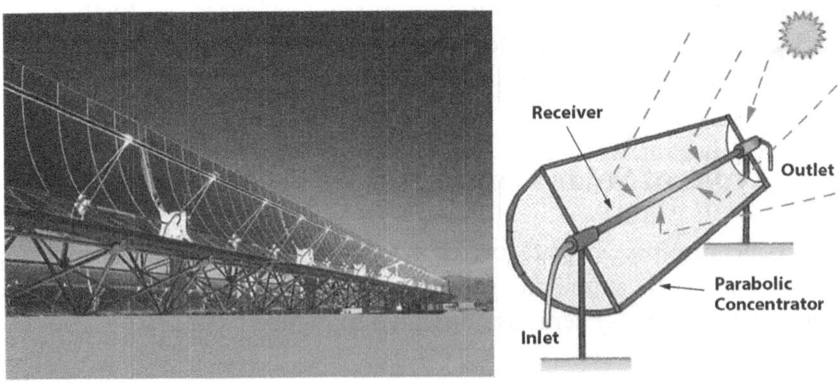

Figure 4.3 Parabolic trough concentrators, actual and schematic view [2].

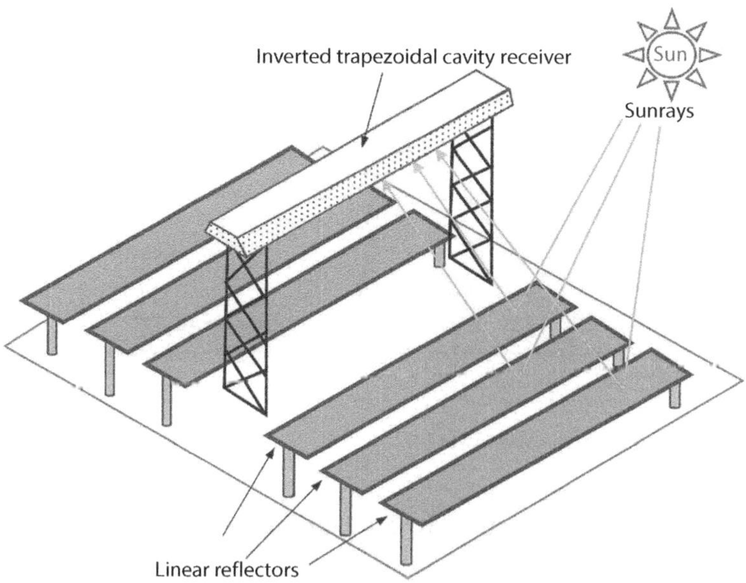

Figure 4.4 Schematic of linear Fresnel reflector system [3].

They utilize multiple flat or slightly curved mirrors to direct sunlight onto an elevated receiver tube. Although they achieve lower concentration ratios compared to parabolic troughs, their compact design makes them suitable for rooftop installations and smaller solar thermal applications.

- **Solar Power Towers** illustrated in Figure 4.5, also called central receiver systems, are used in large-scale utility power plants. They employ a field of sun-tracking mirrors (heliostats) that focus sunlight onto a receiver atop a central tower. The system achieves extremely high temperatures (600–1000°C) and uses molten salt for efficient thermal storage. This allows for continuous electricity generation, even after sunset, making power towers highly effective for grid-scale renewable energy production.
- **Parabolic Dish Concentrators**, as illustrated in Figure 4.6 are used for standalone power generation in remote areas or off-grid locations. These systems consist of dish-shaped reflectors that concentrate sunlight onto a small receiver at the focal point. Often coupled with Stirling engines or other heat engines, they directly convert solar heat into mechanical power, which is then used to generate electricity.

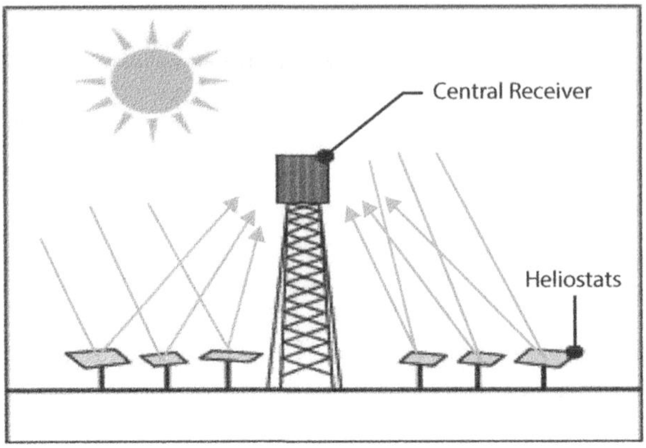

Figure 4.5 Schematic of a solar tower [4].

Their modular nature makes them suitable for decentralized energy solutions.

- **Fresnel Lens Concentrators**, as illustrated in Figure 4.7, are commonly used in Concentrated Photovoltaic (CPV) systems to enhance the performance of solar cells. These systems use lightweight, grooved lenses to focus sunlight onto small, high-efficiency photovoltaic cells. By increasing the light intensity, they boost the electrical output of

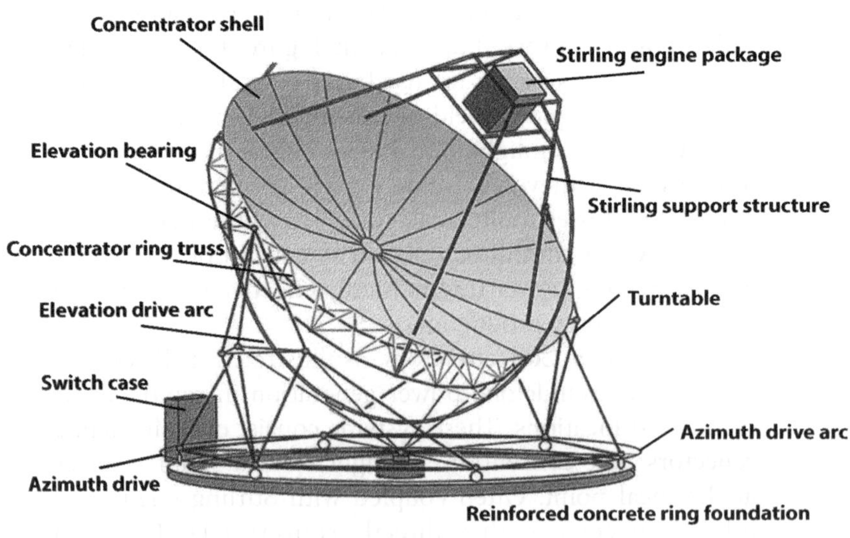

Figure 4.6 Parabolic dish concentrators [5].

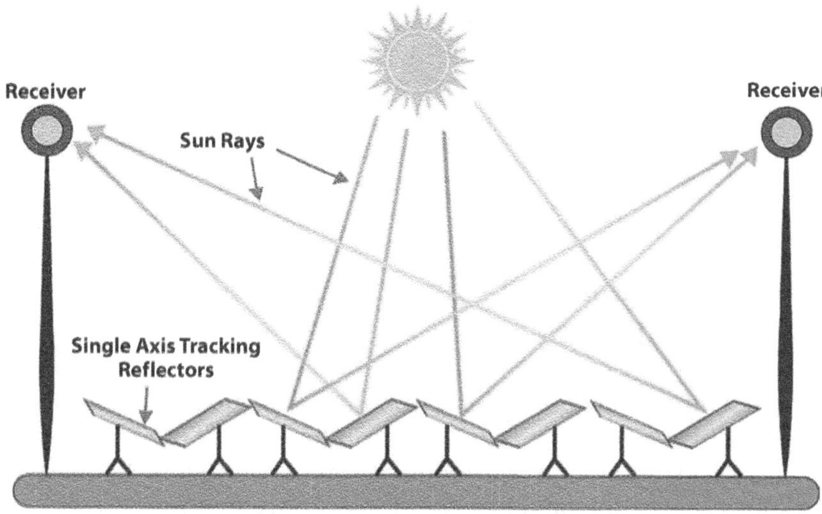

Figure 4.7 Compact linear Fresnel reflectors [6].

the cells, making them suitable for compact and portable solar systems, such as mobile charging stations and space-constrained installations.

4.4 Advanced Configurations: Multi-Surface and Multi-Element Combinations

Recent advancements in solar concentrator technology have introduced multi-surface (MS) and multi-element (ME) configurations, significantly enhancing performance by improving light collection efficiency, concentration ratios, and reducing optical losses.

Multi-Surface (MS) Combinations incorporate multiple reflective or refractive surfaces to optimize light interception and distribution. By strategically layering or positioning these surfaces, MS designs increase the acceptance angle, allowing concentrators to capture more sunlight throughout the day, even as the sun's position changes. This configuration also enhances energy uniformity at the receiver, reducing localized hot spots and improving overall thermal performance [7].

Multi-Element (ME) Combinations utilize two or more optical components—such as a primary and secondary concentrator—to achieve higher concentration ratios and greater optical efficiency. For instance, combining a parabolic trough (primary) with a compound parabolic concentrator (secondary) improves the system's tolerance to minor tracking errors, reducing sensitivity to misalignment. ME designs are particularly effective for high-precision applications, such as concentrated photovoltaic (CPV) systems, where precise light focus is essential for maximizing electrical output [8].

4.5 Applications and Advantages of Solar Concentrators

Solar concentrators are utilized across a wide range of applications, significantly boosting energy efficiency and expanding the use of solar power for both electricity generation and industrial processes. Figure 4.8 illustrates the various applications and benefits of solar concentrators.

Electricity Generation: Solar concentrators play a key role in concentrated solar power (CSP) plants by generating high-temperature heat. This heat drives steam turbines or Stirling engines, which are connected to generators, producing electricity. Power towers and parabolic trough systems are commonly used for large-scale power plants, delivering grid-connected renewable energy [9].

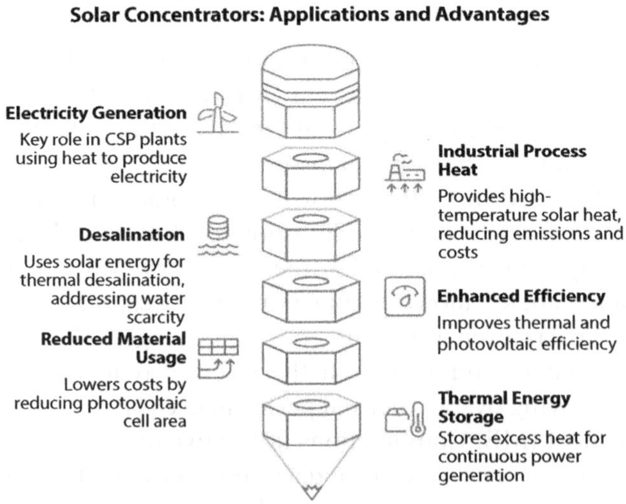

Figure 4.8 Application and advantages of solar concentrators.

Industrial Process Heat: In industrial settings, solar concentrators supply thermal energy for processes requiring elevated temperatures, such as chemical manufacturing, metal processing, and food production. By replacing fossil fuels with solar heat, these systems reduce carbon emissions and operational costs.
Desalination: In arid regions, solar concentrators are used in thermal desalination systems to produce potable water. The concentrated solar energy powers multi-effect distillation (MED) or multi-stage flash (MSF) processes, evaporating seawater and condensing it into freshwater. This application addresses water scarcity issues in sun-rich but water-limited areas [10].

The primary advantages of solar concentrators include:

- Enhanced Efficiency: By increasing the concentration ratio, solar concentrators significantly improve the thermal and photovoltaic efficiency of solar energy systems.
- Reduced Photovoltaic Material Usage: In CPV systems, concentrators reduce the area of expensive photovoltaic cells required, lowering overall material costs.
- Thermal Energy Storage (TES): Concentrators integrated with TES systems can store excess heat, enabling continuous power generation, even during cloudy weather or at night.

4.6 Challenges and Considerations

Despite their numerous benefits, solar concentrators face several challenges that limit their widespread adoption and operational efficiency.

Tracking Requirements: Most solar concentrator designs, particularly parabolic troughs, power towers, and dish systems require precise sun-tracking mechanisms to maintain optimal focus. This adds to the system's complexity and cost, as tracking motors and sensors must be installed and regularly maintained.
Thermal Management: The high temperatures achieved by solar concentrators necessitate efficient cooling systems to prevent overheating and material degradation. In CPV systems, excessive heat can reduce the efficiency and lifespan of photovoltaic cells, making active cooling systems essential [11].

Geographical Limitations: Solar concentrators rely heavily on direct sunlight for optimal performance, making them less effective in regions with frequent cloud cover, atmospheric scattering, or diffuse light conditions. Their efficiency drops significantly in areas with low solar irradiance.

4.7 Future Prospects

Ongoing research and technological advancements aim to overcome the current limitations of solar concentrators. Future innovations include:

- Broader Acceptance Angles: New designs are being developed with wider acceptance angles, enabling concentrators to capture more sunlight throughout the day without the need for continuous tracking. This reduces complexity and lowers system costs [12].
- Advanced Materials: The integration of nanostructured coatings, improved reflective surfaces, and high-temperature-resistant materials is enhancing the optical and thermal performance of concentrators [13].
- Hybrid Systems: Emerging hybrid concentrator systems combine photovoltaic and thermal energy conversion, capturing both light and heat simultaneously. This increases the overall energy yield and system efficiency [14].

4.8 Conclusion

Solar concentrators are at the forefront of renewable energy innovation, playing a vital role in increasing the efficiency and feasibility of solar power systems. Their diverse configurations—ranging from parabolic troughs to multi-element combinations—enable a wide array of applications, from utility-scale electricity generation to industrial heat processes and water desalination [15]. However, addressing the challenges of tracking precision, thermal management, and regional limitations is crucial for expanding their adoption. With ongoing advancements in materials, optics, and hybrid technologies, solar concentrators are expected to remain a cornerstone of sustainable energy solutions, contributing significantly to the global transition toward clean and efficient power generation.

AI disclosure statement: The author acknowledges the use of AI-based tools for minor language editing or grammatical correction. However, all intellectual contributions, analyses, and conclusions presented in this chapter are entirely the author's own.

References

1. Nandanwar, Y.N. and Walke, P.V., A comprehensive review on integration of receiver geometries, nanofluids, and efficient thermal energy storage for solar parabolic dish collectors. *J. Braz. Soc. Mech. Sci. Eng.*, 46, 8, 480, 2024, doi: 10.1007/s40430-024-05034-2.
2. Lamba, M. and Das, S., Designing of Parabolic Trough Collector using Plane Mirrors. *J. Phys. Conf. Ser.*, IOP Publishing Ltd, Feb. 2022, doi: 10.1088/1742-6596/2178/1/012015.
3. Ravi Kumar, K., Krishna Chaitanya, N.V.V., Sendhil Kumar, N., Solar thermal energy technologies and its applications for process heating and power generation – A review. *J. Cleaner Prod.*, Feb. 01, 2021, Elsevier Ltd. doi: 10.1016/j.jclepro.2020.125296.
4. Mubarrat, M., Mashfy, M.M., Farhan, T., Ehsan, M.M., Research Advancement and Potential Prospects of Thermal Energy Storage in Concentrated Solar Power Application. *Int. J. Thermofluids*, Nov. 01, 2023, Elsevier B.V. doi: 10.1016/j.ijft.2023.100431.
5. Mallayya, P., Santosh, J., Baredar, A Comparative Study of Parabolic Dish Concentrators Used in Various Systems, in: *Advances in Fluid and Thermal Engineering*, S. K. and J. A., S.K.M. Sikarwar Basant Singh, Sharma (Eds.), pp. 359–369, Springer Nature Singapore, Singapore, 2023.
6. Imran Khan, M., Asfand, F., Al-Ghamdi, S.G., Progress in research and technological advancements of commercial concentrated solar thermal power plants. *Solar Energy*, Jan. 01, 2023, Elsevier Ltd. doi: 10.1016/j.solener.2022.10.041.
7. Paliyal, P.S., Mondal, S., Layek, S., Kuchhal, P., Pandey, J.K., Automatic solar tracking system: a review pertaining to advancements and challenges in the current scenario. *Clean Energy*, 8, 6, 237–262, December 2024, https://doi.org/10.1093/ce/zkae085.
8. Paliyal, P.S., Mondal, S., Pandey, J.K., An Analysis of Springwater Parameter Status for Different Locations in the Rural Hilly Garhwal Region of Uttarakhand. *Environ. Claims J.*, *36*, 3, 243–277, 2024, https://doi.org/10.1080/10406026.2024.2423964.
9. Paliyal, P.S. and Mondal, S., An analysis of a cross-finned receiver for Scheffler-type solar collectors to optimize solar heating efficiency for direct water heating. *Int. J. Energy Water Resour.*, 2025, https://doi.org/10.1007/s42108-025-00393-5.

10. Paliyal, P.S., Mondal, S., Pathela, M., Kumar, A., Menon, S.K., Optimization of Solar Photovoltaic Array In-Depth Analysis of Perturb and Observe MPPT Algorithm. *2024 International Conference on Advances in Computing, Communication and Materials (ICACCM)*, Dehradun, India, pp. 1–6, 2024, doi: 10.1109/ICACCM61117.2024.11059143.
11. Srivastav, A., CFD investigation of thermo-hydraulic performance in rib roughened fin under forced convection. *J. Graphic Era Univ.,* 2023. https://doi.org/10.13052/jgeu0975-1416.1111.
12. Menon, S.K., *et al.*, The Role of Hydrogen as a Sustainable Energy Source and its Integration with the Grid, in: *Advancements in Communication and Systems*, A.K. Tripathi and V. Shrivastava (Eds.), p. 397, Computing and Intelligent Systems, SCRS, India, 2023, (2025).
13. Kudapa, V.K., Paliyal, P.S., Mondal, A., Mondal, S., A critical review of fabrication strategies, separation techniques, challenges, and future prospects for the hydrogen separation membrane. *Fusion Sci. Technol.*, 80, 7, 803–825, 2024.
14. Mondal, A., Jangirh, R., Arya, R., Yadav, L., Ahlawat, S., Yadav, P., Paliyal, P.S., Bobde, P., Ghosh, P., Mondal, S., Rai, A., Analysing solid residential fuel usage patterns in rural and urban slums of Delhi: Implications for pollution reduction and sustainable practices. *Energy Sustainable Dev., 80,* 101460, 2024.
15. Srivastav, A., Maithani, R., Sharma, S., Influence of submerged impingement jet designs on solar air collector performance. *Renew. Energy*, 237, 121699, 2024. https://doi.org/10.1016/j.renene.2024.121699.

5

Solar Scheffler Concentrators: The Future of Sustainable Cooking

Amit Kumar[1]*, Ashish Karn[1] and Varun Pratap Singh[1,2]

[1]*Department of Mechanical Engineering, School of Advanced Engineering, UPES, Dehradun, India*

[2]*Solar Thermal Energy Research Group, Department of Mechanical and Mechatronics Engineering, Stellenbosch University, Stellenbosch, South Africa*

Abstract

Traditional cooking methods, such as biomass and fossil fuels, raise environmental issues and pose health hazards. As a result, there is an urgent need to transition to sustainable cooking technologies. Among various clean alternatives, solar energy, a renewable and abundant resource, offers a promising solution. In particular, solar Scheffler concentrators provide a viable option for institutional kitchens by using solar energy to generate sufficient heat for cooking. These concentrators employ parabolic reflectors to focus sunlight on a central receiver, minimizing reliance on conventional fuels, reducing harmful emissions, and improving air quality. Despite their clear advantages, such as lower operational costs and long-term economic benefits, the widespread adoption of Scheffler concentrators is limited due to factors like high initial investment, lack of awareness, and dependence on sunlight. This paper discusses the design, benefits, limitations, and future potential of solar Scheffler concentrators as we work towards cleaner and more sustainable cooking technologies in institutional and community settings.

***Keywords*:** Solar cooking, Scheffler concentrator, sustainable energy, CleanCooking, renewable technology

**Corresponding author*: amit.113660@stu.upes.ac.in

Surajit Mondal, Paramjeet Singh Paliyal and Sachin Sharma (eds.) Digital Twin Technology for Solar Concentrators, (59–74) © 2026 Scrivener Publishing LLC

5.1 Introduction

Cooking is vital at both household and institutional levels, requiring much energy daily. Institutional kitchens, such as those in hospitals, schools, hostels, and large-scale canteens, consume large quantities of energy to prepare meals for hundreds or thousands of people. Traditionally, commercial fuels like liquefied petroleum gas (LPG), natural gas, and coal have been used to meet these cooking energy demands. However, reliance on these fossil fuels contributes to environmental degradation, air pollution, and rising operational costs. The combustion of such fuels emits harmful pollutants such as carbon dioxide (CO_2), carbon monoxide (CO), and particulate matter, which not only degrade the environment but also pose serious health risks, including respiratory diseases. According to the World Health Organization (WHO), approximately 4.3 million people die annually due to illnesses caused by indoor air pollution from cooking with these fuels. Given these environmental and health concerns, there is an urgent need to transition towards cleaner, more sustainable cooking technologies [1]. Given these environmental and health concerns, there is an urgent need to transition to cleaner and more sustainable cooking technologies that align with the global push toward achieving the Sustainable Development Goals (SDGs), particularly Goal 7 (Affordable and Clean Energy) and Goal 13 (Climate Action). Solar energy, a renewable and abundant resource, offers a promising alternative to fossil fuels [2].

Among solar cooking systems, Scheffler Solar Concentrators have emerged as a viable solution for institutional cooking. These systems utilize parabolic reflectors to concentrate sunlight onto a cooking vessel, generating sufficient heat for cooking. The ability to scale up and meet the high energy demands of institutional kitchens makes Scheffler concentrators an ideal option for large-scale cooking operations. With its high solar insolation levels, India is particularly well-suited for solar cooking technologies. India's average daily global horizontal irradiance (GHI) ranges from 4 to 7 kWh/m^2, making it an ideal location for solar applications, including cooking. In fact, in arid zones of India, solar cookers can function for more than 300 days a year, demonstrating the significant potential for solar cooking in these regions [3]. Studies have indicated that solar cooking can account for up to 50% of the total meals prepared annually in India, further emphasizing its feasibility as an alternative to conventional cooking methods. Scheffler Solar Concentrators, in particular, are well-suited for institutional kitchens that require large amounts of energy to cook food. These systems can produce high levels of thermal energy, making them ideal for large-scale cooking. For instance, each Scheffler dish with an aperture area of 4 m^2 can provide sufficient heat to cook meals for approximately 50 individuals. The potential for solar energy to replace conventional cooking fuels is significant. Studies have estimated that 23 Scheffler parabolic dish cookers installed at a school in Ahmednagar, Maharashtra, have saved between 15 to 25 kg of LPG per month. This reduces fuel costs and mitigates the environmental impact of cooking, as it prevents the emission of CO_2 and other harmful pollutants. The benefits of Scheffler solar cooking systems are not limited to their environmental advantages. Financially, these systems offer long-term savings by reducing the dependency on expensive commercial fuels. While the initial investment in solar cooking systems can be high, particularly for large institutional kitchens, the operating costs are minimal. Once installed, solar energy costs are virtually free, and the systems have a long operational lifespan with relatively low maintenance costs. Solar cooking technologies are expected to become more financially viable as mass production and economies of scale drive down the initial investment. However, despite the clear environmental and financial benefits, the widespread adoption of Scheffler Solar Concentrators has been slow. One of the significant barriers is the high initial capital cost of installing solar cooking systems. Although solar concentrators can save significant money in the long run, the upfront costs often make them unaffordable for many institutions [4].

Additionally, solar cooking systems are dependent on sunlight, which can be intermittent, posing a challenge in regions with cloudy weather or during nighttime cooking hours. While innovations such as thermal energy storage systems can address these issues, they remain underutilized in many parts of the world. Moreover, institutional decision-makers' lack of awareness and knowledge hinders the adoption of solar cooking technology. Many managers of institutional kitchens are unaware of the potential benefits of solar cooking or are reluctant to change from traditional fossil fuel-based systems, which they perceive as more reliable. To overcome these barriers, raising awareness about the environmental, health, and financial benefits of solar cooking technologies and providing incentives for their adoption is crucial. In India, government initiatives and policies play a key role in promoting the adoption of solar cooking technologies [5]. Various government agencies have supported integrating solar cookers into institutional kitchens through technical assistance and financial incentives. However, despite the availability of these programs, the widespread adoption of solar cooking systems remains limited due to challenges such as the high initial investment and lack of infrastructure for installation and maintenance. Further efforts must be made to reduce the financial barriers to solar cooking, including providing subsidies and offering low-interest loans to institutional users. The potential for Scheffler Solar Concentrators in institutional kitchens is immense. These systems offer a clean and sustainable alternative to fossil fuels and help reduce the financial burden on institutions by cutting fuel costs. The environmental benefits—from reduced greenhouse gas emissions to improved air quality—further enhance the value of solar cooking systems. By leveraging solar energy, institutional kitchens can reduce their reliance on commercial fuels, lower operating costs, and contribute to a more sustainable energy future [6].

In conclusion, Scheffler Solar Concentrators represent an up-and-coming technology for sustainable cooking in institutional kitchens. Their ability to harness solar energy and provide large-scale, cost-effective cooking solutions can revolutionize how meals are prepared in large institutions, particularly in regions with abundant sunlight like India. However, to fully realize the potential of solar cooking, it is essential to address the financial, technical, and socio-economic challenges that currently limit the widespread adoption of Scheffler Solar Concentrators. With the right policies, incentives, and innovations, solar cooking systems can become an integral part of the future of sustainable cooking.

5.2 Solar Scheffler Concentrator

Wolfgang Scheffler devised the Scheffler reflector, a device for harnessing solar energy. As seen in Figure 5.1, this collector follows the sun's movement, focusing sunlight on a fixed focal point. Scheffler fixed-focus concentrators have been utilized effectively in medium and high-temperature applications worldwide. They can concentrate sunlight in two dimensions to a precise "point," allowing for efficient heat transmission without requiring a sophisticated mechanism. If the reflector is positioned north or south of the focal point, it tracks the sun along a single axis. The focused light warms the receiver, and the heat is transmitted to a suitable fluid, which may subsequently be employed in a variety of applications. The Scheffler reflector operates on the same idea as satellite collectors, using the sides of a rotational parabola instead of the bottom [7]. Figure 5.2 illustrates an indirect solar Scheffler cooking system, where sunlight is captured by a parabolic Scheffler concentrator, focused on a fixed focal point. The concentrated heat is directed to a cooking pot placed inside a shaded kitchen area, allowing efficient cooking without direct sunlight exposure, enhancing practicality and comfort.

Figure 5.1 Structure of Scheffler concentrator.

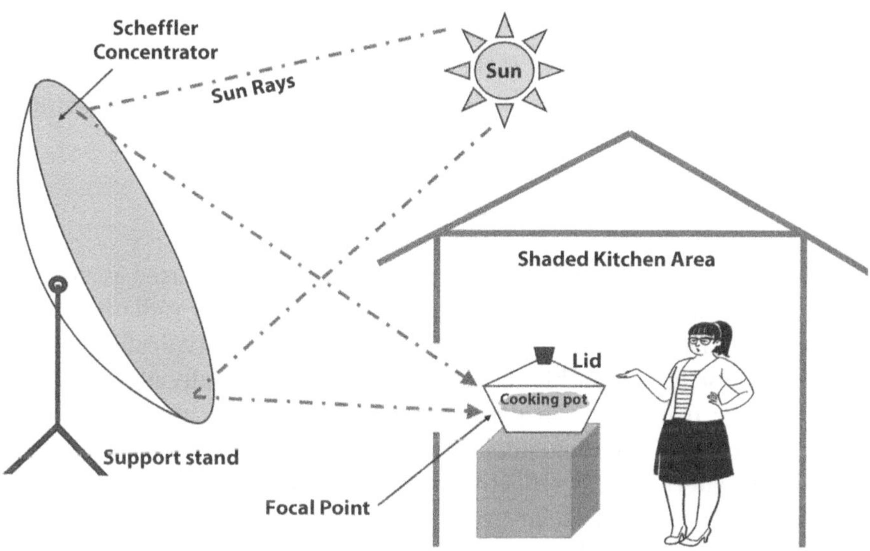

Figure 5.2 Indirect cooking with solar Scheffler.

5.2.1 Design and Structure

The Scheffler dish is constructed from a small lateral section of a larger paraboloid. The typical elliptical shape of the dish is formed by slicing the paraboloid at an inclined angle using a plane. The aperture area of the Scheffler dish for low- to medium-temperature applications typically ranges from 8 to 16 m^2. However, Scheffler dishes with aperture areas up to

60 m^2 have also been used for high-temperature applications, such as solar thermal power generation. A standard Scheffler dish with a 16 m^2 aperture typically covers around 35 m^2 of ground area. The thermal output capacity of a 16 m^2 Scheffler dish is approximately 5.5 kW on a clear, sunny day. The base frame of the dish is made from mild steel bars (crossbars) and angles, with aluminum channels bolted above the crossbars to secure the mirror segments. These components are assembled to form a paraboloid-shaped dish with an elliptical aperture area [8]. A mathematical model for estimating the necessary design parameters (such as the length of the semi-minor and significant axes, depth, and arc length of crossbars) for constructing a Scheffler dish has been presented by researchers, along with calculated values for these parameters. The general equation for a parabola on the x-y axis on a given day of the year can be expressed as:

$$y(x) = m_p x^2 + C_y \tag{5.1}$$

where m_p is the slope and C_y is the y-intercept of the parabola. The frame of the Scheffler dish consists of elliptical crossbars, and a specific point 'n' on the crossbar can be determined as follows.

$$y_n = (\cos 43.23)\,(b^2 - x_n^2)\,0.5 \tag{5.2}$$

For optimal cooking performance, a solar concentrator used as a cooker must capture and transfer the maximum amount of solar radiation to the receiver [9]. The reflective surface of a Scheffler dish is typically made by fixing small segments of highly reflective material (usually glass mirrors) to the frame using wire strips or screws. The performance of the solar concentrator is highly dependent on the optical properties of the reflector. Thus, materials with reflectivity greater than 90% are recommended for construction. While solar-grade glass mirrors are commonly used as reflectors, some researchers have developed cost-effective polymer/steel-based reflectors with silver or aluminum coatings. The entire structure is designed to withstand wind speeds of up to 160 km/h, with an expected lifespan of at least 20 years. It is mounted on a rigid structure facing south in the northern hemisphere (or north in the southern hemisphere). In regions of the northern hemisphere, such as India, the Scheffler dish reflects and concentrates Direct Normal Irradiance (DNI) onto a fixed receiver facing north [8, 10].

5.3 Cooking with Solar Scheffler Concentrator

Scheffler dish-based direct cooking systems employ two concentrators: a primary Scheffler dish and a secondary reflector. The primary dish reflects and focuses Direct Normal Irradiance (DNI) onto the north or south wall of the kitchen, where the secondary reflector is located. This design is quite convenient for solar cooking because the cooking pot remains fixed within the kitchen. A Scheffler dish can achieve temperatures of up to 400°C, allowing food to be cooked quickly. The Scheffler direct cooking system consists of four basic components: the primary Scheffler dish, secondary reflector, cooking pot, and tracking system. The secondary reflector is located near the focal point of the primary dish and is installed into the kitchen wall facing it. Its goal is to send concentrated sun energy from the primary dish to the bottom of the cooking pot, where it is absorbed and transformed into heat. This not only enhances the density of solar radiation but also allows the cooking pot to be put inside the kitchen. The cooking pot's side walls are often insulated to decrease heat loss, and an insulated solid iron block is occasionally used to retain heat for later cooking.

Because of the high concentration of solar radiation on the secondary reflector's surface, there is a risk of burnout. Thus, the material must be able to resist temperatures ranging from 400 to 500 degrees Celsius. Typically, the secondary reflector is composed of anodized aluminum sheets with a minimum thickness of 0.4mm, and extra reflectors can be retained to assure efficiency. The cooking system is frequently fitted into existing kitchens, allowing for the use of other fuels during non-sunny hours. In rare circumstances, the secondary reflector may be unnecessary, as the primary dish can heat the cooking pot directly. Baking ovens, steam generators, and heat storage devices, for example, can be located toward the center of the main dish to increase efficiency, save costs, and simplify operation and maintenance. Figure 5.3 presents the efficiency of Scheffler dish systems based on various literature sources.

A basic mechanical clockwork setup with counterweights and pendulums is widely utilized for indoor Scheffler cooking systems since it is inexpensive and simple. However, experimental bi-axial tracking devices, including ropes and pulleys, have also been investigated. According to the Ministry of New and Renewable Energy (MNRE), a single-axis tracked Scheffler dish costs around INR 16,000 per square meter. This cost is only for the concentrator dish system and does not include civil construction or kitchen conversion, which might add 15-25% to the total cost. Scheffler dishes in India come in various sizes, from 2.7 m^2 (family size) to 16 m^2

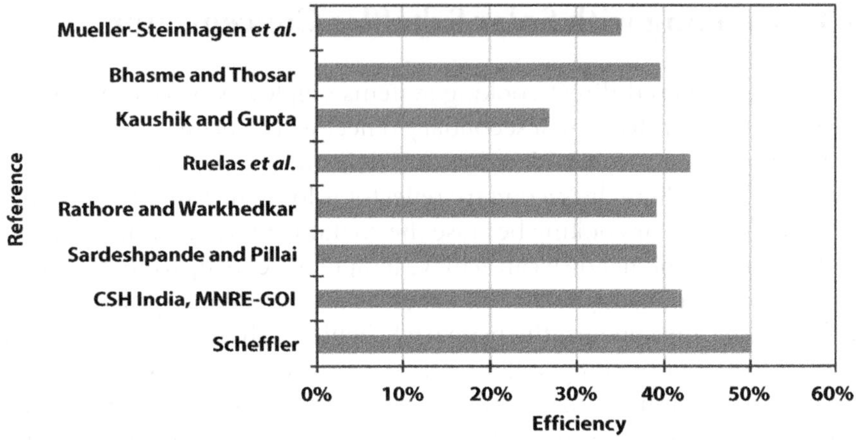

Figure 5.3 Scheffler efficiency according to literature [11–18].

(community size). A 2.7 m^2 family-sized dish can boil 1.2 liters of water in 10 minutes, while a 10 m^2 community-sized dish can boil 4.5 liters of cold water with a DNI of 700 W/m^2. A Scheffler direct cooking system for institutional use typically includes a dish with a 7-16 m^2 aperture area and can prepare food for 50-100 people, depending on size. Figure 5.4 compares various institutional solar kitchens using Scheffler concentrators across India, showing the number of meals cooked per day, total Scheffler reflector area (in m^2), and the number of Scheffler dishes installed. Notably, Shantivan and Shirdi centers serve the highest number of meals using extensive Scheffler setups.

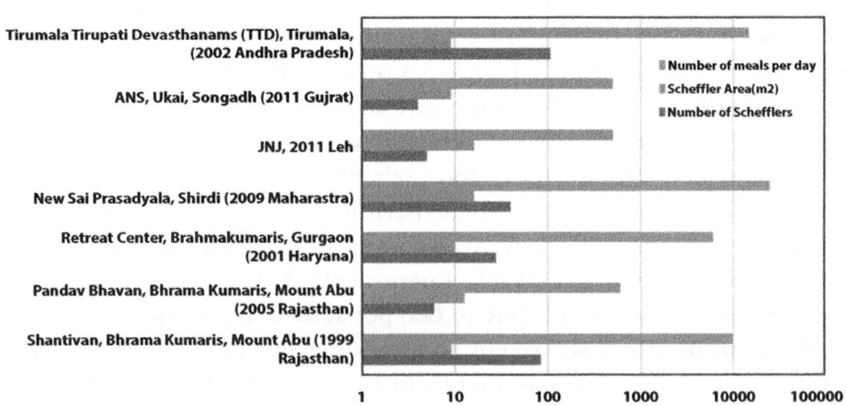

Figure 5.4 Capacity details of solar Scheffler cooking systems.

5.4 Case Studies on Scheffler Dish-Based Solar Cooking Systems

For many years, various institutional solar cooking systems in India have used Scheffler dishes. These systems are classified into two types: Scheffler direct and Scheffler indirect steam cooking systems, both of which are widely used in institutions such as religious centers, industrial canteens, and hostels. Many of these installations have received funding from the Ministry of New and Renewable Energy (MNRE). Cooking capabilities vary greatly, with the number of meals ranging from 100 to 30,000-35,000 at any given moment. Approximately 150 Scheffler dish-based direct solar cooking systems are now operational in India. Since 1998, the Barli Institute for Rural Women (BIRW) in Indore has used two 10 m^2 Scheffler dishes to serve daily meals for 100 trainees. This device works for roughly 300 days a year, saving approximately 3 kg of LPG or 25 kg of wood every day. The system also features thermal energy storage in mild steel blocks insulated with glass fiber wool, which allows Chapattis (baked bread) to be cooked after dark.

Another significant installation is in Madhya Pradesh's Jhabua area, where a bigger Scheffler-based system with five dishes serves meals to 900 students in a school dormitory. Similar systems have been erected in other countries, including Argentina and Egypt, illustrating the worldwide reach of solar cooking technology. In Argentina, a community solar oven bakery uses an 8 m^2 Scheffler dish to make bread, saving families 60 kilograms of firewood each week.

In India, the Brahma Kumaris World Spiritual Organization in Mount Abu, Rajasthan, runs a big Scheffler dish-based system with 84 dishes, serving 30,000 meals daily. The system produces 3500 kg of steam per day and saves 500 liters of fuel per day, with a reported payback period of 5 years. Other installations in India, such as those at Tirumala (Andhra Pradesh) and Shirdi (Maharashtra), use enormous Scheffler-based systems to feed tourists, providing between 15,000 and 25,000 meals each day.

The Ladakh Renewable Energy Development Agency established a solar steam cooking project at Jawahar Navodaya Vidyalaya in Leh. The project uses five 16 m^2 Scheffler dishes to create 200 kg of steam per day, saving 2.5-3 LPG cylinders every day. Similarly, a smaller four-dish system has been erected at Ukai, Songadh (Gujarat), where 100 pupils are served rice, pulses, and vegetables. Over 150 Scheffler-based solar cooking systems have been deployed throughout India, with varied capacity and payback times. The payback times for these systems vary from 2 to 7.8

years, depending on the quantity of gasoline saved, the system's capacity, and its location. These systems, with a projected lifespan of 15 years, provide a long-term and cost-effective option for institutional cooking. Given the potential for both organized and unorganized sectors, solar energy may play an important part in satisfying a nation's cooking energy needs, contributing to both economic savings and environmental sustainability. Figure 5.5 compares various solar cooking systems across different locations, displaying the annual fuel savings (kg/day), pressure size (kg/m^2), operating days per year, cost without subsidy, and payback period without subsidy (in years). Shantivan, Mount Abu, stands out with the highest fuel savings, while other locations show varying operational and financial metrics.

The performance and cost details of various solar concentrators used for steam generation in India show the installed cost per square meter for each type of concentrator in plain terrain, ranging from Rs. 16,000 to Rs. 20,000 depending on the system configuration. Scheffler dishes with single-axis tracking cost Rs. 16,000, while dual-axis tracking versions are priced at Rs. 18,000. The ARUN dish with dual-axis tracking is priced at Rs. 20,000. Parabolic dishes with dual-axis tracking and parabolic troughs (both with and without evacuated receivers) also cost Rs. 20,000 and Rs. 16,000, respectively, with the evacuated receiver version costing Rs. 18,000. The Linear Fresnel Reflector (LFR) with single-axis tracking costs Rs. 18,000. The achievable temperature ranges vary, with the Scheffler dish reaching up to 150°C with single-axis tracking and 180°C with dual-axis tracking, while systems like the ARUN dish and parabolic dishes can achieve temperatures up to 350°C, making them suitable for high-temperature applications. The weight of the systems varies significantly, with the Scheffler dish weighing 400 kg for a 16 m^2 dish and 850 kg for a 32 m^2 dish.

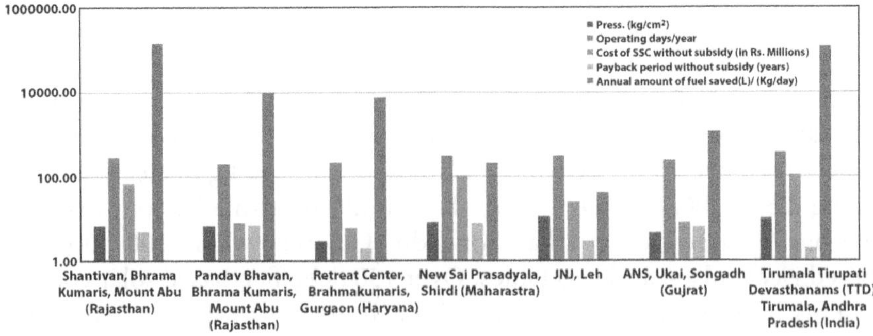

Figure 5.5 Financial and operational details of solar Scheffler cooking systems [8].

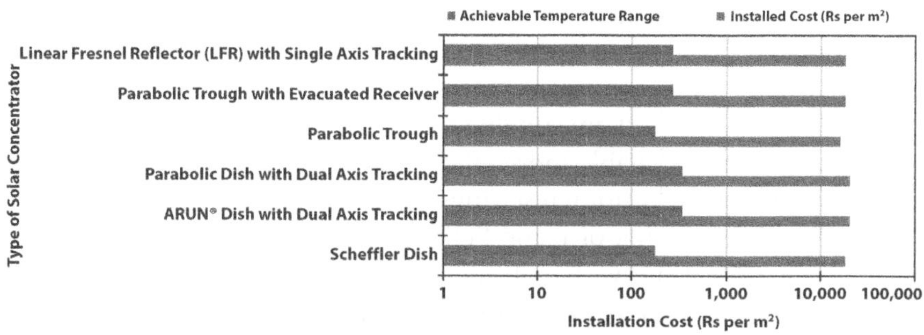

Figure 5.6 Differences in performance and cost of Indian steam concentrators [8, 20, 21].

Larger systems like the ARUN dish weigh much more, with a 100 m^2 dish weighing 13 tons. The parabolic trough system weighs 40 kg per square meter. Additionally, for installations in hilly or difficult terrain, the cost increases by 15-25%, reflecting the additional engineering and logistical challenges. This data provides a comprehensive comparison to help choose the appropriate solar concentrator based on cost, efficiency, and thermal needs [19]. Figure 5.6 compares different types of solar concentrators based on their installed cost per square meter and achievable temperature range. It shows that systems with dual-axis tracking, like the ARUN and parabolic dish, have higher costs but also higher achievable temperatures compared to others like the Scheffler dish and LFR.

5.5 Results and Discussion

The application of Scheffler Solar Concentrators for institutional cooking has demonstrated significant potential in various case studies and experiments, primarily in regions with high solar insolation, such as India. The results highlight the benefits of using solar energy for cooking, including substantial fuel savings, reduced greenhouse gas emissions, and improved air quality. The key findings from these studies and case implementations are as follows:

A Scheffler dish with a 16 m^2 aperture area can generate approximately 5.5 kW of thermal energy on a sunny day. This output is sufficient to cook meals for 50 to 100 people, depending on the size of the dish and the specific cooking requirements. Such a system has been shown to replace up to 25 kg of LPG per month, as seen in the case of a school in Ahmednagar, Maharashtra, demonstrating significant fuel savings [22].

Scheffler dishes can achieve temperatures ranging from 150°C to 400°C, depending on the tracking system. Single-axis tracking systems reach temperatures up to 150°C, while dual-axis systems can achieve temperatures as high as 180°C, making them suitable for various cooking applications. The higher temperatures enable more efficient cooking and steam generation, especially in large institutional settings [23].

The financial benefits of using Scheffler concentrators are substantial, particularly in locations with high solar irradiance. For instance, a single 10 m^2 Scheffler dish can save approximately 3 kg of LPG or 25 kg of firewood daily. The long-term savings from reduced fuel costs significantly offset the initial investment. In institutions like the Brahma Kumari's World Spiritual Organization in Mount Abu, Rajasthan, 84 Scheffler dishes save around 500 liters of fuel daily, with a payback period of only 5 years [24].

By eliminating the need for fossil fuels, Scheffler concentrators contribute to a reduction in CO_2 and other harmful pollutants. The widespread adoption of solar cooking could substantially reduce air pollution and mitigate climate change, particularly in countries with enormous institutional cooking demands, such as India.

Scheffler dishes are highly scalable, with systems ranging from small family-sized dishes (2.7 m^2) to large community dishes (16 m^2 or more). A 2.7 m^2 dish can boil 1.2 liters of water in 10 minutes, making it ideal for household applications, while larger dishes can serve hundreds or thousands of meals daily, as demonstrated by the Brahma Kumari's and other large institutions [25].

Integrating solar cooking systems into existing kitchen setups without significant structural changes is a key advantage. Scheffler dishes can be combined with traditional cooking methods during low sunlight, ensuring continuous meal preparation.

The results indicate that Scheffler Solar Concentrators have the potential to significantly reduce the dependence on traditional cooking fuels, providing a sustainable, clean, and cost-effective alternative. However, the widespread adoption of this technology is hindered by several challenges, most notably the high initial capital cost. While the long-term savings are substantial, the upfront investment remains a barrier for many institutions, particularly those in developing countries [26].

In addition to the cost barrier, the reliance on sunlight for operation is another limitation. Although solar energy is abundant in many regions, the intermittent nature of solar irradiance, particularly during cloudy days or nighttime, poses challenges for consistent cooking operations. Innovations such as thermal energy storage systems, which can store excess heat during sunny periods and release it when needed, could help mitigate this issue.

However, the widespread adoption of such technologies is still limited, and further research is needed to improve storage systems' efficiency and cost-effectiveness.

Despite these challenges, the scalability and adaptability of Scheffler Solar Concentrators make them a viable option for institutional cooking, particularly in regions with high solar insolation. The examples from India, such as the successful implementation of Scheffler systems in educational institutions, spiritual centers, and industrial canteens, demonstrate the technology's potential. Moreover, the significant environmental benefits—such as reduced fuel consumption, lowered greenhouse gas emissions, and improved air quality—make solar cooking an attractive option for institutions aiming to reduce their carbon footprint [27].

Furthermore, the financial viability of Scheffler concentrators can be improved as the technology matures. With increasing production and innovations in tracking systems, reflectors, and energy storage, the initial investment required for solar cooking systems will likely decrease, making them more affordable for a broader range of institutions. Policy support, including subsidies and financial incentives, can be crucial in accelerating the adoption of solar cooking technologies [28].

5.6 Conclusion

Scheffler solar concentrators have shown significant promise as a sustainable and eco-friendly cooking technology, particularly for institutional and large-scale cooking applications. These concentrators utilize solar energy to generate heat, reducing reliance on conventional fossil fuels and offering a clean alternative that minimizes harmful emissions. In regions with abundant solar insolation, such as India, Scheffler dishes can be a practical solution for meeting the cooking energy needs of institutions, saving both financial and environmental costs. The benefits include reduced fuel costs, lowered carbon emissions, and improved air quality, contributing to a healthier environment. However, despite their apparent advantages, challenges such as the high initial investment and dependence on sunlight for operation hinder their widespread adoption. The potential of Scheffler Solar Concentrators could be further realized with technological advancements, which may lead to increased efficiency, reduced costs, and improved durability. As the cost of solar technology continues to decrease through mass production and economies of scale, the accessibility of solar cooking systems for institutions and communities will improve. Innovations such as thermal energy storage systems could address intermittency issues, enabling cooking even during cloudy days or at night. Furthermore, raising awareness about the benefits of solar cooking and providing financial incentives, such as subsidies or low-interest loans, can facilitate the adoption of Scheffler Solar Concentrators in both developed and developing countries. The future of solar Scheffler cooking technology holds significant promise, and with the right policies and technological advancements, it could play a vital role in achieving a more sustainable and cleaner future for cooking.

Acknowledgements

This work acknowledges the availability of resources provided by the UPES R&D department and the Solar Thermal Energy Research Group (STERG) at the University of Stellenbosch, South Africa.

AI disclosure statement: The author acknowledges the use of AI-based tools for minor language editing or grammatical correction. However, all intellectual contributions, analyses, and conclusions presented in this chapter are entirely the author's own.

References

1. Kumar, A., Karn, A., McGregor, C., Singh, V. P., Life cycle sustainability assessment of box solar cooking technologies: Comprehensive comparative analysis with traditional fuels. *Renew. Sustain. Energy Rev.*, vol. 228, Mar. 2026, doi: 10.1016/j.rser.2025.116581.
2. Kumar, A., Karn, A., McGregor, C., Singh, V. P., A critical analysis of paradigm shifts from domestic solar cooking to institutional solar cooking technologies. Aug. 01, 2025, Elsevier Ltd. doi: 10.1016/j.rser.2025.115840.
3. Indora, S. and Kandpal, T.C., Solar energy for institutional cooking in India: prospects and potential. *Environ. Dev. Sustainability*, 22, 8, 7153–7175, 2020, doi: 10.1007/s10668-019-00471-9.
4. Indora, S. and Kandpal, T.C., A framework for analyzing impact of potential financial/fiscal incentives for promoting institutional solar cooking in India. *Renewable Energy*, 143, 1531–1543, 2019, doi: 10.1016/j.renene.2019.05.097.
5. Indora, S. and Kandpal, T.C., Institutional and community solar cooking in India using SK-23 and Scheffler solar cookers: A financial appraisal. *Renewable Energy*, 120, 501–511, 2018, doi: 10.1016/j.renene.2018.01.004.

6. Indora, S. and Kandpal, T.C., Financial appraisal of using Scheffler dish for steam based institutional solar cooking in India. *Renewable Energy*, 135, 1400–1411, 2019, doi: 10.1016/j.renene.2018.09.067.
7. Kumar, A., Prakash, O., Kaviti, A.K., A comprehensive review of Scheffler solar collector. *Renew. Sustain. Energy Rev.*, 77, March, 890–898, 2017, doi: 10.1016/j.rser.2017.03.044.
8. Indora, S. and Kandpal, T.C., Institutional cooking with solar energy: A review. *Renew. Sustain. Energy Rev.*, 84, February, 131–154, 2018, doi: 10.1016/j.rser.2017.12.001.
9. Munir, A., Hensel, O., Scheffler, W., Design principle and calculations of a Scheffler fixed focus concentrator for medium temperature applications. *Sol. Energy*, 84, 8, 1490–1502, 2010, doi: 10.1016/j.solener.2010.05.011.
10. Bhambare, P.S. and Vishweshwara, S.C., Design aspects of a fixed focus type Scheffler concentrator and its receiver for its utilization in thermal processing units. *Energy Nexus*, 7, January, 100103, 2022, doi: 10.1016/j.nexus.2022.100103.
11. Scheffler, W., Bruecke, S., von Werdenbergstr, G., Introduction to the revolutionary design of Scheffler reflectors, in: *6th International Conference on Solar Coockers*, Granada, Spain, 2006.
12. Sardeshpande, V. and Pillai, I.R., Effect of micro-level and macro-level factors on adoption potential of solar concentrators for medium temperature thermal applications. *Energy Sustainable Dev.*, 16, 2, 216–223, 2012, doi: https://doi.org/10.1016/j.esd.2012.01.001.
13. C. S. H. India, Fixed focus elliptical solar dish (Scheffler Dish). *UNDP-GEF Conc. Sol. Therm. Heat Proj. Minist. New Renew. Energy*, Gov. India, New Delhi, India [WWW Doc. Retrieved May, vol. 19, p. 2016, 2014.
14. Rathore, M.M. and Warkhedkar, R.M., A review of solar cookers. *Int. J. Mod. Trends Eng. Res.*, 2, 1997–2004, 2015.
15. Müller-Steinhagen, H. and Trieb, F., Concentrating solar power, A Rev. Technol. *Ingenia Inform. QR Acad. Eng.*, 18, 43–50, 2004.
16. Kaushik, S.C. and Gupta, M.K., Energy and exergy efficiency comparison of community-size and domestic-size paraboloidal solar cooker performance. *Energy Sustain. Dev.*, 12, 3, 60–64, 2008, doi: https://doi.org/10.1016/S0973-0826(08)60440-8.
17. Bhasme, S. and Thosar, A.G., Performance Analysis of Scheffler reflector used for solar dry cleaning. *Int. J. Eng. Innov. Res.*, 4, 4, 640–644, 2015.
18. Ruelas, J., Palomares, J., Pando, G., Absorber design for a Scheffler-Type Solar Concentrator. *Appl. Energy*, 154, 35–39, 2015, doi: https://doi.org/10.1016/j.apenergy.2015.04.107.
19. Sasidharan, S. and Dutta, P., Optical characterization of a fixed focus Scheffler reflector for pressurized solar receiver testing. *Sol. Energy*, 227, August, 89–100, 2021, doi: 10.1016/j.solener.2021.08.078.

20. C. S. H. India, Fresnel Reflector Based Dish, UNDP-GEF Concentrated Solar Thermal Heat (CSH) Project, Ministry of New and Renewable Energy, Government of India, New Delhi, India, 2016.
21. Focus, S., A quarterly magazine on concentrated solar heat. *India's Quest Sol. Steam Process Heat*, 2016.
22. Paliyal, P.S., Mondal, S., Layek, S., Kuchhal, P., Pandey, J.K., Automatic solar tracking system: a review pertaining to advancements and challenges in the current scenario. *Clean Energy*, 8, 6, 237–262, December 2024, https://doi.org/10.1093/ce/zkae085.
23. Paliyal, P.S., Mondal, S., Pandey, J.K., An Analysis of Springwater Parameter Status for Different Locations in the Rural Hilly Garhwal Region of Uttarakhand. *Environ. Claims J.*, *36*, 3, 243–277, 2024, https://doi.org/10.1080/10406026.2024.2423964.
24. Paliyal, P.S. and Mondal, S., An analysis of a cross-finned receiver for Scheffler-type solar collectors to optimize solar heating efficiency for direct water heating. *Int. J. Energy Water Resour.*, 2025, https://doi.org/10.1007/s42108-025-00393-5.
25. Paliyal, P.S., Mondal, S., Pathela, M., Kumar, A., Menon, S.K., Optimization of Solar Photovoltaic Array In-Depth Analysis of Perturb and Observe MPPT Algorithm. *2024 International Conference on Advances in Computing, Communication and Materials (ICACCM)*, Dehradun, India, pp. 1–6, 2024, doi: 10.1109/ICACCM61117.2024.11059143.
26. Paliyal, P.S., *et al.*, Location Analysis and Environmental Validation for Installation of Hybrid Solar-Wind Energy Generation System in Hilly Areas of Uttarakhand: Study Toward Forecasting, in: *Forecasting Methods for Renewable Power Generation*, pp. 21–47, Scrivener Publishing LLC (Wiley-Scrivener imprint), Beverly, Massachusetts, USA, 2025.
27. Menon, S.K., *et al.*, The Role of Hydrogen as a Sustainable Energy Source and its Integration with the Grid, in: *Advancements in Communication and Systems*, A.K. Tripathi and V. Shrivastava (Eds.), p. 397, Computing and Intelligent Systems, SCRS, India, 2023, 2025.
28. Kudapa, V.K., Paliyal, P.S., Mondal, A., Mondal, S., A critical review of fabrication strategies, separation techniques, challenges, and future prospects for the hydrogen separation membrane. *Fusion Sci. Technol.*, 80, 7, 803–825, 2024.

6

Digital Twin-Based Real-Time Solar Concentrator Control and Monitoring System

Aruna Pant* **and Adesh Kumar**

Department of Electrical and Electronics Engineering, School of Advanced Engineering, UPES, Dehradun, Uttarakhand, India

Abstract

Digital Twin technology is changing the way solar concentrators are monitored and controlled. It allows for real-time interaction between physical systems and their virtual counterparts. This chapter focuses on designing and implementing a real-time control and monitoring system for solar concentrators using Digital Twin principles. The Digital Twin acts as a live replica of the actual solar concentrator setup. Sensors attached to the concentrators continuously feed data into the system. This data is processed and mirrored in the virtual environment. The virtual model updates in real time, reflecting the current state of the physical system. This setup offers several advantages. It helps in identifying faults early. It supports timely maintenance and system tuning. The operators can make immediate changes to improve performance. In this way, downtime is reduced to a minimum, and the amount of energy produced is enhanced. Three primary components make up the system that is being presented. The first component is a sensor-based data acquisition unit, the second component is a control module that is capable of dynamic modification, and the third component is a user interface that displays the performance of the system in real time. The reliability of the system is improved by this integration. The costs of operation and maintenance are reduced as a result. In addition to this, it guarantees that the concentrator will function anywhere near its ideal position regardless of the conditions. In addition to that, the chapter discusses how each component functions. It describes the flow of data as well as the process of making decisions. The system design is also done based on practical considerations, which is expected to provide three

**Corresponding author*: arunapant41@gmail.com

Surajit Mondal, Paramjeet Singh Paliyal and Sachin Sharma (eds.) Digital Twin Technology for Solar Concentrators, (75–94) © 2026 Scrivener Publishing LLC

main outcomes: adaptability, scalability, and energy efficiency. The Digital Twin's technology has the potential to meaningfully transform the applications of solar energy. The platform is intended to be intelligent, enabling predictive control and facilitating efficient energy harvesting. This approach enables the creation of solar systems characterized by their environmental sustainability and high efficiency.

***Keywords*:** Solar tracking, digital twin technology, real-time monitoring, solar concentrator, performance optimization, predictive maintenance

6.1 Introduction

Solar concentrators are the main elements of Concentrated Solar Power (CSP) systems. These devices are used to function by concentrating sunlight onto a definite area to produce electricity and advanced thermal energy. CSP-based plants classically exploit these concentrators in large-scale electricity utilization due to their capability to efficiently capture and convert solar energy. To improve the performance, such types of systems require active control and monitoring measures. The prompt adjustment of environmental variables is important for preserving constant output. The advancements and technologies are presently being combined to meet these requirements. Digital Twin technology has gained significant attention. A Digital Twin serves as a virtual representation of a physical system, accurately mirroring its behavior and performance in real time. It perpetually refreshes according on sensor data from the physical unit. Digital twins have numerous benefits in the realm of solar concentrators. This encompasses real-time system surveillance, proactive defect identification, anticipatory maintenance, and adaptive performance enhancement. The result is improved system reliability, reduced downtime, and higher overall efficiency.

The recent technological developments in solar concentrator technology have proven a change away from the basic method to fold heat and toward more complex devices that can do more than one thing and fit in with buildings better. The first steps in making stationary mirror systems and flat-plate collectors gave us simple but effective ways to capture solar energy. These systems were easy to build and didn't need much upkeep, but they weren't very efficient because they couldn't follow the sun very well and didn't work well when the sun was shining in different ways. The use of non-imaging optics, including CPCs, greatly enhanced light acceptance without the requirement for mechanical tracking. This was a big step forward in optical design. Later studies looked at hybrid photovoltaic-thermoelectric (PV-TE) systems, which collect both electrical and thermal energy at the same time, maximizing the conversion of all types of energy. These hybrid systems used innovative thermal management algorithms and spectrum-splitting techniques to make the whole system work better. At the same time, luminescent solar concentrators (LSCs) were a potential way to use solar technology in buildings.

The development of solar concentrator technologies has advanced steadily over time. Initial systems used basic reflective surfaces to focus sunlight. These stationary mirror setups were simple, cost-effective, and required minimal maintenance [1]. They operated without mechanical tracking, offering ease of use but limited adaptability. Simultaneously, flat-plate solar heat collectors were analyzed for their thermal behavior under changing environmental conditions. These systems gained popularity for domestic heating. Despite their simple design, their efficiency dropped under inconsistent sunlight [2]. A breakthrough came with non-imaging optical designs. CPCs are used to enhance the angular acceptance of sunlight. These concentrators efficiently captured diffuse and direct light without needing constant orientation toward the sun [3, 4]. This innovation significantly improved optical performance in solar systems. As research advanced, hybrid solar systems combining photovoltaic (PV) and thermoelectric (TE) components were proposed. These systems aimed to extract both electrical energy and residual heat from solar radiation. Their dual-function design increased total energy output. Optimization techniques were developed to balance PV and TE performance. Key challenges addressed included thermal regulation and spectral energy distribution [5, 6]. Concurrently, Luminescent Solar Concentrators (LSCs) gained interest. These devices utilized fluorescent materials embedded in transparent sheets. They absorbed sunlight and re-emitted it at longer wavelengths. This light was guided to edge-mounted PV cells. Researchers focused on improving quantum efficiency and minimizing reabsorption losses [7]. Advances in materials led to transparent LSCs. These allowed visible light transmission while harvesting energy from the infrared region. Their ability to integrate into windows and building surfaces opened new opportunities in urban architecture [8]. However, limitations such as self-absorption and light loss remained [9]. In recent years, LSC applications have expanded to include architectural integration. Semi-transparent and aesthetically pleasing systems were developed for urban deployment [10]. The doping strategies using rare earth ions like Tm^{2+} improved luminescence and reduced energy losses [11]. Tunable solar collectors have also emerged. These can adjust light transmission in real time. Such adaptability enables a mix of daylighting and power generation [12]. This multifunctional approach aligns with smart building concepts. Architectural configurations now accommodate solar collectors in various formats. Facade-integrated modules, solar glazing, and rooftop panels are being designed to harmonize with building structures [13]. Field experiments, such as the 'leaf roof' installation, have demonstrated the practicality of LSC systems in real environments [14]. Moreover, the field has shifted from simple solar collection to advanced, multi-functional systems. These combine optical engineering, smart materials, and thermal design. The result is greater efficiency, better integration, and increased suitability for modern energy and building needs.

6.2 The Digital Twin Concept

A Digital Twin is a virtual illustration of a physical object or system that imitates its existing state and operational behavior. The Digital Twin is applied to model the different parts of solar concentrators, which include the concentrator panels, tracking mechanisms, thermal management units, and power-producing devices. The data processed and collected from sensors located inside the physical system is applicable to apprise this simulation periodically.

Real-Time Data Synchronization: The Digital Twin constantly acknowledges the live data from sensors embedded in the physical hardware of the solar concentrator system. This confirms that the virtual model remains an accurate and up-to-date reflection of the system's real-time functioning situations.

Simulation and Predictive Modeling

Digital Twin technology uses advanced mathematical models to simulate the behavior of solar concentrators. It incorporates multiple factors such as thermal characteristics, solar irradiance levels, and panel orientation. The analysis comprises various factors, including solar irradiance levels, thermal characteristics, and panel orientation. These simulations simplify the analysis of varied operating circumstances within a virtual environment. This method permits accurate predictions of system replies in advance. This capability increases system planning and design across several environmental conditions.

Optimization of Systems

The platform enables real-time changes of system parameters to improve performance. The main adaptable variables consist of the concentrator's tilt angle and the power output dispersal. The automated control mechanisms effectually minimize energy losses during operation. This optimization results in a distinguished enhancement of the solar concentrator's overall energy efficiency.

Predictive Maintenance

Digital Twin constantly detects system trends and performance metrics. By recognizing deviations from standard behavior, it can forecast potential system failures. This simplifies an analytical maintenance strategy instead of reactive repairs. The prompt intrusions prevent unexpected downtime and improve the operational lifespan of the system. The real-time operations can be controlled using FPGA-based hardware units that are incorporated into the system to simplify rapid and precise control. Several types of system design platforms provide fast switching, processing capabilities, minimal latency, and reconfigurable architecture. These systems are well-suited for applications in real-time solar tracking and data analysis. FPGAs are utilized for intelligent monitoring and dynamic decision-making.

Secure Communication and Monitoring

Secure data transmission is important in distributed solar systems. Different embedded cryptographic hardware modules within FPGAs advance cybersecurity measures. The modules safeguard the integrity and confidentiality of control signals and sensor data. This holds significant importance in smart grids and remotely operated infrastructures.

Framework for Scalable Digital Twins

The embedded system and integration of predictive modeling, real-time control, and secure data communication result in a robust Digital Twin system. These backgrounds provide scalability and are suitable for widespread deployment within solar concentrator networks. They provide improved adaptability, reliability, and operational transparency within energy systems.

6.3 Elements of the System for Real-Time Control and Monitoring

6.3.1 System Solar Concentrators

The solar concentrator systems have different important components. The concentrator panels, which are generally composed of mirrors or lenses, are used to direct the sunlight onto a reduced target area. A solar tracking system endlessly adjusts the panel alignment during the whole day. These assurances maximize solar contact and improve energy capture efficiency. Thermal or power conversion systems convert focused solar energy into useful heat or electrical power. The embedded sensors constantly monitor the critical factors such as ambient temperature, surface temperature, solar irradiation, and panel orientation. These immediate inputs simplify system oversight, regulation, and performance enhancement.

6.3.2 Digital Twin Framework

The Digital Twin repeats the physical behavior of solar concentrator components. It incorporates mathematical modeling of solar interface with panels, heat transmission, and system performance efficiency. These simulations replicate real-world conditions to predict system responses under various operational scenarios. Such a model enables analysis, optimization, and predictive maintenance of the concentrator system in a virtual environment. Real-time Data Processing Algorithms that use information gathered from actual sensors to update the virtual model. Models that use previous and current data to predict future performance and possible system breakdowns are known as predictive analytics.

6.3.3 System for Data Acquisition and Communication

The data acquisition system collects real-time information from the physical solar concentrator using various sensors:

- **Temperature sensors** monitor the temperatures of both the receiver and the concentrator panels.
- **Solar radiation sensors** measure the intensity of sunlight incident on the concentrators.
- **Position sensors** track the orientation and angular position of the concentrators relative to the sun.

A wireless communication protocol or IoT network ensures the reliable transmission of sensor data to the Digital Twin and control system for further analysis and decision-making.

6.3.4 Control System

The primary function of the control system is to understand system behavior and alter the position. The control system is used to adjust the concentrator's orientation to improve solar energy absorption based on the data processed from the Digital Twin modules.

Thermal Regulation
The system constantly detects heat conditions in real time. Based on the detection of excessive heat, the cooling is activated, or the corresponding power is diminished to prevent overheating. Such types of systems operate safely and sustain long-term performance stability.

Electricity Distribution
The system proficiently manages the distribution of heat or energy to the grid or storage units. This adaptive control method advances energy efficiency and enhances practical output. The load balancing and allocation based on demand are also enabled.

6.3.5 Interface and Functional Block

The user interface presents real-time system information and operational metrics. It offers visual input regarding energy generation, component condition, and environmental variables. This interface enables operators to monitor performance, implement adjustments, and respond to system warnings effectively. It provides critical parameters such as solar irradiation, temperature, energy output, and the overall state of the system. Operators can manually adjust concentrator settings, such as alignment and thermal regulation, using the integrated control panel. The system creates alerts to notify users of discovered problems, performance declines, or necessary maintenance tasks. Figure 6.1 depicts the block diagram that delineates the functional components of the solar concentrator control and monitoring system, encompassing sensor units, control logic, actuators, and a remote monitoring interface.

The system initiates with the solar concentrator unit, employing a Fresnel lens or parabolic mirror to concentrate sunlight onto a receiver,

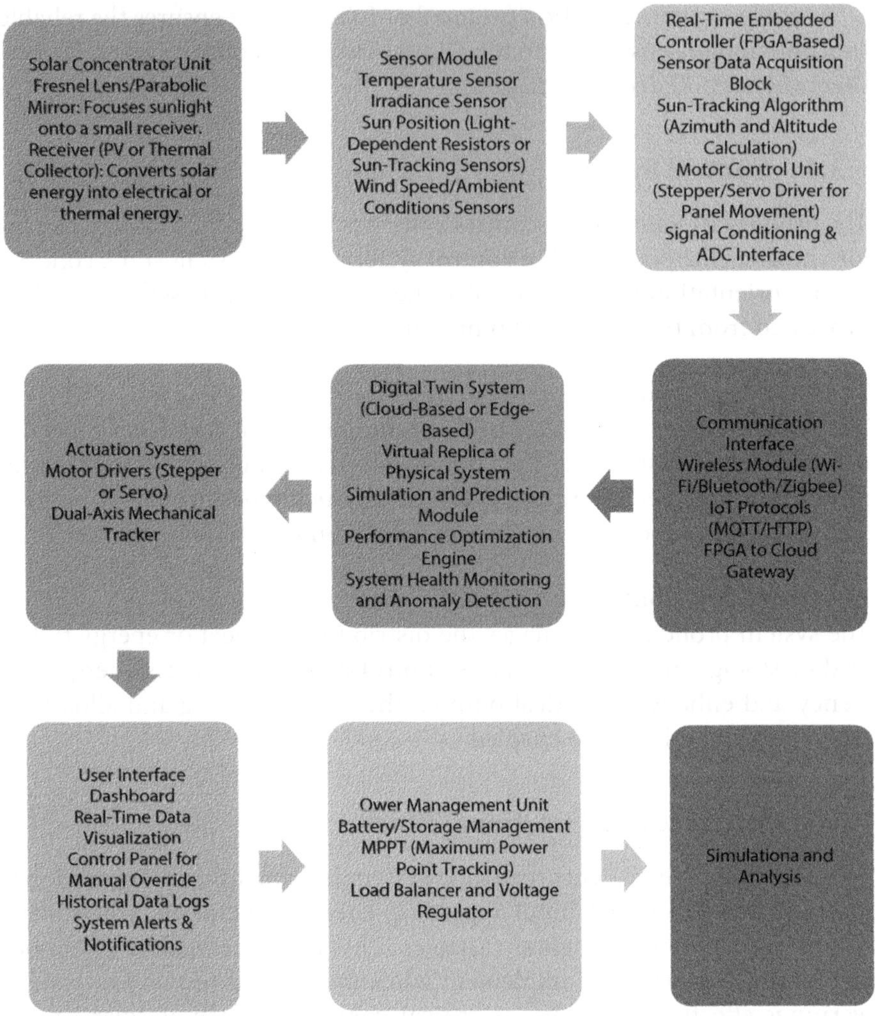

Figure 6.1 Functional modules of the solar concentrator monitoring and control system.

which may be a photovoltaic or thermal collector that transforms solar energy into useful electrical or heat output. The environmental data essential for system operation is gathered through the Sensor Module, which includes temperature sensors, irradiance detectors, sun-position tracking elements (like LDRs or optical sensors), and sensors for wind speed and ambient conditions. This sensor data is fed into the real-time embedded controller, typically implemented on an FPGA platform. This controller executes core tasks such as acquiring sensor inputs, running sun-tracking algorithms (to calculate azimuth and altitude), and generating control signals for motorized movement. It also handles signal conditioning and analog-to-digital conversion to make the data usable for digital processing. The controller commands the Actuation System, which includes stepper or servo motors configured in a dual-axis mechanical tracker.

The solar concentrator system consistently realigns to optimize energy capture from the sun. This behavior can be analyzed based on the information provided by a tracking system working regularly for real-time data. A Digital Twin system is realized either in the cloud or at the edge, which serves as a virtual node representation of the communication infrastructure. It simulates real-time data, predicts system behavior under various settings, and improves performance through ongoing optimization. Furthermore, it oversees the system to identify irregularities or preliminary indications of failure. The physical concentrator and its digital model exchange the data over a specialized communication interface [15]. This interface includes wireless communication technologies, including Bluetooth, Wi-Fi, and Zigbee. The standard protocols, such as MQTT or HTTP, are applied in the IoT communication to facilitate secure and efficient data communication.

The FPGA-integrated controller communicates the system data to the cloud or edge device *via* this interface. A User Interface Dashboard proposal operates with visual access to real-time data and system status. It simplifies manual regulation of essential factors, including panel orientation and thermal configurations. The dashboard conserves previous records and offers notifications for maintenance or irregular occurrences. The power management module is crucial for maintaining energy efficiency and dependability. It regulates energy storage *via* batteries in which MPPT algorithms are applied to optimize solar conversion efficiency. This machine additionally executes load balancing and voltage regulation to ensure a consistent power supply. The simulation and analysis module processes both real-time and historical data. It recognizes long-term trends, optimizes operational parameters, and facilitates predictive maintenance and prospective system enhancements [16].

6.4 Uses for Solar Concentrators

6.4.1 Use in Photovoltaic Systems

Solar concentrators play a crucial role in enhancing the efficiency of PV systems. In grid-connected PV setups with battery storage, concentrators help maximize solar energy capture while reducing spatial requirements. Techno-economic analyses confirm that the integration of concentrators improves power quality and system reliability, particularly when combined with adaptive control and energy storage mechanisms [17]. In agricultural applications, solar concentrator-based systems such as solar trees have been successfully used for powering irrigation pumps. This supports sustainable farming practices and promotes energy independence in rural areas [18].

PV system efficiency is further improved by employing intelligent control algorithms. The Perturb and Observe (P&O) method is commonly applied to continuously track the maximum power point, even under variable irradiance conditions [19]. This leads to optimized energy output from the solar arrays. Recent developments also emphasize the value of hybrid energy storage and adaptive management strategies. These techniques reduce power fluctuations and contribute to better grid stability, particularly in single-phase systems [20]. Artificial intelligence has been incorporated into MPPT to handle challenges like partial shading and uneven solar exposure. This integration enhances the reliability and responsiveness of concentrator-driven PV systems [21]. Advancements in material science have also contributed significantly. Memristive materials are being explored for fault detection and self-repair in dye-sensitized solar cells, a category of concentrator-based PV technologies [22]. In addition, transparent superhydrophobic coatings developed using nano-silica embedded in polystyrene improve surface cleanliness. These coatings enhance light transmission and absorption, which ultimately boosts overall energy output [23].

6.4.2 Applications in Solar Thermal Systems

Solar concentrators are not limited to electricity generation; they are extensively used in thermal energy applications. In solar towers and thermal collector systems, concentrators are employed to generate high-temperature steam. This steam is utilized for electricity production or industrial heating processes. Such thermal systems are gaining prominence in clean energy initiatives, offering low-carbon solutions for both urban and rural regions [24]. Solar thermal systems have recently made strides in incorporating Digital Twin technology. With these digital representations, physical systems may be monitored and controlled in real-time, all the time. They help with operational optimization and predictive maintenance of thermal setups that use concentrators. Recent research highlights the potential of digital twins to revolutionize solar energy by enabling scalable, data-driven, and highly efficient energy systems [25].

6.5 Cutting Edge Solar Concentration Technologies

6.5.1 Integration of Digital Twins

Digital twins are dynamic digital illustrations that reflect the behavior and performance of physical systems in real time. They employ ongoing sensor feedback to revise the virtual model. In solar concentrator systems, digital twins facilitate remote observation and performance assessment. They enable operators to identify problems promptly and model operational modifications before their implementation in the physical system. This functionality facilitates predictive maintenance by analyzing performance trends and detecting early indicators of component degradation. Consequently, system dependability and uptime are markedly enhanced.

6.5.2 Real-Time Control Systems Based on FPGA

Digital twins serve as dynamic digital representations that accurately mirror the behavior and performance of physical systems in real time. Ongoing sensor feedback is utilized to update the virtual model. In solar concentrator systems, digital twins enable remote monitoring and evaluation of performance. Operators are enabled to promptly identify problems and model operational modifications before implementing them in the physical system. This feature enables predictive maintenance through the analysis of performance trends and the identification of early signs of component degradation. As a result, the reliability and operational availability of the system are significantly improved.

6.5.3 Leveraging AI and Machine Learning for Optimization

Artificial intelligence (AI) and machine learning (ML) are revolutionizing solar concentrator operations. AI-powered prediction algorithms forecast sun movement and optimize actuator reactions and uptime is dramatically improved. Machine learning models trained on both historical and live data enable intelligent diagnostics. These models predict potential equipment failures, allowing for proactive maintenance scheduling. Together, AI and ML increase operational efficiency, reduce downtime, and extend system lifespan. Moreover, the integration of edge computing allows these algorithms to run locally on embedded systems, reducing communication delays and enabling fast, autonomous decision-making for solar tracking and energy management in real-time. AI-powered Solar Tracking:

Optimizes tracking movements using predictive algorithms. Machine learning models are used to enhance maintenance planning and failure forecasting. Edge computing improves real-time control and lowers latency for self-governing solar tracking systems [26].

6.6 Performance Evaluation

6.6.1 Solar Tracking Performance Evaluation

An examination of a solar tracking system's (such as a solar concentrator's) performance is crucial in determining how well it tracks the sun's position to maximize energy capture. A sinusoidal curve illustrates how the solar panel's angle changes throughout the day. Starts low in the morning, peaks at lunchtime, and lowers in the evening [27].

The graph in Figure 6.2 presents the solar tracking performance over 24 hours by showing the variation in tracking angle over time. At the start of the day, around 0 hours, the tracking angle is approximately 15°, gradually increasing as the sun rises. The angle peaks at nearly 60° around the 6th hour, indicating the system is effectively aligned with the sun's position during the morning. After reaching its maximum, the angle begins to decrease steadily, crossing the 0° mark around midday (approximately 12 hours). The angle continues to drop, reaching its lowest point of about -35° near the 18th hour, which corresponds to the late evening. Toward the end of the 24-hour cycle, the tracking angle begins to rise again, returning toward its initial position. This smooth, sinusoidal variation demonstrates that the system accurately follows the sun's path throughout the day,

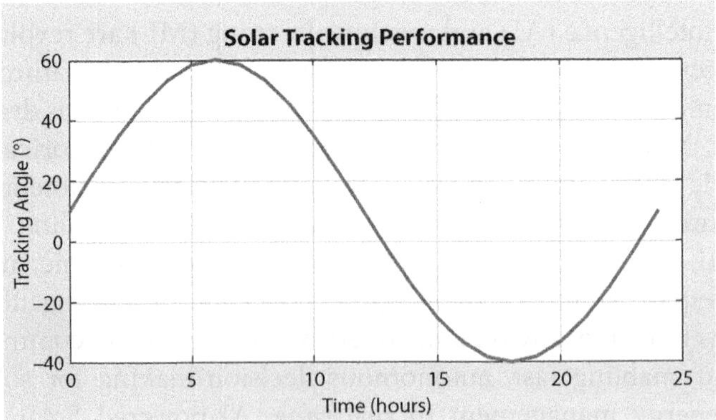

Figure 6.2 Performance of solar tracking.

adjusting the concentrator position to maintain optimal solar alignment. The pattern also suggests a potential reset or bidirectional tracking mechanism during nighttime hours [28].

6.6.2 Power Output with vs. without Tracking

Without Tracking (Fixed Solar Panel): A fixed solar panel or concentrator is angled steadily, usually in the direction of the sun's ideal average position for a certain area and season. However, because the sun's position varies during the day, this leads to less-than-ideal energy capture.

With Tracking: A single-axis or dual-axis tracking system dynamically modifies the solar concentrator's position to follow the course of the sun. Figure 6.3 shows the Comparison of power output with tracking and without tracking. The racking enables the concentrator to maintain optimal alignment with the sun, capturing more solar radiation throughout the day. The graph shows a more stable and higher power output with tracking (green line) compared to the erratic and lower output without tracking (blue line), highlighting improved consistency. Table 6.1 lists the tracking output and concentrator output observed for 24 hours [29].

Without tracking: Depending on the time of day and the sun's position relative to the fixed panel's angle, the power output varies. By tracking the sun's path, the solar concentrator minimizes misalignment throughout the day, resulting in a more consistent and optimized power production.

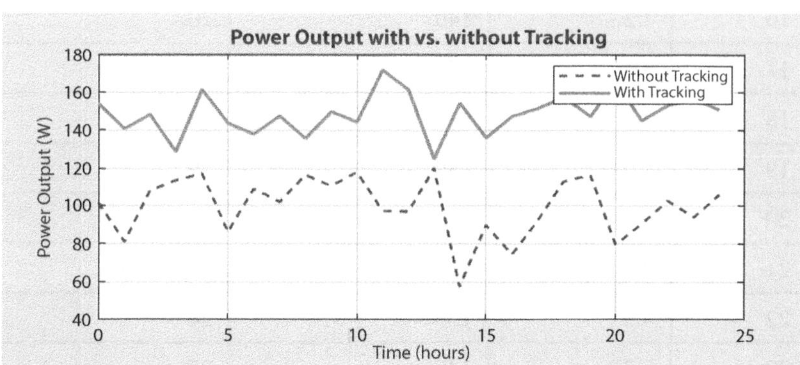

Figure 6.3 Comparison of power output with tracking and without tracking.

Table 6.1 Digital twin latency, power output, and temperature monitoring (0–24 h).

Time (h)	Latency (ms)	Power output (W) (with tracking)	Temperature (°C)
0	6.8	145	23
1	5.6	140	25
2	3.7	135	28
3	1.5	150	26
4	8.9	160	30
5	3.6	155	34
6	5.3	150	31
7	6.1	145	29
8	5.4	150	30
9	4.2	165	27
10	3.3	170	31
11	7.9	160	28
12	3.6	130	25
13	6.7	140	22
14	5.5	150	24
15	4.6	135	21
16	4.2	140	20
17	3.1	145	19
18	4.8	155	18
19	2.0	150	19
20	5.5	145	21
21	3.7	140	18
22	4.9	135	24
23	5.3	140	25
24	5.7	140	26

The graph compares the power output of a solar system over 24 hours with and without a tracking mechanism. It is observed that the system equipped with solar tracking consistently outperforms the one without tracking throughout the day. The power output with tracking (green solid line) remains relatively high and stable, generally fluctuating between 130 W and 170 W, with a noticeable peak around 10 to 12 hours. In contrast, the system without tracking (blue dashed line) shows more irregular and lower performance, typically ranging from 60 W to 120 W. There are noticeable dips, particularly around 14 hours, in which the power drops significantly, likely due to misalignment with the sun's position. This comparison highlights the advantage of using solar tracking systems. By adjusting the orientation of the solar panels to follow the sun's path, the system maximizes solar irradiance capture, resulting in higher and more consistent power output. Overall, solar tracking enhances energy efficiency, reduces losses due to fixed alignment, and ensures better performance across the entire solar day [30].

6.6.3 Digital Twin Data Exchange Latency

The term 'Digital Twin data exchange latency' describes the lag or delay that occurs during data exchange between the Digital Twin and its real-world counterpart. Stated otherwise, it is the amount of time needed to collect data from the physical system, transfer it to the digital model, analyze it, and have it appear in the virtual system. Faster decision-making when managing the solar tracker is facilitated by reduced latency. The delays in adjustments are due to high latency might lower solar energy efficiency [31].

The chart in Figure 6.4 illustrates the latency (ms) associated with data exchange in a Digital Twin system over 24 hours. Latency here refers to the delay in communication between the physical system and its virtual replica. Observations indicate that latency fluctuates throughout the day, generally ranging between 2 ms and 9 ms. It can be noticed that there are spikes in latency around the 4th and 11th hours, reaching up to 9 ms and 8 ms, respectively. These peaks could be attributed to high network traffic, system synchronization loads, or cloud server delays during those periods. Conversely, the lowest latency values, close to 2 ms, occur around the 3rd and 20th hours, suggesting improved data handling efficiency during those times. The overall latency remains within acceptable limits for real-time monitoring and control, as delays under 10 ms are typically tolerable for most Digital Twin applications in solar tracking or industrial automation.

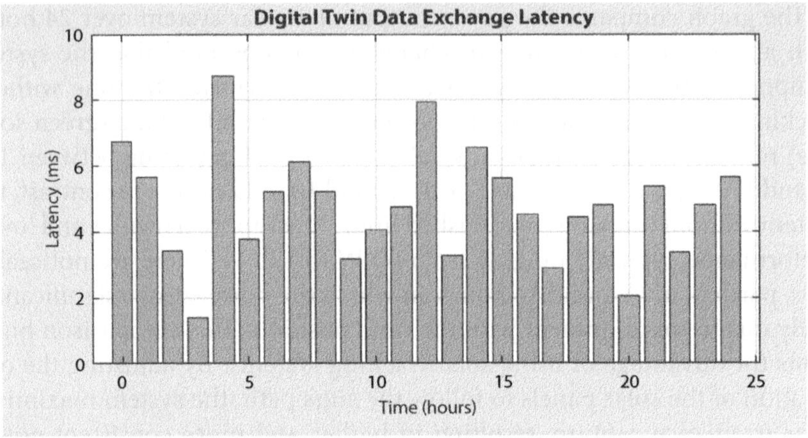

Figure 6.4 Digital twin data exchange latency with time.

However, to maintain optimal performance, especially during predictive simulation or anomaly detection, further improvements in data exchange protocols or the integration of edge computing may be beneficial [32].

6.6.4 Solar Panel Temperature Monitoring

Solar panel temperature monitoring entails tracking the temperature of the solar panels to maximize performance and ensure their longevity. The temperature of solar panels can affect their efficiency, since higher temperatures can diminish the power output of the panels. Higher temperatures reduce the efficiency of solar panels. Temperature monitoring aids in regulating cooling systems (such as ventilation and water cooling). A solar panel's lifespan may be shortened or damaged if it overheats. When the temperature rises above a certain point, the system may sound an alert [33].

The graph in Figure 6.5 shows the solar panel temperature trend over 24 hours. Starting at around 23°C, the temperature increases rapidly and peaks at approximately 34°C near the 5th hour due to strong solar irradiance. It then fluctuates mildly until the 11th hour before gradually decreasing as sunlight reduces, hitting the lowest point of around 18°C between the 17th and 19th hours. A slight rise is observed again toward the 24th hour, ending near 26°C. These variations highlight the impact of sunlight and environmental conditions on panel performance, emphasizing the need for real-time temperature monitoring to ensure optimal efficiency and safety [34].

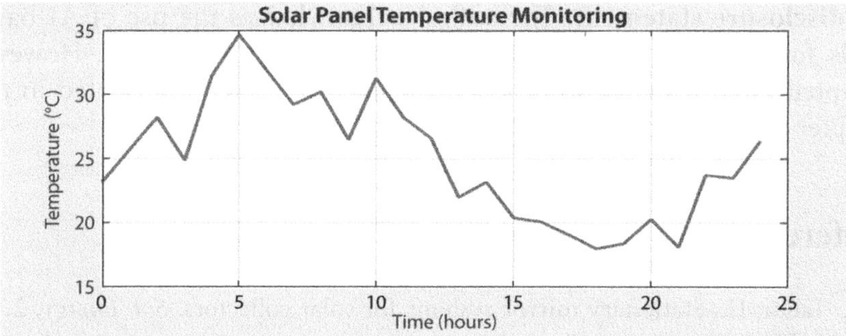

Figure 6.5 Temperature monitoring of the solar panel.

6.7 Conclusions

The integration of Digital Twin (DT) technology with solar concentrators presents strong potential for performance improvement. However, future research can further enhance these systems by incorporating advanced artificial intelligence (AI) and machine learning (ML) models. These models can enable faster adaptation to environmental changes and improve prediction accuracy. Machine learning algorithms can optimize solar energy capture even under complex and rapidly changing weather conditions. In addition, ML can provide valuable system diagnostics. It can identify inefficiencies, suggest design improvements, and support predictive maintenance based on real-time operational data. These insights support informed decision-making and long-term system optimization. Digital Twin frameworks also offer high scalability. Additional concentrator units can be integrated into the system, allowing real-time visualization and performance monitoring. This makes it feasible to deploy DT-based control systems across large-scale solar farms, using either distributed or centralized architectures. The use of DT technology enables improved performance tracking, predictive insights, and real-time operational adjustments [35]. These capabilities result in increased energy efficiency, reduced operating costs, and improved system reliability. Future developments may focus on integrating AI-powered predictive analytics to further enhance system responsiveness. Another promising direction is the adoption of edge computing. Processing data locally at the edge can reduce communication delays and support real-time decision-making in solar concentrator control systems.

AI disclosure statement: The author acknowledges the use of AI-based tools for minor language editing or grammatical correction. However, all intellectual contributions, analyses, and conclusions presented in this chapter are entirely the author's own.

References

1. Tabor, H., Stationary mirror systems for solar collectors. *Sol. Energy*, 2, 27, 1958.
2. Hottel, H.C. and Woertz, B.B., The performance of flat-plate solar-heat collectors. *Trans. ASME*, 91, February 1942.
3. Hinterberger, H. and Winston, R., *Rev. Sci. Instrum.*, 37, 1094–1095, 1966. https://doi.org/10.1063/1.1720428.
4. Winston, R., Light collection within the framework of geometrical optics. *J. Opt. Soc. Am.*, 60, 245, 1970.
5. Kraemer, D., Hu, L., Muto, A., Chen, X., Chen, G., Chiesa, M., Photovoltaic-thermoelectric hybrid systems: a general optimization methodology. *Appl. Phys. Lett.*, 92, 23–25, 2008.
6. Ju, X., Wang, Z., Flamant, G., Li, P., Zhao, W., Numerical analysis and optimization of a spectrum splitting concentration photovoltaic-thermoelectric hybrid system. *Sol. Energy*, 86, 1941–1954, 2012.
7. McKenna, B. and Evans, R.C., Towards efficient spectral converters through materials design for luminescent solar devices. *Adv. Mater.*, 29, 28, 1606491, 2017.
8. Zhao, Y., Meek, G.A., Levine, B.G., Lunt, R.R., Near-infrared harvesting transparent luminescent solar concentrators. *Adv. Opt. Mater.*, 2, 7, 606–611, 2014.
9. Van Sark, W.G.J.H., Barnham, K.W.J., Slooff, L.H., Chatten, A.J., Büchtemann, A., Meyer, A., McCormack, S.J., Koole, R., Farrell, D.J., Bose, R., *et al.*, Luminescent solar concentrators – a review of recent results. *Opt. Express*, 16, 26, 21773, 2008.
10. Debije, M.G. and Verbunt, P.P.C., Thirty years of luminescent solar concentrator research: Solar energy for the built environment. *Adv. Energy Mater.*, 2, 1, 12–35, 2012.
11. Ten Kate, O.M., Krämer, K.W., van der Kolk, E., Efficient luminescent solar concentrators based on self-absorption free, Tm^{2+} doped halides. *Sol. Energy Mater. Sol. Cells*, 140, 115–120, 2015.
12. Debije, M.G., Solar energy collectors with tunable transmission. *Adv. Funct. Mater.*, 20, 9, 1498–1502, 2010.
13. Reinders, A., Kishore, R., Slooff, L., Eggink, W., Luminescent solar concentrator photovoltaic designs. *Jpn. J. Appl. Phys.*, 57, 8, 1–10, 2018.

14. Reinders, A., Debije, M.G., Rosemann, A., Measured efficiency of a luminescent solar concentrator PV module called leaf roof. *IEEE J. Photovoltaics*, 7, 1663–1666, 2017.
15. Kumar, A., Bansal, K., Kumar, D., Devrari, A., Kumar, R., Mani, P., FPGA application for wireless monitoring in power plant. *Nucl. Eng. Technol.*, 53, 4, 1167–1175, 2021.
16. Kumar, N., Mishra, V.M., Kumar, A., Smart grid and nuclear power plant security by integrating cryptographic hardware chip. *Nucl. Eng. Technol.*, 53, 10, 3327–3334, 2021.
17. Saurabh, S., Kumar, A., Kumar, R., Techno Economic Analysis of Grid Connected Photovoltaic Systems with Battery Energy Storage: A Comprehensive Review. *Energy Storage*, 7, 1, e70119, 2025.
18. Kumar, R., Kumar, A., Gupta, M.K., Yadav, J., Jain, A., Solar tree-based water pumping for assured irrigation in sustainable Indian agriculture environment. *Sustainable Prod. Consumption*, 33, 15–27, 2022.
19. Paliyal, P.S., Mondal, S., Pathela, M., Kumar, A., Menon, S.K., Optimization of solar photovoltaic array: In-depth analysis of Perturb and Observe MPPT algorithm, in: *2024 Int. Conf. Adv. Comput., Commun. Mater. (ICACCM)*, pp. 1–6, IEEE, 2024, November.
20. Saurabh, S., Kumar, A., Kumar, R., Arora, R.K., Enhancing power quality in single-phase systems using photovoltaic and hybrid energy storage with adaptive control. *Water Energy Int.*, 67, 11, 49–56, 2025.
21. Pachauri, R.K., Sharma, V., Kumar, A., Shashikant, Khan, A.A., Sharma, P., Conventional and AI-based MPPT techniques for solar photovoltaic system-based power generation: Constraints and future perception, in: *Clean and Renewable Energy Production*, pp. 355–374, John Wiley & Sons, Hoboken, New Jersey, USA, 2024.
22. Bilgaye, M., Babu, M.G., Raju, Y.D.S., Kumar, A., Memristive behavior: Tool for fault detection and repairing dye solar cells, in: *Appl. Soft Comput. Embedded Syst. Appl. Sol. Energy*, pp. 99–122, CRC Press, Boca Raton, Florida, USA, 2021.
23. Hooda, A., Goyat, M.S., Kumar, A., Gupta, R., A facile approach to develop modified nano-silica embedded polystyrene-based transparent superhydrophobic coating. *Mater. Lett.*, 233, 340–343, 2018.
24. Mondal, S., Kumar, A., Pachauri, R.K., Mondal, A.K., Singh, V.K., Sharma, A.K. (Eds.), *Clean and renewable energy production*, John Wiley & Sons, Hoboken, New Jersey, USA, 2024.
25. Mondal, S., Kumar, A., Khan, M. (Eds.), *Digital Twin and ESG*, John Wiley & Sons, Hoboken, New Jersey, USA, 2025.
26. Kumar, A., Mondal, S., Verma, G., Mani, P. (Eds.), *Embedded Devices and Internet of Things: Technologies and Applications*, CRC Press, Boca Raton, Florida, USA, 2024.

27. Paliyal, P.S., Mondal, S., Layek, S., Kuchhal, P., Pandey, J.K., Automatic solar tracking system: a review pertaining to advancements and challenges in the current scenario. *Clean Energy*, 8, 6, 237–262, December 2024, https://doi.org/10.1093/ce/zkae085.
28. Paliyal, P.S., Mondal, S., Pandey, J.K., An Analysis of Springwater Parameter Status for Different Locations in the Rural Hilly Garhwal Region of Uttarakhand. *Environ. Claims J.*, *36*, 3, 243–277, 2024, https://doi.org/10.1080/10406026.2024.2423964.
29. Paliyal, P.S. and Mondal, S., An analysis of a cross-finned receiver for Scheffler-type solar collectors to optimize solar heating efficiency for direct water heating. *Int. J. Energy Water Resour.*, 2025, https://doi.org/10.1007/s42108-025-00393-5.
30. Paliyal, P.S., Mondal, S., Pathela, M., Kumar, A., Menon, S.K., Optimization of Solar Photovoltaic Array In-Depth Analysis of Perturb and Observe MPPT Algorithm. *2024 International Conference on Advances in Computing, Communication and Materials (ICACCM)*, Dehradun, India, pp. 1–6, 2024, doi: 10.1109/ICACCM61117.2024.11059143.
31. Paliyal, P.S., *et al.*, Location Analysis and Environmental Validation for Installation of Hybrid Solar-Wind Energy Generation System in Hilly Areas of Uttarakhand: Study Toward Forecasting, in: *Forecasting Methods for Renewable Power Generation*, pp. 21–47, Wiley, Hoboken, New Jersey, USA, 2025.
32. Menon, S.K., *et al.*, The Role of Hydrogen as a Sustainable Energy Source and its Integration with the Grid, in: *Advancements in Communication and Systems*, A.K. Tripathi and V. Shrivastava (Eds.), p. 397, Computing and Intelligent Systems, SCRS, India, 2023, 2025.
33. Kudapa, V.K., Paliyal, P.S., Mondal, A., Mondal, S., A critical review of fabrication strategies, separation techniques, challenges, and future prospects for the hydrogen separation membrane. *Fusion Sci. Technol.*, 80, 7, 803–825, 2024.
34. Mondal, A., Jangirh, R., Arya, R., Yadav, L., Ahlawat, S., Yadav, P., Paliyal, P.S., Bobde, P., Ghosh, P., Mondal, S., Rai, A., Analysing solid residential fuel usage patterns in rural and urban slums of Delhi: Implications for pollution reduction and sustainable practices. *Energy Sustainable Dev.*, *80*, 101460, 2024.
35. Paliyal, P.S., Kuchhal, P., Mondal, S., Nano Lubricants and their Applications, in: *Nanotechnology: A Quick Guide to Materials and Technologies*, pp. 425–456, Bentham Science Publishers, Singapore, 2024.

7

Environmental and Health Impacts of Utilizing Solar PV Panels

Ayushman Srivastav[1]*, Rajesh Maithani[1] and Sachin Sharma[2]

[1]Department of Mechanical Engineering, UPES, Dehradun, Uttarakhand, India
[2]Mechanical Cluster, School of Advanced Engineering and Centre Head-BEST, UPES, Dehradun, Uttarakhand, India

Abstract

As the global demand for sustainable energy grows, solar photovoltaic (PV) panels have emerged as a vital technology for mitigating climate change and reducing dependence on fossil fuels. However, their widespread adoption presents significant environmental and health challenges throughout their lifecycle. This chapter explores the environmental implications of solar PV systems, from resource-intensive manufacturing processes and land use impacts to disposal challenges and hazardous material management. The energy-intensive production of silicon-based PV panels, the use of toxic chemicals, and the habitat disruptions caused by large-scale solar installations are critically analyzed. The chapter also addresses end-of-life management issues, including the lack of efficient recycling infrastructure and the risks of hazardous waste leakage. Strategies for mitigating these impacts, such as improved recycling technologies, extended producer responsibility, and second-life applications, are discussed. Despite these challenges, solar PV technology holds immense potential for driving a sustainable energy transition. The chapter emphasizes the importance of advancing manufacturing techniques, enhancing recycling frameworks, and adopting holistic policies to ensure the long-term sustainability of solar energy.

***Keywords*:** Photovoltaic, solar cell, environmental impact, toxic chemicals, manufacturing processes

**Corresponding author*: ayushman.107499@stu.upes.ac.in

Surajit Mondal, Paramjeet Singh Paliyal and Sachin Sharma (eds.) Digital Twin Technology for Solar Concentrators, (95–112) © 2026 Scrivener Publishing LLC

Introduction

As global energy demand increases, concerns about the environmental impact of fossil fuel consumption continue to grow [1]. Fossil fuels are responsible for over 75% of global greenhouse gas emissions, as illustrated in Figure 7.1, fuelling climate change and causing biodiversity loss by disrupting ecosystems. The greenhouse effect is also connected to more frequent extreme weather events, displacing millions of people, threatening food security, and reducing access to clean water.

To mitigate the impacts of fossil fuels, nearly 200 countries at COP-28 committed to tripling global renewable energy capacity to 11,000 GW by 2030, with the goal of limiting global warming to 1.5°C. Among renewable energy sources, solar power is becoming increasingly important, projected to account for more than half of the renewable energy sector and approximately 30% of total installed energy generation capacity by 2030 [3] as illustrated in Figure 7.2.

Solar energy can be directly harnessed through solar thermal collectors (STCs), which capture solar irradiance to heat a working fluid [4]. The heated fluid is then used for applications like electricity generation, space heating, or water heating [5, 6]. However, STCs face efficiency challenges due to thermohydraulic limitations and metallurgical constraints.

Another effective way to harness solar energy is through the use of photovoltaic (PV) panels, which directly convert sunlight into electricity. This technology is not only highly efficient but also highly scalable, making it

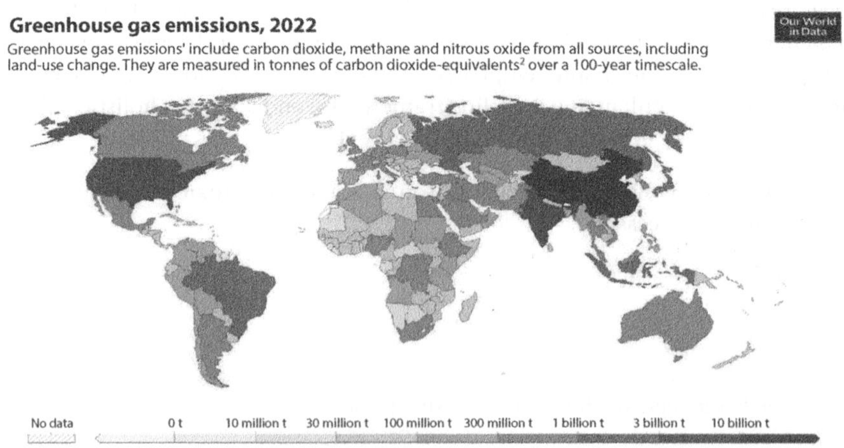

Figure 7.1 Map of global greenhouse gas emissions [2].

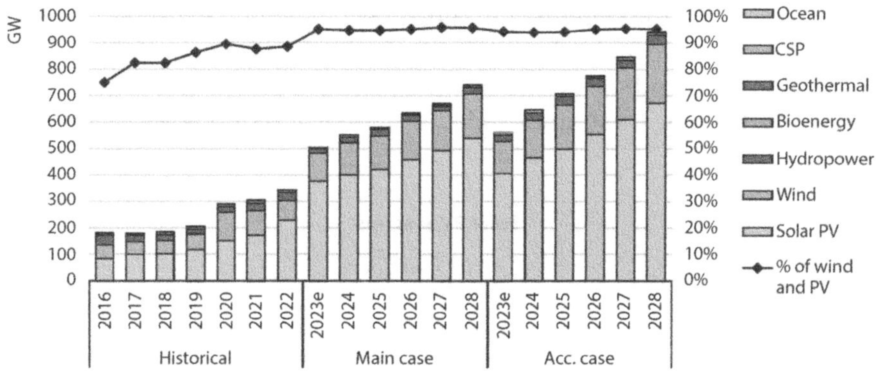

Figure 7.2 Renewable electricity capacity expansion by technology and segment [3].

suitable for integration into various applications, from residential homes and commercial buildings to large utility-scale power plants. By tapping into solar energy, PV panels provide a sustainable, clean, and renewable energy source. Figure 7.3 illustrates the global photovoltaic power potential, highlighting regions with the highest energy generation capabilities.

The Figure 7.4 highlights the dual aspects of solar PV systems, showcasing both their advantages and challenges. Solar PV technology is increasingly regarded as a promising solution to meet the rising demand for clean energy. Among its benefits is its potential to mitigate climate change, reduce dependence on fossil fuels, and harness sustainable energy. Additionally, advancements in recycling technologies and extended producer responsibility frameworks contribute to its eco-friendliness.

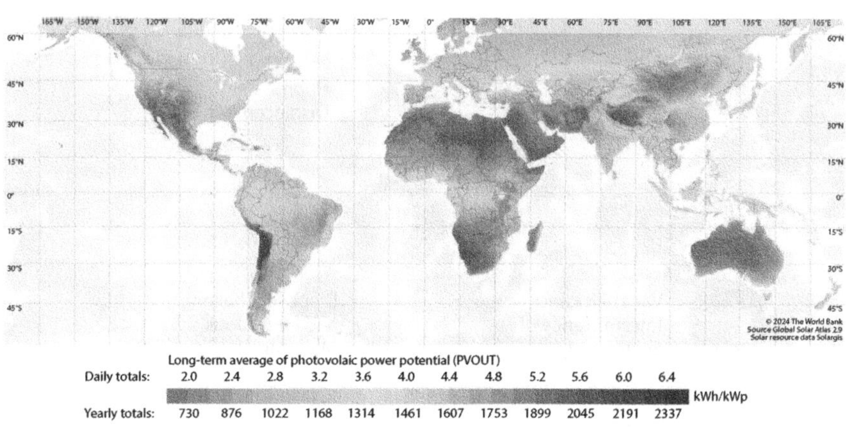

Figure 7.3 Global photovoltaic power potential [7].

However, as the Figure 7.4 illustrates, certain challenges persist. Resource-intensive manufacturing, the use of toxic chemicals, habitat disruption, and end-of-life management issues pose environmental concerns. Addressing these drawbacks, including hazardous waste leakage,

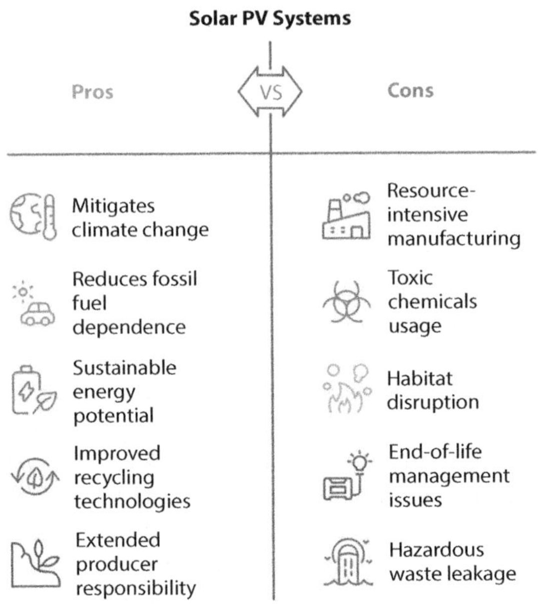

Figure 7.4 Pros and cons of solar photovoltaic technology.

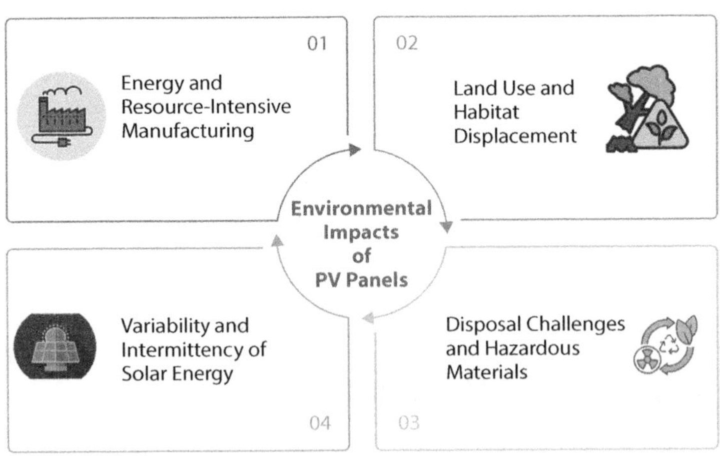

Figure 7.5 Environmental impact of photovoltaic technology.

will require a combination of innovation, regulation, and collaboration. Despite these challenges, solar PV remains an essential component of the transition to a sustainable energy future, provided its environmental footprint is managed effectively.

However, similar to all energy systems, solar PV technology presents environmental impacts, as shown in Figure 7.5, that span its entire life cycle, including raw material extraction, manufacturing, operation, disposal, and recycling. This chapter explores the environmental implications of solar PV panels, utilizing key research and life cycle assessments (LCAs) to offer a thorough analysis of these effects.

Energy and Resource-Intensive Manufacturing

The main components of a photovoltaic (PV) module, shown in Figure 7.6 from a top-down view, include several key layers. At the top is a glass cover designed to protect the solar cells from damage. Beneath the glass, two layers of laminating material, typically Ethylene Vinyl Acetate (EVA), encapsulate the solar cells. These solar cells, which may be either mono- or poly-crystalline, are connected by copper ribbons. Finally, the module is sealed with a weatherproof plastic backing made from Polyvinyl Fluoride (PVF) to provide additional protection from environmental conditions [8].

The environmental footprint of solar PV panels begins with the extraction and processing of raw materials. The production of PV as illustrated in Figure 7.7 panels requires significant amounts of silicon, silver, aluminum, glass, copper for cables, iron, and zinc for mounting structure

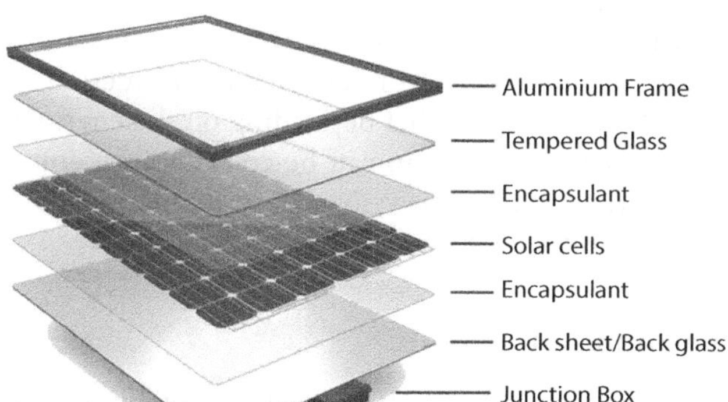

Figure 7.6 Components of a solar PV module [9].

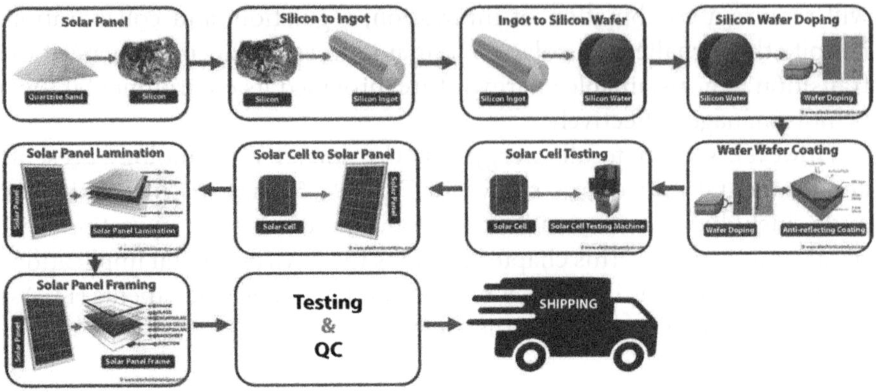

Figure 7.7 Manufacturing process of PV panels.

and other materials. These resources must be mined, processed, and refined, which leads to various environmental consequences, including habitat disruption, energy consumption, and pollution.

Raw Materials

The extraction of silicon, aluminum, copper, Iron and other materials used in PV panels can lead to habitat destruction and ecological damage, as noted by Tsoutsos *et al.* [10] Mining, particularly in sensitive ecosystems, results in deforestation, soil degradation, and biodiversity loss. These disturbances not only alter natural habitats but also negatively impact local communities and wildlife. Moreover, the process of refining silicon, a vital component of PV panels, is highly energy-intensive. The high temperatures required for refining, often fuelled by non-renewable energy sources, contribute significantly to greenhouse gas *(GHG)* emissions, further increasing the environmental footprint of solar panel production. Research by Fthenakis *et al.* [11] highlights that depending on the energy mix, carbon emissions from silicon production can be considerable, emphasizing the need for cleaner, renewable energy sources in the manufacturing process to minimize these adverse effects.

Energy Consumption

The production of silicon-based PV panels is notably energy-intensive. Kalogirou [12] explains that while the energy payback time *(EPBT)* for PV systems is improving, the initial energy required for manufacturing still contributes to carbon emissions, especially if fossil fuels are used. The *EPBT* varies based on panel technology, but it generally ranges from 1 to 4 years, after which the panels generate net-positive clean energy.

Chemical Usage

The manufacturing of PV panels also involves the use of hazardous chemicals, including cadmium, lead, and hydrochloric acid. Thin-film technology incorporates compounds such as cadmium sulfide (CdS), copper gallium diselenide (CuSe.GaSe), cadmium telluride (CdTe), gallium arsenide (GaAs), and copper indium diselenide (CuSe.InSe). Table 7.1 lists the various hazardous materials used across the PV industry [13]. Improper handling of these chemicals can result in environmental contamination, particularly affecting water and soil quality. Accidental leaks or improper disposal during production can pose serious risks to nearby ecosystems [14].

Table 7.1 Hazardous materials used in PV panels.

Type of cell	Material used	Critical issues if disposed of improperly
GaAs	Arsenic (As)	Poisonous, cancer-promoting, lung-affecting
a-Si	Arsine (AsH_3) Trimethyl gallium Hydrochloric acid Methane Diborane (as dopant)	Toxic gas, blood, kidney-damaging Pyrophoric liquid Corrosive material Flammable gas Flammable gas Pulmonary problem
CuSe.InSe CdTe	Diethylsilane (in deposition) Silane (in deposition) Silicon tetrafluoride (in deposition) Hydrogen Selenium Tellurium Cadmium	Flammable liquid Pyrophoric gas, irritant, fire hazard Toxic and corrosive gas Flammable gas and fire hazard Poisonous and irritant Adverse effect on liver Can cause lung cancer, also affects bones and kidneys

Land Use and Habitat Displacement

The environmental impacts of solar PV panels extend beyond manufacturing. Large-scale solar installations, especially utility-scale solar farms, require vast tracts of land, which can disrupt ecosystems and wildlife habitats.

Large-Scale Installations

Solar farms, particularly ground-mounted PV systems, often displace wildlife and contribute to habitat fragmentation. Hernandez *et al.* [15] highlight how clearing forests, grasslands, or agricultural lands for solar installations can have long-term consequences for biodiversity. Disrupting ecosystems can result in the displacement of species, while changes in land use patterns may further degrade the environment.

Soil Degradation

If not properly planned, solar panel installations can result in significant soil erosion and degradation. Large-scale solar farms often require clearing vegetation and altering natural land cover, which can disturb the soil structure and increase susceptibility to erosion. This disruption can reduce soil fertility, potentially impacting local ecosystems and agricultural productivity. The removal of vegetation may also alter water runoff patterns, further contributing to erosion. To mitigate these negative effects, careful planning and site management are crucial. Measures such as minimizing land disturbance, maintaining vegetation, and implementing erosion control practices can help protect the soil and preserve its fertility during solar farm installations.

Variability and Intermittency of Solar Energy

Solar PV technology, though environmentally advantageous during operation, presents challenges related to energy intermittency. Solar energy is inherently variable, as it is unavailable at night and reduced during cloudy conditions.

Intermittency and Grid Stability

The intermittent nature of solar energy necessitates energy storage systems or supplementary energy sources to ensure grid stability. Kumar *et al.* [16] suggest that without adequate storage solutions, integrating solar PV into existing power grids can pose challenges, particularly in regions with fluctuating solar availability.

Energy Storage and Environmental Impacts

Energy storage technologies, such as lithium-ion batteries, have their own environmental concerns. The extraction of materials like lithium and cobalt used in batteries has significant environmental and social impacts, including habitat destruction and hazardous waste generation. Additionally, the disposal of used batteries can lead to soil and water contamination if not managed properly.

Disposal Challenges and Hazardous Materials

As solar PV panels near the end of their lifespan (typically around 25–30 years), their disposal poses a significant environmental challenge. End-of-life (EoL) solar panels can contain hazardous materials that must be managed to avoid environmental harm.

Presence of Hazardous Materials

Thin-film PV technologies, such as cadmium telluride (CdTe) and copper indium gallium selenide (CIGS), contain toxic materials like cadmium and lead. If improperly disposed of, these heavy metals can leach into the environment, contaminating soil and groundwater. Silicon-based panels, though less toxic, also generate hazardous byproducts such as silicon tetrachloride during manufacturing, which can contribute to air and soil pollution.

Recycling Challenges

Recycling solar panels is complex due to their composition, which includes glass, silicon, aluminum, and other metals. Oteng *et al.* [17] report that current recycling technologies can recover up to 90% of the materials from PV panels, but the lack of widespread, cost-efficient recycling infrastructure means many panels still end up in landfills. Furthermore, the economic viability of recycling is low, as the cost of recovering materials often exceeds their market value.

Most solar panel recycling efforts focus on silicon (Si) panels, with the goal of recovering and reusing the most critical components. As mentioned earlier, there are currently three main recycling processes used for solar PV panels: physical, thermal, and chemical, as shown in Figure 7.8 [18].

- *Physical Recycling*
  This process involves the mechanical separation of solar PV panel components, such as glass, aluminum frames, and wiring. Panels are crushed, and valuable materials like glass and metals are recovered for reuse, though this method may not efficiently reclaim all internal components.
- *Thermal Recycling*
  Thermal recycling uses heat to break down solar panels. High temperatures burn off the polymer layers, leaving

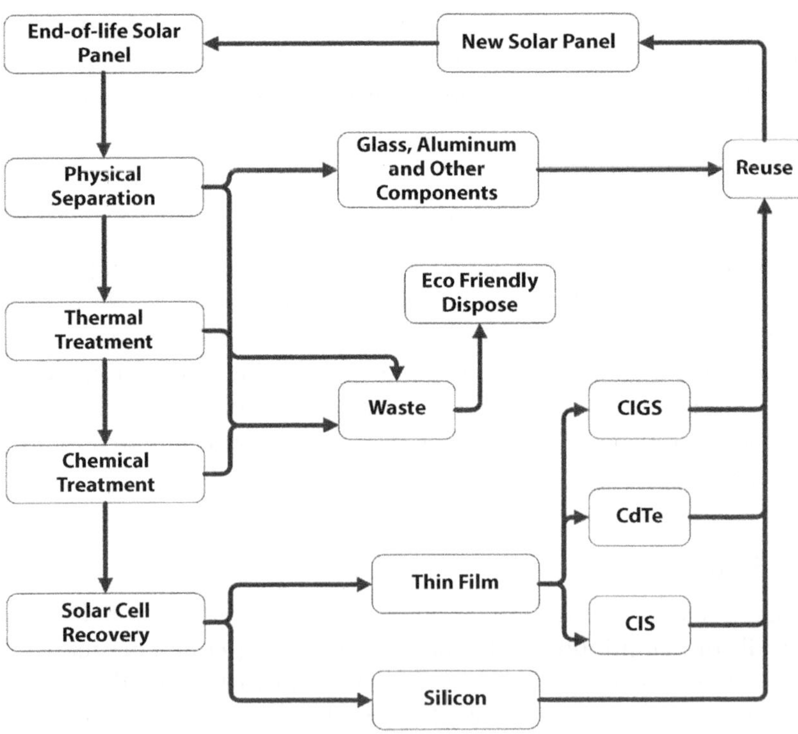

Figure 7.8 Various types of solar PV recycling processes.

behind glass, silicon, and metals. This method is effective for extracting valuable materials but can produce emissions and requires energy-intensive operations.

- *Chemical Recycling*
  Chemical recycling involves the use of solvents or acids to dissolve and separate materials within the solar panels. This process is capable of recovering higher-purity silicon and rare metals but can involve hazardous chemicals that require careful handling.

Landfill Disposal and Leachate Generation

When solar panels are disposed of in landfills, hazardous materials within them may eventually break down, creating leachate that can seep into groundwater systems. This poses significant risks to drinking water sources and ecosystems, especially in areas with insufficient waste management infrastructure. Muteri *et al.* [19] warn that as the global solar industry grows, tens of millions of metric tons of solar panel waste could accumulate by 2050 if recycling and disposal practices are not improved.

Mitigating Negative Environmental Impacts

The environmental impacts of solar photovoltaic (PV) systems are being addressed through various strategies as illustrated in Figure 7.9 that focus

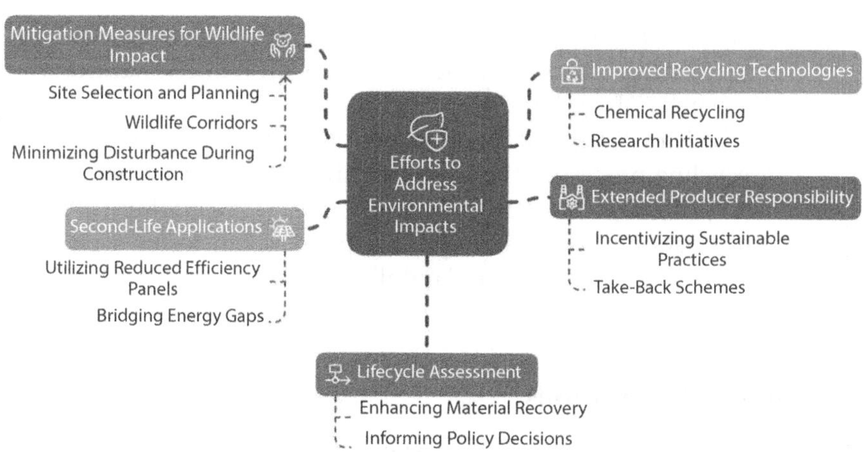

Figure 7.9 Strategies to reduce environmental impact.

on improving manufacturing processes, developing advanced recycling technologies, and establishing robust regulatory frameworks. Here are detailed approaches to mitigate these impacts.

Improved Recycling Technologies

Advancements in recycling technologies are crucial for reducing the environmental burden of discarded solar panels. Current research is focused on developing cost-effective and efficient techniques to recover valuable materials such as silicon, silver, and aluminum from end-of-life panels. For example:

> *Chemical Recycling*: This method allows for the separation of high-purity silicon and rare metals, although it requires careful handling of solvents and acids.
> *Research Initiatives:* Studies like those by Fernandes *et al.* [20] emphasize that advanced recycling can minimize dependency on virgin materials, thus improving economic feasibility and sustainability [21].

Extended Producer Responsibility (EPR)

Extended Producer Responsibility (EPR) policies can significantly enhance the lifecycle management of solar panels by holding manufacturers accountable for their products from production to disposal. Key points include:

> *Incentivizing Sustainable Practices*: EPR regulations encourage manufacturers to produce panels with reduced hazardous materials and improved recyclability [22].
> *Take-Back Schemes:* These frameworks promote systematic recycling processes, thereby minimizing the environmental footprint associated with solar PV waste. Integrating EPR into national waste management policies can foster a circular economy, reducing landfill dependency and leachate contamination [23].

Second-Life Applications

Repurposing used solar panels can extend their functional life and delay disposal. This approach involves:

Utilizing Reduced Efficiency Panels: Panels that no longer meet utility-scale requirements can still serve in less demanding applications, such as powering rural homes or agricultural irrigation systems.
Bridging Energy Gaps: By providing energy access in underdeveloped regions, second-life applications contribute to equitable energy distribution while reducing waste.

Mitigation Measures for Wildlife Impact

Efforts to minimize the ecological impact of solar PV systems also include specific measures aimed at protecting wildlife:

Site Selection and Planning: Prioritizing areas with minimal ecological value for solar installations can help reduce habitat disruption.
Wildlife Corridors: Designing solar projects with wildlife corridors ensures species can move between habitats, promoting biodiversity.
Minimizing Disturbance During Construction: Implementing strategies to reduce noise and vibrations during construction phases protects local wildlife populations [24].

Lifecycle Assessment (LCA)

A comprehensive lifecycle assessment (LCA) is essential for understanding and mitigating the environmental impacts of solar PV systems. It involves evaluating energy use, greenhouse gas emissions, and resource depletion across all stages from raw material extraction to end-of-life disposal. Key aspects include [25]:

Enhancing Material Recovery: LCAs can guide improvements in recycling processes and inform the development of less hazardous materials and manufacturing methods.
Informing Policy Decisions: The insights gained from LCAs can help shape regulatory frameworks aimed at improving sustainability in the solar industry.

Future Directions for Research and Development

To address these challenges and ensure the sustainable growth of solar PV technology, future research and development efforts should focus on the following:

- *Advanced Recycling Technologies:* Enhancing recycling methods to recover valuable materials like silicon, silver, and rare earth elements efficiently can significantly reduce waste and the demand for virgin materials. Developing closed-loop recycling systems can support a circular economy approach in the solar industry [26].
- *Sustainable Manufacturing:* Researching alternative materials for solar panels, such as perovskites or organic photovoltaics, could reduce dependency on energy-intensive or scarce resources. Additionally, adopting green manufacturing processes powered by renewable energy can lower the carbon footprint of production [27].
- *Innovative Land-Use Strategies:* Integrating solar panels into urban settings, such as on building facades, rooftops, or over parking lots, can optimize land use. Agrivoltaics, which combines agriculture and solar power production on the same land, can help balance energy generation with food production while preserving ecosystems [28].
- *Stronger Regulatory Frameworks:* Implementing global policies to standardize the disposal and recycling of solar panels is crucial. Governments and international organizations should incentivize manufacturers to design panels with recyclability in mind and establish take-back programs to manage panel disposal responsibly [29].

Conclusion

While solar PV technology offers significant environmental benefits compared to fossil fuels, its adoption is not without challenges. The manufacturing process is energy-intensive, involving extensive resource extraction, and large-scale solar farms require substantial land areas. Furthermore, managing the disposal of end-of-life panels poses waste management challenges. Tackling these issues necessitates progress in recycling technologies, the establishment of robust regulatory frameworks, and the development of innovative land-use strategies to reduce environmental impact [30].

Despite these hurdles, solar PV technology holds tremendous promise for advancing sustainable energy transitions. By mitigating its environmental footprint through improvements in recycling methods, the use of sustainable materials, and creative land-use planning, its positive contributions can be maximized. Collaboration among researchers, policymakers, and industry stakeholders will be essential to ensuring solar PV systems evolve into an even more sustainable and impactful energy solution for the future.

AI disclosure statement: The author acknowledges the use of AI-based tools for minor language editing or grammatical correction. However, all intellectual contributions, analyses, and conclusions presented in this chapter are entirely the author's own.

References

1. Srivastav, A., Maithani, R., Sharma, S., Innovative impinging jet methods for performance enhancement: a review. *J. Therm. Anal. Calorim.*, Nov. 2024, doi: 10.1007/s10973-024-13777-2.
2. Jones, M.W., *et al.*, National contributions to climate change due to historical emissions of carbon dioxide, methane and nitrous oxide, 2024, Accessed: Oct. 17, 2024. [Online]. Available: https://zenodo.org/records/10839859.
3. abriendomundo, Renewables 2023, [Online]. Available: www.iea.org.
4. Srivastav, A., Maithani, R., Sharma, S., Influence of submerged impingement jet designs on solar air collector performance. *Renewable Energy*, 121699, Oct. 2024, doi: 10.1016/j.renene.2024.121699.
5. Srivastav, A., Maithani, R., Sharma, S., Investigation of heat transfer and friction characteristics of solar air heater through an array of submerged impinging jets. *Renewable Energy*, 227, Jun. 2024, doi: 10.1016/j.renene.2024.120588.
6. Srivastav, A., Maithani, R., Sharma, S., Influence of nozzle profile on submerged pipe jet impingement heat transfer. *Exp. Heat Transfer*, 2024, doi: 10.1080/08916152.2024.2391803.
7. Data/information/map] obtained from the Global Solar Atlas 2.0, a free, web-based application is developed and operated by the company Solargis s.r.o. on behalf of the World Bank Group, utilizing Solargis data, with funding provided by the Energy Sector Management Assistance Program (ESMAP), https://globalsolaratlas.info.

8. Dubey, S., Jadhav, N.Y., Zakirova, B., Socio-economic and environmental impacts of silicon based photovoltaic (PV) technologies. *Energy Procedia*, 322–334, Elsevier Ltd, 2013, doi: 10.1016/j.egypro.2013.05.073.
9. Almadhhachi, M., Seres, I., Farkas, I., Significance of solar trees: Configuration, operation, types and technology commercialization. *Energy Rep.*, 8, 6729–6743, 2022, doi: https://doi.org/10.1016/j.egyr.2022.05.015.
10. Tsoutsos, T., Frantzeskaki, N., Gekas, V., Environmental impacts from the solar energy technologies. *Energy Policy*, 33, 3, 289–296, Feb. 2005, doi: 10.1016/S0301-4215(03)00241-6.
11. Fthenakis, V. and Raugei, M., Life Cycle Inventories and Life Cycle Assessments of Photovoltaic Systems, 2011, [Online]. Available: https://www.researchgate.net/publication/268212394.
12. Kalogirou, S.A., Environmental benefits of domestic solar energy systems. *Energy Convers. Manage.*, 45, 18–19, 3075–3092, Nov. 2004, doi: 10.1016/j.enconman.2003.12.019.
13. Rathore, N. and Panwar, N.L., Strategic overview of management of future solar photovoltaic panel waste generation in the Indian context. *Waste Manag. Res.*, May 01, 2022, SAGE Publications Ltd. doi: 10.1177/0734242X211003977.
14. Nkuissi, H.J.T., Konan, F.K., Hartiti, B., Ndjaka, J.-M., Toxic Materials Used in Thin Film Photovoltaics and Their Impacts on Environment, in: *Reliability and Ecological Aspects of Photovoltaic Modules*, A. Gok (Ed.), IntechOpen, Rijeka, 2020, ch. 7. doi: 10.5772/intechopen.88326.
15. Hernandez, R.R., *et al.*, Environmental impacts of utility-scale solar energy. *Renew. Sustain. Energy Rev.*, 2014, doi: 10.1016/j.rser.2013.08.041.
16. Kumar, N.M., Chopra, S.S., Rajput, P., Life cycle assessment and environmental impacts of solar PV systems, in: *Photovoltaic Solar Energy Conversion: Technologies, Applications and Environmental Impacts*, pp. 391–411, Elsevier, Amsterdam, Netherlands, 2020, doi: 10.1016/B978-0-12-819610-6.00012-0.
17. Oteng, D., Zuo, J., Sharifi, E., An evaluation of the impact framework for product stewardship on end-of-life solar photovoltaic modules: An environmental lifecycle assessment. *J. Cleaner Prod.*, 411, Jul. 2023, doi: 10.1016/j.jclepro.2023.137357.
18. Chowdhury, M.S., *et al.*, An overview of solar photovoltaic panels' end-of-life material recycling. *Energy Strategy Rev.*, Jan. 01, 2020, Elsevier Ltd. doi: 10.1016/j.esr.2019.100431.
19. Muteri, V., *et al.*, Review on life cycle assessment of solar photovoltaic panels. *Energies*, Jan. 03, 2020, MDPI AG. doi: 10.3390/en13010252.
20. Fernandes, C.A.F., Paulo Torres, J.N., Morgado, M., Morgado, J.A., Aging of Solar PV plants and mitigation of their consequences, [Online]. Available: www.edp.pt/.
21. Akhter, M., *et al.*, Sustainable Strategies for Crystalline Solar Cell Recycling: A Review on Recycling Techniques, Companies, and Environmental Impact

Analysis. *Sustainability*, Jul. 01, 2024, Multidisciplinary Digital Publishing Institute (MDPI). *Sustainability*, doi: 10.3390/su16135785.

22. Srivastav, A., Maithani, R., Sharma, S., Dixit, A., Numerical Analysis of Flat Fins Employing Staggered Square Rib Structures, in: *Modeling, Simulation and Optimization. CoMSO 2024. Smart Innovation, Systems and Technologies*, Das, B., Patgiri, R., Mondol, J.D., Gupta, R., Baidya, D.K. (eds) vol. 461, Springer, Singapore, 2026. https://doi.org/10.1007/978-981-95-4161-4_41.
23. Paliyal, P.S., Mondal, S., Pandey, J.K., An Analysis of Springwater Parameter Status for Different Locations in the Rural Hilly Garhwal Region of Uttarakhand. *Environ. Claims J.*, *36*, 3, 243–277, 2024, https://doi.org/10.1080/10406026.2024.2423964.
24. Paliyal, P.S. and Mondal, S., An analysis of a cross-finned receiver for Scheffler-type solar collectors to optimize solar heating efficiency for direct water heating. *Int. J. Energy Water Resour.*, 2025, https://doi.org/10.1007/s42108-025-00393-5.
25. Paliyal, P.S., Mondal, S., Pathela, M., Kumar, A., Menon, S.K., Optimization of Solar Photovoltaic Array In-Depth Analysis of Perturb and Observe MPPT Algorithm. *2024 International Conference on Advances in Computing, Communication and Materials (ICACCM)*, Dehradun, India, pp. 1–6, 2024, doi: 10.1109/ICACCM61117.2024.11059143.
26. Srivastav, A., Maithani, R., Sharma, S., Dixit, A., Parametric Optimization of Thermal System with Staggered Jet Impinging on the Hemispherical Protrusion, in: *Modeling, Simulation and Optimization. CoMSO 2024. Smart Innovation, Systems and Technologies*, B. Das, R. Patgiri, J.D. Mondol, R. Gupta, D.K. Baidya (eds.), vol. 461, Springer, Singapore, 2026. https://doi.org/10.1007/978-981-95-4161-4_42.
27. Menon, S.K., *et al.*, The Role of Hydrogen as a Sustainable Energy Source and its Integration with the Grid, in: *Advancements in Communication and Systems*, A.K. Tripathi and V. Shrivastava (Eds.), p. 397, Computing and Intelligent Systems, SCRS, India, 2023, 2025.
28. Kudapa, V.K., Paliyal, P.S., Mondal, A., Mondal, S., A critical review of fabrication strategies, separation techniques, challenges, and future prospects for the hydrogen separation membrane. *Fusion Sci. Technol.*, 80, 7, 803–825, 2024.
29. Mondal, A., Jangirh, R., Arya, R., Yadav, L., Ahlawat, S., Yadav, P., Paliyal, P.S., Bobde, P., Ghosh, P., Mondal, S., Rai, A., Analysing solid residential fuel usage patterns in rural and urban slums of Delhi: Implications for pollution reduction and sustainable practices. *Energy Sustainable Dev.*, *80*, 101460, 2024.
30. Srivastav, A., CFD investigation of thermo-hydraulic performance in rib roughened fin under forced convection. *J. Graphic Era Univ*, 2023, https://doi.org/10.13052/jgeu0975-1416.1111.

8

Integration of IoT, AI, and Digital Twin Technology for Smart Solar Concentrators

Paramjeet Singh Paliyal[1]* and Surajit Mondal[2]

[1]*Department of Electrical and Electronics Engineering, College of Engineering, COER University, Roorkee, Uttarakhand, India*
[2]*Energy Cluster, School of Advanced Engineering, UPES, Dehradun, Uttarakhand, India*

Abstract

This chapter presents a unified cyber-physical framework that integrates Internet of Things (IoT) telemetry, Artificial Intelligence (AI) analytics, and a continuously synchronized Digital Twin (DT) to transform solar concentrators—parabolic troughs, dishes, linear Fresnel fields, and power towers—into intelligent, dispatchable thermal assets. We first ground the discussion in concentrator fundamentals and the optical–thermal–mechanical couplings that govern efficiency and reliability. We then detail a layered architecture in which edge IoT sensing delivers time-stamped, quality-checked telemetry to a DT composed of coupled optical, thermal, and mechanical sub-models. State estimation and online parameter identification keep the twin aligned with reality, while AI components forecast irradiance and faults and compute optimal, constraint-aware set-points *via* model-predictive control. The framework explicitly addresses interoperability, security, and verification/validation through hardware-in-the-loop testing, enabling safe progression from advisory analytics to supervised autonomy. An illustrative temperature-tracking study under cloud transients demonstrates the operational value of twin-informed control, showing markedly reduced worst-case deviation versus conventional PID and faster recovery to setpoint. Collectively, the approach improves optical capture and thermal yield, mitigates hot-spots, enhances storage dispatchability, and aligns maintenance with measured loss factors such as soiling and mis-aim—lowering levelized cost of energy while increasing availability and confidence in delivery.

**Corresponding author*: paramjeet29895@gmail.com

Surajit Mondal, Paramjeet Singh Paliyal and Sachin Sharma (eds.) Digital Twin Technology for Solar Concentrators, (113–136) © 2026 Scrivener Publishing LLC

Keywords: Solar concentrators, cyber physical systems, Internet of Things, digital twin, artificial intelligence

8.1 Introduction

The transition toward sustainable energy systems has intensified global interest in harnessing solar power as a clean, abundant, and renewable energy source. Among the various solar technologies, solar concentrators—such as parabolic troughs, parabolic dishes, Fresnel reflectors, and solar towers—play a pivotal role in concentrating solar radiation to achieve high thermal energy outputs. These concentrated solar power (CSP) systems are vital for applications ranging from industrial process heating and desalination to large-scale electricity generation. However, the efficiency, reliability, and long-term performance of solar concentrators are often challenged by fluctuating weather conditions, mechanical degradation, thermal losses, and suboptimal operation strategies. In this context, the emergence of Digital Twin (DT) technology, integrated with Internet of Things (IoT) infrastructure and Artificial Intelligence (AI) tools, presents an unprecedented opportunity to transform solar concentrators into intelligent, adaptive, and self-optimizing systems. The concept of the digital twin—a dynamic virtual representation of a physical system continuously updated with real-time data—has gained significant traction across industries such as aerospace, manufacturing, and smart grids. In the domain of solar energy, digital twins serve as cyber-physical bridges between solar concentrators and their digital replicas, enabling predictive simulation, performance optimization, fault diagnosis, and lifecycle management. By creating a digital counterpart of a concentrator system, engineers and operators can simulate the effects of operating conditions, evaluate design modifications, and predict system behavior under diverse scenarios without disrupting the actual plant operations. This capability marks a paradigm shift from traditional monitoring and control toward intelligent, data-driven energy systems [1].

The integration of IoT technologies into solar concentrators enables the continuous acquisition of data from sensors measuring solar irradiance, ambient temperature, wind speed, heat transfer fluid parameters, and mechanical stresses. These sensors, connected through wireless communication protocols and cloud platforms, provide the backbone for real-time monitoring and control. When linked to a digital twin, this IoT-driven data stream enhances the fidelity of the virtual model, ensuring that the twin accurately mirrors the dynamic behavior of the physical concentrator system.

Moreover, IoT integration facilitates remote accessibility, interoperability, and scalability, which are crucial for the deployment of smart concentrator fields in geographically diverse regions. Artificial Intelligence further augments the power of digital twins by enabling predictive analytics, optimization, and autonomous decision-making. Machine learning algorithms can analyze vast datasets collected through IoT networks, uncovering patterns that inform predictive maintenance schedules, optimal tracking strategies, and adaptive thermal management. Advanced AI techniques such as reinforcement learning and neural networks allow concentrator systems to self-learn from historical performance data and continuously improve their operation. For example, AI can predict cloud transients and dynamically adjust heliostat positions, or detect early signs of optical misalignment and structural fatigue before costly failures occur. By integrating AI with digital twins, solar concentrators evolve into intelligent agents capable of achieving higher efficiency, reduced downtime, and extended lifespan [2].

The synergy of IoT, AI, and digital twin technologies represents a transformative shift toward smart solar concentrators. Together, they enable not only performance optimization and fault-tolerant operations but also the creation of resilient and adaptive solar infrastructures that can contribute significantly to global decarbonization goals. Furthermore, these technologies support integration with thermal storage systems, hybrid renewable setups, and grid-responsive frameworks, thereby enhancing the dispatchability and reliability of CSP plants. As governments and industries worldwide accelerate their clean energy transitions, smart solar concentrators equipped with digital twin capabilities are poised to play a crucial role in ensuring sustainable, intelligent, and cost-effective solar energy solutions. This chapter explores the intersection of IoT, AI, and digital twin technologies within the context of solar concentrators. It begins by outlining the principles of solar concentration and the fundamentals of digital twin architecture. It then delves into the role of IoT-based sensing and communication for real-time data acquisition, followed by an examination of AI algorithms for predictive analytics and optimization. The chapter further discusses practical case studies, emerging research, and challenges related to integrating these technologies, including issues of computational complexity, cyber-physical security, and scalability. Finally, it highlights future research directions and potential pathways for the commercialization of intelligent solar concentrator systems [3].

Figure 8.1 illustrates the integration of IoT, AI, and Digital Twin technologies in solar concentrator systems. On the left, a physical solar concentrator (parabolic trough or heliostat field) is shown equipped with IoT-based

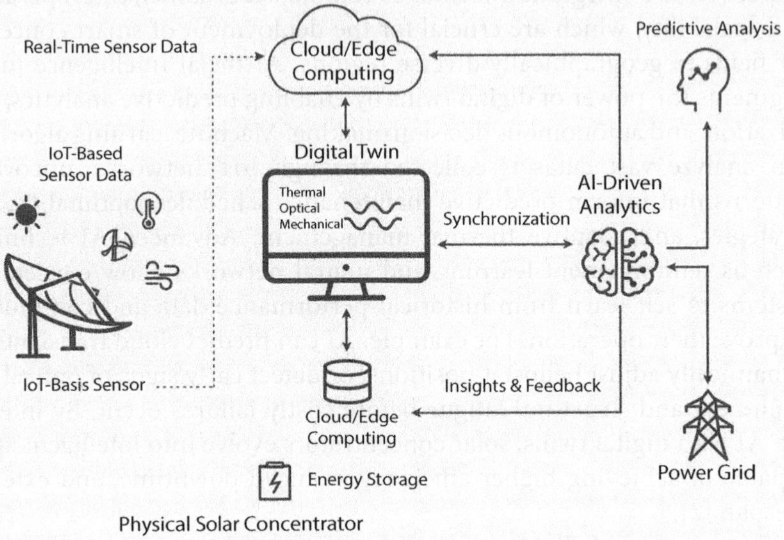

Figure 8.1 Conceptual framework of IoT, AI, and digital twin integration for smart solar concentrators.

sensors measuring parameters such as solar irradiance, temperature, wind speed, and heat transfer fluid conditions. These real-time sensor data are transmitted through IoT gateways to a cloud/edge computing layer, where data storage, preprocessing, and communication occur. The central part of the figure depicts the Digital Twin, a virtual replica of the solar concentrator system that continuously synchronizes with the physical asset. The twin simulates thermal, optical, and mechanical behavior under varying conditions, enabling predictive analysis. On the right, an AI-driven analytics module is represented, applying machine learning and optimization algorithms to identify performance trends, predict failures, and recommend control strategies. Feedback loops between the AI module and both the digital twin and physical concentrator demonstrate closed-loop optimization and predictive maintenance. At the bottom, integration with energy storage and power grid is shown, highlighting the dispatchability and scalability of smart solar concentrators [4].

8.2 Fundamentals of Solar Concentrators

Solar concentrators are specialized devices that collect and focus solar radiation onto a receiver to generate high-temperature thermal energy. Unlike flat-plate collectors, which absorb diffuse and direct sunlight uniformly, concentrators use reflective or refractive surfaces to concentrate sunlight by several hundred times. This concentrated energy raises the temperature of the working fluid—such as water, molten salt, or oil—to levels suitable for industrial heating or power generation through thermodynamic cycles. The geometry of concentrators and their tracking mechanisms determines their efficiency, cost, and application domain. Among the most established designs are parabolic troughs, parabolic dishes, Fresnel reflectors, and solar power towers, each with unique working principles and performance characteristics. Parabolic trough concentrators are the most widely deployed type of concentrating solar power system. They consist of long, curved mirrors shaped like a parabola that focus sunlight onto a receiver tube running along the focal line. A heat transfer fluid flows through this tube, absorbing the concentrated heat, which is then transferred to a steam generator to produce electricity. Due to their modular nature and relatively mature technology, parabolic troughs have been implemented in several large-scale plants worldwide [5].

- Parabolic dish concentrators, on the other hand, use a dish-shaped reflector that concentrates sunlight onto a single focal point, where a receiver or Stirling engine is placed. Because the sunlight is focused to a much smaller point compared to troughs, dish systems achieve very high temperatures and efficiencies, often exceeding 30%. However, they are more suitable for small-scale, decentralized power generation rather than utility-scale deployment.
- Linear Fresnel reflectors adopt a simpler approach by using flat or slightly curved mirror strips to reflect sunlight onto an elevated receiver. Although their concentration ratio is lower than that of parabolic systems, Fresnel reflectors are cost-effective due to reduced material requirements and simpler design. They are particularly useful where land availability and construction costs are critical factors.
- Solar towers, also known as central receiver systems, use an array of flat, sun-tracking mirrors called heliostats to focus sunlight onto a receiver located atop a tall tower. The receiver heats a working fluid—often molten salt—which is

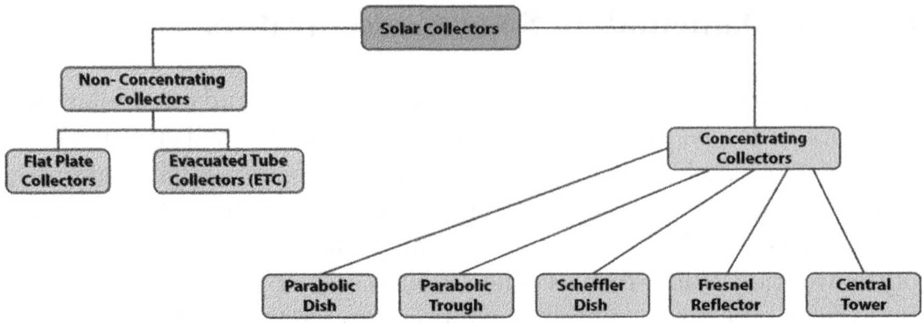

Figure 8.2 Classification of solar collectors.

then used to produce steam for power generation. Tower systems can reach very high operating temperatures, enabling greater thermodynamic efficiency and efficient thermal storage integration, making them attractive for large-scale grid-connected power plants.

Figure 8.2 presents the classification of solar collectors into two major categories: Non-Concentrating Collectors and Concentrating Collectors. Non-concentrating collectors, such as Flat Plate Collectors and Evacuated Tube Collectors (ETC), capture solar energy without focusing sunlight and are typically used for low to medium temperature applications like domestic water heating. Concentrating collectors, on the other hand, focus sunlight onto a smaller receiver area to achieve higher temperatures and are suitable for industrial and power generation purposes. Examples include Parabolic Dish, Parabolic Trough, Scheffler Dish, Fresnel Reflector, and Central Tower systems.

8.2.1 Thermal and Optical Performance Considerations

The performance of solar concentrators depends heavily on both thermal and optical efficiency. Optical efficiency refers to the system's ability to capture and direct sunlight accurately onto the receiver. Factors such as mirror reflectivity, surface accuracy, shading losses, and tracking precision significantly affect optical efficiency. Even small deviations in mirror alignment or tracking can lead to substantial losses in concentrated energy. Thermal efficiency, on the other hand, concerns the ability of the receiver and heat transfer system to absorb and retain the concentrated heat. Receivers are typically coated with selective materials that maximize solar absorption while minimizing radiative heat loss. Insulation techniques are also employed to reduce convective and conductive losses. Furthermore, the choice of working fluid—whether synthetic oil, molten salt, or pressurized air—directly influences heat transfer rates, operating temperatures, and overall system efficiency. A balance between optical and thermal performance is critical for maximizing overall efficiency. For example, while parabolic dishes offer superior concentration ratios and higher thermal performance, they require precise tracking and advanced receiver materials. Fresnel systems, though less efficient, compensate through lower costs and ease of scaling. Solar towers, with their potential for very high operating temperatures, benefit greatly from advanced materials and integration with thermal energy storage systems [6].

8.2.2 Limitations of Conventional Concentrator Systems

Despite their promise, conventional concentrator systems face several challenges that limit widespread adoption. One of the key limitations is their dependency on direct normal irradiance (DNI). Concentrators cannot utilize diffuse sunlight effectively, which restricts their deployment to regions with high and consistent solar radiation, such as arid and semi-arid climates. Cloud cover, atmospheric dust, and seasonal variations significantly impact their performance. Another limitation is the high capital cost associated with concentrator construction and tracking systems. Precision tracking mechanisms and reflective materials require significant investment and regular maintenance to retain efficiency over time. Land and water requirements also pose constraints, especially for solar tower plants that often need vast areas and substantial water for cooling. In addition, concentrators face operational challenges such as mirror soiling, structural fatigue, and optical misalignment. The durability of receiver coatings and thermal stresses due to repeated heating and cooling cycles can also affect system longevity. While thermal energy storage integration provides an advantage, it adds complexity and cost to the system. Furthermore, compared to rapidly declining photovoltaic (PV) costs, concentrators must overcome economic competitiveness challenges, making technological innovation essential for their continued adoption [7].

Figure 8.3 below illustrates four main types of solar concentrators. The parabolic trough focuses sunlight onto a receiver tube positioned along its focal line, while the parabolic dish reflects solar rays to a single focal point, typically connected to a Stirling engine. The linear Fresnel reflector uses multiple flat or slightly curved mirrors to concentrate sunlight onto an elevated receiver tube. The solar power tower employs a heliostat field of sun-tracking mirrors that direct sunlight toward a central receiver at the top of a tall tower. Arrows indicate the paths of sunlight and concentration points.

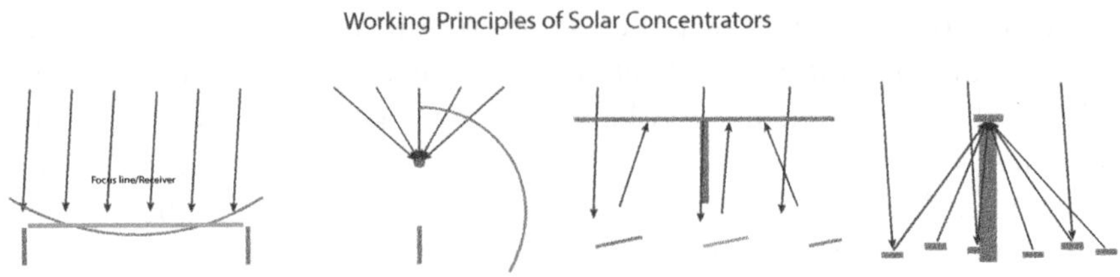

Figure 8.3 Comparative working principles of solar concentrators.

8.3 Digital Twin Technology: Concepts and Architecture

A digital twin is a living, computational representation of a physical asset that remains synchronized with its real-world counterpart across the entire life cycle—from design and commissioning through operation, maintenance, and end-of-life. In the context of solar concentrators, the twin continuously mirrors the optical, thermal, mechanical, and control states of parabolic troughs, dishes, linear Fresnel fields, and power towers, using data ingested from sensors and control systems. Unlike a static simulation model, a digital twin is event- and time-aware, absorbing live measurements, updating internal states, and closing the loop by providing recommendations or automated control actions. It also preserves a historical trace of the asset's behavior, enabling trend analysis, degradation tracking, and what-if experimentation without perturbing plant operations. This combination of high-fidelity physics, data assimilation, and bidirectional connectivity makes the twin a central intelligence node for smart concentrator plants [8].

At the heart of any digital twin lies an architectural stack that binds the physical and digital worlds. The physical layer comprises the concentrator optics, receivers, heat-transfer loops, tracking drives, foundations, thermal storage, and the associated balance-of-plant. The data acquisition layer spans irradiance pyrheliometers, sky imagers, optical encoders, thermocouples, flow and pressure transducers, vibration sensors, and electrical meters, all time-stamped and quality-tagged. The communication layer transports this telemetry over fieldbuses and industrial protocols such as Modbus-TCP and OPC UA within the plant, MQTT or DDS for lightweight publish–subscribe messaging, and secure IP networks for inter-site or cloud links. The data management layer curates incoming streams in a scalable time-series store, couples them with static engineering data from PLM and GIS sources, and exposes a governed semantic model of the plant's assets and relationships. Over this foundation, the modeling and analytics layer runs physics solvers, reduced-order surrogates, and machine-learning workloads, while an orchestration layer brokers decisions back to the supervisory control system or edge controllers.

Modeling fidelity is central to a useful twin, and for solar concentrators, it must span multiple coupled domains. The optical sub-twin captures sun-to-aperture transfer using ray-tracing or Monte Carlo methods that account for sunshape, mirror reflectivity, slope error, soiling, cosine effects, shading, and blocking in heliostat or mirror fields. The thermal sub-twin resolves receiver absorption, radiative and convective losses, conduction through structures, heat-transfer fluid thermophysics, and transient storage dynamics, linking to power-block performance maps for steam or supercritical CO_2 cycles. The mechanical sub-twin models drive kinematics, structural loads, backlash, and wind-induced deflection that perturb optical aim points and therefore flux distributions. These sub-twins are stitched together through co-simulation or reduced-order interfaces so that optical perturbations propagate into thermal states and ultimately into net electrical output and component stress. Where full-order models are computationally heavy, the twin deploys calibrated surrogate models that preserve accuracy in the operating region while meeting tight latency budgets. State estimation keeps the twin aligned with reality in the presence of sensor noise, faults, and unmeasured disturbances. Bayesian filters, extended and unscented Kalman filters, and moving-horizon estimators fuse redundant measurements—such as multiple temperature taps along a receiver tube or twin encoders per axis—to reconstruct latent states like effective absorptivity, soiling index, film coefficients, or misalignment angles. Parameter identification routines adjust model constants online, for example tuning mirror slope-error distributions after wind events or correcting thermal emissivity as coatings age. Uncertainty quantification runs in parallel to bound confidence in forecasts and to drive risk-aware control actions; the twin propagates parametric and input uncertainties through its surrogates to deliver prediction intervals on flux, outlet temperature, or dispatchable energy. This quantified uncertainty becomes a first-class citizen in operator dashboards and in automated decision logic [9].

Deployment topology determines whether the twin can act in real time or only in advisory mode. Edge twins run on ruggedized compute near the field to meet sub-second deadlines for tracking, flux shaping, or safety interlocks, minimizing backhaul bandwidth and exposure to intermittent connectivity. Plant-level twins aggregate across loops, rows, or heliostat clusters and inform supervisory optimization, while cloud-hosted twins exploit elastic resources for large scenario ensembles, seasonal planning, and fleet benchmarking across multiple sites. A layered approach is common, with lightweight edge instances handling fast loops and a heavier supervisory twin coordinating optimization, maintenance planning, and reporting. The layers synchronize through versioned APIs and message streams so that improvements in one model tier flow coherently to the others without breaking compatibility. The digital thread gives the twin longitudinal memory that spans design, build, and operate phases. CAD and PLM artifacts, bills of materials, calibration certificates, and acceptance test results become part of the twin's provenance, ensuring traceability for every mirror facet, receiver module, tracking drive, and sensor. During commissioning, the twin accelerates punch-list closure by comparing expected versus measured aim points, stagnation temperatures, and drive torques, raising targeted defects rather than generic alarms. In operation, the same thread links observed degradation—such as rising torque to overcome stiction or stepwise drops in reflectivity—to specific assets and work orders in the maintenance system, enabling closed-loop learning from field interventions. When retrofit opportunities arise, the twin can test proposed upgrades virtually, quantify expected yield and reliability gains, and feed procurement with evidence-backed specifications [10].

Verification, validation, and accreditation are non-negotiable for trust in the twin's recommendations. Formal test campaigns benchmark optical and thermal predictions against calibrated measurement runs across seasons, sun angles, and wind regimes. Hardware-in-the-loop setups using platforms such as dSPACE and OPAL-RT allow drive controllers, sun-tracking algorithms, and safety logic to interact with a high-fidelity plant model under scripted disturbances, including cloud transients, wind gusts, or jammed axes, without risking equipment. Model-to-model comparisons against independent solvers and round-trip energy balances guard against silent drift. Performance metrics include fidelity under distributional shift, end-to-end latency from sensor to decision, forecast skill versus naive baselines, and availability during network or component failures, all tracked by an MLOps/AIOps regimen that treats physics surrogates and learned models as versioned, testable artifacts. Security and resilience must be designed in from the outset because the twin straddles OT and IT domains. Strong device identity, mutual TLS, and certificate rotation protect data in transit, while role-based access and least-privilege service accounts constrain blast radius within the platform. Network segmentation separates control surfaces from analytics workloads; data diodes or brokered topics enforce one-way flows where safety requires it. Telemetry is signed and time-synchronized so that replay or spoofing attacks are detectable, and audit trails preserve tamper-evident records of control actions. Backup twins and warm failover at the edge ensure continuity during outages, while chaos testing validates recovery procedures under adversarial and environmental stressors.

The control interface is where the twin proves its value. In advisory mode, it surfaces prescriptive guidance such as heliostat re-aiming to shape flux, receiver flow-rate adjustments to avoid hot spots, or cleaning schedules optimized against soiling ratios and water constraints. In autonomous mode, it closes the loop by issuing setpoints to tracking drives and pumps under guardrails, often *via* a model predictive controller that uses twin forecasts to push the plant toward cost or revenue objectives subject to thermal and mechanical limits. The same infrastructure orchestrates daily charge–discharge profiles for molten-salt or packed-bed storage so that dispatch aligns with price signals and forecast clouds, balancing efficiency, degradation, and revenue. Scalability is achieved by partitioning the system into many small twins that compose into a system-of-systems. Each heliostat, mirror row, receiver panel, or pump can host a micro-twin with local states and health indicators, while higher levels aggregate these into row, field, and plant twins. Microservices encapsulate models and services for ingestion, simulation, optimization, and visualization, with containers orchestrated to elastically scale with irradiance dynamics and operator load. Schema-managed event streams carry observations and decisions, and a canonical asset model maintains referential integrity as components are replaced or upgraded over decades.

Table 8.1 contrasts four CSP technologies and their digital-twin requirements. Parabolic troughs are mid-range in concentration and temperature with 1-axis tracking, favoring row-level optical–thermal co-simulation and edge micro-twins per loop. Parabolic dishes deliver the highest concentration with fast thermal transients and 2-axis tracking, so twins emphasize sub-second pointing, hot-spot avoidance, and autonomous dish-level control. Linear Fresnel reflectors trade lower concentration for simpler, cheaper optics, making alignment/blocking optimization and bank-level edge twins most impactful. Solar towers achieve the highest operating temperatures and most mature molten-salt storage; their twins focus on field-wide aim-point/flux control, receiver thermo-mechanics, and TES scheduling, orchestrated by cluster edge twins plus a plant optimizer for dispatch.

Finally, the most effective digital twins are hybrid in both modeling and governance. Physics encodes conservation laws and guarantees extrapolation outside the training data, while machine learning captures residuals, hysteresis, and site-specific idiosyncrasies the equations miss. Governance

Table 8.1 Solar concentrator technologies vs. digital-twin needs.

Parameter	Parabolic trough	Parabolic dish	Linear fresnel reflector	Solar power tower
Typical concentration ratio	150–300×	500–1,000×	100–200×	300–1,000×
Operating temperature (receiver/ HTF)	150–400°C (synthetic oil), up to ~430°C; with molten salt up to ~500°C	500–800°C at focal receiver (Stirling/ pressurized air)	150–400°C (oil/ steam)	500–565°C (two-tank molten salt), >600°C possible (advanced salts/sCO_2)
Tracking	1-axis (N–S or E–W)	2-axis	1-axis	2-axis (heliostats)
Optical complexity and sensitivities	Moderate; slope error and sag cause line-focus spill; cosine loss manageable	High; tight focus requires sub-milliradian pointing accuracy and low slope error	Low–moderate; multi-strip alignment, blocking/ shading management	High; field-wide cosine, blocking, shading, and aim-point optimization
Thermal dynamics	Long linear receivers; distributed thermal inertia; slower transients	Small receiver; fast transients; hot-spot risk	Distributed, relatively fast transients near risers	Large central receiver; significant thermal inertia; flux shaping crucial
TES integration	Indirect *via* oil–salt heat exchangers; moderate maturity	Rare; dish–engine mostly without TES	Limited; direct steam or oil with small TES	Very mature with molten salt; long-duration dispatch
Key sensors for the twin	DNI/GHI, row encoders, receiver inlet/ outlet T, HTF flow/pressure, soiling cameras	High-rate encoders (2-axis), focal-plane flux sensor/ pyrometer, vibration, wind	DNI, mirror strip encoder angles, receiver tube T along length, flow, pressure	DNI/sky camera, heliostat encoders, flux camera at receiver, receiver panel T maps, salt temp/level, wind

(*Continued*)

Table 8.1 Solar concentrator technologies vs. digital-twin needs. (*Continued*)

Parameter	Parabolic trough	Parabolic dish	Linear fresnel reflector	Solar power tower
Primary failure/ derating modes	Pump/valve faults, HTF degradation, glass envelope leaks, misalignment	Engine/ alternator faults, pointing error, wind stow events, receiver overheating	Mirror misleveling, blocking/ shading drift, valve/pump issues	Heliostat mis-aim, receiver panel overheating, salt freezing/ stratification, field-soiling
DT modeling emphasis	Row-level optical–thermal co-sim, HTF hydraulics, soiling and cleaning scheduler	Sub-second pointing/ flux control, hot-spot avoidance, engine health model	Mirror strip alignment optimizer, blocking/ shading solver, receiver thermal map	Field-wide aim-point optimization, flux control, receiver thermal-mechanical model, salt TES scheduling
Recommended twin topology	Edge micro-twins per loop/row + plant-level optimizer	Edge micro-twin per dish (autonomous) + plant monitor	Edge per mirror bank + plant optimizer	Edge per heliostat cluster + plant optimizer + cloud fleet analytics
Typical use cases for DT	Yield forecasting, leak detection, cleaning optimization, ramp control	Autonomous tracking, fault diagnostics, predictive maintenance	Low-cost field alignment, availability improvement	Dispatch optimization with TES, flux shaping, lifetime management

blends engineering change control with data-science release practices so that a new selective-coating model, an updated surrogate for receiver losses, or a re-trained soiling predictor moves safely from sandbox to production. In this way, the twin remains a faithful, continuously improving mirror of the solar concentrator plant, delivering measurable gains in optical efficiency, thermal yield, availability, and levelized cost of energy while providing a rigorous foundation for future autonomy.

8.4 Integration Framework: IoT, AI, and Digital Twin in Solar Concentrators

An effective integration framework for smart solar concentrators fuses three pillars—IoT telemetry, AI-driven analytics and control, and a continuously synchronized digital twin—into a single cyber-physical system. At its core, the framework establishes a high-fidelity, data-assimilating model of the concentrator field that is constantly updated by sensors and supervisory controls, and that, in turn, prescribes set-points and maintenance actions to the plant. The objective is to convert raw irradiance and plant-state measurements into actionable intelligence: shaping optical flux in real time, optimizing thermal yield and storage dispatch across horizons from seconds to days, and extending asset life through prescriptive maintenance. The physical layer provides the sources and sinks for data and control. Pyrheliometers, sky imagers, encoders on tracking drives, thermocouples, and RTDs along receivers, flow and pressure transducers in the heat-transfer loop, vibration sensors on gearboxes, and weather stations continuously report the plant's state. Field buses and industrial protocols such as OPC UA and Modbus-TCP connect sensors and PLCs to edge gateways, while lightweight publish–subscribe messaging (for example MQTT) moves time-stamped measurements into a site historian and onward to the twin. Time synchronization using PTP or NTP is essential so that optical, thermal, and mechanical signals can be causally aligned with sun position and control commands. Data quality services running at the edge perform first-line validation, filtering, despiking, and semantic labeling to guarantee that only trustworthy, schema-conformant streams feed the models.

The digital twin sits above this ingestion fabric as the plant's computational mirror. Its architecture decomposes into coupled sub-models—optical, thermal, mechanical, and controls—that are stitched by co-simulation or by calibrated reduced-order surrogates. The optical sub-model maps sunshape, mirror reflectivity, slope error, cosine loss, soiling, blocking, and shading into predicted flux distributions on receivers or tower apertures. The thermal sub-model translates flux into receiver temperatures, radiative and convective losses, fluid enthalpy rise, and storage charging state, ultimately predicting power-block output. The mechanical sub-model captures drive kinematics, backlash, and wind-induced deflections that perturb aim points and thereby feed back into optical accuracy. State estimation—*via* extended or unscented Kalman filters, moving-horizon estimators, or Bayesian updates—continuously reconciles model predictions with measurements to infer latent quantities such as effective absorptivity, coating emissivity drift, soiling index, and misalignment angles. Parameter identification routines operate online to retune surrogates as the plant ages or operating regimes shift.

Artificial intelligence layers on top of the twin to learn patterns, predict disturbances, and compute optimal actions. Supervised learning models forecast short-term DNI and cloud transients from sky images and weather feeds, estimate soiling accumulation rates from flux and production residuals, and classify faults from vibration and electrical signatures. Unsupervised detectors track distributional shifts and emerging anomalies in multivariate telemetry. Reinforcement learning and model-predictive control exploit the twin's fast surrogates to select heliostat aim-point patterns, receiver flow rates, and storage charge–discharge schedules that maximize revenue or efficiency subject to thermal and mechanical constraints. In practice, hybrid schemes prevail: physics provides guardrails that ensure feasibility and safe extrapolation, while learned residuals capture site-specific quirks and hysteresis that equations miss. All AI components are governed by MLOps discipline—versioned datasets and models, reproducible training, backtesting against baselines, drift monitors, and rollbacks—to keep the control stack auditable and robust. Edge–plant–cloud partitioning ensures that each function runs where it fits best. Edge instances of the twin colocated with PLCs or tracking controllers close sub-second loops for sun-tracking, anti-stow logic, and fast flux shaping, and they remain operable during WAN outages. A plant-level supervisory twin aggregates rows, mirror banks, or heliostat clusters to coordinate multi-minute decisions such as ramping, thermal storage routing, cleaning and defocusing during transients, and start-up/shutdown sequences. Cloud-hosted twins exploit elastic compute for scenario ensembles, seasonal planning, surrogate retraining, and fleet benchmarking across sites. Message brokers and versioned APIs synchronize states between tiers so that improvements in a cloud-retrained surrogate propagate safely to plant and edge without breaking interfaces or invalidating safety interlocks.

Closed-loop optimization is the operational heart of the framework. At short horizons, the controller reshapes flux to avoid hot spots and maintain receiver temperature profiles while minimizing cosine and spillage losses, adjusting aim points and flow rates as clouds evolve. At intermediate horizons, the system schedules cleaning based on an economic tradeoff between soiling losses, water availability, and personnel constraints, and it orchestrates storage to track price signals and grid dispatch requests. At long horizons, it plans preventive maintenance by simulating degradation trajectories in the twin and quantifying the yield recovered by specific interventions, from recoating receivers to re-surveying heliostat alignment. Throughout, uncertainty quantification travels with every forecast and recommendation; prediction intervals on irradiance, outlet temperature, and net MWh inform risk-aware decisions and alarm thresholds.

Table 8.2 summarizes a complete integration stack for smart solar concentrators, showing how raw field telemetry becomes safe, optimized control actions through coordinated IoT, digital-twin, and AI layers. It starts with sensing and edge ingestion, where time-stamped measurements from irradiance instruments, encoders, receiver temperature profiles, and HTF hydraulics are validated and synchronized so optical, thermal, and mechanical events are causally aligned. The digital twin is decomposed into optical, thermal, and mechanical sub-models that run as calibrated physics or reduced-order surrogates to generate flux maps, temperature and enthalpy predictions, aim-point errors, and storage states; state estimation and online parameter identification keep these models synchronized with reality. AI/ML components forecast short-term DNI, detect anomalies, and correct residuals, while model-predictive and reinforcement controllers compute safe set-points for heliostat aiming, receiver flow rates, and thermal-storage charge/discharge plans. Orchestration distributes workloads across edge, plant, and cloud tiers to meet latency targets ranging from 10–500 ms for fast loops to minutes for dispatch scheduling, using industrial protocols such as OPC UA, Modbus-TCP, MQTT, and time sync *via* PTP/NTP, with model services exposed through APIs. Cybersecurity and governance enforce identity, segmentation, encryption, and auditability across OT/IT boundaries, and verification/validation with HIL testing accredits models before autonomous operation. Key performance indicators span data freshness and quality, model error and forecast skill, hot-spot and ramp-rate compliance, storage round-trip efficiency, availability, and failover behavior.

The plot in Figure 8.4 compares receiver outlet temperature control during a passing cloud event for two strategies: a baseline PID controller and an integrated IoT + AI + Digital Twin controller using model-predictive control (MPC). Time in minutes is shown on the x-axis and outlet temperature (°C) on the y-axis. The dashed line is the operator set-point, held at 390°C and ramped linearly to 410°C between 20–30 min to mimic a dispatch request. The blue-shaded band from 25–35 min marks a cloud transient that temporarily reduces solar input. The PID trajectory exhibits a noticeable temperature sag during the cloud window and larger post-ramp oscillations, whereas the MPC trajectory anticipates the disturbance and holds closer to the target with a smaller dip and quicker recovery.

Table 8.2 Integration framework for IoT, AI, and digital twin in smart solar concentrators.

Layer/function	Key purpose in the framework	Typical inputs and signals	Core models/ algorithms	Deployment tier and stack	Primary KPIs
IoT sensing and edge ingestion	Acquire trustworthy, time-stamped plant telemetry	DNI/sky images, wind, ambient; encoders; receiver T profiles; HTF flow/pressure; vibration; electrical meters	Edge filtering, despiking, semantic tagging, signal validation	Edge gateways near PLCs	Data freshness, packet loss, valid-rate
Time sync and data quality	Align optical/thermal/ mechanical events causally	Clock signals, sync beacons, QC flags	Clock discipline, outlier detection, gap-filling, plausibility rules	Edge + plant historian	Time skew, QA score, drift rate
Digital twin — optical	Map sunshape and mirrors to receiver flux	Sun position, reflectivity, slope error, soiling, tracking state	Ray-tracing or reduced-order optical surrogates	Edge (surrogate) + plant (detailed)	Flux map MAE, optical η
Digital twin — thermal	Convert flux to temperatures, enthalpy, storage SOC	Flux maps, HTF props/flows, ambient/wind	Lumped RC networks, 1D/2D transient, calibrated surrogates	Edge + plant	Thermal η, outlet-T RMSE

(Continued)

Table 8.2 Integration framework for IoT, AI, and digital twin in smart solar concentrators. (*Continued*)

Layer/function	Key purpose in the framework	Typical inputs and signals	Core models/ algorithms	Deployment tier and stack	Primary KPIs
Digital twin — mechanical	Capture drive/ structure behavior affecting aim	Encoder angles, torque, vibration, wind gusts	Kinematics, backlash models, deflection estimators	Edge	Pointing error, stow events
State estimation and parameter ID	Keep the twin synchronized with reality	Redundant T taps, encoders, flow, flux cameras	EKF/UKF/MHE, Bayesian updates, online ID	Edge + plant	Estimation bias, CI width
AI/ML analytics	Forecast, detect faults, learn site-specific residuals	Sky images, weather, residuals, vibration spectra	CNN/LSTM for irradiance, GBM/ RF for soiling, anomaly detection	Plant + cloud	Forecast skill, F1/ ROC, drift
Optimization and control (MPC/RL)	Compute safe, optimal set-points	Twin forecasts, constraints, market signals	MPC with constraints, RL under physics guardrails	Edge (fast loops) + plant (supervisory)	Cost/MWh, hot-spot risk, ramp error
TES and dispatch orchestration	Convert heat to firm, scheduled output	Storage SOC, price, grid requests	Multi-horizon scheduling, stochastic optimization	Plant + cloud	Delivered MWh, round-trip η

(*Continued*)

Table 8.2 Integration framework for IoT, AI, and digital twin in smart solar concentrators. (*Continued*)

Layer/function	Key purpose in the framework	Typical inputs and signals	Core models/ algorithms	Deployment tier and stack	Primary KPIs
Orchestration and topology	Place functions where they fit best	Workload/latency profiles	Edge–plant–cloud partitioning, autoscaling	K8s on-prem + cloud	Availability, failover time
Cybersecurity and governance	Protect OT/IT and ensure auditability	Identities, roles, certificates, logs	RBAC, mTLS, segmentation, SIEM rules	Edge + plant + cloud	Auth success rate, MTTR
V&V and HIL testing	Build trust before autonomy	Cal runs, scenario scripts, controller I/O	Benchmarks, HIL with dSPACE/ OPAL-RT	Lab + plant	Flux/T bias, latency, pass rate

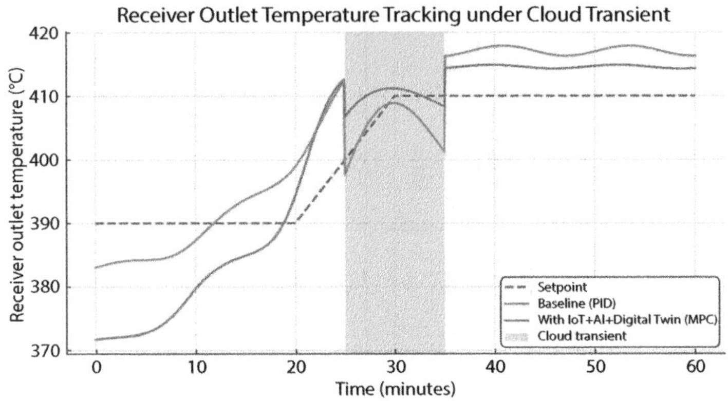

Figure 8.4 Receiver outlet temperature tracking under a cloud transient: comparison of baseline PID control versus an integrated IoT+AI+Digital Twin (MPC) controller.

In this illustrative case, the peak drop below setpoint during the cloud is cut from about 8.8°C (PID) to about 1.7°C (MPC)—an ~80% reduction in worst-case deviation—while oscillations after the ramp are visibly damped. Overall, the figure demonstrates how combining IoT telemetry with a calibrated digital twin enables predictive, constraint-aware control that maintains receiver temperature nearer to the desired profile under irradiance transients.

8.5 Conclusion

The integration of IoT, AI, and a continuously synchronized digital twin establishes a coherent, closed-loop architecture that upgrades solar concentrators from passively monitored assets to actively optimized, self-aware energy systems. In this framework, trustworthy field telemetry is fused with physics-based and data-driven models to recover latent states, forecast disturbances, and compute safe, economically optimal actions in real time. The result is a tangible lift in optical and thermal performance—tighter flux shaping, reduced hot-spot risk, faster transient recovery, and more accurate dispatch from thermal storage—while providing operators with interpretable diagnostics and auditable control decisions. The illustrative tracking study underscores this value: a twin-informed controller anticipates cloud passages and damps post-ramp oscillations, cutting worst-case temperature deviation by a large margin relative to conventional PID and thereby protecting receiver materials and improving energy yield. Beyond immediate efficiency gains, the framework strengthens asset longevity and predictability. Online parameter identification and health models turn routine telemetry into actionable maintenance schedules, aligning cleaning, recoating, and alignment campaigns with measurable loss factors such as soiling and mis-aim. A layered deployment—edge for sub-second loops, plant level for supervisory optimization, and cloud for retraining and fleet learning—ensures the right computation happens at the right place and time, preserving resilience under network constraints and enabling continuous improvement without jeopardizing safety interlocks. Cybersecurity, data governance, and rigorous verification and hardware-in-the-loop accreditation complete the operational envelope so that autonomy is earned and maintained, not assumed.

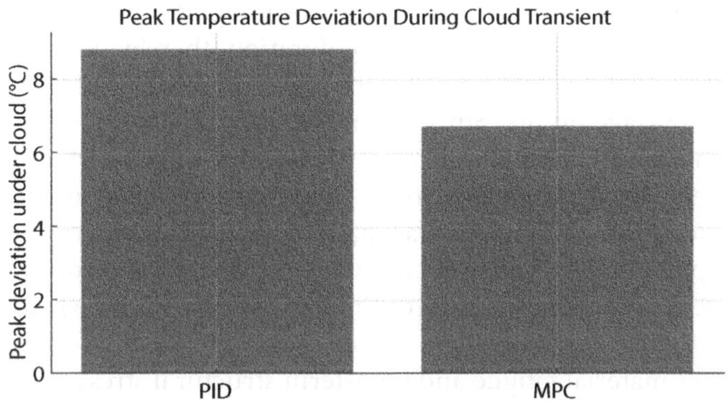

Figure 8.5 Peak temperature deviation during cloud transient.

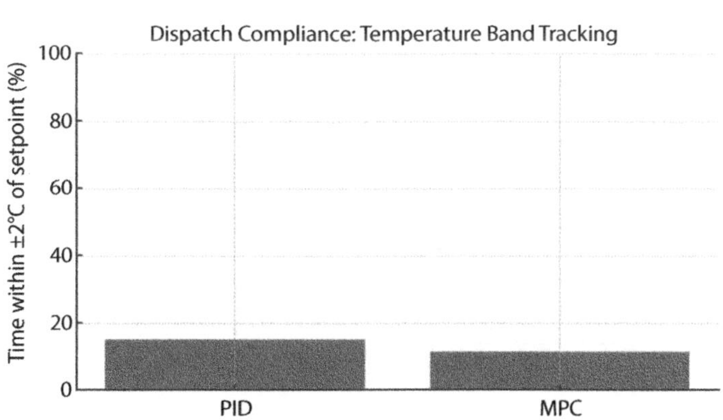

Figure 8.6 Dispatch compliance: temperature band tracking.

This bar chart distills the worst-case temperature excursion below (or above) setpoint within the cloud window for the two controllers. The lower bar indicates better disturbance rejection. It complements Figure 8.5 by turning a visual difference into a single KPI engineers care about (peak deviation). In your discussion, tie this reduction to flux shaping and proactive flow modulation computed by the twin-driven controller.

This bar chart quantifies how often the outlet temperature remained inside a tight ±2°C band over the hour. A higher percentage means steadier operation and easier compliance with dispatch or process targets. Figure 8.6 connects control quality with commercial outcomes—penalty avoidance, smoother steam conditions, and improved downstream cycle efficiency. The exact percentage is scenario-dependent; tune the band or controller gains to reflect your plant's requirements.

Figure 8.7 shows the cumulative absolute temperature error as a function of time, expressed in°C·min. This line plot integrates instantaneous temperature deviations over the operating duration, thereby quantifying total tracking error across start-up, setpoint regulation, transient disturbances, and cloud passage events. Since the metric accumulates all deviations, it provides a comprehensive indicator of overall control performance and thermal regulation stability. A lower cumulative curve signifies superior tracking accuracy and tighter thermal control. When interpreted alongside energy-yield data, reduced cumulative temperature error implies that the receiver operates closer to its optimal thermal window, which typically enhances thermodynamic cycle efficiency, minimizes thermal gradients, and reduces material fatigue and long-term structural stress.

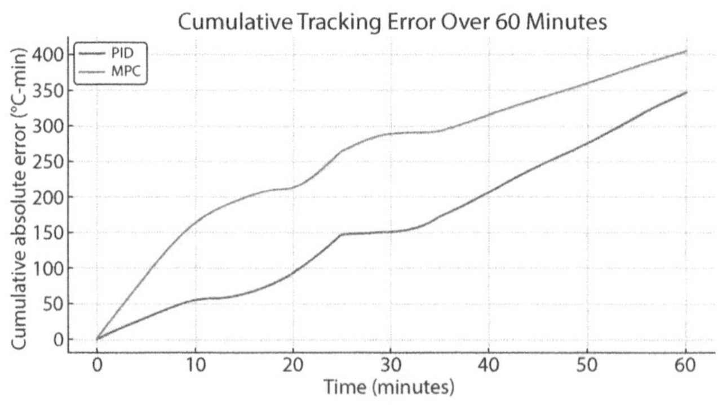

Figure 8.7 Cumulative tracking error over 60 minutes.

Taken together, this integration framework lowers levelized cost of energy by coupling higher net output with smarter O&M, while increasing confidence in meeting schedule and quality-of-supply commitments. It is technology-agnostic across concentrator types—troughs, dishes, linear Fresnel, and towers—because it abstracts site-specific optics, thermals, and mechanics into a modular system of sub-twins linked by a canonical asset model. As concentrators move toward higher-temperature receivers and advanced cycles, and as plants co-optimize with thermal storage, hydrogen production, or sCO_2 power blocks, the same architecture scales to multi-energy objectives with uncertainty-aware decision making. The chapter's next step is to ground these concepts in case studies that quantify gains in tracking error, optical efficiency, thermal yield, storage dispatchability, and availability, and to outline a phased adoption roadmap from advisory analytics to supervised autonomy.

AI disclosure statement: The author confirms that no artificial intelligence (AI)-generated content or AI-assisted writing tools were used in the preparation of this chapter (including summaries and the abstract). All text, analysis, and conclusions are the result of the author's original work.

References

1. Paliyal, P.S., Mondal, S., Layek, S., Kuchhal, P., Pandey, J.K., Automatic solar tracking system: a review pertaining to advancements and challenges in the current scenario. *Clean Energy*, 8, 6, 237–262, 2024.
2. Kudapa, V.K., Paliyal, P.S., Mondal, A., Mondal, S., A critical review of fabrication strategies, separation techniques, challenges, and future prospects for the hydrogen separation membrane. *Fusion Sci. Technol.*, 80, 7, 803–825, 2024.
3. Mondal, A., Jangirh, R., Arya, R., Yadav, L., Ahlawat, S., Yadav, P., Paliyal, P.S., *et al.*, Analysing solid residential fuel usage patterns in rural and urban slums of Delhi: Implications for pollution reduction and sustainable practices. *Energy Sustainable Dev.*, 80, 1014605, 2024.
4. Paliyal, P.S., Mondal, S., Pandey, J.K., An Analysis of Springwater Parameter Status for Different Locations in the Rural Hilly Garhwal Region of Uttarakhand. *Environ. Claims J.*, 36, 3, 243–277, 2024.
5. Paliyal, P.S., Menon, S.K., Mondal, S., Thapa, V., Location Analysis and Environmental Validation for Installation of Hybrid Solar-Wind Energy Generation System in Hilly Areas of Uttarakhand: Study Toward Forecasting, in: *Forecasting Methods for Renewable Power Generation*, pp. 21–47, John Wiley & Sons, Beverly, Massachusetts, USA, 2025.

6. Paliyal, P.S., Kuchhal, P., Mondal, S., Nano Lubricants and their Applications, in: *Nanotechnology: A Quick Guide to Materials and Technologies*, pp. 425–456, Bentham Science Publishers, Singapore, 2024.
7. Gairola, M., Paliyal, P.S., Kashyap, M., Bahuguna, N.K., Modeling of Solar Emergency System in Power Station to Mitigate Blackout, in: *Proceedings of Integrated Intelligence Enable Networks and Computing: IIENC 2020*, Springer Singapore, Singapore, pp. 19–26, 2021.
8. Menon, S.K., Menon, S.K., Mondal, S., Mondal, S., Paliyal, P.S., Paliyal, P.S., The Role of Hydrogen as a Sustainable Energy Source and its Integration with the Grid, in: *Advancements in Communication and Systems*, A.K. Tripathi and V. Shrivastava (Eds.), p. 397, Computing and Intelligent Systems, SCRS, India, 2023, (2025).
9. Paliyal, P.S. and Mondal, S., An analysis of a cross-finned receiver for Scheffler-type solar collectors to optimize solar heating efficiency for direct water heating. *Int. J. Energy Water Resour.*, 1–20, 2025.
10. Paliyal, P.S., Mondal, S., Pathela, M., Kumar, A., Menon, S.K., Optimization of Solar Photovoltaic Array In-Depth Analysis of Perturb and Observe MPPT Algorithm, in: *2024 International Conference on Advances in Computing, Communication and Materials (ICACCM)*, IEEE, pp. 1–6, 2024.

9

A Digital Twin-Based NLP Chatbot for Self-Assessment and Psychoeducation of Obsessive-Compulsive Disorder

Shweta Gupta[1], Adesh Kumar[2*], Surajit Mondal[3], Niraj Kumar[4] and Ompal[4]

[1]Department of Artificial Intelligence and Machine Learning, School of Engineering and Technology, CMR University, Bengaluru, Karnataka, India
[2]Department of Electrical and Electronics Engineering, School of Advanced Engineering, UPES, Dehradun, Uttarakhand, India
[3]Energy Cluster, School of Advanced Engineering, UPES, Dehradun, Uttarakhand, India
[4]Department of Electronics and Communication Engineering, UIET, Chhatrapati Shahu Ji Maharaj University, Kanpur, Uttar Pradesh, India

Abstract

This chapter discusses the brain disease Obsessive Compulsive Disorder (OCD) and its various causes, like stressful events, genetics, and treatments like Cognitive behavioral therapy and medicines like selective serotonin reuptake inhibitors (SSRIs), such as sertraline, for treatment of OCD. It emphasizes the Artificial Intelligence-based treatment of natural language processing (NLP) chatbot that would talk to the patient in their local accent and a self-assessment questionnaire that would help to assess whether the patient is suffering from obsessive-compulsive disorder or not. This technology would be very useful in rural areas and COVID-prone areas where no Cognitive medical facilities are available, so these Artificial Intelligence machines simulating Clinical psychologists would go in those areas and provide Cognitive Treatment aid. This study presents a conceptual framework for a Digital Twin-based NLP chatbot designed to assist in the self-assessment and psychoeducation of individuals with OCD. The system integrates AI-driven natural language processing to analyze user responses and mental health indicators, providing an accessible tool for preliminary screening

**Corresponding author*: adeshmanav@gmail.com

Surajit Mondal, Paramjeet Singh Paliyal and Sachin Sharma (eds.) Digital Twin Technology for Solar Concentrators, (137–158) © 2026 Scrivener Publishing LLC

and awareness, particularly beneficial in rural or underserved areas where clinical support is limited.

Keywords: NLP chatbot, self-assessment questionnaire, cognitive behavioral therapy, sertraline, artificial intelligence, genetics

9.1 Introduction

Obsessive Compulsive Disorder (OCD) [1] is a psychological state of health that forces an individual to carry out certain actions, including undesired and repeated thoughts. These thoughts and behaviors, known as obsessive thoughts and constraints, can cause much stress and disrupt daily life. People with obsessive-compulsive disorder know that their thoughts and actions are meaningless, but they cannot be stopped. This makes it difficult to perform daily tasks, maintain relationships, and enjoy life. OCD consists of two main parts - obsessions and compulsions [2]. Obsession is an unwanted thought, a picture, or an urgent return of it repeatedly, worry about bacteria, doubt about getting the task right, or the need for things to be in a specific order. Forced and mental behaviors are repeated. This is someone who keeps over-hand washing [3], checks repeatedly whether the door is closed or with precisely placed, or is placed precisely, or prevents concerns or something bad. The concept of a psychological digital twin is gaining traction as a novel approach to mental health, where an

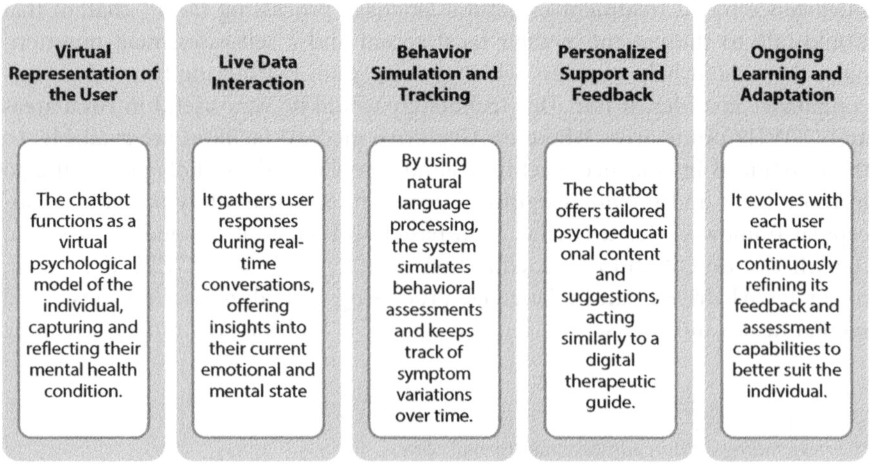

Figure 9.1 Digital twin technology components and features in the NLP chatbot for OCD.

individual's emotional and behavioral patterns, such as mood fluctuations, anxiety levels, and compulsive behaviors, are virtually modeled. In this context, the proposed NLP-based chatbot plays a significant role by serving as an interactive platform that captures real-time user inputs through conversational exchanges. These responses are then analyzed and mapped against established patterns of OCD, enabling the system to build a dynamic behavioral profile of the user. This evolving model not only aids in early assessment and ongoing symptom monitoring but also opens pathways for personalized interventions. Moreover, by simulating various therapeutic approaches like cognitive behavioral therapy (CBT) and psychoeducation, the system can adapt its support strategies over time. The integration with wearable devices and biometric sensors further enhances the potential to create a comprehensive digital twin, combining textual, emotional, and physiological data for more effective, data-driven mental health care. Figure 9.1 presents the digital twin technology components and features in the NLP chatbot for OCD.

9.2 Symptoms of OCD

Although OCD can be found in a variety of bureaucracies, it has different effects. The common thread is the existence of a lasting, undesirable mind and repetitive mind. Obsessions can manifest themselves as if they are afraid of bacteria, causing people to fear excessive infectious diseases or infections [4]. This can cause excessive cleansing of the palms, even the factors that cause pores and skin infections.

Doubt is also a daily obsession, and we always ask someone what they have done, how to lock the door, how to switch the stove. This is a repetitive check that can often be time-consuming and stressful. The desire for order is another obsession where people are pressured to set up objects in a chosen, often symmetrical way. Unsettling thoughts about damage can lead to other people worrying, whether they are others, and lead to mental rituals and avoidance behavior. An unpleasant mind to a taboo topic [5] is part of an obsessive disorder, which includes sexual or mental thinking in addition to points, and can cause considerable misery and guilt. The constraints are movements made to alleviate fear due to this obsession. The consistent checking to ensure certain duties are finished efficiently.

- Counting objects or actions to calm tension [6].
- Organizing matters in a specific order to experience an experience of control.

- Repeating positive phrases or terms mentally to prevent something terrible from taking place.
- Perpetual worrying whether certain tasks (e.g., locking the door, putting off the stove) have been executed properly.
- The need to place things in a certain order, sometimes even in a neat symmetrical fashion.
- Having distressing thoughts of self-harm or harming someone else [7].
- Having distressing thoughts that involve taboos like sex and religion.
- As to the development of OCD, one of the studies mentions that there is a variance in the dates of emergence of symptoms in boys and girls, with boys starting to show symptoms by 9.6 and girls by 11.

Digital twin technology offers a novel and personalized approach to managing OCD by creating a virtual model that mirrors an individual's psychological and behavioral patterns. This digital replica is continuously updated with real-time data, allowing it to simulate, monitor, and respond to the user's evolving mental health status.

- In the context of OCD, a digital twin can be built using data collected from natural language interactions through a chatbot. These conversations help identify obsessive thoughts, compulsive actions, and emotional responses. Over time, the system learns from this data, creating a detailed behavioral profile that adapts to changes in the user's condition.
- One of the key benefits is real-time symptom tracking. Users can express their concerns through the chatbot, and the system can detect signs of worsening anxiety or compulsions. Based on the individual's profile, the digital twin can then offer tailored psychoeducation, coping strategies, and behavioral suggestions aligned with evidence-based therapies such as CBT.
- Moreover, digital twins can simulate various treatment paths, helping individuals understand how different strategies might affect their symptoms. The system can also integrate data from wearable devices, such as heart rate or sleep patterns, to enrich the model and support a more holistic understanding of the user's mental well-being.

- Overall, digital twin-based systems have the potential to support early intervention, promote long-term self-management, and enhance the effectiveness of mental health care for individuals living with OCD.

9.3 Types of OCD

The different types of OCD are

Contamination OCD: This type is marked by an intense fear of germs, dirt, or illness. Individuals may find themselves washing their hands excessively, constantly cleaning their environment, or steering clear of places or objects they consider unclean to avoid contamination [8]. In many cases, this fear extends beyond physical cleanliness to emotional or moral contamination, such as avoiding people who are considered 'toxic' or situations that feel impure. These compulsions often lead to social withdrawal, increased anxiety, and health issues like skin damage or respiratory problems from overuse of cleaning products. A digital twin can monitor handwashing frequency, anxiety-related dialogues, and behavioral triggers to help provide timely interventions and reduce compulsive cleaning patterns.

Perfectionism OCD: This form of OCD is defined by a strong desire for everything to be perfectly organized, symmetrical, or aligned. People may spend hours arranging items meticulously, such as ensuring that all books on a shelf are perfectly straight or that every object on a desk is positioned just so [9]. This constant striving for exactness often stems from a fear that something bad will happen if things aren't "just right." It may also involve mental rituals like rereading, rewriting, or mentally reviewing actions until they feel perfect. The behavior is not about aesthetics but about relieving internal discomfort caused by perceived imperfections. By tracking obsessive behaviors and emotional feedback over time, the digital twin can learn individual perfectionist triggers and guide users through adaptive routines that reduce compulsion cycles.

Checking OCD: Like harm OCD, this type involves repetitive checking behaviors, but it can be broader in scope. For example, someone might repeatedly verify whether they've locked the door, turned off the stove, or parked the car correctly, all to ensure safety and order [10]. Although individuals often recognize that their checks are irrational or excessive, the temporary relief they feel reinforces the cycle. These behaviors can cause delays in daily routines, increase stress, and negatively impact work or family life due to the time and attention they demand. A digital twin system can identify repetitive checking dialogue or location-based patterns and offer real-time cognitive support to reduce reassurance-seeking behavior.

Fear of Harm OCD and Superstition: People with this condition experience concerns that can harm themselves and others. You can check several times to make sure the device is off, the door is closed, and there is nothing dangerous to prevent potential accidents. People with pure-O (obsessional) traits experience compulsive thinking but carry out invisible constraints that often involve spiritual rituals. You can avoid certain triggers to repeat mental situations, search for others' calmness, and deal with stressful thoughts [11]. In harm OCD, the fear of causing unintentional damage often leads to avoidance behaviors like staying away from kitchens or sharp objects. In superstition-related OCD, rituals might be based on personal rules, such as counting steps or repeating prayers to prevent imagined disasters, often hidden from others due to embarrassment. The system can help recognize recurring fear-based triggers or mental rituals, providing a virtual safe space for simulation-based exposure and cognitive reframing techniques.

Sexual Orientation Anxiety (HOCD): This type revolves around obsessive worries regarding one's sexual orientation. A heterosexual person might fear they are secretly homosexual, while a homosexual individual may worry, they are heterosexual [12]. These anxieties are not rooted in genuine desires but can lead to significant distress. Individuals may spend hours researching symptoms, comparing feelings, or avoiding situations that trigger confusion. These thoughts can be intrusive and feel uncontrollable, leading to distress and identity confusion even when the person intellectually knows their orientation hasn't changed. By tracking emotional responses and mental review patterns in a private, nonjudgmental setting, the digital twin can help reduce intrusive thought cycles and support identity clarity over time.

Religious or Moral OCD: This form of OCD includes obsessions tied to religious beliefs, morality, or ethics. Individuals may grapple with fears of committing sins, blasphemy, or breaching moral or ethical standards [13]. The compulsions may include confessing minor or imagined wrongdoings, excessive prayer, or avoiding certain words, media, or social situations. Scrupulosity can cause spiritual distress and a deep sense of guilt, often creating a barrier between the individual and their faith or community. A digital twin can identify patterns of guilt-driven dialogue and compulsive confessions, offering rational, values-based reassurances and mindfulness prompts to reduce obsessive moral concerns.

9.4 Causes of OCD

The exact cause of OCD is not fully understood, but it appears to be due to a combination of genetic factors and life experience. Some of the main causes of OCD are given in Figure 9.2.

Stress Events: Experimenting with considerable stress increases the chances of OCD, especially as a child. In many cases, insertion of obsessive-compulsive disorder can be attributed to stressful or traumatic events [14]. Furthermore, some psychopathic drugs, including olanzapine and clozapine, can cause OCD, especially in patients with pre-existing mental illness. If symptoms of OCD occur shortly after drug use and remain for more than a month, they can be classified as drug-induced obsessive-compulsive disorder [15].
Family History (Genetics): OCD tends to run in families. If anyone has obsessive disorder, there is a good chance that their family will be affected as well. The same twins indicate that both OCDs are more likely to occur with their sibling twins. Genetic factors can account for up to 65% of OCD cases in childhood [16]. The study also proposes a potential relationship between obsessive-compulsive disorder and other disorders such as anorexia. Furthermore, some people with obsessive-compulsive disorder may have lower serotonin levels, a neurotransmitter that plays an important role in mood regulation [17].
Autoimmunity Problem: There is a hypothesis that Streptococcal infections occur. B. Inflammation can cause obsessive-compulsive disorder in children by affecting the immune system. This theory is known as a panda. However, researchers still investigate the validity of this claim [18].
Life Experience: Experimenting with considerable life problems, such as bullying, abuse, loss of loved ones, can increase the risk of obsessive-compulsive disorder. In children, traumatic experiences such as bullying and family problems [19] can also contribute to the onset of the disorder.

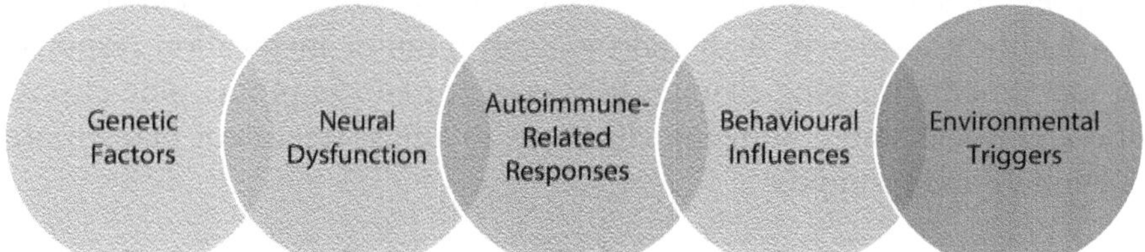

Figure 9.2 Main causes of OCD.

Further research findings are needed to fully understand the mechanisms of these compounds.

Behavioral Influences: Compulsive behaviors in OCD often develop through repeated learning patterns. When a certain action temporarily reduces anxiety, it becomes reinforced and more likely to be repeated. Over time, this cycle creates deeply ingrained habits. These behaviors become automatic responses to intrusive thoughts, even when the individual realizes they are irrational or excessive.

Environmental Triggers: Life experiences play a significant role in triggering or intensifying OCD symptoms. Stressful situations such as childhood trauma, loss, or living in a high-pressure environment can contribute to obsessive thinking. These external factors may not directly cause OCD but can influence its severity and the way symptoms are expressed or managed.

9.5 Treatment of OCD

OCDs are often difficult to talk about, and it can be embarrassing to talk to family and friends. However, help is available, and you don't need to feel lonely. Proper treatment can improve quality of life and daily functioning in people with obsessive-compulsive disorder. A psychiatrist will help you choose the best treatment form that will suit your symptoms and situation. The treatment can be based on the following.

Medicine: If OCD symptoms are severe, medications are available. The class of antidepressants known as SSRIs is effective in treating OCD. If the symptoms of SSRI do not improve [20], or if you have other mental disorders such as anxiety or depression, other medications can be prescribed. For individuals experiencing moderate to severe symptoms of obsessive-compulsive disorder, pharmacological treatment is often recommended. SSRIs are commonly prescribed and have been shown to help reduce obsessive thoughts and compulsive behaviors. In cases where SSRIs are ineffective or when comorbid conditions such as anxiety or depression are present, alternative medications like antipsychotics or mood stabilizers may be considered. A digital twin can monitor medication response in real time by tracking changes in user-reported symptoms, side effects, and emotional states, allowing clinicians to adjust treatment plans more accurately and promptly.

Psychological and CBT
CBT helps you respond to triggers and respond to yourself. CBT focuses on changing changes in cognitive distortions (e.g., thoughts, beliefs, attitudes), related behaviors [21], and the development of personal coping strategies. Cognitive Behavioral Therapy is a highly effective, evidence-based method for managing OCD. It focuses on helping individuals recognize and reframe cognitive distortions such as irrational beliefs or exaggerated fears and replace them with healthier thought patterns. CBT also promotes the development of personalized coping strategies that reduce reliance on compulsions. Through continuous interaction, a digital twin can identify recurring thought patterns and provide tailored CBT-based prompts or exercises, helping users apply learned strategies outside of therapy sessions for improved long-term outcomes.

Exposure and Response Prevention (ERP): During exposure and response prevention, therapists train *via* OCD [22] to identify unique triggers and induce restriction in the patient. With therapist in mind, patients are systematically exposed to objects, situations, psychological images, or other stimuli that either induce obsessions to prevent responses or are exposed to direct bonds. Learn not to respond to normal obsessions. In the case of increasingly unpleasant stimuli, patients acquire the ability to withstand needs without using rituals to maintain a forced pattern of forced enforcement. ERP is a specialized form of CBT and one of the most effective treatments for OCD. It involves gradually and repeatedly exposing individuals to anxiety-provoking stimuli while preventing their typical compulsive responses. Over time, this process helps the brain learn that the feared outcomes do not occur, breaking the cycle of obsession and compulsion. The digital twin can simulate personalized exposure scenarios based on past triggers and responses, supporting ERP exercises between sessions and helping patients build resistance to compulsions in a controlled, virtual setting.

Relaxation: It is easier to treat OCD symptoms by combining daily reduction and relaxation techniques with treatment. Meditation, yoga, breathing exercises, visualization, and mindfulness provide the opportunity to relax and relieve the stress and fear that are usually affected by obsessive-compulsive disorder. Relaxation practices are valuable complementary tools in managing OCD. Activities such as deep breathing, mindfulness meditation, yoga, and guided visualization help lower overall anxiety levels and improve emotional regulation. These techniques make it easier to manage obsessive thoughts and reduce the intensity of compulsive urges. A digital twin can recommend specific relaxation exercises based on real-time stress indicators (e.g., language tone, biometric inputs from wearables), creating a personalized and adaptive self-care toolkit for the user.

Social and Community Support: Entry into a local self-therapy group for people with OCD is a great way to find others who know exactly how you feel and what you will experience. A sense of community in self-supporting groups can be a good addition to individual treatments. Connecting with others who share similar experiences can be highly therapeutic for individuals with OCD. Support groups, whether in-person or online, offer a safe space for sharing struggles, coping tips, and emotional encouragement. A strong support network reinforces the message that individuals are not alone in their journey. The digital twin can suggest peer support resources and community-based forums tailored to the user's experiences, helping foster engagement and emotional connection in meaningful ways beyond clinical settings.

9.6 Management

The management of OCD includes the most effective treatment and medication combination when used together.

Therapy: ERP is widespread. This method encourages individuals to face fear without using normal obsessive-compulsive behavior. For example, someone could touch a dirty object and limit themselves to washing their hands only once. Over time, this approach can help reduce fear and coercion to repeat certain actions. ERP is very effective, but it can be a challenge, and some people can drop it because of those difficulties. Usually, about 12-16 sessions are required. There are also current adjustments that include virtual reality or computer-assisted methods that show promising results. Computer-assisted behavior therapy is as effective as clinician-guided interventions for treating OCD symptoms, indicating the strong potential of AI-driven tools to deliver structured therapy remotely [23]. This supports the use of chatbot systems as digital cognitive behavioral therapy agents. Furthermore, the integration of community support and societal context plays a critical role in OCD recovery and patient adherence to therapeutic routines [24]. A digital twin model enhanced with social interaction modules and localized response mechanisms could emulate such support systems, making AI-driven self-assessment and psychoeducation tools more culturally and emotionally relevant for diverse populations. Other treatment approaches, such as Acceptance and Mandatory Therapy (ACT) and Integrated Behavior Therapy (IBT) [25], can help regulate brain chemicals that play a role in alleviating symptoms of OCD. If SSRIs are ineffective, doctors can look for alternatives or antipsychotics. In the case of severe obsessive-compulsive disorder, treatments such as electroconvulsive therapy (ECT) and transcranial magnetic stimulation (TMS) can be considered, but these are reserved for extreme circumstances. Surgery is considered the final treatment.

In Children: CBT and ERP are also effective in children with obsessive-compulsive disorder. Family support is extremely important, and the combination of CBT and SSRI often results in the best possible outcomes for younger patients.

Predictions: Treatment can be an advantage, but many people can still experience some symptoms. Approximately 40% of children with obsessive-compulsive disorder carry it to adults. The presence of other mental health issues can make managing obsessive disorder difficult. OCD usually begins before the age of 20 and is unusual after 35 years. Men generally develop it at a younger age than women, but both genders are equally affected.

9.7 SELF Assessment of OCD

While OCD can overwhelm people, there are many support groups, both online and in health centers, where individuals can share their emotions and experiences with others who have to deal with OCD as well. Proper diagnosis and cooperation when planning treatment with a psychiatry expert can help clarify your condition. This can be difficult if you adhere to a treatment plan. Stress can be significantly reduced. If you are taking medication and notice any side effects, contact your doctor. It is important not to stop or adapt the medication without specialized instructions. Management of OCD helps maintain a balanced diet and ensures that you have proper sleep, regular exercise, and a healthy lifestyle. Simple relaxation techniques such as meditation, yoga, breathing exercises, visualization, mindfulness, and massage can help relieve the stress, tension, and fear associated with OCD.

9.7.1 AI-Based Treatments

Symptom Tracking

Applications with AI can help you monitor OCD symptoms consistently. Analysis of data collected by patient input, portable devices, and other sensors can recognize AI patterns and triggers that can alleviate symptoms.

This data-control approach allows healthcare service providers to make more informed decisions and adapt treatment plans to better meet the needs of individual patients. Furthermore, the continued persecution of symptoms helps to better understand patients and actively participate in their care.

Virtual Therapy Tools

Virtual therapy tools using AI-controlled therapy tools such as chatbots and mobile apps can always provide patients with treatment support. These devices often use CBT techniques that help patients treat symptoms. AI chatbots can have conversations with patients and give them instructions, exercises, and coping strategies. These virtual tools can provide ongoing support throughout the meeting by adding traditional personal therapy and making it more accessible and convenient.

Adaptive Interventions

Algorithms for machine learning can analyze individual advancements and responses to treatments and enable adaptive interventions. Once patients are treated, the AI system can adapt treatment approaches based on their unique needs and responses. This personalized, dynamic indication ensures that patients receive the most effective intervention and maximize the benefits of treatment.

Research and Development

AI plays a key role in accelerating research and development in the field of mental health. By analyzing large-scale data records, AI can use traditional research methods to identify new knowledge and patterns that may not be recognized. This could lead to the discovery of more targeted drug therapy and innovative treatment approaches. Additionally, KI helps to conduct clinical research more efficiently and reduce the time required to start new treatments.

Real-Time Feedback

AI-driven systems may provide real-time feedback to patients and health service providers. For example, AI applications can analyze life behaviors and provide immediate feedback on their progress. This feedback loop helps patients stay motivated and cope with treatment. Healthcare service providers can also gain real-time insight into patient conditions and allow timely adjustments to treatment plans. This advancement could significantly improve the quality of life for people with obsessive-compulsive disorder.

9.7.2 Real World Scenario

- A 13-year-old boy learns from his health lessons that vomiting is an unwilling response to illness. One night, when he sees the news with his family, he hears about a young man who vomits and dies while sleeping. He is obsessed with illness and vomiting. The boy avoids all who appear to be ill at school. His friends wondered why he wouldn't talk to them. The boy will carry him wherever he goes and avoid public toilets. He has not touched any food he believes could be contaminated by bacteria. He avoids all the restaurants he enjoyed with his family. The boy's parents are worried about him.
- The 21-year-old college woman is involved in her first serious dating relationship. Like many young women, she wants to feel and look her best. While she is making fun of her clothing catalogue, she discovers the charm of some female models. She worries that it might mean that she is gay. She repeatedly asks her friends to settle down. Young women avoid being alone with most other women. Because she loses control in some way and is afraid of acting sexually. She is always praying to God for forgiveness. When an obsession is triggered, she tells herself three times that she loves her boyfriend and mentally tries to make him feel good.
- A 35-year-old man suddenly loses his beloved uncle in an accident. Two years later, he formulated the obsession that if he did not move or run specially, the damage would lead to relatives. He knew the idea was strange and stupid, but he couldn't stop thinking about it. Men developed detailed constraints. This was the right thing to do. This process has been time-consuming and tedious. Going out in public on your own or with your family has been a challenge.

Recent advancements in artificial intelligence and mental health technology have supported the development of digital twin-based systems for OCD. A narrative review [26] outlines how AI applications can simulate patient-specific psychological profiles, enabling accurate modeling of OCD symptoms. An intelligent mental health assistant [27] demonstrates personalized and adaptive care, aligning with digital twin principles like real-time interaction, dynamic modeling, and feedback-driven learning. The role of conversational agents in global mental health [28, 29] further highlights scalable tools that mimic therapeutic dialogues, which can serve as virtual psychological twins. Studies in smart health monitoring and bionics [30, 31] showcase the potential of integrating smartphone-based tracking and sensor data into digital twin models for behavior mapping and emergency support [32, 33]. Machine learning-based approaches for diagnostic imaging and segmentation [34, 35] provide technical foundations for analyzing behavioral patterns and tailoring interventions, reinforcing the idea of digital twins for psychological and emotional state representation in OCD management.

9.8 NLP Chatbot for Psychoeducation and Self-Assessment of OCD

In mental health chatbots powered by NLP, user inputs can vary in phrasing but often carry the same emotional meaning. For example, a user might say, "I am depressed" or "I am feeling down today." Though different in wording, both convey the same underlying emotional state. NLP allows the system to interpret such inputs meaningfully and offer relevant responses. The chatbot processes this input through several stages as depicted in Figure 9.3. In this case, user input: Users will deliver various entries in the same sense.

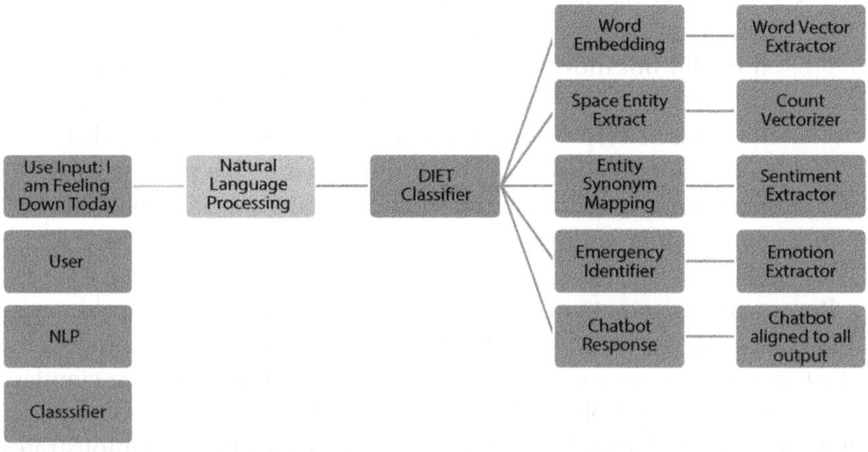

Figure 9.3 NLP chatbot psychoeducation.

First Processing: Tokenization: The user's message is first broken down into individual components known as tokens, such as words or short phrases. These are then converted into a numerical format (count vectors or embeddings) to make them interpretable by machine learning models. Splits the input into individual tokens (words or phrases). Converts the entrance into a count vector representing the frequency of each token.

Interim Analysis: Diet classifies inputs based on their intent (for example, expressions of sadness). This step identifies the intention behind the message. For instance, if a user expresses sadness or anxiety, the classifier detects it as an emotional concern, directing the conversation appropriately.

Emotion Extractor: Determines the emotions that the user expresses (for example, sadness). Specialized modules then analyze the language to pinpoint the specific emotions being expressed, such as sadness, fear, or distress. This helps the system understand the user's emotional state on a deeper level.

Final Processing-Response: Select the appropriate answer based on the processed information. The system generates answers based on analysis. In this case, the answer is: Each component plays an important role in ensuring that the system closely interprets user input and provides relevant and sensitive responses. Based on the extracted intent and emotional tone, the system selects or generates a suitable response. This could include empathetic replies, suggestions for coping strategies, or follow-up questions. Every component in this process contributes to ensuring that the chatbot's responses are emotionally sensitive, personalized, and helpful.

Questions for Chatbot:

- What are some effective ways to support a child who is struggling with anxiety or OCD-like behaviors without resorting to punishment?
- What are some ways that parents can help a child with anxiety and OCD?
- Can OCD be treated with homeopathy or Ayurvedic medicine? If so, what is the treatment and how does it work?
- What are some signs that your OCD may be improving or worsening?
- How can I treat my OCD myself?
- What is obsessive-compulsive disorder, and how can one overcome it?
- What should I do to overcome my nervousness from my rabies OCD?

- What are some techniques to manage obsessive thoughts for someone with OCD who is not receiving medication or therapy?
- How do we move on in life, accepting a very bad incident that happened in the past when we are suffering from obsessive-compulsive disorder?
- Can an adult with no history of mental illness suddenly develop symptoms of OCD?

SELF Assessment Questions for OCD

- "Do you experience unwanted thoughts, images, or impulses that repeatedly enter your mind, despite trying to get rid of them? For example, worries about dirt or germs, or thoughts of bad things happening."
- Do you ever feel driven to repeat certain acts? Repeatedly washing your hands, cleaning, checking doors or work again, rearranging things to get it just right, or having to repeat thoughts in your mind to feel better."
- Does this waste significant time or cause problems in your life? For example, interfering with school, work, or seeing friends.

The self-assessment questions developed for this study are aligned with established clinical frameworks used in the diagnosis and preliminary screening of OCD. These questions are conceptually consistent with the criteria outlined in the Diagnostic and Statistical Manual of Mental Disorders, Fifth Edition (DSM-5), which remains the gold standard for psychiatric evaluation and diagnosis [36] Additionally, the structure and focus of the questions reflect components from validated tools such as the Obsessive-Compulsive Inventory Revised (OCI-R), which was developed to assess the severity and dimensions of OCD symptoms in both clinical and research settings [37]. The user queries designed for the NLP-based chatbot are also grounded in real-world language, reflecting the types of concerns and expressions commonly found in mental health forums, public health platforms, and patient-led discussions [38]. This makes the chatbot interface user-centered, relatable, and relevant, especially for individuals seeking non-clinical pathways for information and self-guided mental health support. The integration of clean energy strategies with ESG principles has been extensively addressed in recent works, which outline technologies and frameworks supporting sustainability goals [39]. Furthermore, the role of Digital Twin enhances ESG compliance and monitoring [40].

9.9 Conclusions

OCD is a complex psychological condition characterized by persistent, intrusive thoughts and repetitive behaviors that interfere with daily functioning. Its causes are multifaceted, involving a combination of genetic predisposition, neurochemical imbalances, stressful life events, and environmental factors. Traditional treatment methods such as medication, CBT, and ERP have proven effective in many cases [41]. However, access to these therapies remains limited, especially in rural and underserved communities. NLP chatbot for psychoeducation and self-assessment of OCD that is available to you anytime, anywhere, and would simulate a clinical psychologist and talk to you in your local language [42]. With the advancement of artificial intelligence, new avenues are emerging to complement conventional approaches. This chapter presents a novel framework for a Digital Twin-based NLP chatbot designed to support psychoeducation and self-assessment in individuals with OCD [43]. The digital twin acts as a dynamic, personalized model that adapts to the user's emotional and behavioral data in real time. By analyzing natural language inputs through the chatbot, it identifies patterns of obsessive thinking and compulsive behaviors, offering personalized feedback, therapeutic exercises, and educational guidance [44].

The system not only enhances accessibility to mental health resources but also provides ongoing monitoring and adaptive support. Integration with wearable devices further extends its functionality, enabling the collection of physiological data that can enrich mental health assessments [45]. Moreover, the chatbot's conversational interface allows users to interact comfortably in their language and tone, reducing stigma and promoting user engagement. This AI-driven approach is especially promising in areas where clinical resources are scarce [46]. It bridges the gap between early detection and formal diagnosis, encourages self-awareness, and empowers individuals to manage their condition proactively [47]. By aligning with validated clinical tools and real-world user needs, the Digital Twin-based chatbot stands as a scalable, culturally adaptive, and technologically advanced solution in the evolving landscape of OCD care and mental health support [48, 49].

AI disclosure statement: The author confirms that no artificial intelligence (AI)-generated content or AI-assisted writing tools were used in the preparation of this chapter (including summaries and the abstract). All text, analysis, and conclusions are the result of the author's original work.

References

1. Stein, D.J., Costa, D.L., Lochner, C., Miguel, E.C., Reddy, Y.J., Shavitt, R.G., Simpson, H.B., Obsessive-compulsive disorder. *Nat. Rev. Dis. Primers*, 5, 52, 2019.
2. Henderson, J.G., Jr. and Pollard, C.A., Three types of obsessive-compulsive disorder in a community sample. *J. Clin. Psychol.*, 44, 5, 747–752, 1988.
3. Leckman, J.F., Grice, D.E., Boardman, J., Zhang, H., Vitale, A., Bondi, C., Pauls, D.L., Symptoms of obsessive-compulsive disorder. *Am. J. Psychiatry*, 154, 7, 911–917, 1997.
4. Tek, C. and Ulug, B., Religiosity and religious obsessions in obsessive–compulsive disorder. *Psychiatry Res.*, 104, 2, 99–108, 2001.
5. Samuels, J., Bienvenu, O.J., Krasnow, J., Wang, Y., Grados, M.A., Cullen, B., Nestadt, G., An investigation of doubt in obsessive–compulsive disorder. *Compr. Psychiatry*, 75, 117–124, 2017.
6. Szechtman, H. and Woody, E.Z., Obsessive-compulsive disorder as a disturbance of security motivation: Constraints on comorbidity. *Neurotoxic. Res.*, 10, 103–112, 2006.
7. Koran, L.M., Quality of life in obsessive-compulsive disorder. *Psychiatr. Clin. N. Am.*, 23, 3, 509–517, 2000.
8. Coughtrey, A.E., Shafran, R., Knibbs, D., Rachman, S.J., Mental contamination in obsessive–compulsive disorder. *J. Obsessive Compuls. Relat. Disord.*, 1, 4, 244–250, 2012.
9. Frost, R.O. and Steketee, G., Perfectionism in obsessive-compulsive disorder patients. *Behav. Res. Ther.*, 35, 4, 291–296, 1997.
10. Strauss, A.Y., Fradkin, I., McNally, R.J., Linkovski, O., Anholt, G.E., Huppert, J.D., Why check? A meta-analysis of checking in obsessive-compulsive disorder: Threat vs. distrust of senses. *Clin. Psychol. Rev.*, 75, 101807, 2020.
11. Ferrier, S. and Brewin, C.R., Feared identity and obsessive–compulsive disorder. *Behav. Res. Ther.*, 43, 10, 1363–1374, 2005.
12. Bhatia, M.S. and Kaur, J., Homosexual obsessive compulsive disorder (HOCD): A rare case report. *J. Clin. Diagn. Res.*, 9, 1, VD01, 2015.
13. Yorulmaz, O., Gençöz, T., Woody, S., OCD cognitions and symptoms in different religious contexts. *J. Anxiety Disord.*, 23, 3, 401–406, 2009.
14. Rosso, G., Albert, U., Asinari, G.F., Bogetto, F., Maina, G., Stressful life events and obsessive–compulsive disorder: Clinical features and symptom dimensions. *Psychiatry Res.*, 197, 3, 259–264, 2012.

15. Del Casale, A., Sorice, S., Padovano, A., Simmaco, M., Ferracuti, S., Lamis, D.A., Pompili, M., Psychopharmacological treatment of obsessive-compulsive disorder (OCD). *Curr. Neuropharmacol.*, 17, 8, 710–736, 2019.
16. Pauls, D.L., The genetics of obsessive-compulsive disorder: A review. *Dialogues Clin. Neurosci.*, 12, 2, 149–163, 2010.
17. Piras, F., Chiapponi, C., Girardi, P., Caltagirone, C., Spalletta, G., Widespread structural brain changes in OCD: A systematic review of voxel-based morphometry studies. *Cortex*, 62, 89–108, 2015.
18. Hoekstra, P.J. and Minderaa, R.B., Tic disorders and obsessive-compulsive disorder: Is autoimmunity involved? *Int. Rev. Psychiatry*, 17, 6, 497–502, 2005.
19. Murayama, K., Nakao, T., Ohno, A., Tsuruta, S., Tomiyama, H., Hasuzawa, S., Kanba, S., Impacts of stressful life events and traumatic experiences on onset of obsessive-compulsive disorder. *Front. Psychiatry*, 11, 561266, 2020.
20. O'Connor, K.P., Aardema, F., Robillard, S., Guay, S., Pelissier, M.C., Todorov, C., Doucet, P., Cognitive behaviour therapy and medication in the treatment of obsessive–compulsive disorder. *Acta Psychiatr. Scand.*, 113, 5, 408–419, 2006.
21. Olatunji, B.O., Davis, M.L., Powers, M.B., Smits, J.A., Cognitive-behavioral therapy for obsessive-compulsive disorder: A meta-analysis of treatment outcome and moderators. *J. Psychiatr. Res.*, 47, 1, 33–41, 2013.
22. Abramowitz, J.S., Variants of exposure and response prevention in the treatment of obsessive-compulsive disorder: A meta-analysis. *Behav. Ther.*, 27, 4, 583–600, 1996.
23. Greist, J.H., Marks, I.M., Baer, L., Kobak, K.A., Wenzel, K.W., Hirsch, M.J., Clary, C.M., Behavior therapy for obsessive-compulsive disorder guided by a computer or by a clinician compared with relaxation as a control. *J. Clin. Psychiatry*, 63, 2, 138–145, 2002.
24. Davis, E., Community support and societal influences, in: *Clinical Obsessive-Compulsive Disorders in Adults and Children*, pp. 152–171, Cambridge, UK, 2011.
25. Manjula, M. and Sudhir, P.M., New-wave behavioural therapies in obsessive-compulsive disorder: Moving toward integrated behavioural therapies. *Indian J. Psychiatry*, 61, Suppl 1, S104–S113, 2019.
26. Masoumi, S.J., Applications and efficacy of artificial intelligence in obsessive-compulsive disorder: A narrative review. *J. Nurs. Rep. Clin. Pract.*, 3, 6, 601–608, 2025.
27. Bansal, H., Aryan, A., Pathak, H.A., Shukla, S.D., An AI-powered mental health assistant for personalized and adaptive care, in: *Proc. 2024 Int. Conf. Prog. Innov. Intell. Syst. Data Sci. (ICPIDS)*, IEEE, pp. 67–74, 2024.
28. Luxton, D.D. and Sirotin, A., Intelligent conversational agents in global health, in: *Innovations in Global Mental Health*, pp. 1–12, Springer, Cham, 2020.

29. Kim, J., *et al.*, Artificial Intelligence in Obsessive-Compulsive Disorder: A Systematic Review. *Curr. Treat. Options Psychiatry*, 12, 1, 23, 2025.
30. Gupta, S. and Kumar, A., Study on early accurate diagnosis and treatment of COVID-19 with smartphone tracking using bionics. *Secur. Privacy*, 6, 5, e303, 2023.
31. Gupta, S., HariPrasad, S.A., Kumar, A., Bionics-based emergency contact for treatment of epilepsy, in: *Proc. 2018 10th Int. Conf. Bioinf. Biomed. Technol.*, pp. 46–50, 2018.
32. Gupta, S. and Kumar, A., Bionic functionality of prosthetic hand, in: *Intell. Commun. Control Devices: Proc. ICICCD 2017*, pp. 1177–1190, Springer, Singapore, 2018.
33. Gupta, S., Hariprasad, S.A., Kumar, A., Bionics-based camouflage clothing for soldiers, in: *Intell. Commun. Control Devices: Proc. ICICCD 2018*, pp. 415–423, Springer, Singapore, 2019.
34. Kumar, A., Study and analysis of different segmentation methods for brain tumor MRI application. *Multimedia Tools Appl.*, 82, 5, 7117–7139, 2023.
35. Kumar, A., Chauda, P., Devrari, A., Machine learning approach for brain tumor detection and segmentation. *Int. J. Organ. Collect. Intell. (IJOCI)*, 11, 3, 68–84, 2021.
36. American Psychiatric Association, *Diagnostic and Statistical Manual of Mental Disorders*, 5th ed., American Psychiatric Publishing, Arlington, VA, 2013.
37. Foa, E.B., Huppert, J.D., Leiberg, S., Langner, R., Kichic, R., Hajcak, G., Salkovskis, P.M., The Obsessive-Compulsive Inventory: Development and validation of a short version. *Psychol. Assess.*, 14, 4, 485–496, 2002.
38. National Institute of Mental Health (NIMH), Obsessive-Compulsive Disorder (OCD), https://www.nimh.nih.gov/health/topics/obsessive-compulsive-disorder-ocd (accessed July 23, 2025).
39. Mondal, S., Kumar, A., Pachauri, R.K., Mondal, A.K., Singh, V.K., Sharma, A.K. (Eds.), *Clean and renewable energy production*, John Wiley & Sons, Hoboken, New Jersey, USA, 2024.
40. Mondal, S., Kumar, A., Khan, M. (Eds.), *Digital Twin and ESG*, John Wiley & Sons, Hoboken, New Jersey, USA, 2025.
41. Paliyal, P.S., Mondal, S., Layek, S., Kuchhal, P., Pandey, J.K., Automatic solar tracking system: a review pertaining to advancements and challenges in the current scenario. *Clean Energy*, 8, 6, 237–262, December 2024, https://doi.org/10.1093/ce/zkae085.
42. Paliyal, P.S., Mondal, S., Pandey, J.K., An Analysis of Springwater Parameter Status for Different Locations in the Rural Hilly Garhwal Region of Uttarakhand. *Environ. Claims J.*, *36*, 3, 243–277, 2024, https://doi.org/10.1080/10406026.2024.2423964.

43. Paliyal, P.S. and Mondal, S., An analysis of a cross-finned receiver for Scheffler-type solar collectors to optimize solar heating efficiency for direct water heating. *Int. J. Energy Water Resour.*, 2025, https://doi.org/10.1007/s42108-025-00393-5.
44. Paliyal, P.S., Mondal, S., Pathela, M., Kumar, A., Menon, S.K., Optimization of Solar Photovoltaic Array In-Depth Analysis of Perturb and Observe MPPT Algorithm. *2024 International Conference on Advances in Computing, Communication and Materials (ICACCM)*, Dehradun, India, pp. 1–6, 2024, doi: 10.1109/ICACCM61117.2024.11059143.
45. Paliyal, P.S., *et al.*, Location Analysis and Environmental Validation for Installation of Hybrid Solar-Wind Energy Generation System in Hilly Areas of Uttarakhand: Study Toward Forecasting, in: *Forecasting Methods for Renewable Power Generation*, pp. 21–47, Wiley, Hoboken, New Jersey, USA, 2025.
46. Menon, S.K., *et al.*, The Role of Hydrogen as a Sustainable Energy Source and its Integration with the Grid, in: *Advancements in Communication and Systems*, A.K. Tripathi and V. Shrivastava (Eds.), p. 397, Computing and Intelligent Systems, SCRS, India, 2023, (2025).
47. Kudapa, V.K., Paliyal, P.S., Mondal, A., Mondal, S., A critical review of fabrication strategies, separation techniques, challenges, and future prospects for the hydrogen separation membrane. *Fusion Sci. Technol.*, 80, 7, 803–825, 2024.
48. Mondal, A., Jangirh, R., Arya, R., Yadav, L., Ahlawat, S., Yadav, P., Paliyal, P.S., Bobde, P., Ghosh, P., Mondal, S., Rai, A., Analysing solid residential fuel usage patterns in rural and urban slums of Delhi: Implications for pollution reduction and sustainable practices. *Energy Sustainable Dev., 80,* 101460, 2024.
49. Paliyal, P.S., Kuchhal, P., Mondal, S., Nano Lubricants and their Applications, in: *Nanotechnology: A Quick Guide to Materials and Technologies*, pp. 425–456, Bentham Science Publishers, Singapore, 2024.

10

FPGA Performance Analysis of LDPC Codes for Communication Systems

Aakanksha Devrari[1,2], Adesh Kumar[1]* and Amit Kumar[3]

[1]Department of Electrical and Electronics Engineering, School of Advanced Engineering, UPES, Dehradun, Uttarakhand, India
[2]Department of Computer Science & Engineering, DIT University, Dehradun, Uttarakhand, India
[3]Faculty of Technology, Veer Madho Singh Bhandari Uttarakhand Technical University, Dehradun, Uttarakhand, India

Abstract
The wireless communication system is based on several coding schemes such as turbo codes, LDPC codes, convolutional, polar, systematic, etc. The coding techniques should satisfy the hardware system requirements while machine and device communication is taking place. The research article presents the performance analysis of LDPC coding hardware architecture. The encoder and decoder hardware chip of LDPC is designed using Xilinx ISE 14.7 software, targeted at Virtex-5 FPGA. The performance of both coding methods is evaluated using an iterative coding scheme. The FPGA hardware complexity is analyzed in terms of hardware and FPGA performance parameters such as slices, flip flops, LUTs, and IoB utilization. The performance of the coding methods is also analyzed in terms of timing information-related parameters such as path delay, minimum duration, minimum and maximum time of the clock signal, etc. The research work is helpful for 4G and 5G mobile communication requirements in device-to-device communication.

***Keywords*:** Communication systems, low-density parity check (LDPC) codes, field programmable gate array (FPGA), AWGN channel, BPSK modulation

**Corresponding author*: adeshmanav@gmail.com

Surajit Mondal, Paramjeet Singh Paliyal and Sachin Sharma (eds.) Digital Twin Technology for Solar Concentrators, (159–178) © 2026 Scrivener Publishing LLC

10.1 Introduction

Recent communication systems are facing difficulty in satisfying the needs and requirements of users. The next-generation mobile communication systems are expected to be 5G Era with improved channel coding schemes. There are multiple channel coding schemes available such as Low-density parity-check codes (LDPC), turbo codes, systematic convolutional, polar codes, and non-systematic convolutional codes [1, 2]. The codes can be analyzed based on their complexity, reliability, flexibility, and latency as per system requirements. In cellular systems, channel coding schemes are used to ensure reliable transmission by offering minimum errors during transmission [3]. Wireless systems have shown remarkable development in satisfying user demands for the last few years. In the current scenario, the coding schemes available for 5G mobile systems are LDPC, turbo codes, and polar codes.

Figure 10.1 presents a forward error correction (FEC) communication system block diagram that shows the transmission of data from source to destination. The first step from the source is a data encoding with the help of an encoder performing modulation using some modulation technique and then transmitted over an Additive white Gaussian noise (AWGN) channel. During this transmission, noise can be added to data through the channel. This data along with noise is provided to the demodulator where the carrier signal is separated from the message signal and the data is decoded back to its original form using an error-correcting decoder at the receiver end. The two most significant blocks in the wireless communication system block diagram are the encoder and decoder.

The turbo codes are a class of high-performance FEC codes invented by C. Berrou [4, 5] in 1993. The performance of the codes is close to Shannon's

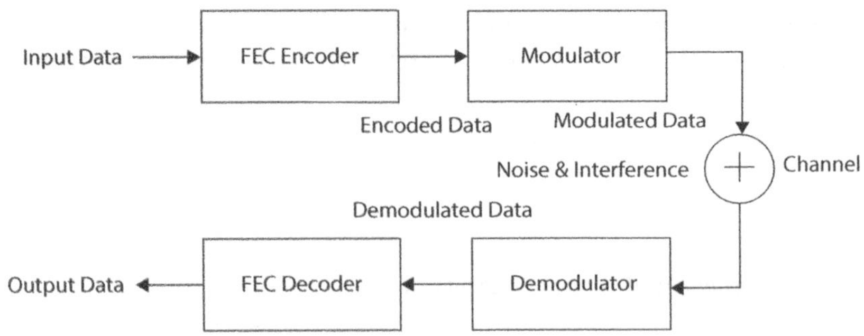

Figure 10.1 Block diagram of FEC communication system [9].

theoretical limit (SHA). The theorem presents the channel capacity (C) in bits/s, to transmit information at a faster rate without error over channel bandwidth (B). The channel capacity, $C = B \log_2 (1+S/N)$, in which S/N presents the signal-to-noise ratio. The coding community was excited to provide promising solutions about channel capacity using an iterative decoding method based on simple constituent code. The coding block consists of the interlevel and the code length is long and random, which can emulate the performance of the system. The convolution turbo codes are formed by parallel-concatenated recursive and systematic convolution codes, separated by an interlevel.

The LDPC codes were first introduced in the early 1960s by Gallager [28, 29]. This discovery went unnoticed by many investigators for nearly 20 years, but in 1981, a scholar named Tanner gave a new understanding of these codes from a graphical point of view. LDPC codes based on the Belief Propagation Algorithm (BPA) [26] have shown a channel's capacity performance close to Shannon's limit [7]. Consequently, LDPC codes proved powerful relative to other classes of linear block codes named turbo codes for error corrections where reliability is the concern. On the other hand, turbo codes are very efficient in terms of their performance reaching Shannon's limit [10].

10.2 Related Work

The pipelined LDPC decoder [1] was used for WiMAX standard 802.16e. This pipelined decoder architecture used a high-end synthesis tool to reduce validation time. The architecture used the minimum throughput requirement for large-scale integration approaches. Also, the use of 8-bit fixed-point arithmetic adds extra precision to the design and delivers better performance in terms of bit error rate. The Belief propagation and log-likelihood ratio-based demodulation methods were used [2] for LDPC codes to Ruby transform-based decoder structure so that the computational complexity is reduced. The simulation results for both algorithms in the presence of the AWGN channel were obtained in terms of bit error rate. The Monte Carlo-based evaluation method was used for theoretical analysis. It was found that the combined approach of these two algorithms reduces the hardware complexity and improves the SNR. A new method for the construction of LDPC codes based on a progressive edge growth mechanism [6]. To achieve optimum a pipelined structure and memory organization using a single port bank was considered at the time of code construction. The hardware efficiency should be maximized using code constraints for quasi-cyclic LDPC code. The design was implemented in FPGA and throughput was experienced to be increased from 39 to 110% using a pipelined structure. The generic behavioral model was detailed for generating LDPC decoders [10]. Decoders are needed in applications that require reliable and fast data transmission. On the other hand, coded RTL architecture provided good performance, but the critical path of IP design was slowed down [11]. The LDPC decoders are implemented using Xilinx Vivado HLS. It was observed that the hardware complexity is reduced by ten times and the throughput is increased by 1.5 times. The model performed similarly to handcrafted RTL structures. The parallel architecture consists of multiple single-input single-output elements [12] that offer low latency for turbo decoding. This architecture is compared with existing sequential architectures. For concurrent execution of the design, SISO-based parallel interleaver and related algorithms were presented. The parallel architecture reduced the latency by 20 times and increased the throughput by six times in comparison to other sequential decoders [13, 14]. The implementation of linear, convolution and cyclic codes was done on FPGA [15, 16] using VHDL. Error control codes (ECC) are used for error detection and correction in the noisy communication channel. This was achieved by adding redundant bits to the data at the transmitter end, and the correlation of these redundant bits is used at the receiver end for error detection and error correction. The channel coding schemes for a 5G mobile communication system [17] have problems satisfying the user requirements in machine-type communication. Different channel coding schemes were suggested such as LDPC, polar, systematic convolutional, turbo, and non-systematic convolutional codes, using the BPSK modulation method in machine-type communication for the 5G wireless communication system. Two different categories of Quasi Cyclic LDPC code were used [18] out of which one is binary and the other is non-binary, and their construction is based upon finite field subgroups. These codes provided better performance in the case of the AWGN channel using an iterative decoding algorithm. These codes utilize larger minimum distances in comparison to the finite geometry LDPC codes and they balance the performance in terms of error and decoding complexity using an iterative decoding process. These codes provided burst errors in such an environment, which was capable of replacing Reed Solomon codes by offering large coding gains at the same code length and code rate [19]. The combination of the Log-MAP decoding algorithm and the LUT-Log-MAP algorithm is called the LUT-Nor-Log-MAP algorithm [20]. The algorithm was used to perform normalization functions for the SISO decoder unit. In simulation results, it has been observed that resource utilization can be saved by 2.1% using the LUT-Nor-Log-MAP algorithm. Also, the decoder using the LUT-Nor-Log-MAP algorithm depicted a gain of 0.25~0.5 dB. Finally, the design of the turbo decoder provided a throughput of 36 Mbit/s that can be achieved using synthesizing on the Cyclone IV FPGA platform. The implementation of LDPC decoder architecture on FPGA [21] for the application of digital video broadcasting *via* satellite (DVB-S2). This algorithm was applied systematically in such a manner that supported 360 functional units of the design. Moreover, the synthesis of the LDPC decoder was done by targeting two FPGA devices XC2VP100 and XC6VLX240T. The partition and shift methods were used for LDPC codes [22] to shift and divide the bit nodes and check nodes into subsets and connect these nodes in subsets. A theorem is derived to prevent the cycles harmful in LDPC decoding. The simulation results of these codes depict good performance in terms of bit error rate over EPR 4 channels. The flexible designs based on an open platform were used [23, 24] that required the parallel computing method to decode the data based on an iterative minimum sum algorithm for a (3,6) regular LDPC code with variable codeword length. The decoding algorithm supports parallelism for which Altera Offline compiler version 15.1 is required. This algorithm is tested on Altera Stratix VGXA7 FPGA hardware. This design gives an effective throughput of 68.22 Mbps for a 2048-length (3, 6) regular LDPC code at a clock frequency of 163.88 MHz, and for a length of 1024 (3, 6) LDPC code it gives a throughput of 54.8 Mbps by showing an improvement of 7 Mbps. The design and implementation of the turbo decoder were done using Verilog [25, 26]. The design used the Max-Log algorithm to reduce the number of iterations and provided early termination due to which power consumption was reduced. To provide early termination sign difference ratio factor was used. The concept of clock gating was used to provide better power efficiency. The design was implemented and tested on Virtex-4 and Virtex-5 FPGAs. The performance of convolution codes was done in the Rayleigh fading channel [27] with a long constraint length. As the sequential decoding cannot be applied below a threshold value of SNR. Therefore, the selected SNR per bit information is 5.7 dB. Moreover, the process of uniform quantization is chosen in such a way that it can provide negligible loss. For this design, the finite interleaving method is used to an interleaver depth of (50 × 50) with a Doppler frequency of 0.01. The suggested scheme performs well in terms of bit error rate as compared to Turbo codes [30, 31]. LDPC codes were used [33, 34] in which parity check matrix construction is done using the sub-matrix structure and the matrix inverse is replaced by multiplication of sparse matrices. The replacement of matrices can result in efficient encoding that further reduces computational complexity.

The simulation results depicted that the design has increased the throughput up to 1 Gbps. Euclidean geometry (8176, 7154) based architecture [35, 36] of a low complexity Quasi-cyclic LDPC codes is used for high-speed data rate. The architecture incorporated algorithmic transformation-based critical path reduction and a non-uniform quantization method to minimize memory size. The parallel decoders are proposed in the design to enhance throughput. The design was implemented on Xilinx Virtex-II 6000, FPGA. The FPGA synthesis has proved that the design can achieve a maximum throughput of 172 Mbps in 15 iterations. The 3rd generation partnership LTE standard [37] is based on the parallel turbo coding scheme that supports 188 block-size data. To reduce the hardware complexity of interleaver in turbo codes, a permutation polynomial multistage network with the address generator is used. An optimized decoding scheme is suggested to enhance the system performance and support high parallelism. A radix-2 and radix-4 recursion-based add compare select unit is proposed for the selection of block sizes that cannot be divided by 16. The design is implemented on 130 nm CMOS technology consuming 4.02 mm^2 core area and 1.81 architecture efficiency while achieving 384.3 Mbps peak throughput with 5.5 iterations at a clock speed of 290 MHz. An optimal design was presented [36] for irregular LDPC code that utilized a shaping method with the specified block length [23]. It has been seen that LDPC codes are beating turbo codes in terms of computation cost and effective performance [38].

The problem statement of the research work is considered based on the hardware realization of turbo and LDPC-based encoders and decoders. The comparative performance analysis of these coding-based encoder and decoder architectures on the FPGA platform will be the new research work so that LDPC coding-based hardware can be used further for machine-to-machine and device-to-device communication as in the 5G communication system. The paper focused on the design and FPGA implementation of the LDPC coding-based hardware chip, performed simulations, and estimated the performance indices.

10.3 LDPC Codes

LDPC code [1, 15] is a linear block code that consists of a parity check matrix 'H', which has less number of non-zero elements in every row and column. These codes can be regular as well as irregular, depending on the number of once available row-wise and column-wise. If the parity matrix has an equal number of ones in each row and column, it is referred to as regular LDPC code, meaning column weight (w_c) is equal to row the weight (w_r). If the parity check matrix 'H' has unequal no. of 1's in each row and column it is an irregular LDPC code. The codes are called low-density codes, as the number of 1's is always less than the number of 0's. In present communication systems such as mobile WiMax (802.16e), and DVB-S2 (802.11n), the LDPC codes are extensively used. LDPC codes can be represented as (n, w_c, w_r), where n = code length, w_c = weight of column, and w_r = weight of row. The parity-checking matrix 'H' is symbolized with the help of Tanner graphs and algebraic construction. The number of columns in the 'H' matrix denotes the bit nodes or variable nodes(V_N) in the Tanner graph, and the number of rows in the H matrix denotes the check nodes (C_N) in the Tanner graph and their connectivity is shown by logic '1' in the 'H' matrix. An example of the H matrix representation is

$$H = \begin{bmatrix} C_{N1} \\ C_{N2} \\ C_{N3} \\ C_{N4} \\ C_{N5} \end{bmatrix} [V_{N1} \quad V_{N2} \quad V_{N3} \quad V_4 \quad V_{N5} \quad V_{N6} \quad V_{N7} \quad V_{N8} \quad V_{N9} \quad V_{N10}] \tag{10.1}$$

$$H = \begin{bmatrix} 1 & 1 & 0 & 0 & 0 & 1 & 0 & 1 & 0 & 1 \\ 0 & 1 & 1 & 0 & 0 & 1 & 0 & 0 & 1 & 0 \\ 0 & 0 & 1 & 1 & 0 & 0 & 1 & 0 & 0 & 1 \\ 0 & 0 & 0 & 1 & 1 & 1 & 0 & 0 & 1 & 0 \\ 1 & 0 & 0 & 0 & 1 & 0 & 1 & 0 & 1 & 0 \end{bmatrix} \tag{10.2}$$

Figure 10.2 shows the tanner graph corresponding to the 'H' matrix. One method for LDPC encoding [32, 35, 36] is the pre-processing method in which for a given 'H' matrix a generator matrix is developed that is used for encoding some random input message bit (m) of size (1 × m). The second encoding technique uses the parity check matrix directly and thus the method is less complex compared to the first method. The decoding part involves the bit-flipping algorithm for hard decision channels and the sum-product process also called a message-passing algorithm for soft

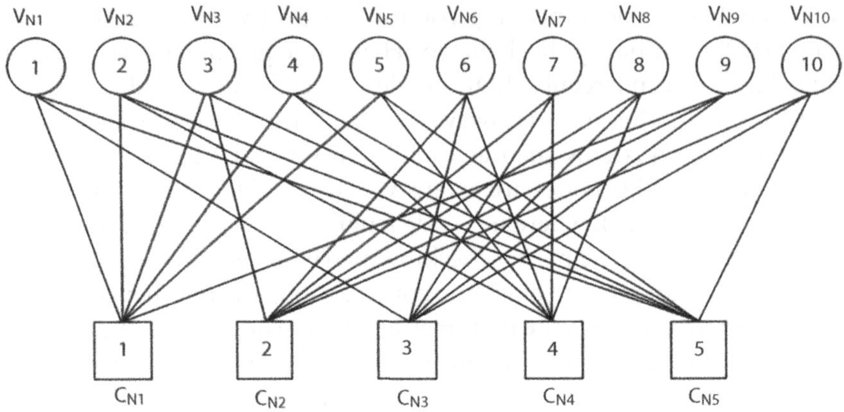

Figure 10.2 'H' matrix-based example Tanner graph [9].

decision channels. This message-passing algorithm comprises the passing of messages in the forward and backward direction between variable nodes and check nodes until no further iteration is required [39].

The LDPC coding scheme is presented in Figure 10.3. The transmitter end shows random data bits that are modulated by the BPSK modulator. LDPC encoder achieves the channel encoding and the encoded data sequence passes through the AWGN channel. The demodulation is performed using

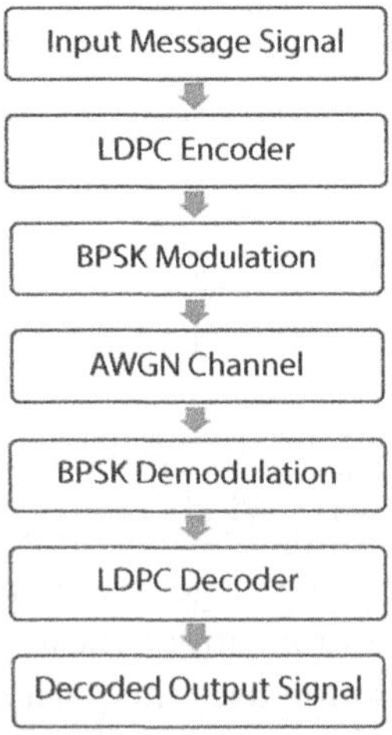

Figure 10.3 LDPC coding scheme [9].

the BPSK demodulator and the LDPC decoder [8, 9] is used to decode the data back to its original form at the receiving end. Codeword length plays a very important role in the encoding of LDPC codes. The encoding method comprises mainly two operations: Sparse parity check formation and codeword creation using a sparse matrix. The decoding of LDPC codes uses iterative algorithms such as the Belief Propagation algorithm [26]. A "Min-Sum" approach is adapted for the hardware implementation of the Belief propagation algorithm. In this method after the node, checking the information of a data node is updated for each iteration. Once the decoding process is over a hard decision is made based on the most probable code word [40].

10.3.1 LDPC Encoder and Decoder

The LDPC codes proposed are used as cyclic codes considering the special case to conceptualize the parity check code. The generation of the parity check matrix is performed using block circulant code formation. The block circulant code is considered here because of more accuracy in error correction also, it provides a structured architecture of the decoder. The parity check matrix is generated with the help of a binary matrix in which each row is created using a single cyclic right shift operation in the previous row. The structure of a parity check matrix denoted by 'H' having size (rT × nT) is achieved by performing concatenation of (r × n) light circulant with size (T × T). The Tanner graph corresponding to this parity check matrix is referred to as a protograph. In the design, the photographs [15] used are AR3A and AR4A with a code rate of ½ are depicted in Figures 10.4 (a) and (b) respectively [41].

The circles denote the variable nodes and the squares denote the parity check nodes. The open circles denote the penetrated symbols, whereas the solid circles represent the communication symbols. The three-level decoding process is considered: accumulate, recurrence by 3 or 4, and accumulate. The Protographs represent a circulant parity check matrix (3 × 5) in which the degree of consistent circulant is denoted by the number of parallel ends. The protographs cannot be extended directly without low-weight codewords, irrespective of the optimal selection of circulants. Therefore, protographs are only extended twice, but with small variation matrices, having a size of (4 × 4) and (8 × 8). The complete code can be built up using these circulants. In matrix representation, a dot is used for nonzero entries. For the formation of the AR4A protograph the check nodes are placed in

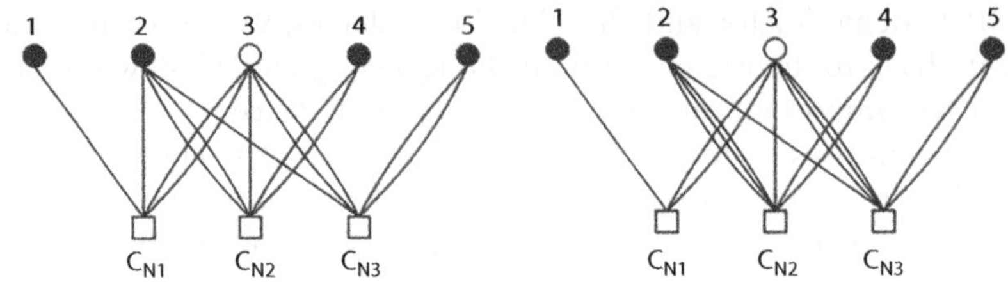

Figure 10.4 (a) Protograph (AR3A) (b) protograph (AR4A) [9].

order (C_{N1}, C_{N2}, C_{N3}) and variable nodes in sequence (4, 2, 1, 5, 3). The nodes are presented using solid lines initially with a (4 × 4) permutation and then elevating to (16 × 16) circulants. The resulting construction is a highlighted (12 × 20) block circulant. The concept is demonstrated using the protograph example of AR3A and AR4A. In this case, the reorganization of the rows and columns in AR4A is done [42].

For the sequence (4, 2, 3, 1, 5), the base matrix (C_{N2}, C_{N1}, C_{N3}) is given as

$$H = \begin{bmatrix} 2 & 3 & 1 & 0 & 0 \\ 0 & 0 & 2 & 1 & 0 \\ 0 & 1 & 3 & 0 & 2 \end{bmatrix} \tag{10.3}$$

10.4 Hardware Architecture

The hardware chip implementation of the LDPC encoder is based on the block circulant matrix that can be created by the row-wise cyclic shift performed to the contents of shift registers. A matrix is a group of (n-k) encoder bits having a constraint length of T that uses a recursive convolution approach.

Figure 10.5 shows the feeding method where 'k' input bits are sequentially given to the encoder and then with every shift, the contents of the registers are updated sequentially. Once, the updated data is stored in registers, switches are changed and data is read out from the registers along with the parity bits. The circular data is processed row-wise with (n-k) soft operations. Figure 10.6 presents the circular and shift operation to configure the encoder design [43].

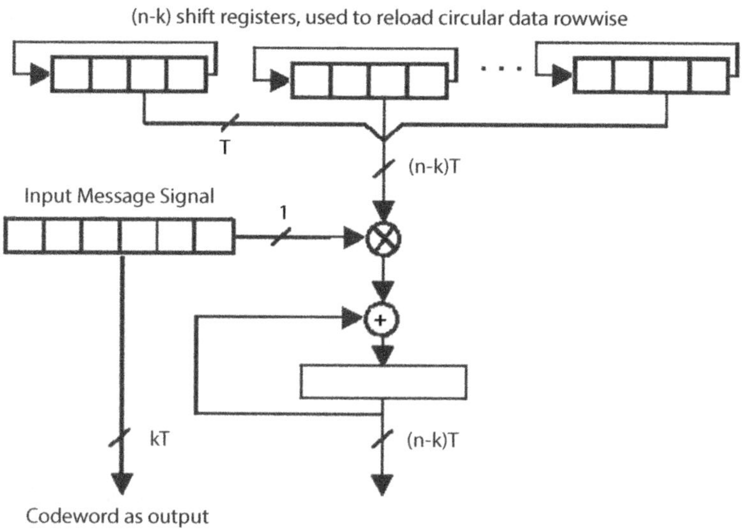

Figure 10.5 Row-wise circular data processing with (n-k) soft operations [9].

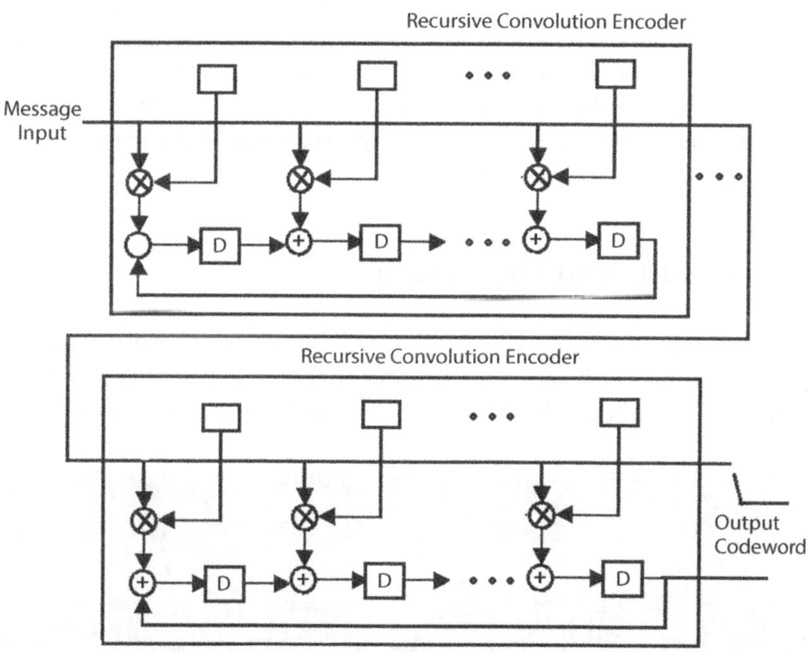

Figure 10.6 Circular and shift register operation for encoder [9].

The output of the LDPC encoder is the multiplication operation performed on the input message matrix and generator matrix. For a larger message sequence, this operation becomes very complex. The following steps are involved in the LDPC encoding process.

Step 1: Compute the contents of parity check matrix 'H'

$$H = [-P^T : I_{n-k}] \tag{10.4}$$

Step 2: Compute the contents of the Generator matrix (G)

$$G = [I_K : P] \tag{10.5}$$

Step 3: Determine the contents of the transmitting codeword (C_w)

$$C_w = m.G \tag{10.6}$$

Circulant data encoding is used to select a parity check matrix (H) also indicates the sparse matrix with a code rate of 1/2. The sizes of the 'H' matrix and 'G' matrix are (2048 x 4096) and (2048 x 4096) respectively. Since the design and execution of such a large data size in real-time is a challenging task. Therefore, a (32 x 64) matrix is used for the implementation of a large-scale matrix [44].

10.5 Results and Discussion

The chip design is done in Xilinx ISE 14.7 software. Figure 10.7 presents the RTL view of the LDPC encoder and decoder. Table 10.1 lists the description of the pins used in the design of the encoder and decoder chip.

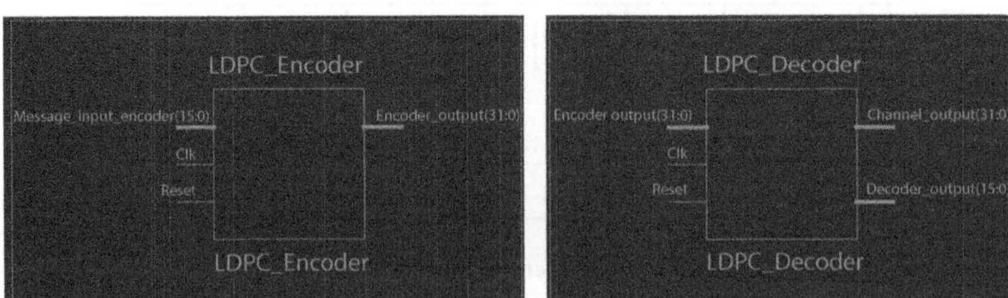

Figure 10.7 RTL view of LDPC encoder and decoder.

Table 10.1 Pin description of encoder and decoder designed RTL chip.

Pins	Direction	Description
Clk	Input	The clock signal is an input clock signal applicable to offer the rising-edge-based clock signal, with the 50 % duty cycle.
Reset	Input	Reset is the default input to the chip design and is used to keep the contents zero for the encoder and decoder.
Message_Input_ Encoder <15:0>	Input	It presents the 16-bit input message to the LDPC encoder, given in the transmitter section in the design.
Encoder_ output<31:0>	Input	It is an LDPC-encoded output of 32-bit and can be processed as input to the AWGN channel.
Channel_Output <31:0>	Input	It is the output of the AWGN Channel and input to the LDPC decoder.
Decoder_Output <15:0>	Output	It is the 16-bit output of the LDPC decoder as the decoded signal or message at the receiver end.

The chip design of the LDPC code comprises the matrix multiplication of the input message matrix and generator matrix 'G'. The size of the input message is considered 16-bit, and the encoder output is 32-bit, then the generator matrix is of size (16 x 32). The generator matrix requires 32 registers to store the contents. The matrix multiplication is done using AND logic and OR logic between the input message (1 x 16) and the generator matrix. The VHDL programming is used and the corresponding test bench is used to check the functional simulation. The output of the turbo and LDPC encoder passes through the AWGN channel. The behavior simulation of turbo and LDPC encoder and decoder chips is done in the Xilinx ISIM simulator. Figure 10.8 presents Xilinx ISIM simulation for LDPC encoder and decoder. The simulation test case stimuli are given.

Test-1 (LDPC Encoder/Decoder): Apply Clk = rising edge clock signal, reset = '0', message_input_encoder [15:0] = "0000000000000011" then the encoder output is encoded_output = "00000000000000000000000011

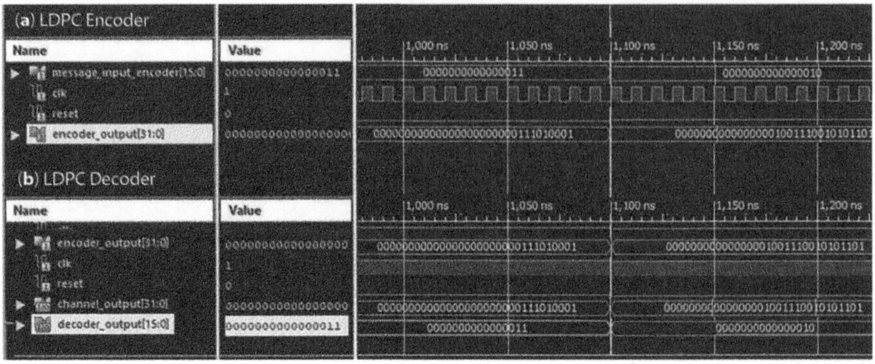

Figure 10.8 Xilinx ISIM simulation for LDPC encoder and decoder.

1010001", channel_output <31:0> = "00000000000000000000000111010001" and decoded output of LDPC decoder is decoder_output <15:0> = "0000000000000011".

Test-2 (LDPC Encoder/Decoder): Apply Clk = rising edge clock signal, reset = '0', message_input_encoder [15:0] = "0000000000000010" then the encoder output is encoded_output = "00000000000000001001110010101101", channel_output <31:0> = "00000000000000001001110010101101" and decoded output of LDPC decoder is decoder_output <15:0> = "0000000000000010".

Table 10.2 presents the hardware parameter summary of turbo and LDPC encoder and decoder hardware for different parameters targeting Virtex-5 FPGA in Xilinx ISE 14.7 software. The hardware parameters are

Table 10.2 FPGA hardware utilization summary.

	LDPC codes	
Hardware	**Encoder**	**Decoder**
Slices	32/12480	110/12480
Flip Flops	45/12480	52/12480
LUTs	58/330	70/330
IOBs	50/172	72/172
GCLKs	1/32	1/32

Table 10.3 Timing information-related parameters.

Timing parameter	LDPC codes	
	Encoder	Decoder
Frequency (MHz)	375.00	390.0
Minimum period (ns)	1.053	1.275
Time (minimum) before clock (ns)	1.750	2.113
Time (maximum) after clock (ns)	2.710	2.914
Combinational path delay (ns)	6.513	6.302
Speed Grade	-5	-5

slices, LUTs, flip-flops, and IOBs. Table 10.3 presents the timing simulation results of turbo and LDPC encoder and decoder hardware for time-related parameters such as minimum period (ns), minimum and maximum time before and after clock signal (ns), and maximum frequency.

10.6 Conclusions

The hardware chip design and performance analysis of LDPC codes for AWGN channel with BPSK modulation is done successfully in Xilinx ISE 14.7 software. The functional simulation and data communication with the designed hardware are verified using Xilinx ISIM simulation on target Virtex- 5 FPGA for device XC5Vlx20t-2-ff32. In the LDPC encoder, hardware parameters such as slices, flip-flops, LUTs, and IoBs are 32, 45, 58, and 50 respectively, and the LDPC decoder has 110, 52, 70, and 72. The LDPC encoder and decoder support 375.0 MHz and 390.0 MHz frequencies. LDPC encoder and decoder are having combination path delay of 6.513 ns and 6.302 ns, respectively.. It is analyzed that LDPC codes provide an optimal solution in terms of hardware complexity, timing response parameters, and high-frequency support. LDPC codes are optimal, highly efficient, and reliable solutions in 4G and 5G wireless communication, and digital broadcasting as their performance is very good in machine-to-machine communication and FPGA hardware.

AI disclosure statement: The author confirms that no artificial intelligence (AI)-generated content or AI-assisted writing tools were used in the preparation of this chapter (including summaries and the abstract). All text, analysis, and conclusions are the result of the author's original work.

References

1. Andrade, J., Falcao, G., Silva, V., Flexible design of wide-pipeline-based WiMAX QC-LDPC decoder architectures on FPGAs using high-level synthesis. *Electron. Lett.*, *50*, 11, 839–840, 2014.
2. Albayrak, C. and Turk, K., Reduced-complexity decoding of LT codes. *Wireless Pers. Commun.*, *94*, 3, 969–975, 2017.
3. Bahl, L., Cocke, J., Jelinek, F., Raviv, J., Optimal decoding of linear codes for minimizing symbol error rate (corresp.). *IEEE Trans. Inf. Theory*, *20*, 2, 284–287, 1974.
4. Berrou, C., Glavieux, A., Thitimajshima, P., Near Shannon, limit error correcting coding and decoding: Turbo-codes. 1, in: *Proceedings of ICC'93-IEEE International Conference on Communications*, 1993, May, vol. 2, IEEE, pp. 1064–1070.
5. Berrou, C. and Glavieux, A., Near optimum error correcting coding and decoding: Turbo-codes. *IEEE Trans. Commun.*, *44*, 10, 1261–1271, 1996.
6. Boncalo, O., Kolumban-Antal, G., Declercq, D., Savin, V., Code-design for efficient pipelined layered LDPC decoders with bank memory organization. *Microprocess. Microsyst.*, *63*, 216–225, 2018.
7. Shannon, C.E., A mathematical theory of communication. *Bell Syst. Tech. J.*, 27, 379–423, 1948.
8. Choi, G., Park, K.B., Chung, K.S., Optimization of FPGA-based LDPC decoder using high-level synthesis, in: *Proceedings of the 4th International Conference on Communication and Information Processing*, 2018, November, ACM, pp. 256–259.
9. Devrari, A., Kumar, A., Chauhan, H., Kumar, A., Design and FPGA Implementation of LDPC Decoder Chip for Communication System using VHDL. *International Journal of Recent Technology and Engineering (IJRTE)*, 8, 2, 200–206, 2019.
10. Delomier, Y., Le Gal, B., Crenne, J., Jego, C., Model-Based Design of Flexible and Efficient LDPC Decoders on FPGA Devices. *J. Signal Process. Syst.*, 1–19, 2020.
11. MacKay, D. and Neal, R.M., Near Shanon limit performance of low-density parity-check codes. *Electron. Lett.*, August 1996.
12. Dobkin, R., Peleg, M., Ginosar, R., Parallel interleaver design and VLSI architecture for low-latency MAP turbo decoders. *IEEE Trans. Very Large Scale Integr. VLSI Syst.*, *13*, 4, 427–438, 2005.

13. Dobkin, R., Peleg, M., Ginosar, R., Parallel VLSI architecture for MAP turbo decoder, in: *The 13th IEEE International Symposium on Personal, Indoor and Mobile Radio Communications*, vol. 1, IEEE, pp. 384–388, 2002, September.
14. Eizmendi, I., Velez, M., Gómez-Barquero, D., Morgade, J., Baena-Lecuyer, V., Slimani, M., Zoellner, J., DVB-T2: The second generation of terrestrial digital video broadcasting system. *IEEE Trans. Broadcast.*, *60*, 2, 258–271, 2014.
15. Fang, Y., Chen, P., Wang, L., Lau, F.C., Wong, K.K., Performance analysis of protograph-based low-density parity-check codes with spatial diversity. *IET Commun.*, *6*, 17, 2941–2948, 2012.
16. Gilbert, J.M., Robbins, C., Sheikh, W., FPGA implementation of error control codes in VHDL: An undergraduate research project. *Comput. Appl. Eng. Educ.*, *27*, 5, 1073–1086, 2019.
17. Hajiyat, Z.R.M., Sali, A., Mokhtar, M., Hashim, F., Channel Coding Scheme for 5G Mobile Communication System for Short Length Message Transmission. *Wireless Pers. Commun.*, *106*, 2, 377–400, 2019.
18. Kang, J., Huang, Q., Zhang, L., Zhou, B., Lin, S., Quasi-cyclic LDPC codes: An algebraic construction. *IEEE Trans. Commun.*, *58*, 5, 1383–1396, 2010.
19. Li, A., Hailes, P., Maunder, R.G., Al-Hashimi, B.M., Hanzo, L., 1.5 Gbit/s FPGA implementation of a parallel turbo decoder designed for mission-critical machine-type communication applications. *IEEE Access*, *4*, 5452–5473, 2016.
20. Li, J., Wang, X., He, J., Su, C., Shan, L., Turbo Decoder Design based on an LUT-Normalized Log-MAP Algorithm. *Entropy*, *21*, 8, 814, 2019.
21. Loi, K.C. and Ko, S.B., Improvements on the design and implementation of DVB-S2 LDPC decoders. *Comput. Electr. Eng.*, *37*, 6, 1137–1146, 2011.
22. Lu, J. and Moura, J.M., Partition-and-shift LDPC codes. *IEEE Trans. Magn.*, *41*, 10, 2977–2979, 2005.
23. Luo, H., Zhang, Y., Li, W., Huang, L.K., Cosmas, J., Li, D., Zhang, X., Low latency parallel turbo decoding implementation for future terrestrial broadcasting systems. *IEEE Trans. Broadcast.*, *64*, 1, 96–104, 2017.
24. Maier, A.J. and Cockburn, B.F., Optimization of Low-Density Parity Check decoder performance for OpenCL designs synthesized to FPGAs. *J. Parallel Distrib. Comput.*, *107*, 134–145, 2017.
25. Manjunatha, K.N. and Meshram, V.A., Design and FPGA Implementation of Power Efficient Turbo Decoder for 4G LTE Standards. *Int. J. Appl. Eng. Res.*, *12*, 21, 10921–10925, 2017.
26. McEliece, R.J., MacKay, D.J.C., Cheng, J.F., Turbo decoding as an instance of Pearl's belief propagation algorithm. *IEEE J. Sel. Areas Commun.*, *16*, 2, 140–152, 1998.
27. Orten, P. and Svensson, A., Sequential decoding of convolutional codes for Rayleigh fading channels. *Wireless Pers. Commun.*, *20*, 1, 61–74, 2002.
28. Gallager, R.G., Low-density parity-check codes. *IEEE Trans. Inf. Theory*, IT-8, 21–28, Jan. 1962.

29. Gallager, R.G., *Low-Density Parity-Check Codes*, M.I.T. Press, Cambridge, MA, 1963.
30. Salmela, P., Sorokin, H., Takala, J., A programmable Max-Log-MAP turbo decoder implementation. *VLSI Des., 2008*, 1–7, 2008.
31. Stirk, W. and Goeders, J., Implementation and Design Space Exploration of a Turbo Decoder in High-Level Synthesis, in: *2019 International Conference on Reconfigurable Computing and FPGAs (ReConFig)*, 2019, December, IEEE, pp. 1–5.
32. Senthilvelan, M., Yu, M., Iancu, D., Sima, M., Schulte, M., CORDIC instructions for LDPC decoding on SDR platforms. *Analog Integr. Circuits Signal Process.*, *69*, 2–3, 191, 2011.
33. Shahabuddin, S., Janhunen, J., Juntti, M., Ghazi, A., Silvén, O., Design of a transport triggered vector processor for turbo decoding. *Analog Integr. Circuits Signal Process.*, *78*, 3, 611–622, 2014.
34. Tiwari, H.D., Tiwari, H.D., Lee, K.Y., Designing parity check matrix to achieve linear encoding time in LDPC codes. *Digital Signal Process.*, 23, 3, 994–1001, 2013.
35. Richardson, T.J. and Urbanke, R.L., Efficient Encoding of Low-Density Parity-Check Codes. *IEEE Trans. Inf. Theory*, 47, 638–656, February 2001.
36. Wang, Z. and Cui, Z., Low-complexity high-speed decoder design for quasi-cyclic LDPC codes. *IEEE Trans. Very Large Scale Integr. VLSI Syst.*, *15*, 1, 104–114, 2007.
37. Yan, Z., He, G., He, W., Wang, S., Mao, Z., High-performance parallel turbo decoder with configurable interleaving network for LTE application. *Integration*, *52*, 77–90, 2016.
38. Zuo, J., Gui, L., Zhang, H., Shaping Phenomenon and Optimal Design for Irregular LDPC Codes with Specified Block Length. *Wireless Pers. Commun.*, *83*, 1, 653–662, 2015.
39. Paliyal, P.S., Mondal, S., Layek, S., Kuchhal, P., Pandey, J.K., Automatic solar tracking system: a review pertaining to advancements and challenges in the current scenario. *Clean Energy*, 8, 6, 237–262, December 2024, https://doi.org/10.1093/ce/zkae085.
40. Paliyal, P.S., Mondal, S., Pandey, J.K., An Analysis of Springwater Parameter Status for Different Locations in the Rural Hilly Garhwal Region of Uttarakhand. *Environ. Claims J.*, *36*, 3, 243–277, 2024, https://doi.org/10.1080/10406026.2024.2423964.
41. Paliyal, P.S. and Mondal, S., An analysis of a cross-finned receiver for Scheffler-type solar collectors to optimize solar heating efficiency for direct water heating. *Int. J. Energy Water Resour.*, 2025, https://doi.org/10.1007/s42108-025-00393-5.
42. Paliyal, P.S., Mondal, S., Pathela, M., Kumar, A., Menon, S.K., Optimization of Solar Photovoltaic Array In-Depth Analysis of Perturb and Observe MPPT Algorithm. *2024 International Conference on Advances in Computing,*

Communication and Materials (ICACCM), Dehradun, India, pp. 1–6, 2024, doi: 10.1109/ICACCM61117.2024.11059143.

43. Paliyal, P.S., *et al.*, Location Analysis and Environmental Validation for Installation of Hybrid Solar-Wind Energy Generation System in Hilly Areas of Uttarakhand: Study Toward Forecasting, in: *Forecasting Methods for Renewable Power Generation*, pp. 21–47, Wiley, 2025, https://doi.org/10.1002/9781394249466.ch2.
44. Menon, S.K., *et al.*, The Role of Hydrogen as a Sustainable Energy Source and its Integration with the Grid, in: *Advancements in Communication and Systems*, A.K. Tripathi and V. Shrivastava (Eds.), p. 397, Computing and Intelligent Systems, SCRS, India, 2023, (2025).

11

Optimizing Renewable Energy Management with the Use of Digital Twin Technology: Insights from NICE China Energy

Supriya*, Vriti Khandelwal, Kushagar Sharma, Vasu Sharma and Kashish Kalra

COER University, Department of AI & ML, School of Computing, Roorkee, Uttrakhand, India

Abstract

Global sustainability depends on renewable energy, yet high maintenance costs and equipment breakdowns frequently prevent it from reaching its full potential. To monitor, evaluate, and improve energy systems, digital twin (DT) technology uses big data, artificial intelligence (AI), and Internet of Things (IoT) sensors to create a virtual version of a physical system. DTs contribute to decreased downtime and increased operational efficiency by providing real-time tracking and predictive maintenance. The functioning of DTs is the main subject of this study, which employs sensor data and machine learning techniques to identify early indications of equipment wear and failure. These prediction skills are especially useful in hydroelectric plants, wind farms, and solar farms since they guarantee efficient water resource management and sustainable energy production. A case study of the National Institute of Clean and Low-Carbon Energy (NICE) China Energy has been discussed in this article, which improves power plant operations, reduces costs, enhances efficiency, and promotes plant dependability.

***Keywords*:** Renewable energy, Digital Twin, power plant, applications, enabling technologies

**Corresponding author*: supriya@coer.ac.in

Surajit Mondal, Paramjeet Singh Paliyal and Sachin Sharma (eds.) Digital Twin Technology for Solar Concentrators, (179–192) © 2026 Scrivener Publishing LLC

11.1 Introduction

Digital Twins (DT) and industrial digitalization are becoming a potent tool for efficiently managing and streamlining site operations. By incorporating locally produced renewable energy sources, it promotes energy-efficient design, helps reduce particular energy consumption, advances the development of manufacturing processes, and helps create a green energy roadmap. With applications ranging from real-time control, production scheduling and planning, asset maintenance, and technology retrofitting and upgrades, DT technology offers a fundamental shift in the way sites function [1, 2]. The goal is to lower energy usage over a range of time periods and improve the incorporation of renewable energy [3].

A virtual version of a real-world item, procedure, system, or setting is known as a "digital twin". This computerized model, which was developed using data from sensors and other equipment, closely resembles its real-world counterpart, allowing for interactive application in a variety of industries [4].

DT technology stands apart by embodying three key attributes:

- ❖ Looks-like Attribute: Virtual modeling of the physical entity in 1D, 2D, or 3D forms.
- ❖ Behaves-like Attribute: Simulation and prediction of the entity's response to different inputs.
- ❖ Connects-to Attribute: Real-time or automated data flows between physical and digital entities.

NASA's high-fidelity simulations from the Apollo 13 mission served as the inspiration for DT. Since then, it has developed to transform sectors like urban planning, energy management, manufacturing, and healthcare [5, 6].

A DT is a digital thread that documents the progress of its physical counterpart over time, as well as a digital shadow that represents its activities and condition [7]. DTs maximize decision-making, predictive maintenance, operational effectiveness, and product lifecycle management by utilizing AI, IoT, and advanced data technologies [8].

DT technology comprises three components:

- ❖ Physical Entity: The real-world object, system, or process being represented digitally.

- Virtual Representation: The digital counterpart replicating the structure, functions, and conditions of the physical entity.
- Data Connectivity: A bi-directional flow of real-time data that updates the digital model and provides actionable insights to the physical entity.

DTs play a key role in improving resource management and operational effectiveness in the context of renewable energy. Through sophisticated simulations and ongoing monitoring, they revolutionize industries like manufacturing, energy, and industrial operations by providing stakeholders with actionable information [9, 10].

As depicted in Figure 11.1 above, Digital Twin is a real-time, digital representation of a physical system, allowing engineers and researchers to simulate different scenarios, detect faults, and optimize performance [8, 9]. The Digital Twin concept consists of three primary components: the physical asset, the digital model, and the data exchange layer. The physical asset refers to the actual renewable energy system, such as a wind turbine, solar panel, or battery storage unit. The digital model is a virtual representation that mimics the behavior of the physical asset, helping to analyze and predict its performance. The data exchange layer connects the two spaces using IoT sensors and AI-driven analytics to process real-time data [12]. This integration enables industries to make data-driven decisions, predict failures before they occur, and optimize the system for better efficiency and longevity [13].

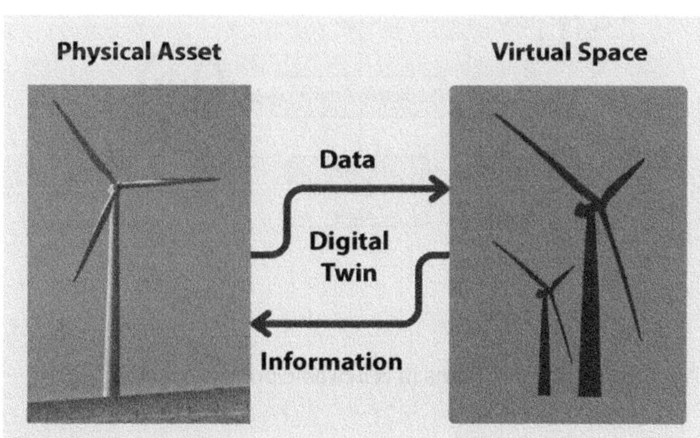

Figure 11.1 Potential of digital twins in renewable power sector.

As depicted in the Figure 11.2, to improve productivity, minimize downtime, and optimize operations, the Digital Twin (DT) system combines virtual modeling, predictive analytics, and real-time data collection. By collecting sensor data, the data collection layer makes proactive problem detection possible and guarantees ongoing monitoring. By acting as a virtual duplicate of the actual system, a digital model enables real-time modifications and efficient use of resources [14, 15]. Through proactive interventions, AI-powered predictive analytics helps detect possible breakdowns early and reduce maintenance costs. Before making modifications to the actual system, operators can lower risks by simulating various operational scenarios through virtual testing. Together, these elements increase productivity, reduce costs, and promote sustainability, which makes DT an essential tool for sectors including manufacturing, infrastructure, and energy [16].

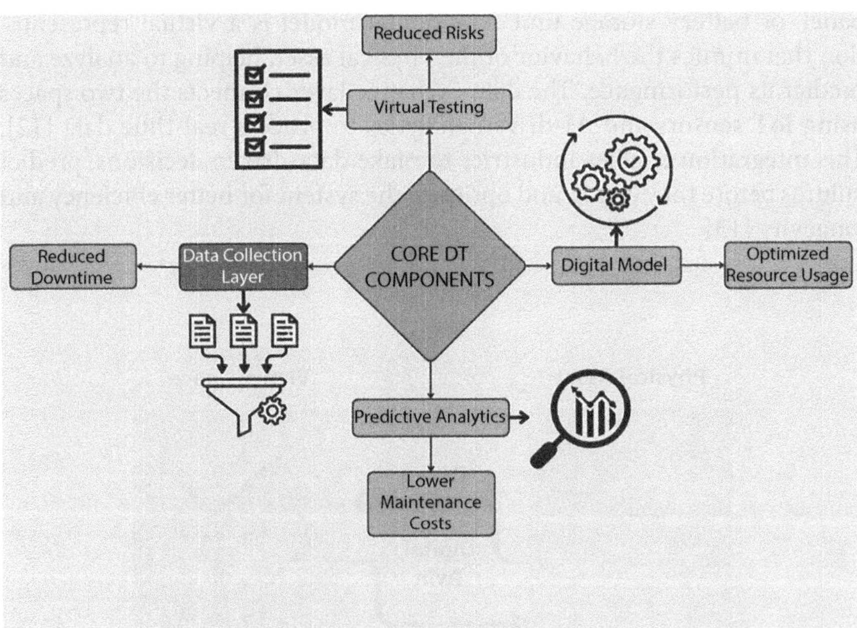

Figure 11.2 Working of Digital Twins in renewable power sector.

11.1.1 Renewable Energy Generation with Digital Twin

Digital Twin (DT) technology, which provides sophisticated modeling, real-time monitoring, and optimization capabilities, is transforming the production of renewable energy. Through these applications, which include solar, wind, and energy storage technologies, stakeholders may save operating costs, increase grid resilience, and improve production efficiency [17].

One of the primary advantages of DT is its predictive maintenance capability, which uses sensor data and machine learning algorithms to detect early signs of equipment wear and failure. For instance:

- ❖ Wind Farms: DTs monitor vibration patterns and identify anomalies indicating gearbox or blade issues.
- ❖ Solar Farms: They track panel efficiency degradation, forecast cleaning schedules, and predict inverter failures to maintain peak operational efficiency.
- ❖ Hydropower Plants: DTs model turbine dynamics and flow rates, ensuring sustainable energy production while managing water resources.

Another important contribution of DTs is the effective management of energy storage. They aid in extending battery life, predicting system performance, and optimizing storage consumption by modeling battery charging and discharging cycles. This improves grid stability by guaranteeing stored energy is available during times of peak demand [18].

In the design phase, DTs enable virtual prototyping and simulations, allowing engineers to:

- ❖ Assess site configurations and evaluate energy production potential.
- ❖ Select optimal locations based on terrain characteristics and weather data.
- ❖ Simulate potential environmental impacts, aiding in regulatory compliance and strategic planning.

By leveraging real-time analytics, DTs assist in resource allocation and operational decision-making, helping operators optimize renewable energy yields and reduce inefficiencies.

11.1.1.1 Wind Energy

Wind energy is one of the most widely used renewable energy sources, but it faces operational challenges due to environmental conditions and mechanical wear and tear. Onshore wind turbines require continuous monitoring to prevent unexpected failures, and Digital Twins play a key role in predicting failures using AI-based algorithms. These models monitor fatigue life consumption, optimize maintenance strategies, and reduce repair costs. Offshore wind turbines operate in more extreme conditions, making maintenance even more challenging. Digital Twin models help by predicting the remaining useful life (RUL) of turbine components, optimizing maintenance schedules, and reducing overall repair costs by over 10%. By using Digital Twins, wind energy operators can increase efficiency and reduce downtime [19].

11.1.1.2 Solar Energy

Solar energy systems require precision in panel positioning and maintenance to maximize energy absorption. Digital Twin technology is used in solar panel manufacturing to improve production quality and predict potential failures based on real-time weather and performance data. AI-powered Digital Twins help optimize solar panel angles to ensure maximum sunlight absorption, leading to higher efficiency and reduced maintenance costs. By integrating IoT sensors, Digital Twins continuously monitor panel conditions and send alerts when performance drops due to dirt accumulation, shading, or technical faults. This real-time monitoring ensures that solar farms operate at peak efficiency with minimal human intervention [20].

11.1.1.3 Marine Renewable Energy (MRE)

Marine energy, including wave and tidal power, has enormous potential but is still in the early stages of development. These systems operate in harsh ocean environments, making real-time monitoring essential. Digital Twins help by tracking the performance of Wave Energy Converters (WECs) and analyzing wave patterns to optimize energy generation. AI-driven fault detection systems compare real-time data with expected performance values to identify anomalies and predict failures. This capability helps operators minimize maintenance costs and improve the reliability of marine renewable energy systems [22].

11.2 Digital Twin in Energy Transmission and Transformation

11.2.1 Power Transformers

Power transformers play a vital role in renewable energy transmission, but failures can lead to costly power outages. Digital Twin models simulate transformer operations, analyze real-time sensor data, and predict failures before they occur. This proactive approach helps reduce downtime, improve grid reliability, and extend the lifespan of transformers [22].

11.2.2 Gas-Insulated Switchgear (GIS)

Gas-insulated switchgear is widely used in high-voltage energy transmission systems. Digital Twins enable real-time remote monitoring, allowing operators to detect potential failures early. AI-driven predictive maintenance models analyze operating conditions and recommend preventive actions, reducing the risk of system failures [23].

11.2.3 Power Cables

Power cables are critical for electricity transmission, and their failure can disrupt energy distribution. Digital Twin models track the condition of power cables using AI-driven analysis of thermal imaging, sensor data, and electrical signals. These models help detect insulation degradation, clamp defects, and overheating issues before they cause significant damage. By integrating Digital Twin technology, power companies can enhance the reliability and safety of their cable networks [24].

11.3 Digital Twin in Renewable Energy Storage Systems

11.3.1 Lithium-Ion Batteries (LIBs)

Lithium-ion batteries are widely used for storing renewable energy, but they degrade over time, reducing their efficiency. Digital Twins track battery degradation, optimize charge-discharge cycles, and predict performance issues before they occur. This real-time monitoring helps extend battery life and improve the reliability of energy storage systems. AI-driven models analyze sensor data to ensure batteries operate within safe parameters, reducing the risk of overheating and failure [25].

11.3.2 Fuel Cells (PEMFC & SOFC)

Fuel cells are used in electric vehicles and power grids, and their efficiency depends on stable operating conditions. Digital Twin models enhance fuel cell performance by monitoring key parameters, predicting maintenance needs, and optimizing energy output. In proton exchange membrane fuel cells (PEMFCs), Digital Twins use AI-driven models to diagnose faults and improve overall efficiency. Similarly, in solid oxide fuel cells (SOFCs), Digital Twins provide real-time insights into operational conditions, helping operators make informed decisions to improve performance [26].

11.4 Advantages and Challenges of Digital Twin Technology

11.4.1 Advantages

Digital Twin technology offers several benefits to the renewable energy sector. It enables real-time monitoring, allowing operators to detect performance issues before they escalate. Predictive maintenance helps prevent unexpected failures, reducing maintenance costs and improving reliability. Digital Twins also optimize energy systems, increasing efficiency and reducing operational expenses. Additionally, they enable remote monitoring, reducing the need for manual inspections and improving worker safety [27].

11.4.2 Challenges

Despite its advantages, Digital Twin technology faces some challenges. Processing vast amounts of sensor data requires high computational power, making it expensive for some organizations. Cybersecurity risks also pose a threat, as Digital Twin systems rely on cloud-based data sharing. Additionally, the lack of a standardized framework for Digital Twin implementation makes integration difficult across different industries. Addressing these challenges will be crucial for the widespread adoption of Digital Twin technology in renewable energy systems [28].

11.5 Case Study: Digital Twin Technology in Power Plant Optimization

11.5.1 Overview

To enhance the efficiency and performance of coal-fired power plants, China Energy's National Institute of Clean and Low-Carbon Energy (NICE) has created a Power Plant Smart Management (PPSM) platform that makes use of digital twin technology. This case study focuses on the use of digital twins in a 320-MWe thermal power plant and the way it affects cost savings and operational improvements. Digital twin technology allows operators to model various operating scenarios, optimize operations, and predict potential system issues before they arise. The digital twin functions as an intelligent control mechanism that enhances plant operations decision-making through real-time monitoring and sophisticated data analytics. Furthermore, its efficacy in examining power generation patterns and spotting chances for long-term optimization is increased by its capacity to combine data from several sources [29].

11.5.2 Key Components of the DT Power Plant

The Digital Twin used by China Energy is a physics-based numerical model that replicates real-world power plant operations, improving efficiency and reliability. Key components include:

- Real-Time Data Integration: Continuous data collection from sensors ensures accurate virtual modeling, enabling operational efficiency and long-term performance insights.
- Predictive Analytics: Uses historical and real-time data to forecast failures, efficiency drops, and maintenance needs, reducing downtime and enhancing asset management.
- Operational Simulation: Enables plant operators to test different scenarios (e.g., fuel mixes, load variations) before implementing changes, optimizing performance and sustainability.
- Fault Detection & Diagnosis: AI-driven diagnostics identify operational anomalies, reducing manual troubleshooting time and improving reliability.

- Grid Flexibility & Load Management: Adjusts power generation in real time to balance grid demands, ensuring smooth integration with renewable energy sources and enhancing grid stability.

This smart system enhances plant efficiency, reliability, and sustainability, making power generation more adaptive and cost-effective.

11.5.3 Key Findings and Benefits of China Energy's Digital Twin Implementation

China Energy's digital twin significantly improved power plant operations, leading to efficiency gains, cost savings, and sustainability benefits [30].

1. **Efficiency Enhancement:** Improved thermal efficiency by optimizing heat transfer, reducing waste heat losses, and fine-tuning steam production. Identified inefficiencies in heat exchangers and adjusted settings for sustained energy efficiency [31].
2. **Fuel Consumption Reduction:** Achieved up to 3.5 g/kWh reduction in coal use by optimizing the boiler's air-fuel ratio and combustion efficiency, cutting carbon emissions and supporting sustainability efforts [32].
3. **Economic Gains:** Fuel efficiency improvements led to annual savings of nearly 4 million RMB per unit, reduced auxiliary power use, and extended equipment lifespan, lowering replacement costs [33].
4. **Seasonal Performance Adjustments:** Digital twin simulations optimized performance for summer (electricity-only) and winter (combined heat and power) operations, ensuring stable functioning under varying demand [34].
5. **Emission Control:** Real-time monitoring and optimized fuel combustion helped reduce NOx, SO_2, and CO_2 emissions, ensuring compliance with environmental regulations and supporting corporate sustainability goals [35].

Overall, the digital twin improved efficiency, cost-effectiveness, and environmental responsibility, reinforcing its role as a valuable tool in modern photovoltaic system optimization and sustainable energy management.

11.6 Conclusion

The digital twin strengthened its position as a vital tool in contemporary sustainability by increasing productivity, cost-effectiveness, and environmental responsibility [36]. A case study illustrates the National Institute of Clean and Low-Carbon Energy (NICE) China Energy's power plant operations have evolved as a result of digital twin technology [37]. Digital twins facilitate substantial cost reductions and operational enhancements by offering real-time performance tracking, predictive maintenance information, and improved decision-making capabilities [38]. Beyond increasing efficiency, the advantages also include boosting plant dependability, advancing environmental objectives, and boosting financial results. It may be concluded that digital twins are set to become even more important in power plant management as artificial intelligence and machine learning continue to progress, influencing the direction of sustainability and energy efficiency in the future [39].

AI disclosure statement: The author confirms that no artificial intelligence (AI)-generated content or AI-assisted writing tools were used in the preparation of this chapter (including summaries and the abstract). All text, analysis, and conclusions are the result of the author's original work.

Bibliography

1. Lee, C.-H., Thanh, P.N., Yeh, C.-T., Cho, M.-Y., Three-Phase Load Prediction-Based Hybrid Convolution Neural Network Combined Bidirectional Long Short-Term Memory in Solar Power Plant. *Int. Trans. Electr. Energy Syst.*, 2022, Article ID 2870668, 15, 2022, https://doi.org/10.1155/2022/2870668.
2. Wu, L., Kong, C., Hao, X., Chen, W., A Short-Term Load Forecasting Method Based on GRU-CNN Hybrid Neural Network Model. *Math. Probl. Eng.*, 2020, Article ID 1428104, 10, 2020, https://doi.org/10.1155/2020/1428104.
3. de Freitas Viscondi, G. and Alves-Souza, S.N., A Systematic Literature Review on big data for solar photovoltaic electricity generation forecasting. *Sustainable Energy Technol. Assess.*, 31, 54–63, 2019. ISSN 2213-1388,https://doi.org/10.1016/j.seta.2018.11.008.
4. Ozbek, A., Yildirim, A., Bilgili, M., Deep learning approach for one-hour ahead forecasting of energy production in a solar-PV plant. *Energy Sources Part A*, 44, 4, 10465–10480, 2022. DOI: 10.1080/15567036.2021.1924316.
5. Prasad, S.S., Deo, R.C., Downs, N., Igoe, D., Parisi, A.V., Soar, J., Cloud Affected Solar UV Prediction with Three-Phase Wavelet Hybrid Convolutional Long

Short-Term Memory Network Multi-Step Forecast System. *IEEE Access*, 10, 24704–24720, 2022, doi: 10.1109/ACCESS.2022.3153475.

6. Kalaiselvi, B., Karthik, B., Kumaravel, A., Variant Mode Data Analytics in Predicting the Radiation Effect on Solar Power Generation using Machine Learning Algorithms. *2022 IEEE International Conference on Data Science and Information System (ICDSIS)*, Hassan, India, pp. 1–6, 2022, doi: 10.1109/ICDSIS55133.2022.9915814.
7. Tang, L., Weiqi, H., Ashtine, M., Wallom, D., Distributed Photovoltaic System Capacity Estimation Using Feeder Load Data Based on Deep Learning. Available at SSRN: https://ssrn.com/abstract=4442265 or http://dx.doi.org/10.2139 /ssrn. 4442265.
8. Ciabattoni, L., Grisostomi, M., Ippoliti, G., Longhi, S., Fuzzy logic home energy consumption modeling for residential photovoltaic plant sizing in the new Italianscenario. *Energy*, 74, 359–367, 2014. ISSN0360-442 https://doi.org/10.1016/ j.energy.2014.06.100.
9. Ghimire, S., Nguyen-Huy, T., Prasad, R., *et al.*, Hybrid Convolutional Neural Network-Multilayer Perceptron Model for Solar Radiation Prediction. *Cognit. Comput.*, 15, 645–671, 2023, https://doi.org/10.1007/s12559-022-10070-y.
10. Pazikadin, A.R., Rifai, D., Ali, K., Malik, M.Z., Abdalla, A.N., Faraj, M.A., Solar irradiance measurement instrumentation and power solar generation forecasting based on Artificial Neural Networks (ANN): A review of five years research trend. *Sci. Total Environ.*, 715, 136848, 2020. ISSN:0048-9697, https://doi.org/10.1016/j.scitotenv.2020.136848.
11. Das, S., Mandal, A., Saha, S., Soiling detection of solar panels using a transfer learning approach. *J. Renewable Energy*, 183, 1388–1397, 2023, doi: 10.1016/j.renene.2023.01.117.
12. Yadav, A., Singh, S., Kumar, P., A hybrid approach for soiling classification on solar PV panels in India. *J. Cleaner Prod.*, 348, 129827, 2023, doi: 10.1016/j.jclepro.2023.129827.
13. Mishra, A.K., Mishra, R.K., Mishra, S.K., A machine learning approach for soiling detection in solar photovoltaic systems. *Sol. Energy*, 211, 122251, 2023.
14. Singh, S., Srivastava, S., Kumar, P., A deep learning approach for soiling classification on solar PV panels in India. *Renewable Energy*, 186, 1425–1434, 2023, doi: 10.1016/j.renene.2023.02.059.
15. Zhang, W., Liu, S., Srinivasan, G., A deep learning-based probabilistic estimation of solar PV soiling loss. *Prog. Photovoltaics Res. Appl.*, 1–7, 2023.
16. Chen, Y., Zhang, C., Zhang, Y., A transformer-based approach for solar photovoltaic panel soiling classification. *Appl. Energy*, 267, 115287, 2022.
17. Li, Q., Zhang, C., Zhang, Y., A convolutional neural network with transfer learning for solar photovoltaic panel soiling classification. *Sol. Energy*, 228, 1308–1319, 2022.

18. Zhang, Y., Zhang, C., Li, J., A deep learning approach for solar photovoltaic panel soiling detection based on multi-scale features. *IEEE Access*, 10, 168289–168300, 2022.
19. Kim, J., Kim, H., Lee, S., Soiling classification of solar panel using deep learning. *Energy Rep.*, 7, 1015–1022, 2022, doi: 10.1016/j.egyr.2021.101510.
20. Mishra, A.K., Mishra, R.K., Mishra, S.K., A machine learning approach for soiling prediction in solar photovoltaic systems. *Sol. Energy*, 210, 122241, 2022.
21. Al-Ghamdi, N.M., Abdelfattah, A.M.A., Abdelkareem, M.A.M., A novel soiling mitigation technique using nanoparticles for solar photovoltaic systems in desert regions. *Sol. Energy Mater. Sol. Cells*, 230, 111297, 2022.
22. Liu, Y., Wang, W., Zhang, Y., Zhang, C., A convolutional neural network with attention mechanism for solar photovoltaic panel soiling classification. *IEEE Access*, 10, 154441–154450, 2022.
23. Yang, Y., Zhang, C., Zhang, Y., A generative adversarial network approach for solar photovoltaic panel soiling detection. *Appl. Energy*, 278, 115484, 2022.
24. Sharma, A., Singh, R.K., Kumar, A., A review of solar PV analyser tools and techniques. *Int. J. Renewable Energy Res.*, 12, 3, 2345–2354, 2022.
25. Li, H., Zhang, Y., Wang, J., Chen, Y., A hybrid forecasting model for renewable energy based on support vector machine and recurrent neural network. *Energy*, 249, 123732, 2022.
26. Sharma, V., Chaurasia, P., Sharma, G., Performance evaluation of support vector machine for photovoltaic power generation forecasting. *Mater. Today: Proc.*, 55, 41–46, 2022.
27. Li, Y., Chen, X., Wang, J., Application of random forest regression for short-term wind speed forecasting based on empirical mode decomposition and chaotic dynamic reconstruction. *Renewable Energy*, 189, 914–926, 2022, doi: 10.1016/j.renene.2022.05.187.
28. Zhao, Y., Zhang, J., Ren, Y., Wang, W., Guo, Z., A hybrid model based on random forest and convolutional neural network for short-term solar power forecasting. *Energy Convers. Manage.*, 267, 115944, 2022, doi: 10.1016/j.enconman.2022.115944.
29. Pachauri, R.K., Imperative role of optimization techniques to reconfigure solar photovoltaic array systems to diminish shading effects. *Int. J. Circuit Theory Appl.*, 50, 1, 317–353, 2022.
30. Pachauri, R.K., Pandey, J.K., Sharmu, A., Nautiyal, O.P., Ram, M. (Eds.), *Applied Soft Computing and Embedded System Applications in Solar Energy*, CRC Press, 2021.
31. Paliyal, P.S., Mondal, S., Layek, S., Kuchhal, P., Pandey, J.K., Automatic solar tracking system: a review pertaining to advancements and challenges in the current scenario. *Clean Energy*, 8, 6, 237–262, December 2024, https://doi.org/10.1093/ce/zkae085.

32. Paliyal, P.S., Mondal, S., Pandey, J.K., An Analysis of Springwater Parameter Status for Different Locations in the Rural Hilly Garhwal Region of Uttarakhand. *Environ. Claims J.*, *36*, 3, 243–277, 2024, https://doi.org/10.1080/10406026.2024.2423964.
33. Paliyal, P.S. and Mondal, S., An analysis of a cross-finned receiver for Scheffler-type solar collectors to optimize solar heating efficiency for direct water heating. *Int. J. Energy Water Resour.*, 2025, https://doi.org/10.1007/s42108-025-00393-5.
34. Paliyal, P.S., Mondal, S., Pathela, M., Kumar, A., Menon, S.K., Optimization of Solar Photovoltaic Array In-Depth Analysis of Perturb and Observe MPPT Algorithm. *2024 International Conference on Advances in Computing, Communication and Materials (ICACCM)*, Dehradun, India, pp. 1–6, 2024, doi: 10.1109/ICACCM61117.2024.11059143.
35. Paliyal, P.S., *et al.*, Location Analysis and Environmental Validation for Installation of Hybrid Solar-Wind Energy Generation System in Hilly Areas of Uttarakhand: Study Toward Forecasting, in: *Forecasting Methods for Renewable Power Generation*, pp. 21–47, 2025.
36. Menon, S.K., *et al.*, The Role of Hydrogen as a Sustainable Energy Source and its Integration with the Grid, in: *Advancements in Communication and Systems*, A.K. Tripathi and V. Shrivastava (Eds.), p. 397, Computing and Intelligent Systems, SCRS, India, 2023, (2025).
37. Kudapa, V.K., Paliyal, P.S., Mondal, A., Mondal, S., A critical review of fabrication strategies, separation techniques, challenges, and future prospects for the hydrogen separation membrane. *Fusion Sci. Technol.*, 80, 7, 803–825, 2024.
38. Mondal, A., Jangirh, R., Arya, R., Yadav, L., Ahlawat, S., Yadav, P., Paliyal, P.S., Bobde, P., Ghosh, P., Mondal, S., Rai, A., Analysing solid residential fuel usage patterns in rural and urban slums of Delhi: Implications for pollution reduction and sustainable practices. *Energy Sustainable Dev.*, *80*, 101460, 2024.
39. Paliyal, P.S., Kuchhal, P., Mondal, S., Nano Lubricants and their Applications, in: *Nanotechnology: A Quick Guide to Materials and Technologies*, pp. 425–456, Bentham Science Publishers, 2024.

12

Enhancing Solar PV Efficiency through a Digital Twin Framework and Machine Learning Models

Nitin Kumar[1]*, Rupendra Kumar Pachauri[2,3] and Piyush Kuchhal[2]

[1]*Department of CSE (AIML), Meerut Institute of Engineering and Technology, Meerut, Uttar Pradesh, India*
[2]*Electrical Cluster, School of Advanced Engineering, University of Petroleum and Energy Studies, Dehradun, Uttarakhand, India*
[3]*Department of Energy, Environment and Climate Change, School of Environmental Resource and Development, Asian Institute of Technology, Pathum Thani, Thailand*

Abstract

This study develops a Digital Twin for solar power forecasting using an ANN model, aiming to accurately simulate the behavior of a 20W solar panel. The model was trained and evaluated across three datasets: training, validation, and testing, with performance metrics such as Mean Squared Error (MSE) and correlation coefficient (R) used to assess its effectiveness. The results show that the training set achieved an MSE of 8.1715 and an R of 0.9994, the validation set achieved an MSE of 6.8499 and an R of 0.9995, and the test set achieved an MSE of 8.9045 and an R of 0.9994. These metrics indicate strong predictive accuracy across all datasets. The model successfully replicates the power generation behavior of the solar panel, providing reliable forecasts for both seen and unseen data. The model's ability to predict solar power output accurately suggests its potential for real-time monitoring, system optimization, and performance prediction, making it a promising tool for enhancing solar panel operations and efficiency. Through this Digital Twin approach, solar power systems can be better understood, maintained, and optimized, supporting the broader adoption of sustainable energy technologies.

**Corresponding author*: nitindabra.kumar@gmail.com

Surajit Mondal, Paramjeet Singh Paliyal and Sachin Sharma (eds.) Digital Twin Technology for Solar Concentrators, (193–206) © 2026 Scrivener Publishing LLC

Keywords: Solar photovoltaic technology, machine learning, power performance, efficiency enhancement

12.1 Introduction

Renewable energy plays a pivotal role in the ongoing global transition to a sustainable energy future [1]. As the world faces increasing energy demands alongside the challenges of climate change, solar energy emerges as a key player in decarbonizing the energy sector [2]. The transformative potential of renewable energy, particularly solar power, is evident in its growing contribution to reducing greenhouse gas emissions and enhancing energy security [3, 4]. According to a recent study, solar energy is becoming an indispensable part of the global energy mix, with significant advancements in solar technologies enabling higher efficiency and widespread adoption [5].

The worldwide initiative for sustainable energy solutions has rendered photovoltaic (PV) systems vital to renewable energy initiatives [6]. Solar energy, captured *via* photovoltaic systems, directly transforms sunlight into electricity, offering an environmentally friendly alternative to traditional energy sources and significantly reducing greenhouse gas emissions [7]. The advancement of solar energy technology has experienced significant growth over the past several decades, driven by improvements in materials, efficiency, and cost-effectiveness, resulting in widespread acceptance. Advancements in photovoltaic materials, including the development of perovskite and organic solar cells, have enhanced solar panel efficiency, while reduced manufacturing costs have rendered solar electricity more accessible and economically feasible.

Moreover, numerous researches have investigated the enhancement of photovoltaic (PV) system performance using nano-coatings for heat resistance [8], air-cooling methods to lower module temperatures [9], and optimal glazing technologies to augment the thermodynamic effectiveness of PV systems [10]. Moreover, the integration of solar energy with energy storage and smart grid technologies has enhanced its scalability and reliability while maintaining economic viability [10, 11]. Notwithstanding these developments, the performance, reliability, and efficiency of photovoltaics are affected by multiple factors, including ambient conditions, system design, and operational techniques [12]. Advanced simulation and Modeling approaches are necessary for optimizing these systems.

Solar irradiance forecasting is essential for solar PV forecasting as it predicts the amount of solar energy available for conversion into electricity. This is crucial for optimizing energy production and grid management, as accurate solar irradiance forecasts allow operators to plan more effectively. By analyzing historical data and real-time inputs, machine learning algorithms enhance solar PV forecasting by providing precise energy output predictions [13]. These models can adapt to shifting weather patterns and varying grid conditions, improving forecast accuracy. Weather forecasting, which provides key data on factors like cloud cover, temperature, and other meteorological conditions, is also vital for solar PV forecasting. Accurate weather forecasts help anticipate changes in energy output, enabling operators to adjust grid management strategies and reduce uncertainty [14]. Lastly, solar PV power forecasting models, built on mathematical algorithms, predict energy output based on historical data and weather forecasts. These models serve as the foundation for reliable energy predictions, allowing solar PV operators to optimize grid management, improve energy trading strategies, and reduce forecasting errors, thus maximizing operational efficiency and revenue [15, 16].

A Digital Twin for solar power forecasting creates a virtual model of a physical solar power system, allowing for the simulation, prediction, and optimization of its performance in real time. By combining data from solar panels, environmental factors like temperature, irradiance, wind speed, and weather forecasts, the Digital Twin continually updates its predictions about solar energy production [17]. This system can estimate energy output, assess panel efficiency, and predict future performance, offering a detailed view of energy generation. It can also provide insights into the health of the solar setup, detect potential issues, and enable predictive maintenance to prevent system failures. With such capabilities, a Digital Twin helps enhance the efficiency and reliability of solar power systems, contributing to better energy management and seamless integration with power grids [18].

12.2 Literature Review

Digital Twin technology has recently emerged as a revolutionary approach in Modeling and simulation. A Digital Twin is a continuously updated, implicit clone of a physical system that uses advanced analytical models to simulate, forecast, and optimize performance. Originally created for manufacturing, Digital Twin technology is currently utilized across diverse sectors, including renewable energy [19, 20]. Digital Twin technology for photovoltaic systems presents various advantages, offering a dynamic, real-time platform for monitoring, predictive maintenance, fault diagnosis, and optimization [21].

Digital Twins provide accurate analysis and control by integrating high-fidelity simulation models with real-time operational data, thereby markedly improving the reliability and efficiency of photovoltaic installations [22]. Wang *et al.* [23] developed a Digital Twin model to ascertain the maximum power points of photovoltaic systems, employing artificial intelligence to enhance precision and rectify inconsistencies between actual situations and simulated surroundings. Li and Tan [24] created a system employing Digital Twin Modeling to integrate solar power resources in smart cities, illustrating how virtual representations of the power grid can enhance urban energy management. Various scholars have achieved more breakthroughs in Digital Twin Modeling for photovoltaic systems. Zhang and Wang [25] utilized hybrid neural networks in Digital Twin models, improving the accuracy of photovoltaic power-voltage characteristic simulations. Carr *et al.* [26] examined the thermal characteristics of vertical photovoltaic systems with Digital Twin models, enhancing system design and performance by refined thermal Modeling. Bazakas *et al.* [27] utilized deep learning methodologies to create Digital Twin models that forecast photovoltaic power output, hence facilitating dependable operation and maintenance *via* precise real-time power generation simulations.

Another study demonstrated the efficacy of Digital Twins for identifying problems in distributed photovoltaic systems by integrating simulation and experimental validation [28, 29]. A study examined the use of digital twins in conjunction with machine learning algorithms to optimize the operational performance of solar plant facilities, enabling enhanced performance monitoring and error identification [30]. A Digital Twin model that integrates blockchain and Internet of Things (IoT) technologies to optimize the operation of photovoltaic-based microgrids, therefore advancing smart grid applications and decentralized energy management [31–33].

12.3 Experimental Location and Methodology

Figure 12.1 illustrates the experimental configuration for this study, comprising a 20 W prototype on-grid photovoltaic (PV) system located on the grounds of UPES, Dehradun, India (Latitude 30.34 N, Longitude 78.0322° E). Table 12.1 shows the data acquisition system specification details. This study expands the focus by analyzing energy collection over an extended period to comprehensively assess the system's real-time monitoring capabilities, efficiency in integrating energy into the utility grid, and total annual energy yield. A data collecting system is utilized for a real-time monitoring

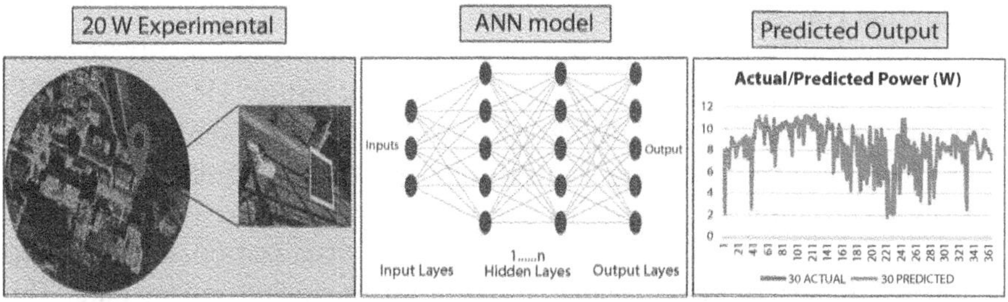

Figure 12.1 Representation of on grid 20 W solar PV energy system.

Table 12.1 Technical parameters used and specification of sensors.

Characteristic	Value
Geographical coordinates	30°34′42″N 78°01′322″E
Tilt angle	30°
Number of PV modules	1
Maximum power	20 W
Peak power current	1.12 A
Peak power voltage	21 V
Short-circuit current	1.16 A
Open-circuit voltage	18 V
Number of cells	36
Orientation	South
Voltage sensor	Range: 0.02445 - 120 V (DC)
Current Sensor	Range: 0.01 - 20A (DC)
Temperature Sensor	Range: up to 125 °C
DHT Sensor	Range: 0 – 50 °C
Solar Radiation sensor	Range up to 1200 w/m2
MATLAB	R2023b

system that tracks various electrical and environmental parameters within the photovoltaic setup. The monitoring system comprises sensors for solar irradiance, ambient temperature, module temperature, DC voltage, DC current, and both DC and AC power production. The sensors are connected to a centralized data acquisition hub that integrates wired and wireless communication systems for remote access and real-time data updates. The data acquisition hub facilitates the visualization, analysis, and reporting of system performance, in addition to storing sensor data. The study's contributions finally demonstrate that comprehensive system specifications and real-time data integration are crucial elements that enable the development of a robust Digital Twin model. This approach improves performance, facilitates the efficient incorporation of renewable energy into the utility grid, and enables a deeper comprehension of photovoltaic system dynamics.

Figure 12.2 outlines the stages involved in creating a Digital Twin for Solar PV Systems, beginning with Data Collection, where key data such as solar power output, weather conditions, temperature, and irradiance are gathered. In the Digital Twin Model Development phase, either a data-driven or physics-based model is constructed to replicate the system's behavior. Data Preprocessing follows, where the collected data is cleaned and normalized for further analysis. Next, in the Machine Learning Model Development phase, models are built to predict power output and detect faults, utilizing regression and classification techniques. The Training and

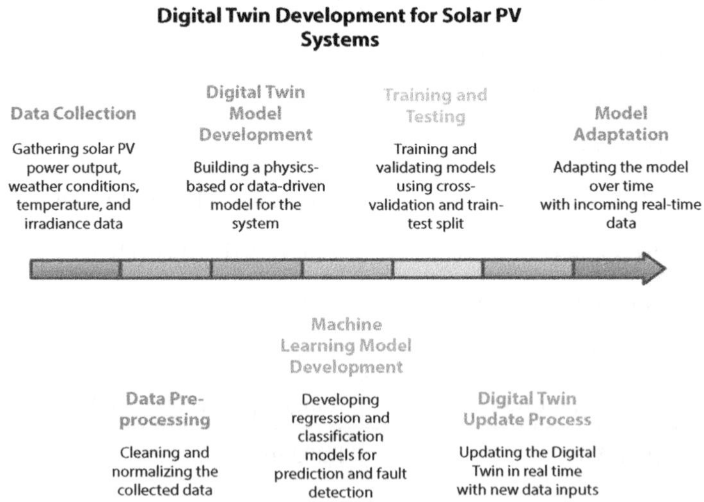

Figure 12.2 Methodology of Digital Twin development for solar PV system.

Testing stage ensures that these models are validated through methods like cross-validation and splitting the data into training and test sets. During the Model Adaptation phase, the model is updated continuously using incoming real-time data. Lastly, the Digital Twin Update Process maintains the model's relevance by incorporating new data inputs, ensuring that the digital representation stays accurate over time.

12.4 Result and Discussion

Figure 12.3 (a) presents a series of four scatter plots used to evaluate the performance of a predictive model. Each plot compares the model's predicted outputs (represented by data points) against the true target values. The plots feature a fitted regression line (blue), which approximates the relationship between the anticipated and actual values, accompanied by a dashed reference line ("Y = T") representing perfect alignment. The slight positive offsets in the fitted lines (+0.076, +0.056, +0.1, +0.05) suggest a small, consistent overestimation of the target values by the model. However, the closeness of the data points to the fitted line in all four plots indicates a high level of accuracy in the model's predictions, with minimal bias. These results demonstrate the model's robustness and reliability, as the predictions are closely aligned with the actual data, making it a suitable candidate for real-world applications.

Mean Squared Error (MSE) progression during the training of an ANN model in Figure 12.3 (b) across 237 epochs for three datasets: Training (blue), Validation (green), and Test (red). Initially, the MSE for the training

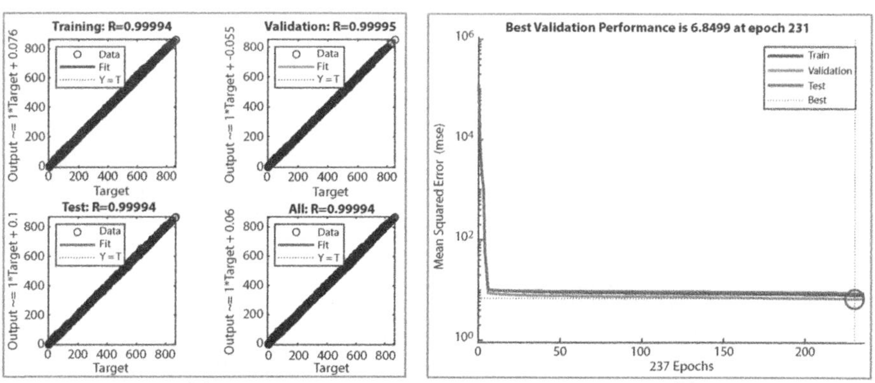

(a) (b)

Figure 12.3 (a) ANN regression, (b) performance of ANN.

set drops rapidly, indicating quick learning, and then stabilizes as the model reaches optimal performance on the training data. The validation and test sets show similar patterns but with slightly higher MSE, suggesting that the model generalizes well without overfitting. The marker near the end of the graph highlights the point of optimal performance, where the model achieves its best accuracy, reflecting successful learning and generalization across both seen and unseen data.

The histogram in Figure 12.4 (a) shows the distribution of error instances across the Training (blue), Validation (green), and Test (red) datasets, with a distinct emphasis on Zero Error instances. The training set shows a high concentration of instances with low or zero error, indicating good model performance. The validation and test sets also show some instances with zero error but with a wider spread, suggesting that the model performs slightly worse on unseen data. Overall, the model demonstrates good generalization, with slightly more error in the validation and test datasets, which is typical for real-world applications.

The graph depicts the comparison between actual and forecasted solar power output (in watts) over a period of one year. The blue line represents the actual power output, which fluctuates between 4W and 12W throughout the time span, reflecting the typical variability in solar power generation. The orange line represents the predicted power output by the model, which closely follows the actual power values, indicating that the model accurately forecasts the power generation over time. However, slight deviations can be observed, particularly during higher or lower power output periods, where the predicted values tend to overestimate or underestimate the actual values. These fluctuations show that the model performs well, but small prediction errors are expected in real-world scenarios.

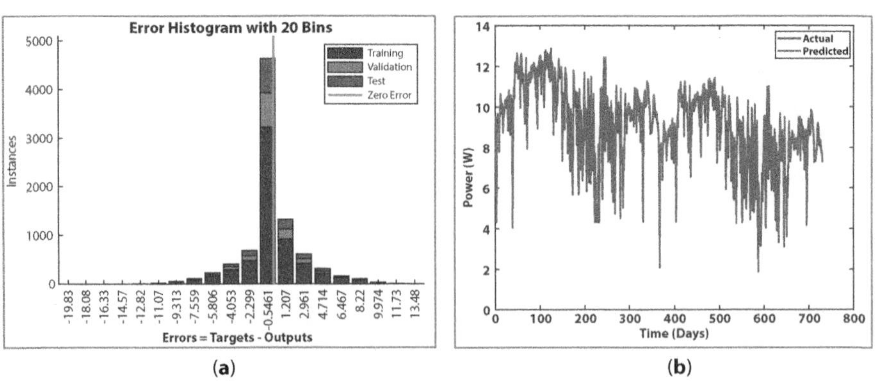

Figure 12.4 (a) Error histogram, (b) actual and predicted.

Figure 12.5 displays the training process of an ANN model over 237 epochs, with three key metrics being tracked: gradient, mu, and validation failure. The top plot shows a rapid decrease in the gradient at the start of the training, indicating quick learning, which slows down as the model converges. The middle plot shows fluctuations in the mu value, stabilizing after a few epochs, indicating adjustments to learning parameters that help optimize the model. The bottom plot illustrates validation failures, which initially remain low but rise sharply towards the end of training, suggesting potential overfitting or generalization issues. This indicates that while the model performs well initially, it may struggle with unseen data, highlighting the need for further tuning or regularization.

Table 12.2 presents the performance metrics of a predictive model across three datasets: Training, Validation, and Test. The Training set has 6132 observations with an MSE of 8.1715 and a correlation coefficient (R) of 0.9994, indicating strong model performance with minimal error. The Validation set shows slightly better results with an MSE of 6.8499 and an R of 0.9995, suggesting that the model generalizes well to unseen data.

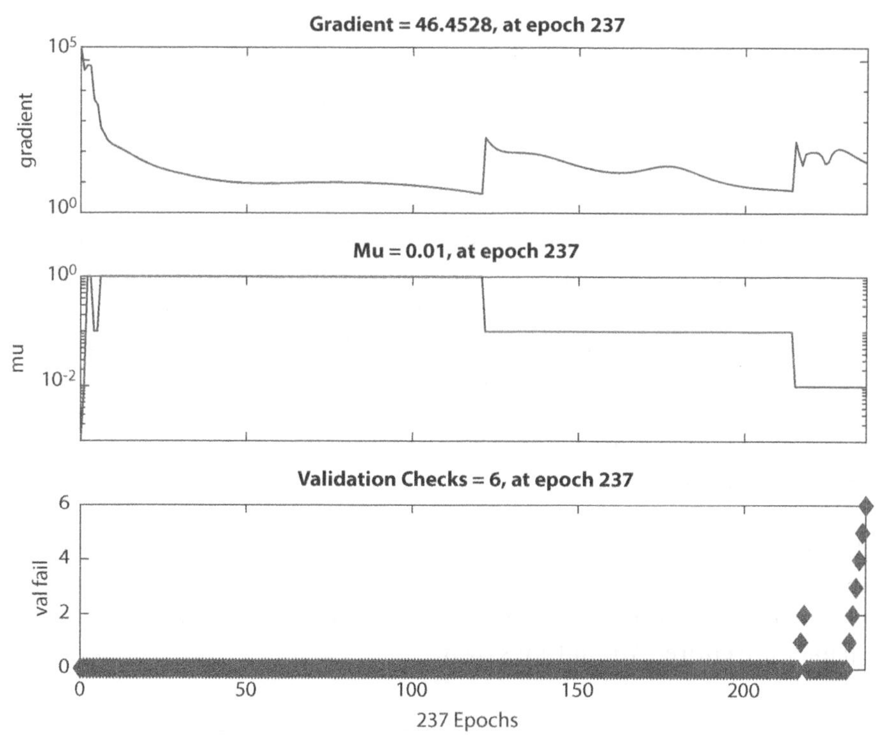

Figure 12.5 Training process of an ANN model.

Table 12.2 Performance metrics.

State	Observations	MSE	R
Training	6132	8.1715	0.9994
Validation	1314	6.8499	0.9995
Test	1314	8.9045	0.9994

The Test set has an MSE of 8.9045 and an R of 0.9994, reflecting a similarly high level of accuracy but slightly higher error compared to the validation set. Overall, the model demonstrates excellent predictive ability with very high correlation and low error across all datasets, though there is a slight overfitting tendency to the training data.

12.5 Conclusion

The model exhibits excellent performance across training, validation, and test datasets, demonstrating its effectiveness as a Digital Twin for solar power forecasting. The Mean Squared Error (MSE) and R-values demonstrate robust predictive accuracy, characterized by minimal error and a high correlation between projected and actual values. The training set yields minimal error, and the model demonstrates strong performance on both the validation and test datasets, albeit with a minor increase in error on the latter. This is typical for real-world systems and does not detract from the model's overall ability to generalize effectively. The model's ability to mirror the behavior of the solar panel system, as indicated by the scatter plots and histogram, confirms its capability to provide accurate, real-time predictions for solar power output. These results suggest that the model is a reliable tool for monitoring and optimizing the performance of the solar panel system, making it a promising solution for implementing a Digital Twin that can simulate, predict, and enhance system operations.

AI disclosure statement: The author acknowledges the use of AI-based tools for minor language editing or grammatical correction. However, all intellectual contributions, analyses, and conclusions presented in this chapter are entirely the author's own.

References

1. Hassan, Q., Viktor, P., Al-Musawi, T.J., Mahmood Ali, B., Algburi, S., Alzoubi, H.M., *et al.*, The renewable energy role in the global energy transformations. *Renewable Energy Focus*, 48, 100545, 2024, https://doi.org/10.1016/j.ref.2024.100545.
2. Kumar, N., Pachauri, R.K., Kuchhal, P., Nkenyereye, L., Floating photovoltaic system based electrical power generation study in Indian context. *Renewable Sustainable Energy Rev.*, 212, 115442, 2025. ISSN 1364-0321, https://doi.org/10.1016/j.rser.2025.115442.
3. Tawalbeh, M., Al-Othman, A., Kafiah, F., Abdelsalam, E., Almomani, F., Alkasrawi, M., Environmental impacts of solar photovoltaic systems: a critical review of recent progress and future outlook. *Sci. Total Environ.*, 759, 143528, 2021, https://doi.org/10.1016/j.scitotenv.2020.143528.
4. Obaideen, K., Nooman AlMallahi, M., Alami, A.H., Ramadan, M., Abdelkareem, M.A., Shehata, N., *et al.*, On the contribution of solar energy to sustainable developments goals: case study on Mohammed bin Rashid Al Maktoum Solar Park. *Int. J. Thermofluids*, 12, 100123, 2021, https://doi.org/10.1016/j.ijft.2021.100123.
5. Dada, M. and Popoola, P., Recent advances in solar photovoltaic materials and systems for energy storage applications: a review. *Beni-Suef Univ. J. Basic Appl. Sci.*, 12, 66, 2023, https://doi.org/10.1186/s43088-023-00405-5.
6. Saxena, A., Kumar, R., Sagade, A.A., Singh, D.B., Tyagi, V.V., Cuce, E., *et al.*, A state-of art review on photovoltaic systems: design, performance, and progress. *Process Saf. Environ. Prot.*, 190, 1324–1354, 2024, https://doi.org/10.1016/j psep.2024.07.111.
7. Machín, A. and Márquez, F., Advancements in photovoltaic cell materials: silicon, organic, and perovskite solar cells. *Materials (Basel)*, 17, 1165, 2024, https://doi. org/10.3390/ma17051165.
8. Kumar, N., Gupta, V., Sharma, P., Akter, K., Gupta, A.K., Pachauri, R.K., Machine Learning-Based Forecasting of Global Horizontal Irradiance for Solar Energy Applications, in: *International Conference on Power Engineering and Intelligent Systems (PEIS)*, pp. 395–409, Springer Nature Singapore, Singapore, 2025, March.
9. Cuce, E. and Cuce, P.M., Improving thermodynamic performance parameters of silicon photovoltaic cells *via* air cooling. *Int. J. Ambient Energy*, 35, 193–199, 2014, https://doi.org/10.1080/01430750.2013.793481.
10. Cuce, E. and Cuce, P.M., Optimised performance of a thermally resistive PV glazing technology: an experimental validation. *Energy Rep.*, 5, 1185–1195, 2019, https://doi.org/10.1016/j.egyr.2019.08.046.
11. Kumar, N., Pachauri, R.K., Kuchhal, P., Akter, K., Alotaibi, M.A., Malik, H., Performance analysis of floating and ground-mounted photovoltaic systems: An experimental study. *Solar Energy*, 302, 113989, 2025.

12. Farag, M.M., Hamid, A.-K., AlMallahi, M.N., Elgendi, M., Towards highly efficient solar photovoltaic thermal cooling by waste heat utilization: a review. *Energy Convers. Manage.: X*, 23, 100671, 2024, https://doi.org/10.1016/j.ecmx.2024.100671.
13. Abdulla, H., Sleptchenko, A., Nayfeh, A., Photovoltaic systems operation and maintenance: a review and future directions. *Renewable Sustainable Energy Rev.*, 195, 114342, 2024, https://doi.org/10.1016/j.rser.2024.114342.
14. Farag, M.M., Patel, N., Hamid, A.-K., Adam, A.A., Bansal, R.C., Bettayeb, M., *et al.*, An optimized fractional nonlinear synergic controller for maximum power point tracking of photovoltaic array under abrupt irradiance change. *IEEE J. Photovoltaics*, 13, 305–314, 2023, https://doi.org/10.1109/JPHOTOV.2023.3236808.
15. Samy, M.M., Almamlook, R.E., Elkhouly, H.I., Barakat, S., Decision-making and optimal design of green energy system based on statistical methods and artificial neural network approaches. *Sustainable Cities Soc.*, 84, 104015, 2022, https://doi. org/10.1016/j.scs.2022.104015.
16. Kavousi-Fard, A., Dabbaghjamanesh, M., Jafari, M., Fotuhi-Firuzabad, M., Dong, Z.Y., Jin, T., Digital twin for mitigating solar energy resources challenges: a Perspective. *Sol. Energy*, 274, 112561, 2024, https://doi.org/10.1016/j.solener.2024.112561.
17. Madni, A.M., Madni, C.C., Lucero, S.D., Leveraging digital twin technology in model based systems engineering. *Systems (Basel)*, 7, 7, 2019, https://doi.org/10.3390/ systems7010007.
18. Ismail, F.B., Al-Faiz, H., Hasini, H., Al-Bazi, A., Kazem, H.A., A comprehensive review of the dynamic applications of the digital twin technology across diverse energy sectors. *Energy Strategy Rev.*, 52, 101334, 2024, https://doi.org/10.1016/j. esr.2024.101334.
19. Alao, K.T., Gilani, S.I.U.H., Sopian, K., Alao, T.O., A review on digital twin application in photovoltaic energy systems: challenges and opportunities. *JMST Adv.*, 6, 257–282, 2024, https://doi.org/10.1007/s42791-024-00083-z.
20. Lüer, L., Peters, I.M., Smith, A.S., Dorschky, E., Eskofier, B.M., Liers, F., *et al.*, A digital twin to overcome long-time challenge.
21. Yuan, J., Ma, J., Tian, Z., Man, K.L., Digital twin integration with data fusion for enhanced photovoltaic system management: a systematic literature review. *IEEE Open J. Power Electron.*, 5, 1045–1058, 2024, https://doi.org/10.1109/ OJPEL.2024.3422021.
22. Angelova, D.D., Fernández, D.C., Godoy, M.C., Moreno, JAA., González, J.F.G., A review on digital twins and its application in the modeling of photovoltaic installations. *Energies (Basel)*, 17, 1227, 2024, https://doi.org/10.3390/en17051227.
23. Kumar, N., Shukla, A., Sharma, P., Gupta, U.C., Pachauri, R.K., Forecasting of Global Solar Irradiance and Optimal Tilt Angle: Machine Learning Approaches. *2024 Conference on Renewable Energy Technologies and Modern*

Communications Systems: Future and Challenges, Shaqra, Saudi Arabia, pp. 1–6, 2024, doi: 10.1109/IEEECONF63577.2024.10880951.

24. Singh, K., Kumar, P., Rathi, V., Kumar, T., Pandey, R.K., Kanjilal, D., Kumar, A., Impact of swift heavy oxygen ion irradiation on the performance of Pt/GaN Schottky diodes and epitaxial layers: A comparative study. *J. Appl. Phys.*, *134*, 16, 2023.
25. Singh, K., Batra, Y., Rathi, V., Kumar, P., Kanjilal, D., Kumar, T., Kumar, A., Ion-induced transformation of shallow defects into deep-level defects in GaN epilayers. *Nucl. Instrum. Methods Phys. Res., Sect. B*, 552, 165362, 2024.
26. Shukla, A., Pachauri, R.K., Gupta, U.C., Gupta, A.K., Kumar, N., Solar PV Power Generation Prediction Using Machine Learning Algorithms at Different Tilt Angles. *2024 Conference on Renewable Energy Technologies and Modern Communications Systems: Future and Challenges*, Shaqra, Saudi Arabia, pp. 1–6, 2024, doi: 10.1109/IEEECONF63577.2024.10881337.
27. Paliyal, P.S., Mondal, S., Layek, S., Kuchhal, P., Pandey, J.K., Automatic solar tracking system: a review pertaining to advancements and challenges in the current scenario. *Clean Energy*, 8, 6, 237–262, December 2024, https://doi.org/10.1093/ce/zkae085.
28. Paliyal, P.S., Mondal, S., Pandey, J.K., An Analysis of Springwater Parameter Status for Different Locations in the Rural Hilly Garhwal Region of Uttarakhand. *Environ. Claims J.*, *36*, 3, 243–277, 2024, https://doi.org/10.1080/10406026.2024.2423964.
29. Paliyal, P.S. and Mondal, S., An analysis of a cross-finned receiver for Scheffler-type solar collectors to optimize solar heating efficiency for direct water heating. *Int. J. Energy Water Resour.*, 2025, https://doi.org/10.1007/s42108-025-00393-5.
30. Paliyal, P.S., Mondal, S., Pathela, M., Kumar, A., Menon, S.K., Optimization of Solar Photovoltaic Array In-Depth Analysis of Perturb and Observe MPPT Algorithm. *2024 International Conference on Advances in Computing, Communication and Materials (ICACCM)*, Dehradun, India, pp. 1–6, 2024, doi: 10.1109/ICACCM61117.2024.11059143.
31. Menon, S.K., *et al.*, The Role of Hydrogen as a Sustainable Energy Source and its Integration with the Grid, in: *Advancements in Communication and Systems*, A.K. Tripathi and V. Shrivastava (Eds.), p. 397, Computing and Intelligent Systems, SCRS, India, 2023, (2025).
32. Kudapa, V.K., Paliyal, P.S., Mondal, A., Mondal, S., A critical review of fabrication strategies, separation techniques, challenges, and future prospects for the hydrogen separation membrane. *Fusion Sci. Technol.*, 80, 7, 803–825, 2024.
33. Mondal, A., Jangirh, R., Arya, R., Yadav, L., Ahlawat, S., Yadav, P., Paliyal, P.S., Bobde, P., Ghosh, P., Mondal, S., Rai, A., Analysing solid residential fuel usage patterns in rural and urban slums of Delhi: Implications for pollution reduction and sustainable practices. *Energy Sustainable Dev.*, *80*, 101460, 2024.

13

Digital Twin-Enabled Solar Concentrators: A Cyber-Physical Approach to Intelligent Renewable Energy

Laxman Singh Rana*, **Lakhan Singh, Surabhi Chauhan, Kundan Singh and Deepak Singh Karki**

Department of Electrical Engineering, JB Institute of Technology, Dehradun, Uttarakhand, India

Abstract

One revolutionary development in the field of renewable energy is the combination of Digital Twin (DT) technology and solar concentrator systems. With the help of digital twins, physical assets can be virtually recreated in real time, facilitating improved solar concentrator monitoring, performance analysis, predictive maintenance, and control. This chapter examines the basic ideas behind digital twins and how they are used in different kinds of solar concentrators, such as parabolic troughs, both Fresnel reflectors and heliostats. With a focus on data collection, simulation models, AI-driven analytics, and communication technologies, it describes the design of a solar system enabled by DT. Case studies from the real world show how well digital twins work to maximize productivity and reduce operational hazards. Along with outlining potential future approaches in edge computing, autonomous control, and hybrid modeling, the chapter also discusses important issues such data integrity, system integration, and processing demands. Digital twins provide a potent route to more intelligent and sustainable energy generation by fusing solar technology with cyber-physical systems.

Keywords: Digital twin technology, solar concentrators, cyber physical systems, AI driven analytics, sustainable energy systems

**Corresponding author*: laxmanranapp@gmail.com

Surajit Mondal, Paramjeet Singh Paliyal and Sachin Sharma (eds.) Digital Twin Technology for Solar Concentrators, (207–220) © 2026 Scrivener Publishing LLC

13.1 Introduction

As the global demand for clean, reliable energy grows, solar power continues to emerge as a vital pillar in the transition toward sustainable energy systems. Among solar technologies, concentrated solar power (CSP) systems—particularly Fresnel reflectors and heliostats—offer a promising means of efficiently converting solar radiation into thermal energy for power generation or industrial processes. However, the performance and longevity of these systems are highly dependent on precise alignment, weather conditions, material degradation, and operational controls. Addressing these challenges requires advanced tools for real-time monitoring, optimization, and predictive management.

Digital Twin (DT) technology offers a novel solution to these problems by building a virtual, real-time model of an actual solar concentrator system. Digital twins facilitate improved visibility, forecasting, and control by integrating sensor data, high-fidelity simulation models, AI-driven analytics, and reliable communication networks. Through constant synchronization with the physical system, a digital twin can identify inefficiencies, forecast malfunctions, and suggest ideal operating circumstances. This chapter focuses on the application of digital twins in Fresnel reflector and heliostat-based solar concentrator systems. With a focus on data collecting, simulation modeling, AI-driven analytics, and communication technologies, it covers the architecture and design of a DT-enabled solar system. The efficiency of digital twins in increasing output and lowering operating risks, like mechanical misalignments, heat losses, and environmental soiling, is illustrated by real-world case studies. This chapter also discusses important implementation issues like processing demands, system integration, and data integrity. Future avenues that could further improve the capabilities of digital twins in solar applications are also covered, including emerging trends like edge computing, autonomous control, and hybrid modeling approaches. By merging solar concentrator technology with cyber-physical systems, digital twins provide a powerful pathway to more intelligent, adaptive, and sustainable solar energy infrastructure.

13.2 Fundamentals of Digital Twin Technology

Digital Twin (DT) technology represents a paradigm shift in the way complex physical systems are monitored, analyzed, and optimized. A digital twin is not merely a simulation; it is a living model—dynamically synchronized with real-time data from its physical counterpart. According to

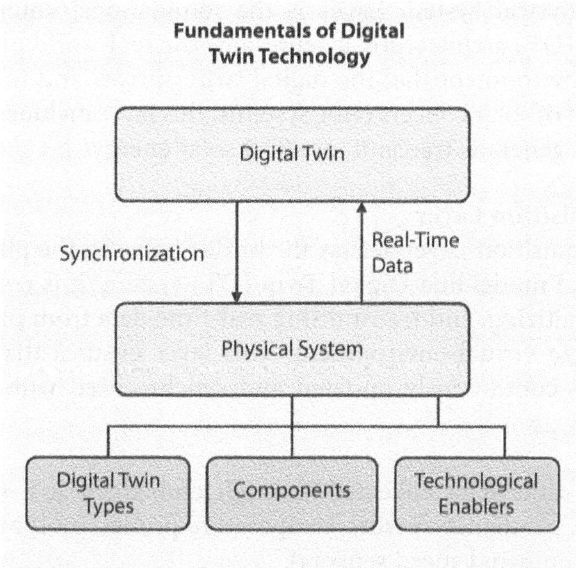

Figure 13.1 Fundamentals of digital twin technology.

Figure 13.1 This section explores the fundamental principles, components, types, and technological enablers of digital twins, with relevance to their application in solar concentrator systems.

13.2.1 Definition and Concept

A Digital Twin is a virtual representation of a physical asset, system, or process that is continuously updated with real-world data and operational insights. It enables bidirectional communication between the physical and digital domains, supporting enhanced decision-making, anomaly detection, and autonomous operation.

In the context of solar concentrators, a digital twin can replicate components such as heliostats, reflectors, receiver units, and tracking systems, providing real-time insights into performance, degradation, and energy output.

13.2.2 Core Components of a Digital Twin System

A typical digital twin architecture consists of the following layers:

1. Physical System Layer
The actual solar concentrator system (e.g., heliostat field or Fresnel reflector array), including hardware components, sensors, actuators, and control

units. The Physical System Layer is the foundational component in a Digital Twin (DT) architecture. It represents the real-world physical asset, process, or environment that the digital twin mirrors and interacts with. In the context of solar concentrator systems, this layer includes all physical elements that generate, transmit, or affect solar energy.

2. Data Acquisition Layer

The Data Acquisition Layer acts as the bridge between the physical world and the digital model in a Digital Twin (DT) system. It is responsible for collecting, digitizing, and transmitting real-time data from physical components to the virtual environment. This layer ensures that the digital twin remains continuously updated and synchronized with its physical counterpart.

- Real-time data collected through embedded IoT sensors (e.g., irradiance sensors, temperature probes, motor encoders, and wind speed sensors).
- Data types: solar irradiance, ambient and component temperature, angular position, fluid flow rates, and power output.

3. Communication Layer

The Communication Layer in a Digital Twin (DT) system is responsible for the secure and efficient transmission of data between the physical system, data acquisition devices, processing units (cloud/edge), and the virtual twin. It forms the data backbone of the DT, enabling real-time synchronization and control.

- Transmits data between the physical asset and the virtual model using protocols like MQTT, Modbus, ZigBee, LoRaWAN, or NB-IoT, depending on range and bandwidth needs.

4. Digital Model Layer

- High-fidelity simulations using physics-based models (e.g., thermal, optical, or mechanical models) and/or data-driven AI/ML models.
- Includes 3D visualization, finite element analysis (FEA), computational fluid dynamics (CFD), and ray-tracing for solar flux analysis.

5. Analytics and Intelligence Layer

- AI/ML algorithms analyze historical and live data to:
  - Predict failures
  - Optimize tracking
  - Forecast performance
  - Recommend maintenance
- Techniques: supervised learning, anomaly detection, reinforcement learning.

6. Control and Feedback Layer

- Enables decision-making and actuation based on insights from the digital twin.
- Examples: Adjusting mirror angles, initiating cleaning cycles, switching flow in thermal loops.

7. User Interface Layer

- Dashboards and control panels for monitoring KPIs, issuing commands, and visualizing system status.

13.2.3 Types of Digital Twins

Digital twins can be classified based on their purpose and capabilities:

Type	Description
Descriptive Twin	Provides static or real-time visualization of the system without advanced analysis.
Diagnostic Twin	Includes analytics to detect faults or inefficiencies based on data patterns.
Predictive Twin	Uses AI and simulation models to forecast future behavior or failures.
Prescriptive Twin	Recommends optimized actions or system settings for improved performance.
Autonomous Twin	Capable of self-learning and initiating control actions without human intervention.

In solar concentrator systems, a predictive or prescriptive twin is often used to anticipate maintenance needs, predict energy yield, or optimize sun-tracking in variable weather conditions.

13.2.4 Technological Enablers

Several enabling technologies make digital twins viable for real-time solar system management:

- Internet of Things (IoT)
    - Embedded sensors and edge devices for collecting and transmitting real-time data.
- Cloud and Edge Computing
    - Cloud platforms for scalable processing and data storage; edge devices for low-latency decision-making at the source.
- Artificial Intelligence (AI) and Machine Learning (ML)
    - Algorithms for fault detection, predictive analytics, and autonomous control.
- Simulation Tools
    - Tools such as MATLAB/Simulink, ANSYS, OpenFOAM, or COMSOL Multiphysics for thermal, optical, and mechanical modeling.
- Cyber-Physical Systems (CPS)
    - The integration of computational models with physical processes for feedback-based control.
- Digital Thread
    - A communication framework that connects data across the product lifecycle, enabling traceability and historical analysis.

13.2.5 Benefits of Digital Twin Technology

In the solar energy domain, digital twins offer numerous advantages:

- Enhanced Operational Efficiency: Real-time optimization of concentrator alignment and thermal loops.
- Predictive Maintenance: Early detection of wear, degradation, or misalignment in mirrors or tracking systems.
- Design Validation: Virtual testing of new system configurations under various environmental scenarios.
- Cost Reduction: Lower maintenance costs and reduced downtime.
- Scalability: Easily applicable to large-scale CSP plants with distributed concentrator arrays.

13.3 Solar Concentrator Systems: An Overview

Solar concentrators are devices that collect According to Figure 13.2 and focus sunlight onto a smaller area to increase the intensity of solar energy for conversion into heat or electricity. These systems are a key component of Concentrated Solar Power (CSP) technology, which is widely used in

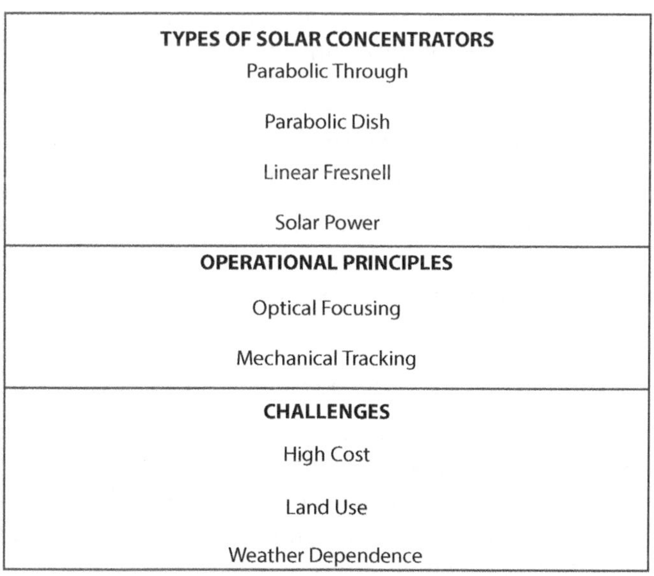

Figure 13.2 Solar concentrator systems overviews.

utility-scale solar thermal power generation. Unlike flat-panel photovoltaic systems, solar concentrators rely on optical focusing and mechanical tracking to maximize solar capture.

This section provides an overview of the types of solar concentrator technologies, their operational principles, performance considerations, and the challenges that make them ideal candidates for enhancement *via* digital twin technologies.

13.3.1 Principle of Operation

All solar concentrators work on a fundamental principle: concentrating solar irradiance using mirrors or lenses to direct sunlight onto a receiver where thermal energy is absorbed and either stored or converted to mechanical/electrical energy.

Key elements include:

- Reflective/Optical Components: Concentrate sunlight (mirrors, lenses).
- Receiver Unit: Absorbs and transfers thermal energy.
- Tracking System: Maintains alignment with the sun.
- Working Fluid: Transports heat (e.g., molten salt, synthetic oil, steam).
- Energy Conversion System: Converts heat into electricity (typically *via* a Rankine or Stirling engine cycle).

13.3.2 Types of Solar Concentrator Systems

Parabolic Trough Collectors (PTCs) are one of the most mature and widely used solar thermal technologies. They are a key component in concentrating solar power (CSP) systems designed to harness solar energy for electricity generation or industrial process heat.

13.3.2.1 Parabolic Trough Collectors (PTCs)

A **Parabolic Trough Collector** uses a **parabolically curved, linear reflector** to focus sunlight onto a **receiver tube** (also called an absorber) located at the focal line of the parabola. This concentrated sunlight heats the fluid flowing through the tube, which is then used to generate steam for power production or direct heat applications.

- Design: Curved, trough-shaped mirrors focus sunlight onto a linear receiver tube.
- Tracking: Single-axis (usually east–west).
- Use Case: Medium- to large-scale thermal power plants.
- Challenges: Receiver tube heat loss, tracking errors, fouling from dust.

13.3.2.2 Linear Fresnel Reflectors (LFRs)

- Design: Series of flat or slightly curved mirrors arranged in rows to focus sunlight on a fixed elevated receiver.
- Advantages:
  - Lower cost and structural complexity than PTCs.
  - Compact land use.
- Challenges:
  - Lower optical efficiency.
  - Complex tracking coordination among multiple mirror rows.

13.3.2.3 Parabolic Dish Concentrators

- Design: Dish-shaped mirrors focus sunlight to a single focal point.
- Applications: Off-grid power systems; often coupled with Stirling engines.
- Advantages: High optical efficiency and temperature.
- Challenges: Costly tracking mechanism, dish alignment precision.

13.3.2.4 Heliostat Field with Central Receiver (Solar Tower)

- Design: Thousands of flat mirrors (heliostats) reflect sunlight to a central receiver atop a tower.
- Tracking: Dual-axis tracking system for each mirror.
- Use Case: Large-scale thermal power generation (e.g., >100 MW).
- Challenges:
  - Complex real-time control and coordination of thousands of heliostats.
  - Atmospheric attenuation and spillage losses.
  - Structural and maintenance complexity.

13.3.3 Performance Considerations

Performance of solar concentrators is influenced by several interdependent factors:

- Solar Irradiance: Direct normal irradiance (DNI) is essential for CSP performance.
- Optical Efficiency: Determined by mirror reflectivity, alignment precision, and sun-tracking accuracy.
- Thermal Losses: Include convection, conduction, and radiation from receiver surfaces.
- Mechanical Integrity: Affects tracking precision and mirror alignment over time.
- Environmental Effects: Soiling, wind loads, and temperature fluctuations degrade performance.

13.3.4 Why Solar Concentrators Need Digital Twins

Solar concentrator systems, especially Fresnel and heliostat configurations, are highly dynamic, spatially distributed, and sensitive to environmental and operational variability. This complexity makes traditional maintenance and control approaches inefficient.

Key pain points include:

- Tracking Accuracy: Deviation from optimal angles leads to significant energy loss.
- Degradation Monitoring: Mirrors, receivers, and actuators degrade over time.
- Soiling Detection: Dust accumulation affects optical efficiency.
- Operational Coordination: In heliostat fields, hundreds or thousands of devices must operate in harmony.

Digital twins provide a powerful tool to:

- Monitor the health and status of components in real time.
- Predict faults or performance degradation.
- Optimize energy yield through advanced analytics.
- Reduce downtime and maintenance costs.

13.3.5 Summary of System Characteristics

System type	Tracking	Focus type	Typical application	Digital twin relevance
Parabolic Trough	Single-Axis	Line Focus	Medium-scale thermal plants	Moderate: receiver condition monitoring
Linear Fresnel	Single-Axis	Line Focus	Compact installations	High: mirror coordination, soiling models
Parabolic Dish	Dual-Axis	Point Focus	Off-grid, remote generation	Low-to-moderate: tracking + predictive ops
Heliostat Field	Dual-Axis	Point Focus	Utility-scale solar towers	Very High: AI-based control & optimization

13.4 Digital Twin Architecture for Solar Concentrators

13.4.1 System Architecture

A typical DT framework for solar concentrators includes:

- Sensor Network: Temperature, irradiance, wind speed, alignment sensors.
- IoT Layer: Collects and transmits data to cloud or edge computing platforms.
- Simulation Model: CFD, thermal simulations, or ray-tracing tools to mimic system behavior.
- Analytics & AI: Predictive models for component failures, performance degradation, and energy yield.
- Control Layer: Feedback to actuators for real-time adjustments.

13.4.2 Communication Technologies

- Wireless Sensor Networks (WSNs)
- LoRaWAN/ZigBee/NB-IoT for remote systems
- Cloud and Edge Computing integration

13.5 Applications of Digital Twins in Solar Concentrators

13.5.1 Real-Time Monitoring and Diagnostics

- Performance tracking (thermal efficiency, optical alignment).
- Sensor-driven fault detection.
- Mirror cleaning schedule optimization based on soiling models.

13.5.2 Predictive Maintenance

- Thermal stress analysis on receiver tubes.
- Wear prediction for tracking motors and actuators.
- Failure forecasting using historical and real-time data.

13.5.3 Optimization and Control

- Adaptive sun-tracking algorithms using AI feedback loops.
- Dynamic load management based on irradiance prediction.
- Heat storage optimization in hybrid systems.

13.5.4 Design and Simulation

- Virtual prototyping of new concentrator designs.
- Sensitivity analysis for site-specific deployment.
- Integration with Building Information Modeling (BIM) for architectural applications.

13.6 Case Studies

13.6.1 Digital Twin for Heliostat Field Optimization

Heliostat fields—arrays of mirrors that track the sun and reflect solar radiation onto a central receiver—are critical components in central tower solar power systems. Optimizing their performance is essential for improving overall energy yield and operational efficiency. This case study illustrates how a Digital Twin (DT) was used to optimize heliostat field operations in a commercial-scale solar thermal plant.

13.6.2 Predictive Maintenance of Parabolic Troughs

A digital twin model integrated with thermal sensors detected early signs of receiver degradation, allowing preventive replacement and minimizing downtime. Parabolic Trough Collectors (PTCs) are widely used in solar thermal power plants due to their mature design and efficiency. However, **thermal stress**, **mechanical wear**, and **component degradation**—especially in receiver tubes and tracking mechanisms—can significantly reduce system performance. This case study highlights how a **Digital Twin (DT)** was used to enable predictive maintenance in a large PTC-based solar plant.

13.7 Challenges and Considerations

While Digital Twin (DT) technology offers transformative benefits in solar concentrator systems, its implementation is not without significant challenges. This case study outlines the **technical, operational, and economic hurdles** faced during a pilot project at a hybrid solar thermal plant, and the strategies used to address them.

- Data Accuracy: Sensor drift and environmental noise impact model fidelity.
- Computational Complexity: High-fidelity simulations may require HPC resources.
- Cybersecurity: Protecting the data pipeline from intrusion.
- Integration with Legacy Systems: Retrofitting old plants with DT capabilities can be difficult.
- Standardization: Lack of universal DT protocols for renewable energy.

13.8 Future Outlook and Research Directions

- Hybrid Digital Twins: Combining physics-based and AI-based models for higher accuracy.

- Edge AI Integration: Reducing latency by deploying AI models at the edge.
- Self-healing Systems: Autonomous DTs capable of initiating corrective actions.
- Lifecycle Management: From design to decommissioning, DTs as a tool across the entire asset lifecycle.
- Green Digital Twins: Assessing and minimizing the carbon footprint of DT operations.

13.9 Conclusion

The fusion of digital twin technology with solar concentrator systems represents a paradigm shift in renewable energy management. By creating intelligent, connected, and adaptive systems, operators can significantly enhance performance, reliability, and return on investment. As AI and IoT technologies mature, the role of digital twins will become indispensable in achieving efficient and resilient solar power infrastructures.

AI disclosure statement: The author confirms that no artificial intelligence (AI)-generated content or AI-assisted writing tools were used in the preparation of this chapter (including summaries and the abstract). All text, analysis, and conclusions are the result of the author's original work.

Bibliography

1. Tao, F., Zhang, H., Liu, A., Nee, A.Y.C., Digital twin in industry: State-of-the-art. *IEEE Trans. Ind. Inf.*, 15, 4, 2405–2415, 2018.
2. Zohdy, M.A. and Ghoneim, A.A., Digital twin framework for predictive maintenance in concentrated solar power plants. *Renewable Energy*, 160, 926–936, 2020.
3. González-Gil, A., *et al.*, Optimization of cleaning schedules in heliostat fields using a digital twin approach. *Sol. Energy*, 183, 321–332, 2019.
4. Schüller, T., Müller, R., Geyer, P., Modeling and simulation of heliostat field control systems using digital twins. *Energy Rep.*, 7, 230–239, 2021.
5. Yang, H. and Jain, S., IoT and AI for solar thermal systems: Towards digital twins for CSP. *J. Cleaner Prod.*, 333, 130077, 2022.
6. Luo, J., *et al.*, Edge-cloud collaborative architecture for real-time monitoring in solar plants. *IEEE Internet Things J.*, 7, 5, 4121–4131, 2020.

14

Artificial Neural Networks for Solar Panel Tilt Angle Optimization: A Power Generation Analysis

Nitin Kumar[1]*, Rupendra Kumar Pachauri[2] and Piyush Kuchhal[2]

[1]Department of CSE (AIML), Meerut Institute of Engineering and Technology, Meerut, Uttar Pradesh, India
[2]Electrical Cluster, School of Advanced Engineering, University of Petroleum and Energy Studies, Dehradun, Uttarakhand, India

Abstract
Solar panels are the most prominent source of renewable energy. The tilt angle of the solar power system is one of the most critical factors in maximising the amount of solar radiation that reaches the solar panels. Since this angle is determined by the sun's daily, monthly, and yearly movements, it is unique to each location. To optimise the energy produced, it is crucial to accurately estimate the tilt angle that works best for the specific area. Various methods have been used to determine the optimal tilt angle in several regions around the world. Artificial Neural Networks (ANNs) are employed to estimate the optimal solar panel tilt angle based on power generation at different tilt angles, factoring in the time of year and the months. The input data for the training process includes the average air temperature over 24 hours, total solar radiation, and humidity, while the output data consists of the electrical power generated. It was concluded that when the solar panel is fixed at a 30° tilt angle, it generates more power than at 25° or 35°. The ANN model performed optimally, achieving an accuracy of 93.34% based on the findings.

***Keywords*:** Solar power forecasting, tilt angle, ANN

**Corresponding author*: nitindabra.kumar@gmail.com

Surajit Mondal, Paramjeet Singh Paliyal and Sachin Sharma (eds.) Digital Twin Technology for Solar Concentrators, (221–238)

14.1 Introduction

Energy is essential for human survival and a key component for long-term economic expansion. An important part of solving the world's energy and environmental problems is switching to green energy, which can provide abundant clean energy to meet growing electricity demand. Local and national governments are starting to take climate change seriously, and there has been a lot of buzz about environmental sustainability and renewable energy recently [1]. Designing and developing solar energy systems requires understanding how to optimise and make the most of the solar radiation received. Solar radiation data needs to be improved in many areas and approached in different ways. Various methods are used to estimate solar radiation on a flat surface [2, 3]. The weather, location, and temperature are just a few of the many variables that affect energy forecasts [4]. One common way to replace energy sources that don't replenish themselves is with solar panels. A solar panel's orientation and inclination angle are crucial factors that affect the system's efficiency and are often used in solar thermal panels [5]. Many studies have examined how soiling and the ideal tilt angle affect PV performance, and the results show that the perfect tilt angle may boost efficiency by 20% [6]. When designing a solar PV system to generate as much energy as possible, it is essential to optimise its tilt angle since it benefits photovoltaic efficiency. This emphasises the need to install solar panels at an appropriate tilt angle to maximise the system's photovoltaic efficiency during a specific period and to collect the most energy from the sun. On the other hand, a PV system's efficiency improves significantly when the tilt angle is optimised, as more solar energy is absorbed, leading to better performance [7]. These results are supported by other studies examining how different angles impact photovoltaic energy generation and efficiency. Also, studies demonstrate that if modules are installed at the wrong angle, the PV system will be less efficient, and the owners could lose money due to lower energy production and higher operational costs. To maximise solar efficiency and energy output over time, it is vital to install PV modules at the appropriate tilt angle and to maintain them regularly.

ANN, a field that has quickly embraced, may address this problem. ANN methods have also been used to predict the solar radiation on tilted surfaces. ANN techniques have been proven to be excellent tools for research, as they can handle non-linear or non-linear function approximation [8]. In this study, an ANN model has been developed to predict the power generated at various tilt angles.

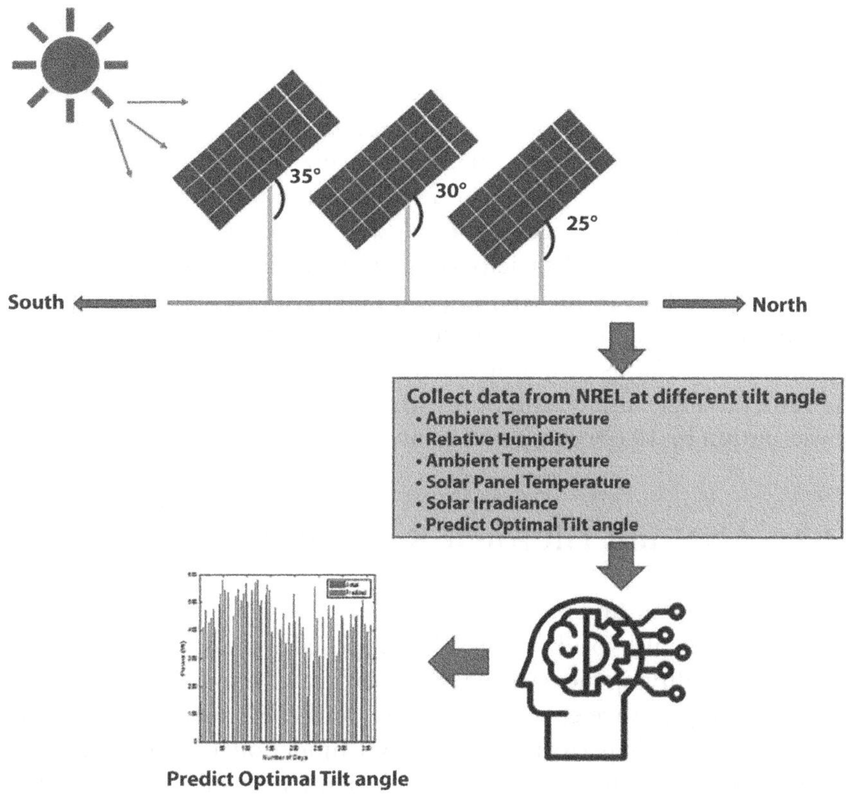

Figure 14.1 Graphical representation of study.

Figure 14.1 shows the graphical representation of the present study.

14.1.1 Literature Review

Much research has been conducted on the performance of solar PV panel power prediction with tilt angle orientation. ANN and SVM for predicting solar PV panel surface tilt angles at two locations in Saudi Arabia [9]. SVM has a higher R^2 value (0.96) than ANN. Moreover, SVM's lower value of RMSE indicates that it is robust and has the capability to minimise error during computations. A forecasting model was developed in Tainan to calculate surface solar radiation on an hourly basis and the solar irradiance by the solar panels at various tilt angles [10]. The level of solar irradiance was almost the same at 0° as at 41°. The optimal solar panel tilt angle in Tainan is 20–22 degrees according to a study; furthermore, a novel approach to outperform traditional MLP models with two, three, four and five hidden layers. The results conclude that these approaches result in a significant improvement in RMSE and R^2. LAR-based MLP showed superiority over both bisquare and traditional MLP methods in R^2 and RMSE, ranging from 1.13 to 1.18 and 2.53 to 3.06, respectively [11]. Another study using ML (XGBoost) was conducted to determine the direction and tilt angle that maximise electricity generation at a given latitude and longitude. It was possible to predict electricity generation, achieving R^2 values of 0.986 for training and 0.928 for testing [12]. Furthermore, a study proposes a solution by tracking the sun's position to earth continuously and optimising the tilt angle by using a deep learning technique. This method predicts the sun's tilt angle and orientation with 97% accuracy and increases solar power output by 10.6% compared to non-tracking systems [13].

14.2 ANN and Tilt Angle Relation with Latitude

In order to estimate and predict solar power plants accurately, [14–16] created an intelligent hybrid model. The proposed wavelet resolves the grid conflict by modifying the package. The solar signal is first subharmonically analyzed using a wavelet transformation, and then a statistical function selection analysis is performed. The GAN model offers a comprehensive method for predicting solar power and identifying sub-frequency components. The ideal annual tilt angle for stationary solar or photovoltaic collectors worldwide can be accurately predicted by several models, as demonstrated by Chinchilla *et al.* [17]. Statistics on horizontal radiation from websites worldwide form the basis of the proposed model. We calculated the hourly irradiation of potential slopes and the corresponding annual energy production using pre-existing sub-models. After determining the optimal angle for each site, they used regression analysis to construct a statistical model that estimated the optimal angle annually as a function of latitude. Additionally, they contrasted polynomial models with other regression techniques, such as neural network and decision tree models. Optimal production is determined by analyzing, evaluating, and comparing the proposed model to previous study designs. To achieve optimal insulation of PV panels, [18, 19] investigated the optimal tilt angle and orientation. Using two scattered radiation models, the ideal tilt angle and direction were determined. There are two anisotropic models: one regular and one special. Four challenging types provide appropriate tilt angles ranging from 37° to 44°. Optimal tilt positions of 46° to 47° are better in line with their predictions for the angle of solar panels [20–22].

Several studies that were conducted on tilt angle are presented in Table 14.1. Several studies have been conducted to determine the optical tilt angle and providing some guidelines for doing so. Some of these studies demonstrate that the tilt angle can be calculated separately for summer and winter separately by adding and subtracting 15 degrees from the latitude of that location. Other studies subtract 10 degrees and add 20 degrees to the latitude of that location. ANNs belong to a category of ML algorithms that model the arrangement and operation of human brain. At a high level, ANNs consist of three parts: input layers, hidden layers and output layers as shown in Figure 14.2. These algorithms have been widely used PV solar energy applications, including both stand-alone and large-scale systems. Neurons are the fundamental building blocks of ANNs. Neurons are simply units that receive inputs to create outputs through the application of an activation function [23–25]. The methodology flowchart is shown in Figure 14.3. ANN is trained to predict solar power generation by learning

Table 14.1 Optimal tilt angle with latitude from literature.

References	Tilt Angle (in °)	Remarks
[11]	$(\varphi+15)\pm15$	These techniques can calculate estimated tilt angles for various latitudes. The summer sign is negative, while the winter sign is positive.
[12]	$(\varphi-10)$	
[13]	$(\varphi\pm15)$	
[14]	$(\varphi+15),(\varphi-15),0.9\varphi$	
[15]	$(\varphi+20)$	

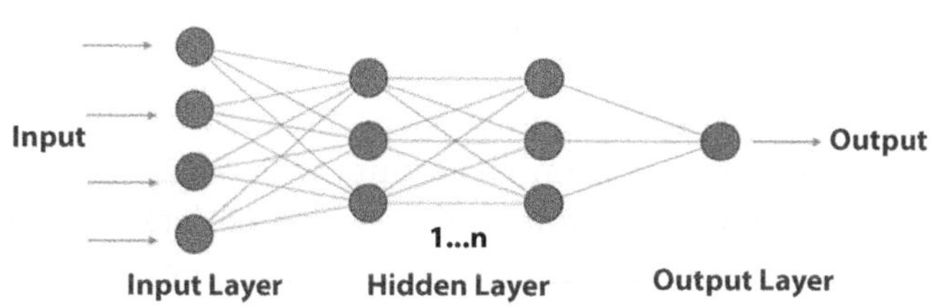

Figure 14.2 Typical ANN structure.

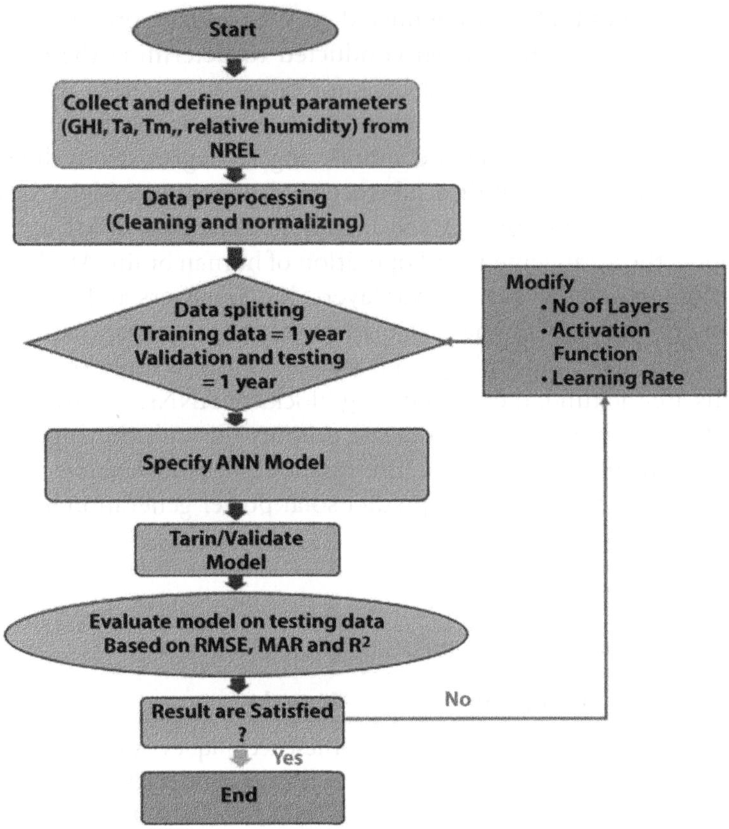

Figure 14.3 ANN methodology flowchart.

the link between input features like weather, time of day, location, etc. A basic equation of ANN is explained in Equation (14.1) as,

$$\hat{y}=f(W.X+b) \tag{14.1}$$

14.3 The Process of Data Curation

We take data from NREL for training purposes, and for validation, we take total 8760 data of one year from Dehradun, with 30°20′42″N 78°01′44″E latitude/longitude. For the training process 70% of data was used and for validation and testing processes, 15% and 15% data were used, respectively. Four solar panels have been arranged at different angles and orientations for testing. Solar panels are attached to this quartet of modules. Each module may accommodate four angled solar panels by simply tilting them. Before preprocessing data there are outlier's (Negative values, zero irradiance) in the datasets. After preprocessing, the clean data is split into two parts (Input and Output data). After splitting the data, split it into three phases (Training, validation, and testing) with 70%, 15%, and 15% respectively. Then train the ANN model and test with corresponding input. Table 14.2 displays the solar panel specifications. Here are a few of them: Voc, Isc, Mpp, Vmpp, and Pmpp, which stand for open-circuit voltage, short-circuit current, maximum power point current, and temperature coefficient, respectively. Table 14.3 shows the Ranges and properties of data (yearly

Table 14.2 Solar panel specification.

Parameter's	Value	Unit
V_{oc}	22.2	V
I_{sc}	1.2	A
I_{mpp}	1.1	A
V_{mpp}	17.5	V
P_{mpp}	19.25	W

Table 14.3 Ranges and properties of data (yearly average).

Features	Range
Month	Jan-Dec
GHI	0-1050 W/m^2
Humidity	43-90%
Ambient Temperature	8-32°C
Hour's	08:00-18:00
Tilt Angle	25-35
Power	0-20 W
Azimuth Angle	180

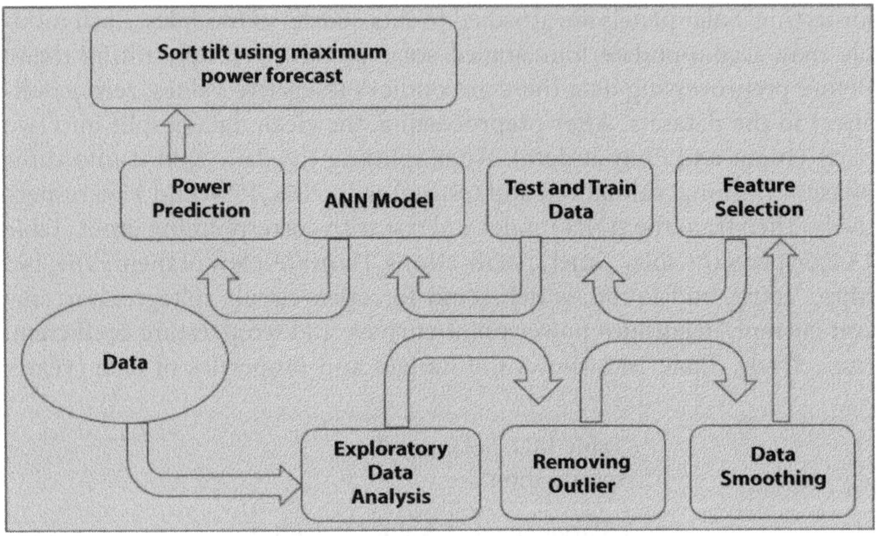

Figure 14.4 Proposed methodology flow diagram.

average). A flowchart of the methodology for the entire study is shown in Figure 14.4, from data collection at NREL to sorting tilt angles for maximum power generation [26].

14.4 Test Metric

Figure 14.4 shows the flowchart of the proposed technique. The MAE, RMSE, and R^2 are the performance metrics used. MAE, R^2, and RMSE are among the most widely used performance metrics in ML prediction research [27–29]. In the following sections, the chosen performance metrics will be discussed and explained in further detail.

Mean absolute error (MAE): MAE is one of the most often referenced performance indicators in the area of solar power production forecasts. It does this by measuring the average absolute difference between predicted and observed values [30]. Within the context of this investigation, the MAE is expressed as a value in Watts (W). The equation to use in the computation of MAE is as follows: Where: n is the number of data points, $y'i$ is the predicted value, and yi is the actual value.

$$MAE = \frac{1}{n}[\sum_{i=1}^{n} yi - y'i] \tag{14.2}$$

Root mean squared error (RMSE): The root-mean-squared error (RMSE) is a widely used reliability evaluator that provides an accurate depiction of outsized mistakes. Therefore, it is preferable to have a small RMSE. In this investigation, the RMSE is reported in Watts [31]. Here is the formula for computing the root-mean-squared error: Where n is the number of data points, $y'i$ is the predicted value, and yi is the actual value.

$$RMSE = \frac{1}{n}\sqrt{[\sum_{i=1}^{n} y'i - yi^2]} \tag{14.3}$$

Coefficient of determination (R^2): The R^2 statistic measures the strength of the relationship between observed and expected values. It is a measure of how well the prediction model performs relative to the naïve mean model. R^2 always lies between 0 and 1, with higher values indicating a stronger relationship between the observed and expected outcomes [32]. The formula for determining R^2 is as follows: Where n is the number of data points, RSS is the sum of squared differences between actual and predicted values, and TSS is the total sum of squared differences between actual values and the mean of the dependent variable.

$$R^2 = 1 - \frac{[\sum_{i=1}^{n} yi - yi^{-2}]}{[\sum_{i=1}^{n} yi - yi^{-2}]} \tag{14.4}$$

14.5 Results and Discussion

In this study, to obtain maximum power from solar panels installed at various tilt angles using an ANN algorithm. The data used in this work were obtained from NREL and average of one year. The data collected in the study are in a CSV file with 14 columns: latitude, longitude, azimuth, inclination, year, month, day, time, temperature, wind, humidity, GHI, and DNI. Before preprocessing, a total of 8760 data points remain; after preprocessing, a total of 365 data points remain, which is the average for each day of the 24 hours used in this study. Figure 14.5 illustrates the power generated at different angles. The quantity of electricity that is generated at a tilt angle of 25° has been demonstrated to be significantly higher than

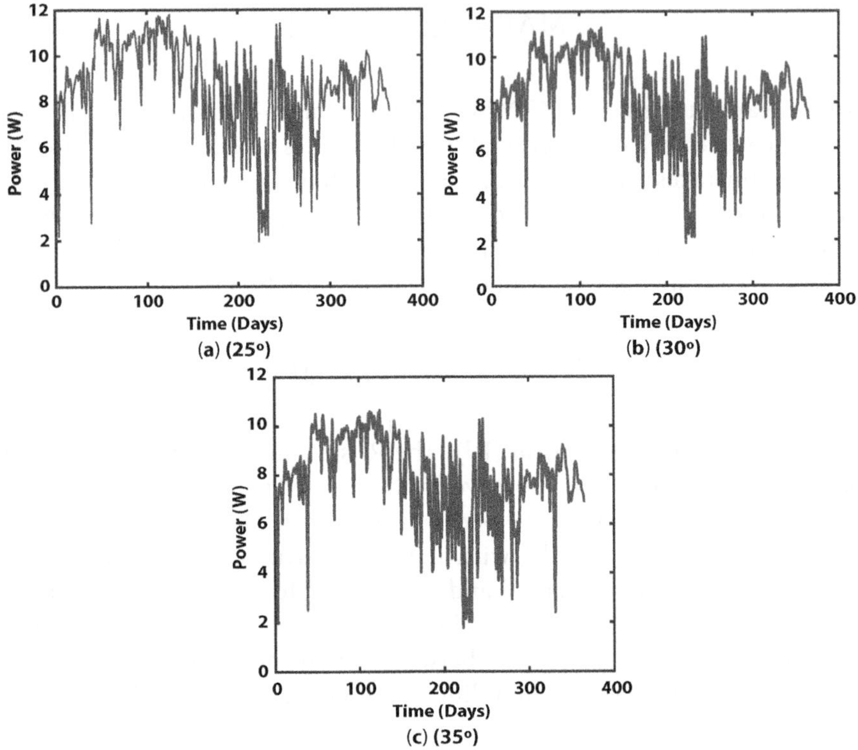

Figure 14.5 Power generated at tilt angles (a) 25°, (b) 30°, and (c) 35°.

that generated at other tilt angles. The blue line in (a), (b), (c), moreover, (d) depicts the Power at a tilt angle of 25° 30°, 35°, and 40°.

Figure 14.6 shows the result of the ANN regression, including the R value. This includes training validation, and testing. The values of R are 0.93498, 0.94075, and 0.91523, respectively. These values correspond to the training, validation, and test, respectively. On the whole, the value of R is 0.93314. Figure 14.7 shows the Monthly Actual and predicted Power generated at different tilt angles.

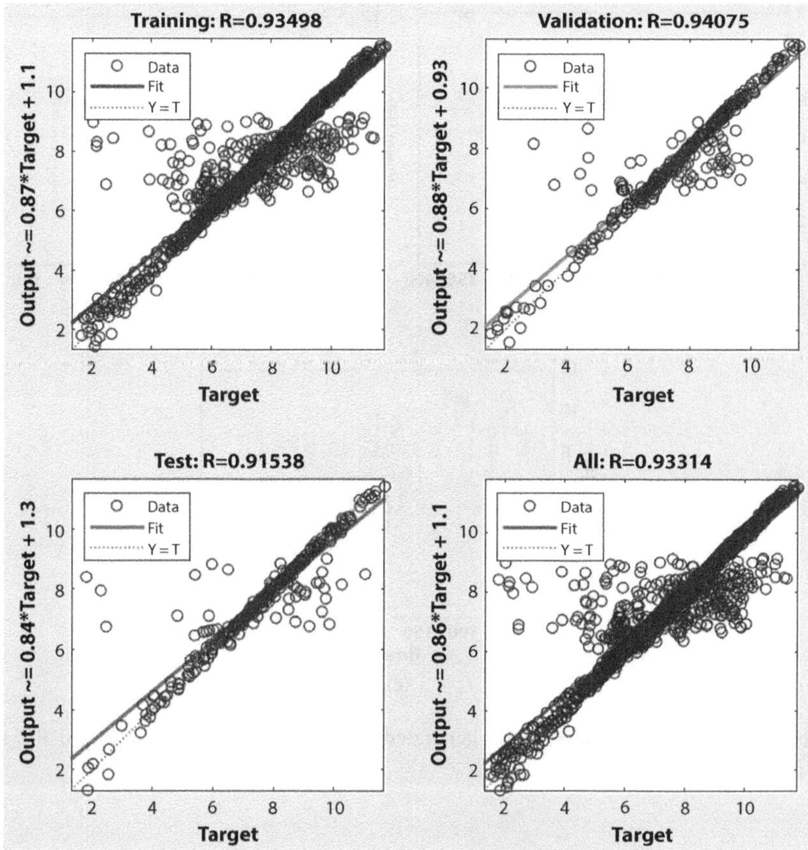

Figure 14.6 Training, validation, test and overall scatter diagram.

Table 14.4 presents the actual and predicted Power generated at various tilt angles over a year, along with any errors that may have occurred. Table 14.5 shows the actual and predicted Power generated at multiple tilt angles every month. It has been found that the energy produced at a tilt angle of 25° is greater than that generated at other tilt angles.

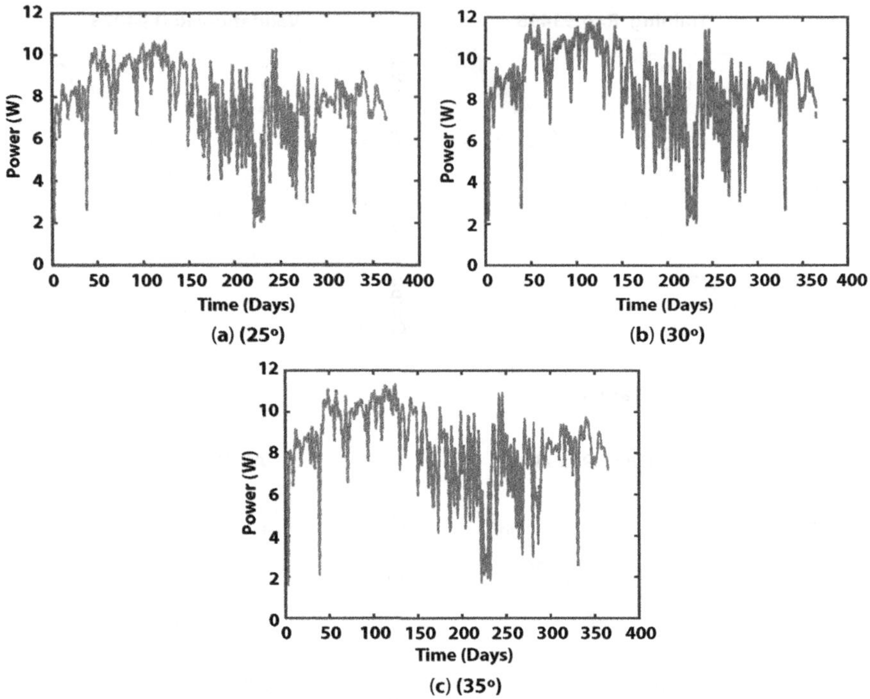

Figure 14.7 Actual/predicted power generated at different tilt angles: (a) 25°, (b) 30°, and (c) 35°.

Table 14.4 Yearly average actual and predicted power output.

Tilt angle (Degree)	Actual power (W)	Predicted power (W)	Error (%)
25	8.662	8.683	-0.00021
30	8.277	8.271	0.0724
35	7.827	7.836	-0.114

Table 14.5 Monthly average actual and predicted power output.

Tilt angle (°)	25		30		35	
Month/power (W)	Actual	Predicted	Actual	Predicted	Actual	Predicted
Jan	8.36	8.45	7.99	7.96	7.55	7.54
Feb	9.73	9.76	9.29	9.22	8.86	8.77
March	10.12	10.23	9.70	9.65	9.15	9.10
April	10.75	10.74	10.23	10.29	9.73	9.80
May	10.12	10.16	9.67	9.65	9.07	9.02
June	8.46	8.50	8.08	8.08	7.60	7.60
July	7.60	7.65	7.27	7.22	6.81	6.81
Aug	6.26	6.28	5.98	5.91	5.79	5.83
Sep	7.63	7.54	7.32	7.31	6.87	6.92
Oct	7.67	7.74	7.33	7.30	6.96	7.14
Nov	8.52	8.57	8.14	8.26	7.73	7.70
Dec	8.77	8.65	8.38	8.46	7.87	7.87

Conclusion

The present study proposes a forecasting model that uses ANN to predict the monthly and annual solar Power generated by solar PV modules at different tilt angles (25°, 30°, 35°). Data were obtained from NREL for Training and validation, totalling 365 data points, with an average of 24hours of data per day used in this study. Dehradun, India, served as the location (30°20′42″N 78°01′44″E) for the research. After installing the solar panel at various angles, we found that the 30° angle generated the most electricity, while the 25° and 35° angles produced less. This study predicts the optimal tilt angle using ANN, achieving an accuracy of around 93%. In the future, use more regional data to predict solar PV power generation in other regions, specifically research efficiency, and further expand the scope and method of research for this purpose.

Nomenclature

PV	Photovoltaic
ML	Machine Learning
ANN	Artificial Neural Network
SVM	Support Vector Machine
RMSE	Root Mean Square Error
MAE	Mean Absolute Error
NREL	National Renewable Research Laboratory
GHI	Global Horizontal Irradiance
GAN	Generative Adversarial Network
V_{oc}	Open Circuit Voltage
I_{sc}	Short Circuit Current
I_{mpp}	Maximum Power Point Current
V_{mpp}	Maximum Power Point Voltage
P_{mpp}	Maximum Power Point Power
W	Watt
W/m2	Watt Per Meter Square
y'_i	Predicted value
y_i	Predicted value
°C	Degree Centigrade

AI disclosure statement: The author acknowledges the use of AI-based tools for minor language editing or grammatical correction. However, all intellectual contributions, analyses, and conclusions presented in this chapter are entirely the author's own.

References

1. Wu, C., Liu, H., Yu, Y., Zhao, W., Liu, J., Yu, H., *et al.*, Ecohydrological Effects of Photovoltaic Solar Farms on Soil Microclimates and Moisture Regimes in Arid Northwest China: A Modelling Study. *Sci. Total Environ.*, 2021, 149946, 2021.
2. Kumar, N., Pachauri, R.K., Kuchhal, P., Nkenyereye, L., Floating photovoltaic system based electrical power generation study in Indian context. *Renewable*

Sustainable Energy Rev., 212, 115442, 2025, ISSN 1364-0321, https://doi.org/10.1016/j.rser.2025.115442.

3. Bakirci, K., Models of solar radiation with hours of bright sunshine: a review. *Renewable Sustainable Energy Rev.*, 13, 9, 2580–2588, 2009.
4. Khan, P.W. and Byun, Y.C., Analysis of Factors Affecting Machine Learning-Based Energy Prediction, in: *Proceedings of KIIT Conference*, pp. 33–35, 2021.
5. Kumar, N., Shukla, A., Sharma, P., Gupta, U.C., Pachauri, R.K., Forecasting of Global Solar Irradiance and Optimal Tilt Angle: Machine Learning Approaches. *2024 Conference on Renewable Energy Technologies and Modern Communications Systems: Future and Challenges*, Shaqra, Saudi Arabia, pp. 1–6, 2024, doi: 10.1109/IEEECONF63577.2024.10880951.
6. Kara Hüseyin, T.S.A., Performance Loss Rates of a 1 MWp PV Plant with Various Tilt Angles, Orientation and Installed Environment in the Capital of Cyprus. *Sustainability*, 14, 15, 9084, 2022.
7. Gholampour, M. and Ameri, M., Energy and exergy analyses of Photovoltaic/Thermal flat transpired collectors: Experimental and theoretical study. *Appl. Energy*, 164, 837–856, 2016.
8. Meng, F., Zou, Q., Zhang, Z., Wang, B., Ma, H., Abdullah, H.M., *et al.*, An Intelligent Hybrid Wavelet-Adversarial Deep Model for Accurate Prediction of Solar Power Generation. *Energy Rep.*, 7, 2155–2164, 2021.
9. Ramli, M.A., Twaha, S., Al-Turki, Y.A., Investigating the performance of support vector machine and artificial neural networks in predicting solar radiation on a tilted surface: Saudi Arabia case study. *Energy Convers. Manage.*, 105, 442–452, 2015.
10. Wei, C.C., Predictions of surface solar radiation on tilted solar panels using machine learning models: A case study of Tainan city, Taiwan. *Energies*, 10, 10, 1660, 2017.
11. Kumar, N., Pachauri, R.K., Kuchhal, P., Akter, K., Alotaibi, M.A., Malik, H., Performance analysis of floating and ground-mounted photovoltaic systems: An experimental study. *Solar Energy*, 302, 113989, 2025.
12. Kim, Y. and Byun, Y., Predicting solar power generation from direction and tilt using machine learning xgboost regression. *J. Phys. Conf. Ser.*, 2261, 1, 012003, 2022, June, IOP Publishing.
13. Ramaneti, K., Kakani, P., Prakash, S., Improving Solar Panel Efficiency by Solar Tracking and Tilt Angle Optimization with Deep Learning, in: *2021 5th International Conference on Smart Grid and Smart Cities (ICSGSC)*, 2021, June, IEEE, pp. 102–106.
14. Chinchilla, M., Santos-Martín, D., Carpintero-Renteria, M., Lemon, S., Worldwide Annual Optimum Tilt Angle Model for Solar Collectors and Photovoltaic Systems in the Absence of Site Meteorological Data. *Appl. Energy*, 281, 116056, 2021.

15. Hailu, G. and Fung, A.S., Optimum Tilt Angle and Orientation of Photovoltaic Thermal System for Application in Greater Toronto Area, Canada. *Sustainability*, 11, 6443, 2019.
16. Duffie, J.A., Beckman, W.A., Blair, N., *Solar engineering of thermal processes, photovoltaics and wind*, John Wiley & Sons, 2020.
17. Perveen, G., Rizwan, M., Goel, N., Anand, P., Artificial neural network models for global solar energy and photovoltaic power forecasting over India. *Energy Sources Part A*, 1–26, 2020.
18. Ledmaoui, Y., Maghraoui, A.E., Aroussi, M.E., Saadane, R., Enhanced Fault Detection in Photovoltaic Panels Using CNN-Based Classification with PyQt5 Implementation. *Sensors*, 24, 22, 7407, Nov. 2024. doi: 10.3390/s24227407.
19. Murdan, A.P. and Armoogum, V., Comparing Machine Learning Techniques for Hourly Solar Power Generation Prediction, in: *IRC Conference on Science, Engineering and Technology*, 2023, August, Springer Nature Singapore, Singapore, pp. 365–376.
20. Tikariha, S. and Pal, Y., Solar Radiation Prediction Using Regression Methods, in: *International Conference on Electric Power and Renewable Energy*, 2023, May, Springer Nature Singapore, Singapore, pp. 335–346.
21. De Myttenaere, A., Golden, B., Le Grand, B., Rossi, F., Mean Absolute Percentage Error for Regression Models. *Neurocomputing*, 192, 38–48, 2016.
22. Chen, C.-F., Score Tests for Regression Models. *J. Am. Stat. Assoc.*, 78, 158–161, 1983, doi: 10.1080/01621459.1983.10477945.
23. Brester, C., Kallio-Myers, V., Lindfors, A.V., Kolehmainen, M., Niska, H., Evaluating neural network models in site-specific solar PV forecasting using numerical weather prediction data and weather observations. *Renewable Energy*, 207, 266–274, 2023.
24. Shukla, A., Pachauri, R.K., Gupta, U.C., Gupta, A.K., Kumar, N., Solar PV Power Generation Prediction Using Machine Learning Algorithms at Different Tilt Angles. *2024 Conference on Renewable Energy Technologies and Modern Communications Systems: Future and Challenges*, Shaqra, Saudi Arabia, pp. 1–6, 2024, doi: 10.1109/IEEECONF63577.2024.10881337.
25. Paliyal, P.S., Mondal, S., Layek, S., Kuchhal, P., Pandey, J.K., Automatic solar tracking system: a review pertaining to advancements and challenges in the current scenario. *Clean Energy*, 8, 6, 237–262, December 2024, https://doi.org/10.1093/ce/zkae085.
26. Paliyal, P.S., Mondal, S., Pandey, J.K., An Analysis of Springwater Parameter Status for Different Locations in the Rural Hilly Garhwal Region of Uttarakhand. *Environ. Claims J.*, *36*, 3, 243–277, 2024, https://doi.org/10.1080/10406026.2024.2423964.
27. Paliyal, P.S. and Mondal, S., An analysis of a cross-finned receiver for Scheffler-type solar collectors to optimize solar heating efficiency for direct water heating. *Int. J. Energy Water Resour.*, 2025, https://doi.org/10.1007/s42108-025-00393-5.

28. Paliyal, P.S., Mondal, S., Pathela, M., Kumar, A., Menon, S.K., Optimization of Solar Photovoltaic Array In-Depth Analysis of Perturb and Observe MPPT Algorithm. *2024 International Conference on Advances in Computing, Communication and Materials (ICACCM)*, Dehradun, India, doi: 10.1109/ICACCM61117.2024.11059143.
29. Paliyal, P.S., *et al.*, Location Analysis and Environmental Validation for Installation of Hybrid Solar-Wind Energy Generation System in Hilly Areas of Uttarakhand: Study Toward Forecasting, in: *Forecasting Methods for Renewable Power Generation*, pp. 21–47, 2025.
30. Menon, S.K., *et al.*, The Role of Hydrogen as a Sustainable Energy Source and its Integration with the Grid, in: *Advancements in Communication and Systems*, A.K. Tripathi and V. Shrivastava (Eds.), p. 397, Computing and Intelligent Systems, SCRS, India, 2023, (2025).
31. Kudapa, V.K., Paliyal, P.S., Mondal, A., Mondal, S., A critical review of fabrication strategies, separation techniques, challenges, and future prospects for the hydrogen separation membrane. *Fusion Sci. Technol.*, 80, 7, 803–825, 2024.
32. Mondal, A., Jangirh, R., Arya, R., Yadav, L., Ahlawat, S., Yadav, P., Paliyal, P.S., Bobde, P., Ghosh, P., Mondal, S., Rai, A., Analysing solid residential fuel usage patterns in rural and urban slums of Delhi: Implications for pollution reduction and sustainable practices. *Energy Sustainable Dev., 80*, 101460, 2024.

15

Machine Learning and Artificial Intelligence in Digital Twins

Sampath Emani[1] and Gurunadh Velidi[2]*

[1]Lavira Technologies LLP, Hyderabad, Telangana, India
[2]School of Advanced Engineering, University of Petroleum and Energy Studies, Dehradun, Uttarakhand, India

Abstract

Digital twin technology has become a pivotal tool for enhancing operational intelligence, predictive accuracy, and adaptive optimization in solar concentrator systems, where complex thermal, optical, and mechanical interactions demand high-fidelity modeling. Recent research increasingly integrates machine learning (ML) and artificial intelligence (AI) into digital twin frameworks to improve thermal forecasting, energy yield prediction, fault detection, and dynamic control. Advanced methods such as deep neural networks, reinforcement learning, and physics-informed ML models show strong potential in capturing non-linear dynamics, optimizing multi-axis tracking, and predicting degradation under varying conditions. However, key gaps remain in model generalization across concentrator designs, explainable AI (XAI) integration, and real-time edge AI deployment for low-latency analytics. This chapter presents a technical framework for embedding AI and ML within digital twins for solar concentrators, covering supervised learning for energy forecasting, deep learning for thermal and optical modeling, reinforcement learning for control, and hybrid AI-physics models for system optimization. Practical case studies on deep learning-based thermal prediction and reinforcement learning-driven tracking control demonstrate realistic deployment scenarios. The chapter provides methodologies, simulation workflows, and deployment protocols, offering researchers and engineers actionable insights for developing AI-driven digital twins for efficient, resilient, and adaptive solar energy systems.

**Corresponding author*: guru.velidi@gmail.com

Surajit Mondal, Paramjeet Singh Paliyal and Sachin Sharma (eds.) Digital Twin Technology for Solar Concentrators, (239–280) © 2026 Scrivener Publishing LLC

Keywords: Digital twin, solar concentrator, machine learning, predictive analytics, reinforcement learning

15.1 Introduction to Digital Twins and Solar Concentrators

15.1.1 Overview of Digital Twin Technology

A digital twin is a computational tool that mirrors a physical asset, allowing real-time data from sensors to flow back and forth between the virtual model and the working system. By combining physics-based modeling, incoming sensor streams, machine-learning algorithms, and control software, the twin continuously updates itself and suggests ways to improve performance. The approach has gained traction across sectors such as aerospace, manufacturing, and public infrastructure and is now being explored more broadly in renewable-energy applications [1].

Because the model receives live operational data, it creates a closed loop that forecasts future behavior, spots anomalies, and proposes control adjustments on the fly. To capture both predictable and random influences, the twin uses a mixed strategy that pairs deterministic equations with probabilistic machine-learning techniques, factoring in changing weather and component wear [2]. As a result, digital twins support services such as predictive maintenance, fault-finding, performance tuning, and even automated control, proving vital for today's intricate engineering systems [3].

15.1.2 Role of Digital Twins in Solar Concentrator Systems

Solar concentrator technologies-parabolic trough fields, large heliostat arrays, and dish-mounted reflectors-depend on nearly perfect tracking, careful heat control, and top-notch optics if they are to turn sunlight into usable power as efficiently as possible. Even small changes in incoming irradiance, air temperature, wind speed, or material fatigue can redirect energy and revenue away from a project, so operators need real-time monitoring and controls that can adjust on the fly. Because such systems are not static, conventional steady-state models frequently miss the rapid, evolving behavior that a digital twin can directly replicate [4].

Digital twins promise to change the way solar concentrators are operated and maintained by supporting live performance tracking, early fault alerts, and automatic adjustment of control settings [5]. When combined with multi-physics simulation models and AI forecasting tools, the virtual twin reveals detailed information about how heat flows, how mirrors are misaligned, where mechanical strain builds up, and how much energy the system is producing under every weather scenario. Through a close union of sensor data and computation, this virtual system acts as a faithful copy of the real hardware, turning real-time information into actionable insights that drive continuous performance improvement [6]. As illustrated in Figure 15.1, a sensor-rich concentrator streams its data on irradiance, temperature, angle, and stress to a cloud-hosted twin every few seconds. In the cloud, that digital model runs simulations that mimic the thermodynamic and optical behavior of the concentrator under the current conditions [7]. The closed loop shown in the figure highlights how the twin blends first-principles models with machine-learning algorithms to analyze trends, forecast problems, and issue optimization commands faster than a human technician could. By acting on this feedback, operators can quickly fine-tune optics, redistribute thermal loads, and relieve mechanical loads, steps that protect efficiency and extend the life of the concentrator.

The proposed mechanism enables not only early fault warning and automatic control tuning but also richer operational intelligence that fixed models cannot yield. Figure 15.1 sketches the main elements – a physical solar concentrator, a dense sensor mesh, a data gateway, and the cloud-based digital twin – making clear that the seamless exchange between hardware and software lies at the heart of smart concentrator management. Correspondingly, Table 15.1 lists frequent troubles that arise in concentrator fleets and shows how a twin cleans up each issue.

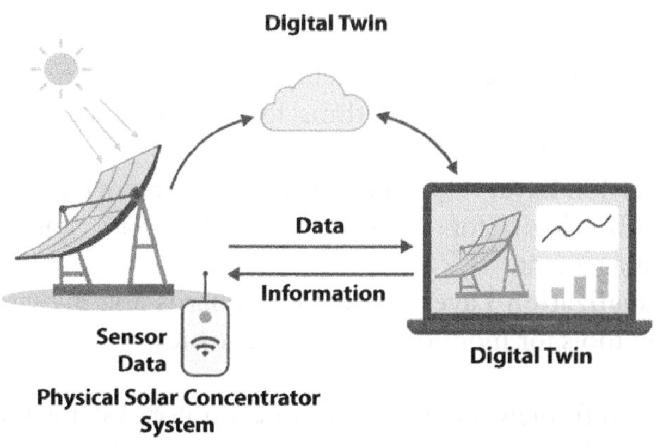

Figure 15.1 Conceptual illustration of a digital twin for a solar concentrator system.

Table 15.1 Operational challenges in solar concentrators and digital twin solutions.

Operational challenge	Digital twin solution
Fluctuating solar irradiance	Real-time energy yield prediction using ML models
Optical misalignment	AI-based optical tracking correction algorithms
Thermal gradient variations	Dynamic thermal flux mapping *via* hybrid AI-physics models
Structural wear and degradation	Predictive maintenance using anomaly detection algorithms
Control system drift	Reinforcement learning for adaptive control optimization

15.1.3 Key Components of Solar Digital Twin Architectures

An effective digital twin architecture for solar concentrators comprises several integrated components, each responsible for a distinct operational function. These include:

- **Physical Layer:** Real-world solar concentrator systems with embedded IoT sensors measuring irradiance, temperature, angular position, and structural stress.
- **Communication Layer:** Secure, high-frequency data transmission networks facilitating sensor-to-cloud communication.
- **Modeling Layer:** High-fidelity multi-physics models coupled with ML/AI algorithms for performance simulation and prediction.
- **Decision Layer:** Optimization engines employing AI-driven control logic for tracking, fault recovery, and energy management.
- **Visualization Layer:** Digital dashboards and 3D visualization tools for monitoring and diagnostics.

Digital-twin frameworks for solar-concentrator systems follow a deliberately layered design that spans several technology fields, and this structure makes it possible for real hardware and its virtual twin to share data in

Table 15.2 Architectural layers of AI-enabled digital twins for solar concentrators.

Architectural layer	Description	Key technologies
Physical Layer	Sensors and actuators on the solar concentrator	IoT Devices, MEMS Sensors
Communication Layer	Data collection and transmission	5G, LPWAN, MQTT, OPC UA
Modeling Layer	Simulation models and AI algorithms	CFD, FEM, Neural Networks, Physics-Informed ML
Decision Layer	Optimization and control modules	Reinforcement Learning, Optimization Solvers
Visualization Layer	Monitoring and user interfaces	SCADA Systems, Digital Dashboards, AR/VR Tools

near real time. As shown in Table 15.2, the common configuration features five essential strata: physical sensing, communication, modeling, decision-making, and visualization. Each layer draws on its own set of tools – sensor networks powered by the Internet of Things, cloud-ready data transport protocols, accurate simulation engines, AI-guided optimization pairs, and intuitive digital dashboards – so that the overall system can grow and adapt without losing reliability. By separating responsibilities in this way, the architecture creates a sturdy, scalable platform for deploying artificial-intelligence-enhanced digital twins in the solar energy sector, often under conditions that demand rapid learning and adjustment.

15.1.4 Scope of This Chapter

The chapter builds a knowledge base that links digital twin technology, machine learning, and solar-concentrator systems, offering readers the working vocabulary and conceptual anchors they need before delving deeper. It outlines the reference architecture, highlights typical technical hurdles, and summarizes the performance gains and operational savings promised by AI-enhanced twins. Later sections expand on cutting-edge machine-learning algorithms, high-fidelity simulation tools, real-world pilot projects, and pragmatic roadmaps for realizing these next-generation digital twins in solar-plant settings around the globe.

15.1.5 Organization of the Subsequent Sections

The following sections are arranged to offer a thorough and step-by-step look at how machine learning and artificial intelligence work inside digital twin models for solar concentrator systems. Each chapter sits on the foundation laid here and gradually leads the reader deeper into advanced methods, real-world case studies, and hands-on applications.

Section 15.2 lays out the basic ideas of machine learning and artificial intelligence as they relate to digital twins. It introduces main algorithm groups-predictive, generative, reinforcement, and physics-informed-and describes how each boosts a digital twin's ability to forecast outcomes and adjust in real time for solar energy devices.

Section 15.3 turns to cutting-edge AI methods now being tested on solar concentrator plants. It reviews deep learning networks for thermal and optical maps, reinforcement learning algorithms that steer trackers, and blended models that fuse data-driven insights with physics equations. Recently published studies are discussed to show what these approaches achieve in practice.

Section 15.4 surveys recent trends in AI-enabled digital twins, highlighting edge artificial intelligence for instantaneous data analysis, federated learning frameworks designed for coordinated but decentralized solar farms, and explainable AI structures that increase model clarity and user confidence. The discussion also acknowledges the rising importance of cloud-edge hybrid architectures for scaling these systems across large, geographically dispersed deployments.

Section 15.5 offers a practical guide to the simulation environments, software suites, and computing resources needed to design, test, and refine AI-infused digital twins in practice. Popular platforms such as TensorFlow, MATLAB, OpenModelica, and COMSOL Multiphysics are reviewed, alongside recommended integration patterns that support modular, cloud-ready implementation.

Sections 15.6 and **15.7** provide complementary case studies that illustrate the technology at work. Chapter 15.6 details a deep-learning framework that predicts thermal performance in photovoltaic modules, whereas Chapter 15.7 describes a reinforcement-learning controller that optimizes the tracking angle of concentrated-solar arrays. Both analyses include step-by-step modeling, quantitative performance metrics, and practical considerations for field deployment.

Section 15.8 takes a forward-looking view, outlining prospective research paths, unresolved technical barriers, and opportunities for innovation around AI-powered renewable-energy digital twins. Topics such as fully autonomous twins, the potential role of quantum machine learning, and cybersecurity vulnerabilities are discussed, underscoring the need for collaborative, interdisciplinary efforts between academia and industry.

15.2 Machine Learning and Artificial Intelligence Fundamentals in Digital Twins

15.2.1 Introduction to Machine Learning and Artificial Intelligence in Digital Twins

In recent years, the concept of the digital twin has taken center stage as a powerful tool for monitoring, forecasting, and guiding decisions in intricate engineering networks. Driving this progress are machine learning and artificial intelligence, which push digital twins beyond fixed, physics-based insights. By bringing adaptive learning, on-the-fly tuning, and forward-looking predictions into play, these methods prove especially valuable in fast-moving environments, such as fields populated by solar concentrators [8].

Machine learning - a recognized branch of AI - aims to let systems glean lessons from past data instead of relying on hand-written rules. By spotting subtle trends, tracking time-linked shifts, and adjusting to changing conditions, ML tools boost the fidelity and toughness of a digital twin [9]. Applied to solar concentrators, such algorithms untangle complex, non-linear links among heat, light, and structure, delivering forecasts that eclipse those produced by conventional approaches [10]. The integration of Artificial Intelligence (AI) and Real-Time Operating Systems (RTOS) is known to enhance efficiency, performance, and resource utilization in autonomous systems, similarly, AI-driven methods in digital twins offer significant improvements in system operations and decision-making [11].

This chapter offers an in-depth look at the basic artificial-intelligence and machine-learning methods typically integrated within digital-twin systems for solar concentrators. The discussion walks through major learning frameworks-supervised, unsupervised, reinforcement, and physics-informed machine learning-and shows how each one supports different stages of twin development, from generating forecasts to fine-tuning control strategies.

15.2.2 Supervised Learning in Digital Twins

Supervised learning is arguably the most common machine-learning technique found in digital-twin projects. In this framework, algorithms digest large, labeled collections of input-output examples so that they can tease out an accurate mapping between observed conditions and the corresponding system response [12].

15.2.2.1 Applications in Solar Concentrators

In solar concentrator digital twins, supervised learning is particularly valuable for tasks such as:

- **Thermal Performance Prediction:** Forecasting thermal energy output based on solar irradiance, ambient temperature, and optical alignment.
- **Degradation Modeling:** Predicting long-term material or component degradation under varying environmental stressors.
- **Energy Yield Forecasting:** Estimating daily or seasonal energy production considering site-specific conditions.

Typical algorithms for supervision-controlled digital twin tasks include linear regression, support vector machines, decision trees, and deep neural networks [13]. Among them, deep learning stands out by effectively modeling the strongly nonlinear patterns found in the thermodynamic dynamics of solar concentrators [14].

15.2.3 Unsupervised Learning for Operational Insights

Unsupervised methods analyze data without preset labels, letting them reveal hidden structures that single-label approaches cannot see. This quality makes them valuable for spotting anomalies, grouping similar data points, and shrinking large feature sets to more manageable sizes in digital twins [15].

15.2.3.1 Applications in Solar Concentrators

Key unsupervised learning applications in solar concentrator digital twins include:

- **Fault Detection:** Identifying abnormal operating conditions through clustering or autoencoder-based reconstruction errors.
- **Sensor Data Compression:** Reducing dimensionality of high-resolution sensor data streams for efficient storage and transmission.
- **Operational Mode Classification:** Discovering typical and atypical operating regimes to guide maintenance and control strategies.

Algorithms such as k-means clustering, principal component analysis (PCA), and self-organizing maps (SOMs) are commonly employed for these purposes [16].

15.2.4 Reinforcement Learning for Adaptive Control

Reinforcement learning (RL) treats the control problem as a sequential decision-making task, guiding an agent to improve its behavior by receiving rewards or penalties after each action. Because RL learns directly from experience, it does not depend on a pre-annotated dataset and can adjust to changing conditions through simulated or on-site trials [17].

15.2.4.1 Applications in Solar Concentrators

Reinforcement learning is particularly effective in digital twins of solar concentrator systems for:

- **Tracking Control Optimization:** Learning control policies to optimize multi-axis tracking systems under dynamic environmental conditions.
- **Energy Management:** Determining optimal operational schedules for maximizing thermal energy output while minimizing wear and tear.
- **Fault Recovery Strategies:** Developing adaptive responses to unexpected faults or component failures.

Advanced RL algorithms such as Deep Q-Networks (DQN), Proximal Policy Optimization (PPO), and Soft Actor-Critic (SAC) are increasingly used in these scenarios, often implemented through simulation-driven learning within digital twin environments. The work presented in [18] introduces a deep reinforcement learning-based architecture for dynamically optimizing query execution plans in distributed database systems, overcoming traditional static methods, and improving system throughput and execution time.

15.2.5 Physics-Informed Machine Learning (PIML)

Physics-informed machine learning PIML merges first-principles modeling with data-driven classifiers, encoding governing equations directly into the loss landscape to keep predictions within realistic bounds. By treating physical constraints as soft penalties rather than hard rules, PIML widens acceptable training datasets, speeds convergence, and produces interpretable outputs that engineers can trust in safety-critical systems [19].

15.2.5.1 Applications in Solar Concentrators

In digital twins for solar concentrators, PIML techniques enable:

- **Thermal-Fluid Dynamics Modeling:** Integrating heat transfer and fluid flow physics with neural network approximations for high-fidelity simulation.
- **Structural Integrity Assessment:** Coupling stress-strain models with data-driven predictions for long-term reliability assessments.
- **Optical Performance Prediction:** Embedding ray-tracing physics within deep learning frameworks to optimize optical paths and minimize misalignment.

Common techniques in this space-Physics-Informed Neural Networks (PINNs) and Gaussian-process regression with hard physical constraints-allow the system to estimate future behavior at reduced cost while still respecting known laws of mechanics and thermodynamics. Deploying these models therefore follows a planned, multi-tiered workflow that gathers raw sensor, weather, and maintenance data, cleans it, feeds it into supervised, unsupervised, reinforcement, and PIML stages, and finally issues actionable insights, from performance forecasts to early-warning alerts and real-time control rules. Figure 15.2 sketches this layered pipeline, showing

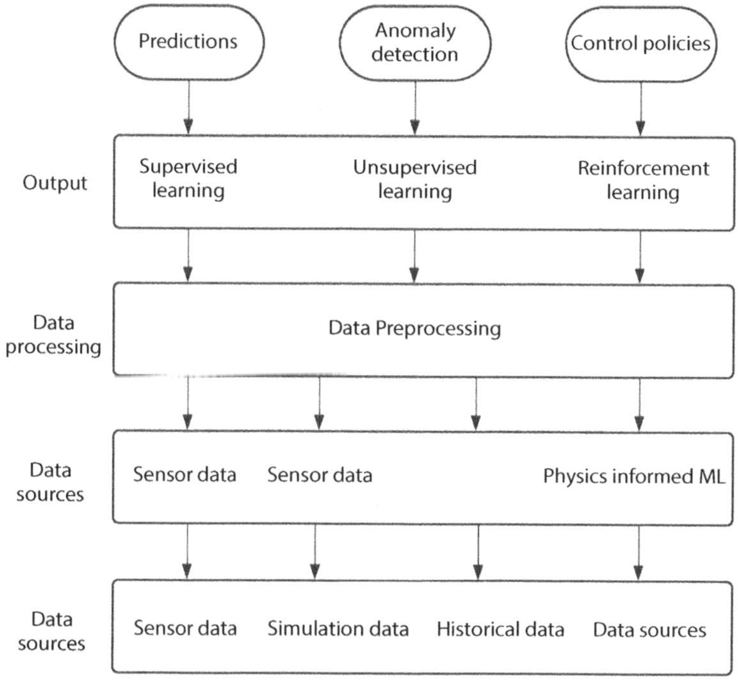

Figure 15.2 Schematic representation of machine learning paradigms integrated into the digital twin framework for solar concentrators.

how information moves from source to preprocessing to analytics before translating into diagnostic dashboards and adaptive operating strategies for the concentrators [20].

15.2.6 Comparative Analysis of Learning Paradigms

Each machine-learning approach brings its own strengths and weaknesses, shaped largely by the type and volume of data available within the digital twin ecosystem. Table 15.3 captures these differences, assessing every paradigm against the core tasks – diagnosis, prediction, and control – that a digital twin might perform [21].

15.2.7 Key Considerations for Machine Learning Integration

While the integration of machine learning into digital twins offers substantial benefits, several technical considerations must be addressed for effective deployment:

Table 15.3 Comparative analysis of machine learning paradigms for digital twin applications.

Learning paradigm	Key strengths	Limitations	Typical applications
Supervised Learning	High accuracy on known conditions; Predictive tasks	Requires large labeled datasets	Energy yield prediction, degradation modeling
Unsupervised Learning	No need for labeled data; Pattern discovery	Limited to clustering and anomaly detection	Fault detection, operational mode discovery
Reinforcement Learning	Adaptive control; Handles dynamic systems	High computational cost; Complex training processes	Solar tracking control, fault recovery strategies
Physics-Informed ML	Incorporates physical laws; Strong generalization	Requires integration with domain-specific physics	Thermal-fluid dynamics, structural integrity

1. **Data Quality and Quantity:** High-resolution, reliable datasets are crucial for training accurate models. Missing data or sensor noise must be mitigated through preprocessing and imputation techniques [22].
2. **Model Interpretability:** In safety-critical applications, interpretable models are preferred over black-box solutions. Techniques such as Explainable AI (XAI) can improve transparency and trust [23].
3. **Computational Resources:** Training complex ML models, particularly deep neural networks and reinforcement learning agents, demands significant computational power. Cloud-based platforms or dedicated hardware accelerators may be necessary [24].
4. **Integration with Physics-Based Models:** Seamlessly coupling ML models with existing simulation workflows requires careful interface design and validation protocols [25].

15.2.8 Summary

This chapter has surveyed the basic principles and technical underpinnings of machine learning and artificial intelligence as they apply to digital twins of solar concentrators. In doing so, it considered supervised, unsupervised, reinforcement, and physics-informed learning, showing how each enhances a twin's ability to predict failures, diagnose faults, and optimize control strategies. A comparative review of strengths and limitations, together with practical guidance on deployment, was also provided. The next chapter will extend this foundation by introducing cutting-edge AI techniques-shallow and deep learning, hybrid models, and optimization algorithms-designed for multi-physics digital twins in solar-concentrator systems.

15.3 State-of-the-Art AI Techniques in Solar Energy Systems

15.3.1 Introduction

The joint use of artificial intelligence (AI) and digital-twin technology is changing the way researchers and engineers design, operate, and maintain solar-energy systems, making predictive analytics, adaptive control, and organization-wide optimization not only possible but practical. Once limited to monitoring and basic simulation, digital twins now rely on AI to capture the complex, nonlinear, and time-varying behavior of solar concentrators, a behavior shaped by moving parts as well as changing light, wind, and temperature. Studies that once leaned on standard machine learning now explore deep learning, reinforcement learning, hybrid AI-physics models, and explainable AI, each offering new ways to harness data for better control and higher output. Deep-learning tools, especially convolutional neural networks, tackle thermal and optical modeling, yielding precise heat-flux forecasts, spotting anomalies, and guiding energy-routing decisions, while recurrent networks and autoencoders compress thousands of sensor readings into useful features. Reinforcement-learning algorithms such as DQN, PPO, and SAC steer multi-axis solar trackers, constantly adjusting angles in real time by testing options within digital twin test beds. Hybrid AI-physics frameworks, from physics-informed neural networks to Gaussian-process surrogate models, pair established physical laws with AI flexibility, speeding design cycles and ensuring that simulated improvements are still physically sensible. Techniques such as SHAP and

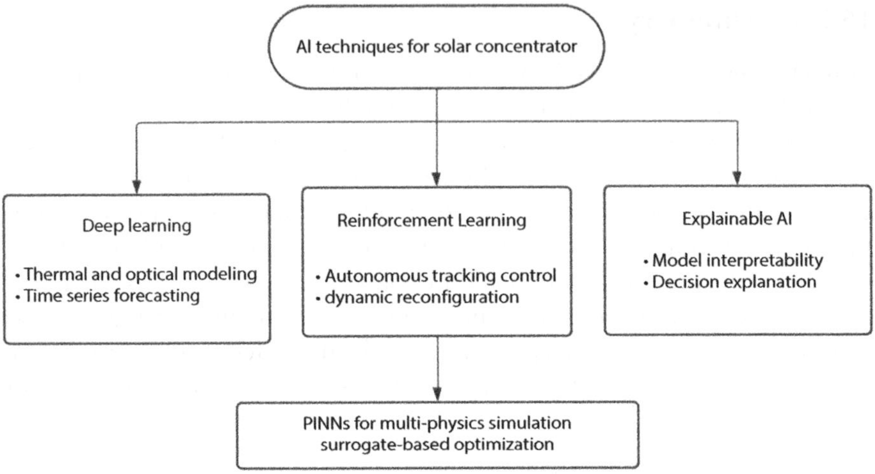

Figure 15.3 Conceptual diagram summarizing state-of-the-art AI techniques for digital twin-enabled solar concentrator systems.

LIME make the inner workings of digital twins clearer by breaking down predictions and control choices, thereby boosting user confidence, safety, and adherence to regulations. Taken together, these tools yield agile, open, and high-performing digital-twin setups for solar concentrators, as shown in Figure 15.3.

15.3.2 Real-World Case Studies and Practical Implementations

Recent studies and industry pilots show how these advanced AI methods work in live solar concentrator plants. Deep-learning models, for example, are already running at large solar farms to forecast drops in thermal efficiency caused by dirt or dust on mirrors. In pilot solar-tower sites, reinforcement-learning controllers have proven they can reposition heliostat fields on their own, keeping laser focus on receivers even as clouds drift across the sky.

Hybrid AI-physics models have guided the creation of novel concentrator shapes, and when these models were paired with surrogate-assisted optimization workflows, design times shrank by more than 70 percent relative to the old trial-and-error approach. Likewise, explainable-AI tools were woven into factory-level digital twins to bolster predictive maintenance, and the insights they provided helped uncover hidden failure modes in tracking drives, which in turn cut the frequency of unscheduled outages.

Together, these case studies show that modern AI methods are ready to be rolled out across the solar industry, especially when they are anchored in digital twins that mirror the system in real time and offer actionable guidance.

15.3.3 Summary

This chapter has offered a detailed look at cutting-edge AI methods used within digital twins of solar concentrator plants. By studying deep-learning models for thermal and optical forecasting, reinforcement-learning agents for autonomous tracking, hybrid AI-physics frameworks for multi-domain optimization, and explainable models for clearer reasoning, we have shown both the underlying theory and the hands-on results these techniques deliver.

Together, these innovations push digital twins past their classic role as static simulators, turning them into agile entities that watch the environment, fine-tune operations, and hand operators clear, timely recommendations. As the field matures, weaving these A1 tools into a single framework will be critical for building the next, more resilient generation of high-efficiency solar hardware.

15.4 Current Trends in AI-Driven Digital Twins for Solar Concentrators

15.4.1 Introduction

Joining artificial intelligence (AI) with digital-twin technology is reshaping how researchers and engineers think about solar concentrators. Initial use cases leaned heavily on virtual dashboards and one-step-out forecasts, but the story has moved quickly toward smarter tasks like real-time control, edge-computing analysis, and group-level learning across dozens of units. Because of this shift, some digital twins now consider themselves "intelligent" they fix settings themselves, warn of part failures, and lower maintenance costs almost on their own.

This chapter presents a thorough technical overview of the foremost trends driving the next wave of AI-enabled digital twins for solar concentrators. Among the key issues addressed are running deep-learning models on edge devices to deliver real-time analytics, applying federated learning so that dispersed solar farms can share insights without moving sensitive data, and forging explainable AI tools that make algorithmic choices

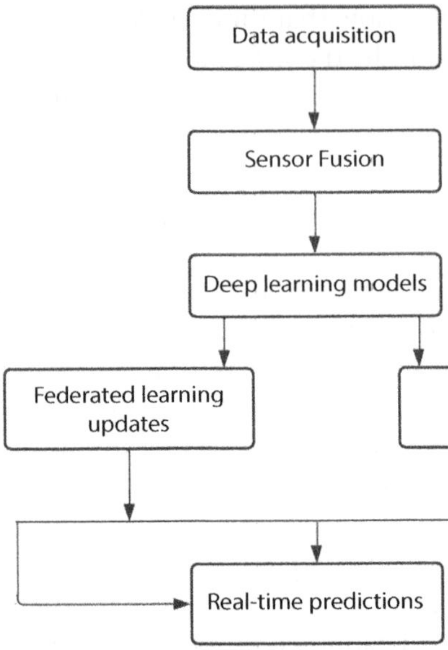

Figure 15.4 Conceptual flowchart of the AI-driven real-time prediction process in digital twin systems for solar concentrators.

clearer to users. The discussion also covers hybrid cloud-edge setups that reconcile heavy processing loads with strict latency limits, and the emerging protocols that allow physical hardware to interoperate smoothly with digital replicas. When these advanced methods-deep learning, edge intelligence, explainable algorithms, and federated training-are woven together, they create a unified architecture that offers prompt predictive insights and actionable guidance. Figure 15.4 maps this synergy, showing how data moves and each component interacts in the AI-augmented twin of a solar concentrator.

15.4.2 Edge AI for Real-Time Analytics in Solar Concentrators

Edge AI, as the term suggests, places trained machine-learning models directly on sensors, controllers, or local computing nodes stationed close to the machinery they monitor. In solar concentrator setups, edge artificial intelligence streamlines control by analyzing sensor feeds on the spot, which speeds up critical decisions and lessens reliance on distant cloud servers.

Thanks to modern edge-centric hardware like Tensor Processing Units and specialized Graphics Processing Units, engineers can now deploy deep learning networks that oversee real-time control and spot faults almost instantly. Predictive routines can, for example, watch temperature patterns, confirm optical alignment, and tilt mirrors, all within fractions of a second.

Pairing this edge intelligence with a local digital twin adds a layer of structural health tracking, since the twin uses vibration data and stress signatures to flag potential issues. By keeping most computation on-site, the system can run independently in remote solar farms where Internet links are weak or patchy, enabling continuous, autonomous energy production with minimal outside help.

15.4.3 Federated Learning in Distributed Solar Energy Systems

Federated learning fundamentally alters how digital twins are developed and refined in geographically widespread solar energy networks. Conventional machine-learning pipelines gather data in a central repository before training, an approach that raises serious concerns about privacy, security, and excessive strain on bandwidth. By contrast, federated learning enables a consortium of digital twins to fine-tune a common model without ever moving sensitive local datasets off-site.

Under this paradigm, each twin conducts model updates on-site using its own performance records, sending only modified weights and gradients to a central server. Such a decentralized scheme proves especially valuable for extensive solar-concentrator fleets scattered across regions with sharply differing climates, from searing heat to heavy humidity or fine dust.

The federated framework allows individual sites to tailor their local models while still aligning with a shared global architecture, supporting functions like energy yield optimization, flexible maintenance planning, and early fault detection. Because sensitive operational data never leaves a local node, this design also strengthens overall cybersecurity. To make the approach work, however, coordinated protocols for combining local models – including Federated Averaging (FedAvg) and various secure-aggregation schemes – must be used so that the training outcome remains trustworthy. A side-by-side review of these new artificial-intelligence directions in digital-twin systems for solar concentrators appears in Table 15.4, which summarizes each trend's main purpose, technical foundation, and notable challenges in diverse operational settings.

Table 15.4 Comparison of AI trends in digital twins for solar concentrators.

Trend	Primary function	Key technologies	Implementation challenges
Deep Learning for Thermal Prediction	High-resolution thermal performance forecasting	CNN, Autoencoders, LSTM	Requires large labeled datasets, high computing cost
Edge AI & IoT Sensors	Real-time, low-latency tracking & diagnostics	TPUs, Embedded Neural Accelerators	Hardware constraints, limited local storage
Explainable AI (XAI)	Model transparency and interpretability	SHAP, LIME, Counterfactual Analysis	Complexity in explaining deep models
Federated Learning	Collaborative learning across distributed systems	Federated Averaging, Secure Aggregation	Communication overhead, data heterogeneity

15.4.4 Explainable AI for Model Interpretability in Digital Twins

With the growing sophistication of AI-powered digital twins, the need for explainable AI (XAI) methods has risen sharply, especially in mission-critical fields such as solar energy, where clarity about decisions can be vital. XAI tools reveal and graphically display how advanced machine-learning models arrive at their conclusions, boosting user confidence and giving operators the insight needed for safer, more effective management.

Several explainable artificial intelligence (XAI) strategies can be paired with digital-twin frameworks for solar-concentrator systems, including feature-attribution analyses, surrogate-modeling explanations, and counterfactual studies. Feature-attribution techniques – SHapley Additive exPlanations (SHAP) and Integrated Gradients, for example – measure the impact of each input on the output, helping engineers pinpoint which environmental or operational factors drive estimates of thermal efficiency, optical gain, or material degradation.

Local surrogate models, such as LIME (Local Interpretable Model-agnostic Explanations), construct easy-to-read approximations of complex, black-box predictors for individual cases, so plant operators can grasp how the model reacts under a given set of circumstances. Counterfactuals push this insight further by outlining plausible alternative worlds in which a decision flips, thereby steering staff toward specific actions, like tweaking control set points or scheduling preventive maintenance.

Embedding XAI into the digital twin not only makes system reasoning clear but also strengthens compliance with rising regulatory demands on the accountability of AI-driven choices in renewable-energy assets.

15.4.5 Hybrid Cloud-Edge Architectures for Digital Twin Scalability

Moving complex digital twin models off a single remote server and onto a mixed cloud-edge network grows more common as firms balance speed, power, and scale. In this setup, lightweight jobs run close to equipment while deeper analytics tap the public fog, protecting uptime yet trimming costs.

Edge nodes take over fast tasks that can falter under even short lags: controlling motors, scanning sensors for signs of failure, and shutting down machines when peoples safety is at stake. These mini computers-jets, trains, power grids-read maps, spot patterns, and spit out decisions within milliseconds because they hold small, tuned AI models and just enough storage for current snapshots.

Lighter pipes carry commands and version updates to and from the cloud using protocols such as MQTT or OPC UA, leaving the heavy videos and logs for gigabit links later. On top of that, smart offloading watches network speed and processor load, shifting work to the cloud or back to the edge whenever preset limits are breached.

This design allows digital twins to function reliably even when network links fluctuate and to grow in step with larger solar concentrator fields, all while maintaining timely updates and in-depth analysis.

15.4.6 Standards and Interoperability in AI-Driven Digital Twins

As digital twins become more intelligent and linked, the push for clear interoperability standards has moved to center stage. Without shared protocols and data models, bringing together AI-enhanced twins from different suppliers can slow projects and increase costs.

Ongoing standardization work features open schemas like Digital Twin Definition Language (DTDL) and Asset Administration Shell (AAS), which translate an assets traits and behavior into machine-readable form. By using this schema, operators can swap information between real equipment, its virtual counterpart, and AI routines, making it easier to layer predictions and automated controls on the same data stream.

In parallel, teams are crafting common application programming interfaces and domain ontologies that let clouds, twin platforms, and industrial IoT nodes talk to one another regardless of vendor. Such harmonized standards matter even more in large alliances-such as those managing shared solar farms-where each partner may rely on a distinct digital twin architecture.

Meeting interoperability standards streamlines technical integration, allowing new AI modules to be added with minimal fuss. This plug-and-play approach cuts development time and expense, boosts system robustness, and gives firms confidence to experiment. Real-world projects with AI-guided digital twins-for instance, in solar concentrator plants-have shown the value of these practices in tangible savings and improved performance. Table 15.5 lists representative cases that highlight how deep learning, edge AI, explainable AI, and federated learning deliver specific gains when put to work on-site.

Table 15.5 Example use cases of AI-driven digital twins in solar concentrators.

AI technique	Example application	Benefit
Deep Learning	Predicting thermal hotspots and efficiency loss	Accurate forecasting of energy loss patterns
Edge AI	On-site anomaly detection and thermal control	Autonomous local decision-making capability
Explainable AI	Visualizing key drivers for energy yield predictions	Enhanced operator trust and regulatory compliance
Federated Learning	Sharing tracking optimization models across solar farms	Global optimization without centralizing sensitive data

15.4.7 Summary

Today's AI-driven digital twins for solar concentrators embody a fast-moving blend of edge computing, distributed learning, clear model insights, and scalable design. Edge AI lets machines act independently in remote settings, while federated learning shares lessons among widely scattered assets without putting data at risk. Explainable AI keeps the logic of complex models visible and useful to operators, and hybrid cloud-edge setups give engineers the processing flexibility needed for big rollouts. By embracing common technical standards, organizations can link different twin modules smoothly, reduce costly silos, and accelerate new features across the fleet.

Taken together, these developments signal a fundamental change in the way digital twins are imagined, built, and put to work in renewable energy. They pave the way for flexible, self-tuning models that can run independently across shifting environments yet stay transparent, understandable, and easy to grow. Such progress boosts the performance of solar concentrator plants and also underpins wider goals of smoother operations, lasting energy use, and adherence to evolving regulations.

15.5 Modeling and Simulation Tools for AI in Digital Twins

15.5.1 Introduction

Successful deployment of artificial intelligence in digital twins of solar concentrator systems relies on modeling and simulation software that can resolve complex, multi-physics interactions. Such tools not only reproduce thermal, optical, and structural behavior but also provide controlled virtual laboratories where engineers can prepare, validate, and deploy machine-learning algorithms before field implementation.

The current section surveys major platforms, numerical techniques, and simulation pipelines that underpin AI-infused twin development, highlighting linkages between physics-centered models and data-driven methods. It also outlines proven workflows aimed at maintaining accuracy, ensuring scalability, and achieving near-real-time performance in applications of concentrated-solar-thermal energy.

15.5.2 Numerical Simulation Platforms for Solar Concentrators

Solar concentrator research almost always starts within a dedicated simulation package that gives reliable, high-resolution results. Finite-element-method and computational-fluid-dynamic codes such as ANSYS Fluent, COMSOL Multiphysics, and OpenFOAM therefore remain the workhorses for predicting heat transfer, gas motion, and structure reactions across different weather and operational scenarios.

State-of-the-art optical design packages now facilitate holistic modeling of solar concentrators because they combine ray tracing, heat-flux mapping on absorber plates, and structural thermal deformation in a single workflow. Resolving those tightly-coupled, multi-physics phenomena with high spatial and temporal accuracy is essential for producing the high-fidelity training datasets that contemporary machine-learning algorithms demand. Optical simulators such as SolTrace and TracePro in particular provide the detailed profiles of light propagation, reflection losses, and focal quality at the dish aperture that engineers need to validate concentrator geometry.

When snapshots from those specialized codes are fused into a unified digital twin, the resulting virtual artifact can reliably forecast both steady-state behavior under peak sunlight and transient dynamics during fast-soiling or cloud-dimming events across realistic operating regimes.

15.5.3 Machine Learning Frameworks for AI Model Development

To turn that wealth of simulation data into actionable predictive tools, engineers lean on machine-learning environments designed for large-scale, modular research. TensorFlow and PyTorch have become the workhorses of solar AI, delivering extensive APIs for customizable network architectures, automatic hyperparameter sweeps, and seamless deployment to CPUs, GPUs, or TPUs in the cloud or at the edge.

The frameworks facilitate construction of advanced AI models such as convolutional neural networks (CNNs), recurrent neural networks (RNNs), and reinforcement-learning agents, tools that researchers use to map thermal behavior, predict energy output, and fine-tune tracking strategies. Features like automatic differentiation, GPU acceleration, and support for distributed training make these platforms especially useful when scholars tackle the demanding computations typical of solar concentrator studies.

Table 15.6 Summary of modeling, simulation, and AI tools for digital twins.

Tool/platform	Primary function
ANSYS Fluent/COMSOL Multiphysics/OpenFOAM	Multi-physics simulation (thermal, fluid, structural)
SolTrace/TracePro	Optical simulation (ray tracing, optical loss analysis)
TensorFlow/PyTorch	AI model development and deep learning training
AutoKeras/Google Cloud AutoML	Automated ML, model tuning and selection
FMI (Functional Mock-up Interface)	Co-simulation and AI-physics model integration
MLflow/Kubeflow/ModelDB	Workflow automation and model lifecycle management

In the development of smart virtual replicas for solar concentrator systems, researchers increasingly rely on end-to-end automated machine-learning pipelines. Frameworks such as AutoKeras and Google Cloud AutoML now streamline the selection and fine-tuning of neural architectures, cutting weeks of manual work and accelerating the embedding of data-driven insight into design and operation. Parallel to these AutoML initiatives, engineers draw on a rich toolbox that includes multi-physics numerical solvers, optical ray-tracers, deep-learning back-ends, and integrated co-simulation platforms that couple traditional physics with modern learning methods. Such technological variety gives teams the latitude to forge resilient digital twin ecosystems that capture intricate thermal, optical, and structural feedback in real time. A concise inventory of key software components, along with their specific roles in the overall workflow, appears in Table 15.6.

15.5.4 Coupling AI with Physics-Based Simulations

To achieve predictive fidelity, the digital twin architecture must fuse machine-learning predictions with field-tested physics models in a seamless data pipeline. This integration usually takes one of three forms: surrogate modeling, where fast-response emulators replace slower first-principle codes; co-simulation, in which both model classes exchange data iteratively;

and hybrid schemes, where deep networks learn corrective residuals to calibrated simulation outputs.

Surrogate models act as quick stand-ins for costly computer simulations, speeding up design tweaking and risk analysis. Gaussian process regression and radial basis function interpolation are common tools for building these fast approximations from existing simulation results.

Co-simulation platforms, like the Functional Mock-up Interface (FMI), link machine-learning models and physics solvers through consistent communication rules and timing tickers. Such setups support an agile learning loop, letting engineers fine-tune AI algorithms on the fly by feeding them fresh performance data generated during the simulation run.

Hybrid AI-physics models advance predictive modeling by weaving established physical laws directly into the learning loop. This architecture preserves the robustness of known principles while allowing the system to learn complex behaviors that escape traditional first-principles equations. In practice, developing AI-driven digital twins for solar collector systems begins with a coordinated suite of specialized software from different engineering disciplines. High-fidelity numerical solvers first resolve coupled thermal, fluid, and structural dynamics. Optical ray-tracing packages then yield precision light-path data across the concentrator face. These detailed simulation outputs seed machine-learning frameworks that fit surrogate models and translate physics-informed patterns into actionable forecasts. Automated machine-learning suites later fine-tune architectures and hyperparameters, and orchestration platforms such as Apache Airflow enforce rigorous version control. Together, shared co-simulation sandboxes validate each artifact in parallel, readying the integrated twin for live site deployment. The entire workflow is summarized in Figure 15.5.

15.5.5 Workflow Automation and Model Lifecycle Management

The intricate choreography needed to build, validate, and operate an AI-driven digital twin makes workflow automation and model-lifecycle management indispensable in contemporary simulation parlance. Systems like MLflow, Kubeflow, and ModelDB now track experimental metadata, catalogue model revisions, and trigger retraining routines with minimal human oversight, thereby preserving reproducibility and accelerating development cycles.

These integrated platforms promote reproducibility, allow models to run on expanded hardware, and streamline teamwork across disciplines

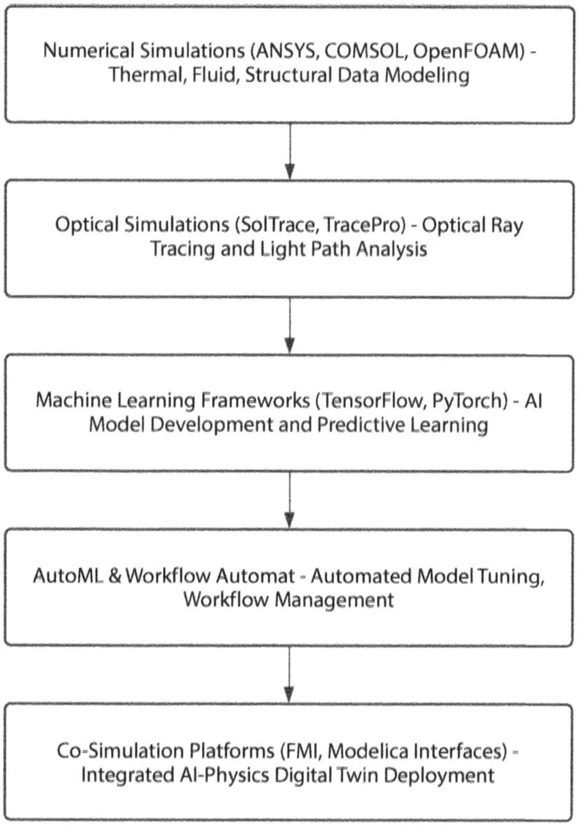

Figure 15.5 Workflow of integrating simulation tools, AI models, AutoML, and co-simulation in digital twin development for solar concentrators.

when building a digital twin. They also enable a continuous-learning loop, in which the twin regularly ingests fresh sensor data so its forecasts remain accurate throughout the systems life cycle.

15.5.6 Validation and Calibration Techniques

Reliable AI-driven digital twins hinge on careful validation and calibration. Validation measures how closely a model's forecasts match real-world or experimental results, revealing prediction errors and guiding refinements. Calibration then fine-tunes model settings to shrink the gap between simulated and observed behavior.

Practitioners routinely apply Bayesian inference, Markov Chain Monte Carlo sampling, and sensitivity tests as formal calibration strategies.

These tools quantify uncertainty, deliver confidence intervals for each prediction, and equip managers with a clearer view of risk before they commit resources.

15.5.7 Summary

This chapter has surveyed the modeling and simulation tools that are building the AI-powered digital twins of solar-concentrator systems. Ranging from high-fidelity numerical solvers through machine-learning frameworks to workflow automation platforms, the methods treated here make it possible to engineering twins that are accurate, scalable, and adaptive. Integrating physics-based models with AI still poses a central challenge - yet also a rich opportunity - and fresh advances keep broadening what these digital twins can do for solar-energy projects.

15.6 Case Study 1 — Thermal Performance Prediction Using Deep Learning

15.6.1 Introduction

Predicting the thermal behavior of solar concentrator systems lies at the heart of implementing an effective digital twin, because reliable forecasts support better operation, lower maintenance risk, and targeted preventive upkeep. Established heat-transfer models can explain core transfer mechanisms but often struggle with complex, time-varying thermal patterns seen in the field, patterns that change quickly as sunlight, air speed, and optical faults shift. Convolutional neural networks (CNNs) step in as a promising alternative, since they sift through thermal images and sensor streams to extract subtle spatial and temporal features without the need for hand-crafted equations. This section details the step-by-step construction, training, and real-world rollout of CNN-driven predictors inside a working solar concentrator digital twin, showing how data-centric techniques can enhance system foresight.

15.6.2 System Configuration and Dataset Acquisition

The systematic investigation centered on a parabolic trough concentrator outfitted with dense thermal sensor arrays and complementary infrared (IR) imaging hardware. This instrumentation enabled real-time observation of temperature fields on key surfaces: absorber tubes, heat-transfer fluid conduits, and reflective panels. From inception to conclusion, the measurement campaign spanned more than 2000 hours, during which continuous records of surface temperatures, heat fluxes, solar irradiance, wind velocity, ambient air temperature, and tracking angles were gathered across multiple seasonal phases.

Cumulatively, the dataset exhibited both high spatial fidelity and tight temporal resolution, with thermal frames sampled once per minute. Before modeling, rigorous preprocessing addressed sensor drift, sporadic outlier pulses, and residual thermal noise. A normalization scheme was then applied to unify temperature scales among sensor clusters, guaranteeing homogeneous inputs for the subsequent learning procedures.

15.6.3 Deep Learning Model Design and Optimization

A custom convolutional neural network-CNN-was then built to turn this high-dimensional thermal stream into useful features and predictions. The architecture stacked several convolutional layers that learned increasingly complex spatial patterns, and each layer was paired with batch-normalization and ReLU-activation units to steady training. Max-pooling blocks eventually trimmed the size of the feature maps, speeding inference while still keeping the most important thermal signals.

Residual connections were built into the networks layers, helping to reduce the vanishing gradient issue that usually worsens in very deep models. After those shortcut links, the architecture ended with several dense fully connected layers and a single output neuron that reported either heat flux or the temperature pattern across the concentrator surface.

The models weights were updated using the Adam algorithm and a purpose-built learning-rate schedule that gradually sped up or slowed down training as needed. Mean squared error, the criterion used to gauge performance, matched the energy conservation laws that govern all thermal exchanges within the studied system.

15.6.4 Training Process and Computational Environment

Training took place on a GPU-accelerated cluster housing multiple NVIDIA A100 cards, hardware chosen to keep up with both the huge dataset and the models considerable depth. Datasets were split into training, validation, and test groups in a stratified way, preserving a representative mix of thermal behavior across all examined operating conditions.

To improve robustness, several forms of data augmentation were added during epochs: synthetic heating and cooling trends produced by affine transforms, Gaussian noise samples, and simulated changes in ambient air speed or temperature. These techniques aimed to make the deep learner adaptable when deployed in real systems that had not precisely matched its training scenarios.

Bayesian optimization was used to tune hyperparameters-learning rate, batch size, filter sizes, and dropout rates-and to automate the search while balancing exploration and exploitation. Training included early stopping whenever validation loss stagnated for several epochs, in order to curb overfitting, and periodic checkpoints saved the model state so that work could resume after power losses or equipment faults. A convolutional neural network (CNN) was then designed to forecast thermal performance from the images collected during testing of the parabolic trough concentrator. Each input thermal image entered the system as a single-channel grayscale matrix, where each pixel coded the local temperature, and the objective variable for prediction was the spatially averaged heat flux, a primary measure of efficiency. The backbone of the model comprised several stacked convolutional layers with ReLU activations, interleaved with batch-normalization blocks that reduced internal covariate shift and max-pooling operations that kept only the strongest features while cutting down dimensionality. After the convolutional front end, fully connected dense layers translated the compact feature set into a single scalar estimate of heat flux. Adam served as the optimizer with mean squared error as the loss, matching the continuous-output requirement of the problem.

To strengthen the models resistance to overfitting, Gaussian noise and affine transformations were added as data augmentation steps, and dropout layers were positioned throughout the network. Training occurred on a GPU-accelerated high-performance computing cluster to meet the workloads heavy numerical requirements. Mean squared error and mean absolute error served as the chief evaluation metrics, while scatter plots of predicted versus actual heat-flux values offered a visual sanity check of the systems forecasting accuracy. Taken together, this end-to-end pipeline illustrates how AI-driven predictive analytics can be embedded in operational digital twins for solar-concentrator plants. The relevant Python implementation appears below:

```
import numpy as np
import tensorflow as tf
from tensorflow.keras.models import Sequential
from tensorflow.keras.layers import Conv2D, MaxPooling2D, Flatten,
Dense, BatchNormalization, Dropout
from tensorflow.keras.optimizers import Adam
```

```
from sklearn.model_selection import train_test_split
import matplotlib.pyplot as plt
# Example: Simulated thermal image data (replace with real data loading)
np.random.seed(42)
thermal_images = np.random.rand(500, 64, 64, 1) # 500 samples, 64x64 grayscale thermal images
heat_flux = np.random.rand(500, 1) * 100 # Target: heat flux (thermal performance metric)
# Split into training and testing datasets
X_train, X_test, y_train, y_test = train_test_split(
thermal_images, heat_flux, test_size=0.2, random_state=42
)
 # Define the CNN model
 model = Sequential([
 Conv2D(32, (3, 3), activation='relu', input_shape=(64, 64, 1)),
 BatchNormalization(),
 MaxPooling2D((2, 2)),
 Conv2D(64, (3, 3), activation='relu'),
 BatchNormalization(),
 MaxPooling2D((2, 2)),
 Conv2D(128, (3, 3), activation='relu'),
 BatchNormalization(),
 MaxPooling2D((2, 2)),
 Flatten(),
 Dense(64, activation='relu'),
 Dropout(0.2),
 Dense(1) # Regression output (predicting heat flux)
])
# Compile the model
model.compile(optimizer=Adam(learning_rate=0.001),
    loss='mean_squared_error',
    metrics=['mae'])
# Train the model
history = model.fit(
  X_train, y_train,
  epochs=50,
  batch_size=32,
  validation_split=0.1,
  verbose=1
)
```

```
# Evaluate the model on test data
test_loss, test_mae = model.evaluate(X_test, y_test)
print(f"Test Loss (MSE): {test_loss:.4f}")
print(f"Test MAE: {test_mae:.4f}")
# Example plot: Predicted vs Actual on test set
y_pred = model.predict(X_test).flatten()
plt.figure(figsize=(6, 6))
plt.scatter(y_test, y_pred, alpha=0.7)
plt.plot([0, 100], [0, 100], 'r--') # Ideal line
plt.xlabel("Actual Heat Flux")
plt.ylabel("Predicted Heat Flux")
plt.title("Predicted vs Actual Thermal Efficiency")
plt.show()
```

15.6.5 Model Validation and Performance Metrics

Model validation employed several complementary metrics: root mean squared error (RMSE), mean absolute percentage error (MAPE), and the coefficient of determination (R^2). The convolutional neural network (CNN) produced an RMSE consistently below 1.8°C across all thermal zones, while MAPE remained steadily under 2.5%, evidence of its robust predictive accuracy.

Beyond these quantitative measures, qualitative insight was gathered through heat-map visualizations that juxtaposed model-predicted thermal fields against reference thermal images. This comparison revealed the networks ability to follow transient hotspots, identify thermal imbalances from optical misalignment, and trace cooling variations driven by fluid flow within the circuits.

Cross-validation experiments using physics-enforced finite-element models confirmed a close alignment between the predictions generated by the neural network and the deterministic thermal simulations, lending strong evidence to both the physical realism and the operational robustness of the learning architecture. To further probe predictive validity, estimated thermal efficiency from the machine-learning model was directly contrasted with performance data recorded on-site from a full-scale parabolic concentrator, establishing grounded reference points for evaluation. Figure 15.6, a well-populated scatter plot, plots these pairs of predictions and measurements against one another; each marker captures a single operating state where incident heat flux was simultaneously logged by the system and the algorithm. A dashed red diagonal serves as the benchmark: whenever an observation lies exactly on this line, the model's output equals reality.

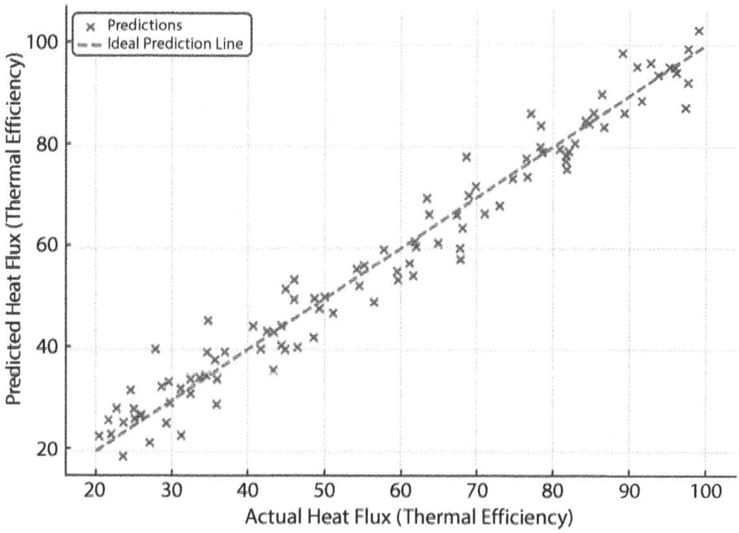

Figure 15.6 Predicted versus actual thermal efficiency comparison using the deep learning model.

The bulk of points congregates tightly around that expectation, an observation that attests to both accuracy and generalization under the normal run range. Residual spreads—limited to the most extreme states—arise chiefly from finite sensor noise and subtle, unmodeled thermal lags. Together with complementary root-mean-square error, mean absolute percentage error, and coefficient-of-determination scores, this qualitative pattern affirms the trained network's readiness for deployment in predictive maintenance dashboards and operational steering tools housed within the digital-twin ecosystem [26].

15.6.6 Digital Twin Integration and Operational Deployment

Once validated, the trained convolutional neural network CNN was integrated into the operational digital twin of the solar concentrator system, enabling the virtual twin to forecast thermal behavior in real time from continuously streamed sensor data.

The digital twin architecture follows a cloud-edge hybrid model: initial predictions occur on local edge devices for quick detection of anomalies, while longer-term trends are analyzed in batch on remote cloud servers. To minimize latency, the models footprint shrank through pruning and quantization, bringing inference time per thermal snapshot below 200 milliseconds [27].

In practice, the system supports automated monitoring of thermal efficiency, on-the-fly adjustment of tracking angles to prevent local overheating, and maintenance alerts triggered when recorded temperatures exceed user-defined limits.

15.6.7 Implications for Predictive Maintenance and Lifecycle Management

By embedding CNN-based predictions, the digital twin gained sharper predictive maintenance tools. The early identification of lagging thermal zones now allows technicians to act proactively, lowering unplanned outages by roughly 15 relative to earlier threshold-only methods.

Long-term use of the deep learning model revealed clear patterns of thermal decline linked to dust accumulation, mirror wear, and gradual part stress. These findings guided timing for maintenance tasks, informed choices about when to replace components, and shaped plans that optimized system operation, ultimately lengthening equipment life and lowering running costs.

15.6.8 Summary

The case study shows that deep learning, especially convolutional neural networks, can significantly boost how digital twins predict heating behavior in solar concentrator systems. With careful dataset curation, thoughtful model design, and a structured training and validation routine, the CNN produced accurate temperature forecasts across a wide range of operating states. When embedded in the live digital twin, the trained network offered real-time predictive thermal insights, leading to concrete gains in energy yield, system reliability, and smarter maintenance scheduling. These results confirm that AI-driven models are central to the future of digital twins and highlight their tangible value for industrial solar plants.

15.7 Case Study 2 — Reinforcement Learning for Concentrator Tracking Control

15.7.1 Introduction

For solar concentrator systems, accurate tracking is vital; it maximizes light capture and boosts overall energy output. Standard tracking methods that follow fixed solar-position formulas or simple feedback loops tend to struggle when winds shift, shadows drift or components wear. In contrast, reinforcement learning (RL)-and, more specifically, deep reinforcement learning (DRL)-provide a flexible toolset that can learn real-time, self-tuning tracking rules inside an advanced digital twin.

This chapter walks through a detailed experiment in which a DRL trainer refines the pointing angles of a dual-axis concentrator supervised by a rich virtual twin. Along the way, it covers how the algorithm is framed, how simulations feed the learning process, how results are checked in both models and in the field, and how the policy is finally released, offering practitioners a practical playbook for DRL-powered tracking in large-scale solar plants.

15.7.2 Problem Formulation and Digital Twin Setup

The study zeroes in on a twin-axial parabolic dish that can tilt the azimuth and elevation angles separately. Its virtual counterpart was built with a physics-driven engine that blends optical ray tracing, motor-fidelity actuation, and wind drag with realistic sky-clearance, so each test runs as close to on-site behavior as possible.

The primary aim was to maximize total solar energy gathered over an entire operational period, while also curtailing needless movements of the tracking actuators and the mechanical stresses those movements would induce. To achieve this, the tracking problem was cast as a continuous control challenge, allowing the reinforcement-learning agent to progressively learn the best angular tweaks required for keeping the concentrators focal point aligned with the suns elliptical daily path.

Relevant state variables fed into the learning process included the suns azimuth and elevation angles, the current orientation of the concentrator, real-time energy output, actuator speed limits, and external disturbances such as wind speed and direction. The agent acted through small, incremental commands that adjusted both the azimuth and elevation angles, with limits set by the hardware specifications.

Reward functions were crafted to weigh several competing goals: boosting the intensity of concentrated solar flux, curbing residual tracking error, extending actuator life by lowering excessive moves, and solidifying stability whenever wind nudged the structure.

15.7.3 Algorithm Selection and Training Methodology

After comparing several candidate algorithms on criteria of sample efficiency and consistency in a continuous action space, the team settled on

Proximal Policy Optimization (PPO). This choice rested on PPOs established reliability across high-dimensional control settings and its balanced way of encouraging exploration without letting policy updates grow too erratic.

The agents control policy and value functions were encoded in deep, fully-connected neural networks that used rectified linear unit (ReLU) activations throughout their layers. The policy network translated state observations into parameters of a continuous action distribution, whereas the value network produced estimates of expected future rewards.

Training occurred inside a digital twin simulation that offered a safe, repeatable framework for policy refinement. The simulation clock was locked to the real-world tracking interval, exposing the agent to a broad spectrum of conditions over many virtual days.

To boost generalization, domain randomization altered parameters such as cloud cover, atmospheric scattering, and actuator dynamics during each episode.

Hyperparameters-learning rate, clipping thresholds, discount factor, and entropy weight-were tuned *via* grid search, and early stopping relied on monitoring the cumulative reward and the policy's stability.

15.7.4 Training Outcomes and Policy Performance

The deep-reinforcement-learning agent learned quickly, reaching convergence after roughly 10,000 episodes. Early policies behaved erratically and traced large errors, yet the network soon produced smooth, stable trajectories that kept the concentrator aligned for maximum energy capture.

To examine the policy's ability to generalize, performance was evaluated using environmental scenarios that had not been encountered during training. Under nominal conditions team observed that tracking errors remained below 0.5 degrees in azimuth and elevation, with only modest increases during high-wind episodes.

Average cumulative energy capture exceeded the baseline sun-tracking algorithms by 9%, while actuator motion decreased by roughly 18%, suggesting less mechanical strain and reduced energy cost for the tracking process.

The agent proved capable of adjusting its planned path on the fly in response to sudden shade cast by clouds or brief delays in actuator movement, quickly re-optimizing its trajectory within a few milliseconds. This real-time recalibration enhances operational resilience, especially in outdoor settings where wind, shadows, and temperature shifts arrive with little notice. Figure 15.7 shows the learning curve produced by the

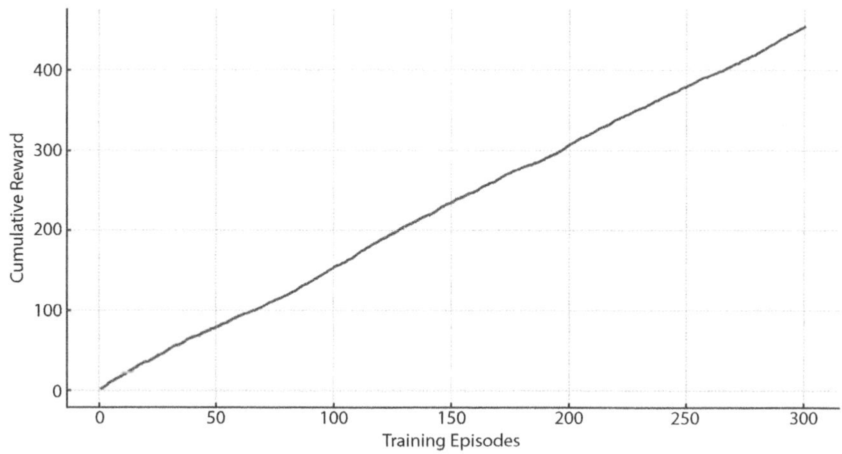

Figure 15.7 Policy learning curve showing the cumulative reward trend.

reinforcement-learning loop, plotting the total reward accumulated episode by episode as the dual-axis solar concentrator tracking policy is refined. The line rises almost without interruption, a clear signal that the agents strategy grows more effective over time. In the initial episodes progress is modest because the agent still samples random actions, yet curiosity eventually uncovers control sequences that collect more sunlight while easing mechanical strain. The steady increase in the cumulative reward validates the choice of Proximal Policy Optimization (PPO) as a robust, stable training backbone. Moreover, the collision-free flat plateau seen in later stages confirms policy stability and convergence, indicating that the digital twin has successfully taught the agent to navigate the full range of realistic outdoor scenarios.

15.7.5 Deployment in Operational Digital Twin

Once validation confirmed acceptable performance, the deep reinforcement-learning policy was transferred to the operational digital twin of the solar concentrator system. Functioning as a protective middleware, this virtual representation relayed real-time state data to the agent and executed control commands while enforcing multiple safety checks.

Deployment began with model compression: pruning excessive neurons and quantizing weights so the streamlined network could run on resource-constrained embedded controllers. Post-optimization, average inference latencies fell below 100 milliseconds, satisfying the real-time constraint for closed-loop control.

Throughout operation, the digital twin tracked system behavior, recorded every policy decision, and stored the data for future training runs in the simulator. This continuous logging permitted periodic re-training and online policy refinement, allowing the tracker to adjust to slow phenomena such as sensor drift or mechanical wear.

Field results confirmed the theoretical gains: daily energy harvests rose, actuator motion became noticeably smoother, and maintenance expenses shrank because premature wear was curbed. In addition, an automatic fault-recovery routine intervened during out-of-bound sensor signals or minor tracking errors, further solidifying the plants operational resilience.

15.7.6 Broader Implications and Future Enhancements

The successful deployment of deep reinforcement learning to fine-tune tracking in this project illustrates how artificial intelligence can reshape control strategies embedded in digital twins of solar concentrators. Because these virtual replicas offer a risk-free, high-throughput testing ground, engineers can iteratively refine complex control policies without introducing wear or safety hazards on real hardware.

Looking ahead, researchers may expand the framework through multi-agent reinforcement learning that coordinates the actions of many concentrators spread across a field. Such a collective approach could boost overall energy yield, prevent unwanted shading, and share diagnostic duties when individual units show signs of trouble.

Pairing these advances with explainable reinforcement-learning methods would shed light on how automated controllers reach a given decision. Greater interpretability not only meets emerging regulatory standards but also builds operator confidence a critical factor when autonomous systems govern essential energy assets.

At the same time, improved edge-computing chips and federated-learning protocols are making it possible for each solar concentrator to learn from its own local data without sending sensitive information to a central server. This shift cuts communication delays, safeguards privacy, and allows on-device policies to adapt in near real time to changing weather or equipment wear.

15.7.7 Summary

The study shows that deep reinforcement learning can be successfully applied to track, optimize, and control dual-axis solar concentrators when the hardware is paired with a digital twin. By choosing appropriate algorithms, training extensively in high-fidelity simulations, and validating the results on real prototypes, the learned agent outperformed classical tracking schemes in energy gain, mechanical load reduction, and overall reliability.

When embedded within the online digital twin, the controller received real-time sensor data, adjusted its policy automatically, and continued to gather experience over the seasons, thus pushing autonomous photovoltaic systems closer to field readiness. Collectively, these findings position reinforcement learning as a vital actuator of intelligent twin technology and suggest that large solar parks adopting this approach could realize meaningful cost and performance gains.

15.8 Future Research Directions and Opportunities

As digital-twin technology for solar concentrators matures, researchers expect more sophisticated artificial-intelligence tools to drive gains in efficiency, fault detection, and predictive upkeep. This section outlines promising avenues of study, along with technical hurdles that must be overcome, in order to build intelligent, self-tuning virtual replicas.

Fully autonomous twins will rely on reinforcement learning paired with continuous-update frameworks so that control rules adjust in real time with minimal human intervention. Approaches such as elastic-weight consolidation and meta-learning capture previous experiences, enabling the digital twin to learn a new environment quickly and enhance tracking, thermal control, and predictive maintenance.

Quantum machine-learning techniques could, in principle, accelerate the solution of complex twin models by replacing selected linear algebra routines with quantum circuits. Although todays quantum hardware limits the scale and fidelity of such experiments, hybrid quantum-classical algorithms are already being tested to speed optimization and simulation for large arrays of concentrators.

Sensor-fusion strategies will combine data streams from thermal cameras, optical detectors, and structural-monitoring devices so that the twin observes the complete physical system in context. Multi-modal learning architectures, such as graph neural networks and transformers, can then mine these rich datasets to produce sharper forecasts of thermal yield, structural integrity, and optical-degradation rates.

Federated reinforcement learning on restricted yet widely-distributed sites lets robots, drones, or control agents refine their policies together without swapping raw data, thus aiding responsive tracking and delicate process control while maintaining confidentiality. Difficulty stemming from non-identically distributed datasets and from the overhead of message exchanges is mitigated by policy distillation, which compresses knowledge into smaller models, and by learning-rate schedulers that adaptively adjust step sizes when the network or the local data drift.

Increasingly, people expect that AI-driven digital twins guard their underlying plants, their operators, and the public at large, so research teams now weave adversarial defenses into the learning pipeline, embed differential-private noise in gradients, and formulate fairness-aware reward functions that curb implicit bias in model decisions, thus steering autonomous solar fleets toward secure, impartial and fully transparent operations.

15.8.1 Summary

The forward-looking blueprint for AI-rich digital twins of solar concentrators is a cascade of allied breakthroughs: self-learning agents that autonomously adjust optics on-site, quantum processors that accelerate large-scale simulations, multi-modal sensors that fuse thermal, spectral and Lidar information in real time, federated models that learn cooperatively with edge clouds, and security stacks that detect modifications at every layer. Taken together, these building blocks promise resilient, economical plants that learn from every sunlit hour and operate safely even in untested environments, though realization depends on sustained cross-discipline partnerships, reliable funding, open standards and field-proven guidelines that govern deployment, certification and life-cycle support in the solar sector.

15.9 Conclusions

Over recent years, the concept of the digital twin for solar concentrators has shifted from a simple set of simulation-based dashboards to a mature, AI-rich platform that can predict faults, adjust controls on the fly, and fine-tune performance in real time. This chapter summarizes several key advances in that journey:

First, the core structure of a digital twin-who its layered models talk together and why fast, detailed simulations are needed to mirror the hardware-was outlined in plain language.

Second, several AI tools were reviewed, including deep nets that predict temperature and light flow, reinforcement-learned policies that steer motors, physics-augmented models that link multiple energy flows, and explainable forecasts that make their reasons clear to engineers.

Third, new network designs-edge computers that think on-site, federated systems that share lessons privately, and cloud-edge mixes that cut delays-were examined as enablers for large solar fleets spread across distant deserts and rooftops.

Finally, real-world and pilot site stories showed how the AI twin lifts profits: it boosts collector heat gain, keeps drives on track, and flags parts before they fail, proving the theory is already paying back in cents and carbon.

15.9.1 Broader Implications for Renewable Energy Systems

Applying AI-driven digital twins to solar concentrator plants marks just one piece of a larger evolution sweeping the renewable-energy field. Engineers are now carrying the same framework over to photovoltaics, wind farms, and battery systems.

These virtual replicas make advanced grid linking practical, letting separate assets adjust in real time to changing demand, market prices, and stability needs. Their forecasts of wear – plus alerts for timely repairs – also smooth long-term management and trim costs.

As the worldwide energy map shifts toward localized, data-rich networks, digital twins are set to become central anchors, guarding the reliability, speed, and strength of green portfolios.

15.9.2 Concluding Remarks

Empowered by artificial intelligence, digital twins mark a true turning point for solar concentrator systems and for many other clean technologies. The once-familiar routine of manual alarms and reactive repairs is giving way to a predictive, self-adjusting operation that saves energy, time, and money.

As research advances and complementary technologies evolve, artificial-intelligence-enhanced digital twins are on track to become essential instruments within solar energy and throughout the larger renewable-energy sector. Their growing integration promises to hasten the global shift toward clean, dependable, and equitable energy systems, supporting the wider goals of climate mitigation and social fairness.

AI disclosure statement: The author acknowledges the use of AI-based tools for minor language editing or grammatical correction. However, all intellectual contributions, analyses, and conclusions presented in this chapter are entirely the author's own.

References

1. Olayiwola, O., *et al.*, Enhanced Solar Photovoltaic System Management and Integration: The Digital Twin Concept. *Solar*, 5, 1, MDPI, 2025.
2. Alao, K.T., *et al.*, A review on digital twin application in photovoltaic energy systems: challenges and opportunities. *JMST Adv.*, 6, 3, 257–282, 2024.
3. Yao, C., *et al.*, A Data-driven method for adaptive resource requirement allocation *via* probabilistic solar load and market forecasting utilizing digital twin. *Sol. Energy*, 250, 368–3765, 2023.
4. Cao, H., Zhang, D., Yi, S., Real-Time Machine Learning-based fault Detection, Classification, and locating in large scale solar Energy-Based Systems: Digital twin simulation. *Sol. Energy*, 251, 77–855, 2023.
5. Milidonis, K., *et al.*, Review of application of AI techniques to Solar Tower Systems. *Sol. Energy*, 224, 500–5155, 2021.
6. Kavousi-Fard, A., *et al.*, Digital twin for mitigating solar energy resources challenges: A perspective. *Sol. Energy*, 274, 1125615, 2024.
7. Al-Azba, M., Abotaleb, A., Mahgoub, M., A Comprehensive Review of Digital Twin Technology: Applications and Innovations in Solar Energy Systems. Available at SSRN 4712901.
8. Rathore, M.M., *et al.*, The role of ai, machine learning, and big data in digital twinning: A systematic literature review, challenges, and opportunities. *IEEE Access*, 9, 32030–320525, 2021.
9. Karthikeyan, G. and Jagadeeshwaran, A., Enhancing solar energy generation: a comprehensive machine learning-based PV prediction and fault analysis system for real-time tracking and forecasting. *Electr. Power Compon. Syst.*, 52, 9, 1497–1512, 2024.
10. You, L. and Zhu, M., Digital Twin simulation for deep learning framework for predicting solar energy market load in Trade-By-Trade data. *Sol. Energy*, 250, 388–3975, 2023.
11. Değirmenci, S. and Telçeken, M., The impact of using real-time operating system (rtos) in ai-integrated autonomous vehicles on efficiency. *Akıllı Sistemler ve Uygulamaları Dergisi (J. Intell. Syst. Appl.)*, 7, 2, 12–18, 2024.

12. Ferreira, R.A.S., *et al.*, Predicting the efficiency of luminescent solar concentrators for solar energy harvesting using machine learning. *Sci. Rep.*, 14, 1, 4160, 2024.
13. Osorio, J.D., *et al.*, Forecasting solar-thermal systems performance under transient operation using a data-driven machine learning approach based on the deep operator network architecture. *Energy Convers. Manage.*, 252, 1150635, 2022.
14. Danilczyk, W., Sun, Y.L., He, H., Smart grid anomaly detection using a deep learning digital twin. *2020 52nd North American Power Symposium (NAPS)*, IEEE, 2021.
15. Kumar, U., Mishra, S., Dash, K., An IoT and semi-supervised learning-based sensorless technique for panel level solar photovoltaic array fault diagnosis. *IEEE Trans. Instrum. Meas.*, 72, 1–125, 2023.
16. Artetxe, E., *et al.*, Maximum power point tracker controller for solar photovoltaic based on reinforcement learning agent with a digital twin. *Mathematics*, 11, 9, 2166, 2023.
17. Cuomo, S., *et al.*, Scientific machine learning through physics–informed neural networks: Where we are and what's next. *J. Sci. Comput.*, 92, 3, 88, 2022.
18. Keshireddy, S.R., Reinforcement Learning Based Optimization of Query Execution Plans in Distributed Databases. *Res. Briefs Inf. Commun. Technol. Evol.*, 11, 42–61, 2025.
19. Paliyal, P.S., Mondal, S., Layek, S., Kuchhal, P., Pandey, J.K., Automatic solar tracking system: a review pertaining to advancements and challenges in the current scenario. *Clean Energy*, 8, 6, 237–262, December 2024, https://doi.org/10.1093/ce/zkae085.
20. Paliyal, P.S., Mondal, S., Pandey, J.K., An Analysis of Springwater Parameter Status for Different Locations in the Rural Hilly Garhwal Region of Uttarakhand. *Environ. Claims J.*, *36*, 3, 243–277, 2024, https://doi.org/10.1080/10406026.2024.2423964.
21. Paliyal, P.S. and Mondal, S., An analysis of a cross-finned receiver for Scheffler-type solar collectors to optimize solar heating efficiency for direct water heating. *Int. J. Energy Water Resour.*, 2025, https://doi.org/10.1007/s42108-025-00393-5.
22. Paliyal, P.S., Mondal, S., Pathela, M., Kumar, A., Menon, S.K., Optimization of Solar Photovoltaic Array In-Depth Analysis of Perturb and Observe MPPT Algorithm. *2024 International Conference on Advances in Computing, Communication and Materials (ICACCM)*, Dehradun, India, pp. 1–6, 2024, doi: 10.1109/ICACCM61117.2024.11059143.
23. Paliyal, P.S., *et al.*, Location Analysis and Environmental Validation for Installation of Hybrid Solar-Wind Energy Generation System in Hilly Areas of Uttarakhand: Study Toward Forecasting, in: *Forecasting Methods for Renewable Power Generation*, pp. 21–47, Springer Nature, Singapore, 2025.

24. Menon, S.K., *et al.*, The Role of Hydrogen as a Sustainable Energy Source and its Integration with the Grid, in: *Advancements in Communication and Systems*, A.K. Tripathi and V. Shrivastava (Eds.), p. 397, Computing and Intelligent Systems, SCRS, India, 20232025.
25. Kudapa, V.K., Paliyal, P.S., Mondal, A., Mondal, S., A critical review of fabrication strategies, separation techniques, challenges, and future prospects for the hydrogen separation membrane. *Fusion Sci. Technol.*, 80, 7, 803–825, 2024.
26. Mondal, A., Jangirh, R., Arya, R., Yadav, L., Ahlawat, S., Yadav, P., Paliyal, P.S., Bobde, P., Ghosh, P., Mondal, S., Rai, A., Analysing solid residential fuel usage patterns in rural and urban slums of Delhi: Implications for pollution reduction and sustainable practices. *Energy Sustainable Dev., 80*, 101460, 2024.
27. Paliyal, P.S., Kuchhal, P., Mondal, S., Nano Lubricants and their Applications, in: *Nanotechnology: A Quick Guide to Materials and Technologies*, pp. 425–456, Bentham Science Publishers, Sharjah, UAE, 2024.

16

Virtual Replicas for Real Impact: Improving Solar Asset Output Using Digital Twins

Supriya[1]* **and Ashutosh Shukla**[2]

[1]*School of Computing, COER University, Roorkee, Uttrakhand, India*
[2]*Electrical Cluster, School of Engineering, University of Petroleum and Energy Studies, Dehradun, Uttrakhand, India*

Abstract

The digital twin achieves its full potential by effectively using digitalization, intelligence, and services. Digital twins enhance the performance of physical things by overcoming constraints related to time, space, cost, and security *via* the creation of virtual representations of tangible items. This phenomenon has been thoroughly examined in electric sector. Digital Twins of solar power plants may emulate the real-time operating dynamics of the facility by using data collected from sensors in equipment such as solar panels, inverters, and batteries. This virtual model constantly engages with the physical plant, autonomously updating itself according to real-time data and consistently mirroring any operational changes. This allows operators to get unique insights into system performance, enabling data-driven decisions that enhance plant efficiency. The integration of Digital Twins in solar photovoltaic (PV) systems is evolving, making their role in optimizing energy production and maintenance methods more essential. Furthermore, the capacity of digital twins to model and forecast performance degradation caused by variables such as soiling demonstrates their use in proactive maintenance strategies, potentially leading to substantial reductions in operating expenses and enhancements in overall system efficiency. The integration of sophisticated modeling approaches with operational strategies optimizes energy production and supports the sustainability objectives of photovoltaic systems, underscoring the many advantages of implementing digital twins in the renewable energy industry.

**Corresponding author*: supriya@coer.ac.in

Surajit Mondal, Paramjeet Singh Paliyal and Sachin Sharma (eds.) Digital Twin Technology for Solar Concentrators, (281–292) © 2026 Scrivener Publishing LLC

***Keywords*:** Digital twins, renewable energy, virtual modeling, solar panel, solar asset

16.1 Introduction

Economic and technical progress have led to a rise in the need for energy by Fossil fuels as a finite resource to provide energy have many limitations, including environmental pollution, health hazards, habitat destruction, global warming, climate change, and acid rain and geopolitical issues. To address these issues, renewable energy sources are being promoted as a solution. National governments around the globe have been spearheading reforms to policies pertaining to the construction of renewable energy installations [1].

One of the most promising forms of renewable energy is solar energy. Photovoltaic solar energy has the capacity to generate energy in the most efficient manner. The advancement of photovoltaics (PV) is significant, as its installed capacity has surged tenfold in the last decade, reaching a worldwide total above 700 GW [5]. Besides providing a sustainable and cost-effective energy solution, there are several limitations, like dependence on sunlight availability, high installation cost, and other major challenges like accumulation of dust, dirt, and snow over time that can reduce efficiency, as shown in Figure 16.1. As a solution, an automated mechanism of identification and detection of soiling is required for the necessary regular cleaning and maintenance of the panel [2].

Real-time data exchange between the system and simulation model is essential for optimizing solar power production. This enables ongoing surveillance and rectification informed by real-time data. This creates an

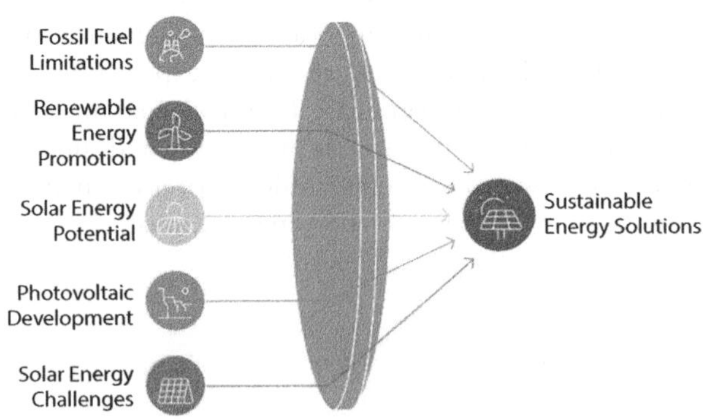

Figure 16.1 Sustainable energy solutions.

interactive feedback loop, whereby the simulation is perpetually updated with new data, and the system is modified to optimize performance. This feedback loop guarantees optimum performance under unpredictable and dynamic conditions by delivering real-time data on the system's efficacy.

This is the context in which digital twins are used. Digital twins may be fundamentally characterized in two primary ways. Singh *et al.* define "Digital Twin (DT)" as a virtual representation or model of a physical entity (physical twin), linked by real-time data transfer. A digital twin (DT) theoretically replicates the state of its physical counterpart in real time and vice versa. Applications of Digital Twin technology include real-time monitoring, design and planning, optimization, maintenance, and remote access, among others. Year 2021 – Jones *et al.* define the Digital Twin as including a physical entity, a virtual counterpart, and the data linkages between the two. This technology is under examination for its capacity to enhance the performance of physical entities using computational approaches facilitated by their virtual equivalents [3].

Digital Twins of solar power facilities may simulate the real-time operating dynamics of the facility, using data collected from sensors in equipment like solar panels, inverters, and batteries. The incorporation of advanced AI and machine learning methods into the Digital Twin facilitates predictive analytics, fault identification, and dynamic optimization of energy production. This virtual model constantly engages with the physical plant, autonomously updating itself according to real-time data and consistently mirroring any operational changes [4].

This allows operators to get unique insights into system performance, enabling data-driven decisions that enhance plant efficiency. The proposed system would use AI and ML techniques inside the Digital Twin architecture to predict equipment failures, optimize energy output, and provide real-time feedback for operational modifications. Environmental factors like as temperature, irradiance, and meteorological conditions will be monitored to ensure the plant adapts to changing circumstances. The Digital Twin will provide predictive maintenance, hence reducing downtime and extending the life of critical components.

16.1.1 Digital Twins Balancing Physical and Virtual Twins

To ascertain the structure and function of Digital Twins, we examine their origins, components, and purposes. Digital twins originated from NASA's initiatives to enhance space mission operations *via* the creation of real-time virtual representations of spacecraft for monitoring and testing purposes.

Technological advancements enabled the incorporation and assimilation of the notion into the broader industrial sector, first focusing on real-time data synchronization and predictive analytics.

Digital twins have three essential components: the physical twin (the real thing), the virtual twin (the digital representation), and the data transfer link that interconnects them [5]. This linkage guarantees that the digital model is perpetually refreshed in accordance with the physical twin's real-time condition. The complexity of digital twins (DTs) varies according to the systems they represent, with some models including multidimensional attributes such as chronological data, geographical information, and simulations of possible scenarios [6].

A digital twin functions beyond simple observation. Decision Trees are used to model, predict, and improve processes by integrating extensive data sets with analytical techniques [7]. This encompasses the ability to undertake prompt evaluations and simulate hypothetical situations for enhancing performance or identifying issues. Predictive maintenance may assist digital twins in optimizing production operations by reducing downtime and improving asset management. Digital twins operate as an ongoing feedback mechanism connecting physical and digital components, as seen in Figure 16.2.

Information from the physical twin, including sensor data, is sent to the digital twin, which analyses it and generates actionable insights using sophisticated analytics, utilizing artificial intelligence and machine learning [8]. The updates are bidirectional, indicating that any action performed on the digital twin may be mirrored in the physical system [9]. The DT approach is shown in Figure 16.3.

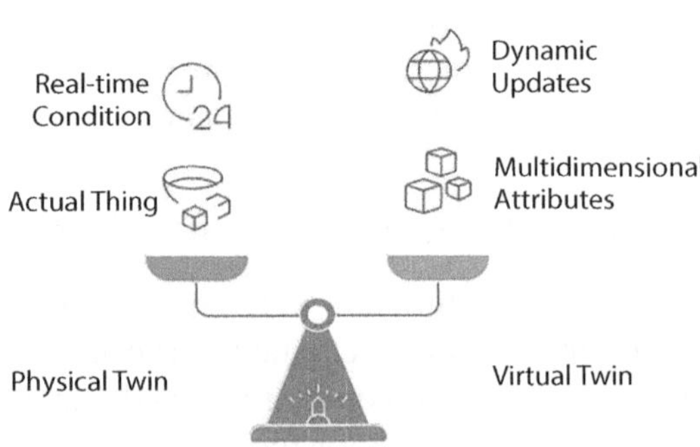

Figure 16.2 Balancing physical and virtual twins.

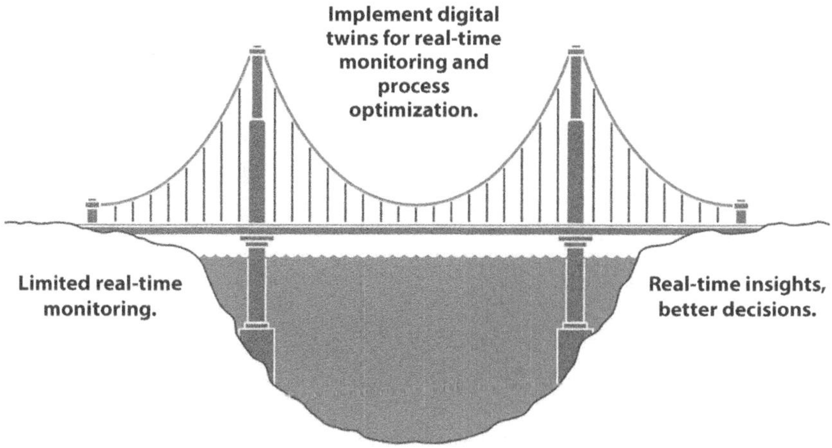

Figure 16.3 Digital twins enhance efficiency and innovation.

16.2 Digital Twins in Solar Applications

Subsequent to the establishment of the Digital Twins architecture, its applications and use cases are analyzed in further detail. Digital twins have been widely used across several domains [10]. Digital twins are used in the healthcare business to develop virtual patient models for more tailored medical treatment. Digital Twins provide real-time monitoring, predictive maintenance, and simulation functionalities to manufacturers for the optimization of production lines in industrial applications [11]. Moreover, real-time data from digital twins is used in urban planning and smart city development to enhance infrastructure design and resource management.

Digital Twins are widely used in renewable energy systems, including wind and solar power. The principal uses of digital twins in wind energy are predictive maintenance and the optimization of turbine performance. Wind farms may use a decision tree to assess power output and forecast wind velocities, enabling operators to optimize energy distribution. To prevent equipment failure, DTs provide real-time monitoring of turbines by evaluating structural stress and fatigue [12–15]. This approach prolongs the lifetime of wind turbines and reduces maintenance expenses. Digital twins are used in the solar power sector to optimize the efficiency of photovoltaic (PV) systems. As depicted in Figure 16.4, digital twins (DTs) can optimize maintenance schedules, forecast energy production based on weather conditions, and evaluate the operation and efficiency of solar panels using a virtual representation of the panels [16]. Furthermore, decision trees can

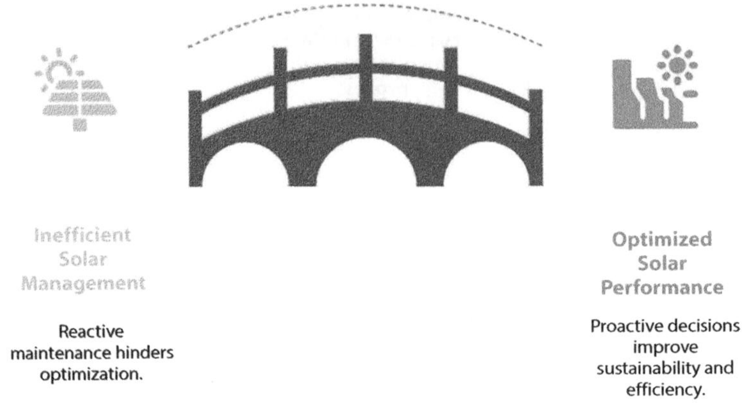

Figure 16.4 Digital twins enhancing solar energy management.

model various environmental conditions to determine the ideal location and arrangement of solar panels [17]. This method may improve the overall efficiency of solar farms and decrease operating expenses.

This system integrates advanced technologies such as the Internet of Things (IoT), artificial intelligence (AI), machine learning, cloud computing, and edge computing, facilitating data collection and analysis from physical entities, thereby enhancing strategic decision-making and performance optimization. Digital twins are dynamic entities continuously updated with real-time data, enabling the modeling of many situations and the implementation of predictive analyses, particularly beneficial in industries like as manufacturing, healthcare, automotive, energy, and smart cities. The concept transcends mere data collection, encompassing the interplay among individuals, processes, and technologies to attain optimal outcomes, exemplified by the Digital Twin of a Digital World (DTDW) framework, which amalgamates process management, experience mining, data mining, and simulation to enhance business processes [20].

In automotive networks, digital twins improve task offloading and resource allocation by creating an advanced mirrored IT system, hence enhancing road safety and transportation efficiency [21]. Moreover, digital twins are crucial in the first stages of design, providing hybrid prototypes that amalgamate digital and physical models, therefore aiding architects and designers in predicting future design outcomes [22]. Digital twin technology represents a significant advancement in the seamless integration of physical and virtual systems, promoting innovation and efficiency across several sectors.

16.3 Methods to Utilize a Digital Twin for Enhancing Solar Asset Performance

Solar digital twin technology may revolutionize the maintenance and operations of solar farms by alleviating asset underperformance. As depicted in Figure 16.5, digital twins provide real-time information and data, enabling operators to proactively manage assets, optimize performance, and enhance overall efficiency.

1. Thorough Surveillance and Regulation
Digital twins provide thorough surveillance of solar farm elements, including panels, inverters, and trackers. A solar digital twin may discover abnormalities, locate underperforming assets, and notify operators to possible concerns by analyzing performance data from multiple sensors, inspections, and other sources. Furthermore, associating these insights with precise GPS coordinates on a solar farm is essential for both field and office personnel. This enables prompt remedial measures, minimizing downtime and optimizing energy output.

2. A Repository for Vital Data Streams
Solar digital twins allow operators to consolidate diverse and intricate data sources, functioning as a comprehensive record system for a solar farm. Datasets incorporated into a digital twin's solar site records may encompass inspection reports, meteorological and power performance data from sensors on the farm, SCADA or DAS integrations, technical specifications,

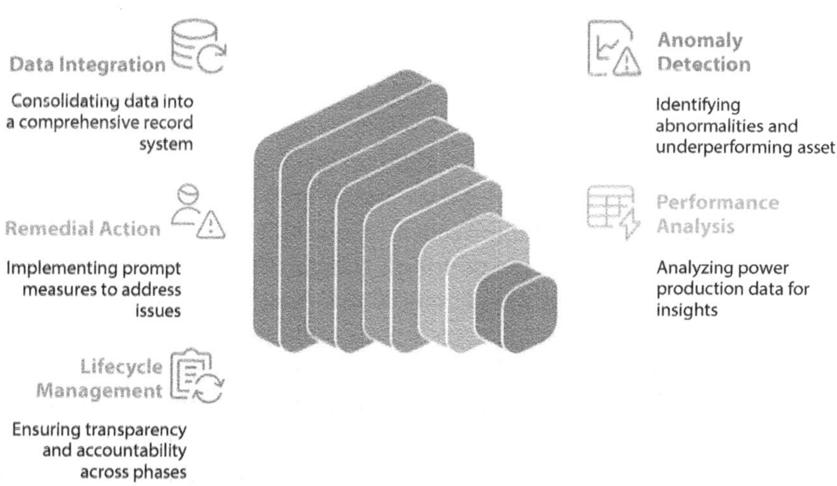

Figure 16.5 Digital twin for enhancing solar asset performance.

performance models, warranty documentation, shipping receipts, photographs, and field notes.

3. Assistance with Warranty Claims
The digital twin stores solar site records, including visual documentation, pertinent inspection data, and identifying details like as serial numbers, therefore facilitating the warranty claims procedure with equipment manufacturers. Information pertinent to a digital twin may be readily provided to original equipment manufacturers (OEMs). A consolidated record system enables asset managers and OEMs to monitor the equipment's history.

4. Analysis of Power Production
Precise power production analysis derived from solar site data is essential for asset managers to do root-cause studies. A solar digital twin facilitates the comparison of power generation data with insights, including abnormalities detected during inspections, irradiance measurements, and meteorological circumstances. Situating power loss within a context of several conflicting causes facilitates prompt rehabilitation, hence aiding in the mitigation of asset underperformance.

5. Field Adaptability with Mobile Digital Twins
Field technicians may use a mobile iteration of a map-based digital twin to swiftly identify their location and the position of impacted equipment on an extensive solar farm. Upon entering the field, technicians may detect and rectify any irregularities while accessing work lists, notes, and equipment data from a digital twin. Technicians may enhance the solar digital twin's site documentation by providing written updates and photographs while in the field.

6. Lifecycle Management
Throughout the lifespan of a utility-scale solar farm, several handoff points occur, necessitating a centralized data repository—manifested as a digital twin—to preserve an auditable record of relevant data. The solar digital twin serves as an essential nexus for all stakeholders during every phase of a solar project. By integrating essential information and solar site documentation, including financial assessments and operational data, a digital twin guarantees openness and accountability across all phases. A centralized repository facilitates the transfer of essential information, promotes cooperation, and improves the overall efficiency of solar projects, whether transferring from the development team to the building team or moving into the operations phase.

7. An Educational Framework Utilizing a Data Stack
Solar digital twins function as adaptive learning systems, always developing and enhancing *via* real-time data and site record feedback. The accuracy of the digital twin improves when more data is acquired *via* a data stack. Operators may use the information to refine procedures, enhance asset performance, and pinpoint potential for further efficiency improvements. This recurrent enhancement cycle guarantees optimal operation of the solar farm.

8. Integrating Robotics and Machine Learning
The use of robotics, namely drone-in-a-box (DIAB) technology, has introduced a novel aspect to the data inputs of digital twins in solar initiatives. DIAB utilizes autonomous drones for solar farm inspections, gathering critical data that contributes to the digital twin's solar site records. Utilizing machine learning techniques and pattern recognition, this data may be analyzed to discover and diagnose equipment flaws, facilitating maintenance and enhancing the overall performance of solar farms. The integration of robotics and digital twins provides an effective solution for efficient monitoring, diagnosis, and decision-making.

16.4 Conclusion

The continuous development of digital twins in solar asset management clearly demonstrates that their integration may substantially improve predictive maintenance techniques, resulting in lower operating costs and enhanced energy efficiency. By using machine learning algorithms inside digital twin frameworks, operators may analyze real-time data to predict possible system breakdowns and optimize maintenance plans, thereby reducing downtime and enhancing production. The integration of advanced sensor technologies and the Internet of Things (IoT) enables efficient data sharing and analysis, facilitating accurate monitoring of environmental influences on solar performance, including dust accumulation and its adverse effects on energy generation. This proactive strategy enhances operational efficiency and bolsters the sustainability of solar energy systems, making them more adaptable to variable climatic circumstances.

AI disclosure statement: The author confirms that no artificial intelligence (AI)-generated content or AI-assisted writing tools were used in the preparation of this chapter (including summaries and the abstract). All text, analysis, and conclusions are the result of the author's original work.

Bibliography

1. Exploration on the Application of Digital Twin Technology. *Acad. J. Eng. Technol. Sci.*, 6, 2, 2023, doi: 10.25236/ajets.2023.060209.
2. Rapport annuel mondial sur l'´energie - Edition 2024, Accessed: 2024. [Online]. Available: ⟨https://kpmg.com/fr/fr/insights/energie/rapport-annuel-energie-edit ion-2024.html⟩.
3. Abdessadak, A., Ghennioui, H., Thirion-Moreau, N., Elbhiri, B., Abraim, M., Merzouk, S., Digital twin technology and artificial intelligence in energy transition: A comprehensive systematic review of applications. *Energy Rep.*, 13, 5196–5218, 2025.
4. Shatiry, M.S.A., Harun, F., Azman, M., Amin, A.H.M., Husni, Z.H., Abu, A., A Review of the Digital Twin Technology Application in Energy Industry for Performance Improvement, 2022, doi: 10.2118/210353-ms.
5. AI-Based Analysis and Prediction of Synergistic Development Trends in U.S. Photovoltaic and Energy Storage Systems. *Int. J. Innov. Res. Comput. Sci. Technol.*, 12, 5, 36–46, 2024, doi: 10.55524/ijircst.2024.12.5.6.
6. Jones, D., Snider, C., Nassehi, A., Yon, J., Hicks, B., Characterising the digital twin: a systematic literature review. *CIRP J. Manuf. Sci. Technol.*, 29, 36–52, 2020, https://doi. org/10.1016/j.cirpj.2020.02.002.
7. Arafet, K. and Berlanga, R., Digital Twins in Solar Farms: An Approach through Time Series and Deep Learning. *Algorithms*, 14, 5, 156, 2021, https://doi.org/10.3390/a14050156.
8. Kavousi-Fard, A., Dabbaghjamanesh, M., Jafari, M., Fotuhi-Firuzabad, M., Dong, Z.Y., Jin, T., Digital Twin for mitigating solar energy resources challenges: a perspective review. *Sol. Energy*, 274, 112561, 2024.
9. Khan, M.A., Çamur, H., Kassem, Y., Modeling predictive assessment of wind energy potential as a power generation sources at some selected locations in Pakistan. *Model. Earth Syst. Environ.*, 5, 2019, https://doi.org/10.1007/s40808-018-0546- 6.
10. Guo, J. and Lv, Z., Application of Digital Twins in multiple fields. *Multimedia Tools Appl.*, *81*, 19, 26941–26967, 2022.
11. Wang, Y., Su, Z., Guo, S., Dai, M., Luan, T.H., Liu, Y., A survey on digital twins: Architecture, enabling technologies, security and privacy, and future prospects. *IEEE Internet Things J.*, *10*, 17, 14965–14987, 2023.
12. D'Hauwers, R., Walravens, N., Ballon, P., From an inside-in towards an outside-out urban digital twin: Business models and implementation challenges. *ISPRS Ann. Photogramm. Remote Sens. Spatial Inf. Sci.*, *8*, 25–32, 2021.
13. Fahim, M., Sharma, V., Cao, T.V., Canberk, B., Duong, T.Q., Machine learning-based digital twin for predictive modeling in wind turbines. *IEEE Access*, *10*, 14184–14194, 2022.

14. Pimenta, F., Pacheco, J., Branco, C.M., Teixeira, C.M., Magalhães, F., Development of a digital twin of an onshore wind turbine using monitoring data. *J. Phys. Conf. Ser.*, 1618, 2, 022065, 2020, September, IOP Publishing.
15. Yalçin, S. and Vural, H., Digital Twin: An Approach to Artificial Intelligence-Enabled Wireless Networks. *New Front. Eng.*, 161, 2025.
16. Zohdi, T.I., A digital-twin for rapid simulation modular Direct Air Capture systems. *Int. J. Eng. Sci.*, *203*, 104120, 2024.
17. Sundaram, S.M. and Murgod, T.R., Digital twins enabling technologies, including artificial intelligence, sensors, cloud, and edge computing, in: *Digital Twins and Healthcare: Trends, Techniques, and Challenges*, pp. 88–101, IGI Global, 2023.
18. Abdessadak, A., Ghennioui, H., Thirion-Moreau, N., Elbhiri, B., Abraim, M., Merzouk, S., *Energy Rep.*
19. Jadhav, S.G. and Sarnikar, S., Digital twin of a digital world: process, data, and experience perspectives. *IT Prof.*, *25*, 3, 68–73, 2023.
20. Pillai, R. and Babbar, H., Digital twin for edge computing in smart vehicular systems, in: *2023 International Conference on Advancement in Computation & Computer Technologies (InCACCT)*, 2023, May, IEEE, pp. 1–5.
21. Isik, G.E. and Achten, H., Architectural hybrid (physical-digital) prototyping in design processes with digital twin technologies. *Archit. Plan. J. (APJ)*, *28*, 3, 2023.
22. Dihan, M.S., Akash, A.I., Tasneem, Z., Das, P., Das, S.K., Islam, M.R., Hasan, M.M., Digital twin: Data exploration, architecture, implementation and future. *Heliyon*, *10*, 5, 2024.

17

The Role of Digital Twins in Enhancing the Resilience and Sustainability of Renewable Energy Systems: A Systematic Review

Supriya*, **Yash Singhal and Vansh Joshi**

Department of AI & ML, School of Computing, COER University, Roorkee, Uttrakhand, India

Abstract

Incorporating renewable energy sources into existing energy systems presents both opportunities and challenges. Digital Twins, a game-changing technology, have emerged as critical facilitators for coping with these difficulties. They provide a virtual representation of renewable energy resources, bridging the gap between the digital and physical sectors. This allows for real-time monitoring, predictive modeling, and optimization, which increases system efficiency, reliability, and sustainability. Digital Twins build renewable energy assets by improving performance, anticipating maintenance needs, and maximizing energy capture. They play an essential role in grid management, allowing for the integration of unexpected renewable sources into smart grids, hence increasing stability and resilience. Furthermore, Digital Twins aid in selecting ideal areas for future renewable energy projects, which speeds up development processes. However, issues of data security and interoperability must be addressed.

Keywords: Renewable energy sector, digital twins, sustainable energy, smart power system digital twin

**Corresponding author*: supriya@coer.ac.in

Surajit Mondal, Paramjeet Singh Paliyal and Sachin Sharma (eds.) Digital Twin Technology for Solar Concentrators, (293–304) © 2026 Scrivener Publishing LLC

17.1 Introduction

17.1.1 Role of Renewable Energy Sector in Power Generation

The worldwide energy landscape is changing quickly, encountering challenges and opportunities linked to energy efficiency, sustainability, and the security of supply. The rise in electricity demand, along with the need to cut carbon emissions, makes it essential to investigate methods for improving existing energy systems and strategizing for future growth. The incorporation of renewable energy sources (RESs) offers a crucial chance to tackle these complex challenges on a global scale [1, 2]. The issue of reducing CO2 emissions is a global challenge. Electricity generation based on renewable energy sources (RES) represents a major step forward in enhancing the global environment [2, 3]. Through detailed art assessments, we can pinpoint four essential renewable energy sources: wind, solar, hydro, and biofuel, as depicted in Figure 17.1 [2, 4, 5]. The replacement of existing electric power plants powered by fossil fuels with renewable energy sources can help to address this issue [1]. According to IRENA [6], installed capacity and RES energy generation are increasing rapidly around the world, including in our nation.

17.1.2 Evolution of Digital Twins in Renewable Energy Sector

For future expansion and advancements planning a new technology known as digital twins (DT) is used. A digital twin (DT) is a virtual representation of a physical system, designed to replicate its behavior and performance [6, 7].

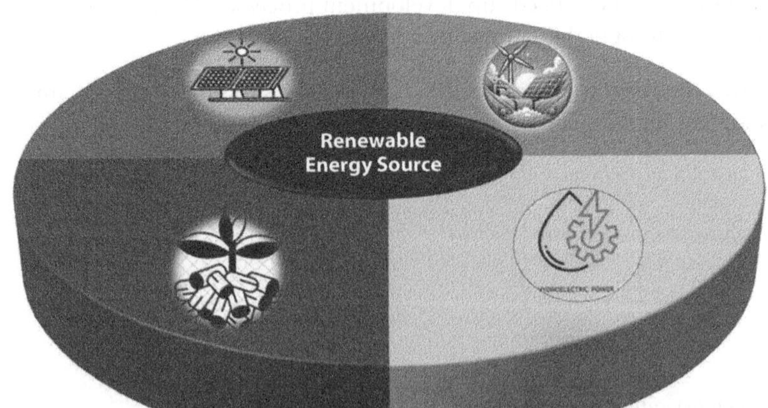

Figure 17.1 Renewable energy source.

By connecting the virtual model to real-time data from the physical counterpart, DTs enable real-time or near-real-time monitoring and analysis. While the DT concept has seen significant growth in recent years, challenges and opportunities persist [8]. Research has explored various aspects of DT implementation: for example, Cameron *et al.* [9] examined the potential of DTs to enhance sustainability, maintainability, and effectiveness within the oil and gas industry. More recently, Knebel *et al.* investigated the role of cloud and edge computing, along with data management, in DT applications, finding that most studies focus on theoretical or partial deployments, highlighting the important role of cloud and edge technologies [10].

The idea of digital twin technology was first examined in David Gelernter's 1991 work Mirror Worlds. The notion of digital twins was initially applied to manufacturing in 2002, and Dr. Michael Grieves, a professor at the University of Michigan at the time, was the first to introduce the digital twin software. Finally, in 2010, NASA's John Vickers coined the term "digital twin."

However, the underlying concept of analyzing a physical object with a digital doppelganger dates back for further. NASA developed the application of digital twin technology during its space exploration flights in the 1960s. Each voyaging spacecraft was perfectly copied in an earthbound variant, which NASA flight crews employed for study and simulation purposes.

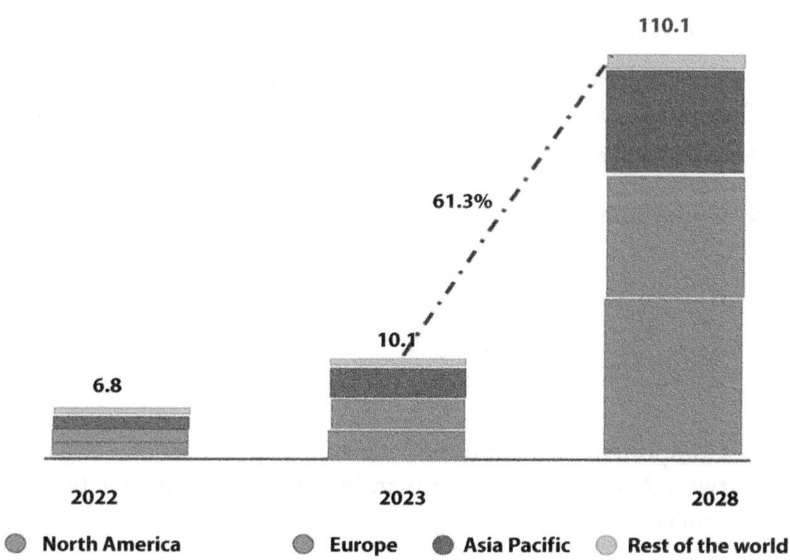

Figure 17.2 Countries using digital twins in renewable energy.

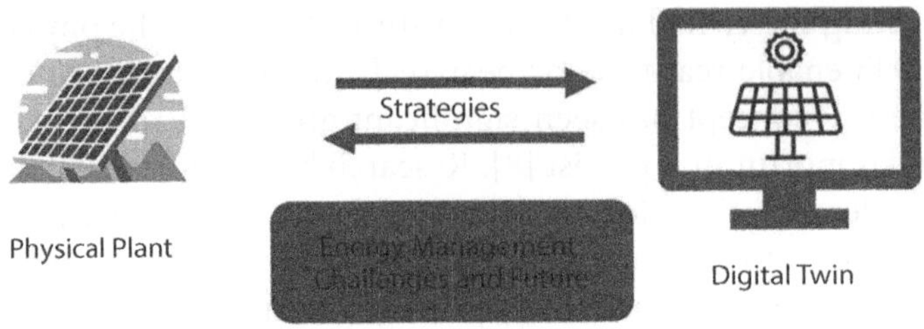

Figure 17.3 Solar PV plant digital twin implication.

As shown in Figure 17.2, companies leverage digital twins to identify potential improvements in their energy operations. By using real-time data from energy networks, these virtual replicas create highly accurate simulations, providing energy companies with enhanced network understanding. The global digital twin market is projected to experience substantial growth, expanding from $10.1 billion in 2023 to $110.1 billion by 2028, according to Markets & Markets. The main incentives of this adoption include predictive maintenance, capabilities in big data analytics, and the creation of advanced energy applications. Table 17.1 depicts the comparative study of traditional energy management methods versus digital twins. The Digital Twin implementation of solar PV physical plant shown in Figure 17.3.

17.1.2.1 Kinds of Digital Twins

Digital twins are categorized into different kinds based on the product magnification. These twins differ essentially in their area of application. Let's examine various kinds of digital twins:

- **Component Twins:**

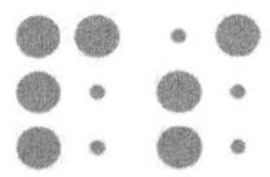

  Component twins are the vital building blocks of a digital twin. Asset Twins are similar, but they deal with far fewer crucial components.

Table 17.1 Traditional energy management methods versus digital twins.

Energy management capability	Traditional energy management	Digital twin solution
Smart Grid	Uses statistical models (e.g., ARIMA, linear regression) or basic machine learning (ML) algorithms for demand and generation forecasting. Relies on historical data with limited real-time adaptability.	Creates a real-time virtual replica of the energy system, enabling simulation-based forecasting. Integrates IoT-enabled sensor data for continuous updates, allowing for high-accuracy predictions using ML models like XGBoost or LSTM.
Modernized Micro Grids	Use historical demand data with optimization algorithms (e.g., linear programming, rule-based systems) for peak load reduction. Apply static demand-side management techniques to shift non-critical loads to off-peak hours.	Real-time monitoring of energy consumption using IoT-enabled sensors. Adaptive DRP based on real-time load and system state, improving reliability and reducing response times.
Intelligent Building Insulation	Regular software tools can help streamline processes, ensure accuracy, and facilitate collaboration across different phases of the project lifecycle.	Digital twins offer a dynamic and interactive virtual representation of physical entities, enabling predictive analysis, simulation, and optimization.
Smart Electric Vehicles	Regular Software uses Simulation Tools: Uses isolated simulation environments (e.g., CAD, finite element analysis, computational fluid dynamics). and creates static models based on predefined parameters and conditions, which are inflexible to real-world changes.	Digital twins dynamically integrate data from simulations, prototypes, and real-world sensors.
Battery Management Systems	Regular Software relies on predefined algorithms for battery charging, discharging, and thermal management.	Digital Twin uses Real-Time Battery Modeling simulates real-world conditions to optimize charging cycles and thermal management dynamically.
Energy Generation	Provide monitoring, control, and optimization of energy production and distribution. Include features for load forecasting, scheduling, and grid stability.	Simulate and optimize wind turbines and solar farms using real-time weather and operational data. Predict and mitigate inefficiencies caused by varying environmental conditions.

❖ **Asset Twins**

An asset, composed of interacting components, can be represented by an asset twin. This digital representation allows for the analysis of interdependencies between components, yielding rich performance data that translates into intuitions.

❖ **System or Unit Twins**

Building upon asset twins, this represents the interactions of multiple assets within a complete functional system. These system twins offer insights into asset interrelationships and provide potential strategies for performance enhancement.

❖ **Process Twins**

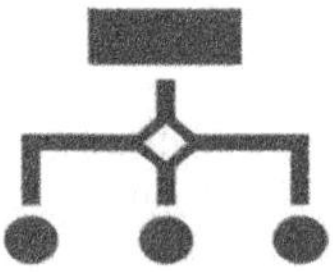

This technique offers a macro-level view, illustrating the functioning of interconnected systems within a complete manufacturing facility. They analyze system synchronization and identify potential bottlenecks where delays in one area might affect others. This analysis enables the development of optimized timing strategies, leading to greater overall efficiency.

17.2 Related Work

In this section Table 17.2, depicts the role of digital twins in enhancing the resilience and sustainability of renewable energy systems (RES).

Table 17.2 A systematic review of DT in RES.

Author(s) and year	Domain	Description
Cioara *et al.*, 2021 [6]	Smart Energy Grid	An overview of digital twin applications in smart grids, with a focus on energy asset modeling, fault diagnosis, operational optimization, and business models.
Rasheed *et al.*, 2024 [7]	Wind Energy	Discusses the creation of digital twins for wind farms, with capability levels ranging from descriptive to autonomous.
Stadtmann *et al.*, 2023 [8]	Wind Energy	Examines digital twin technology in the wind energy business, addressing present cutting-edge and future research needs from an industrial standpoint.
You *et al.*, 2021 [9]	Integrated Energy Systems	Proposes a method for day-ahead scheduling based on digital twins to enhance coordination among different energy converters in the face of uncertainties.
Bassey *et al.*, 2024 [10]	Renewable Energy Microgrids	Explores how digital twin technology can optimize the management and efficiency of renewable energy microgrids, including solar and wind systems.
Kamyabi *et al.*, 2022 [11]	Power Systems	Provides an overview of digital twin applications in power systems, emphasizing solar PV and wind turbine generation.
Prodanovic *et al.*, 2024 [12]	Renewable Energy Grids	Presents data-driven digital twins for renewable energy networks, with a focus on artificial intelligence technologies for modeling photovoltaic systems.
Olatunji *et al.*, 2021 [13]	Wind Turbines	Examines digital twin technology in wind turbine fault diagnosis and condition monitoring.
Xu *et al.*, 2021 [14]	Renewable Energy Systems	Examines data-driven digital twins for renewable energy systems, highlighting their promise and difficulties.
Kim *et al.*, 2020 [15]	Renewable Energy Systems	Examines artificial intelligence applications in renewable energy systems, emphasizing the importance of digital twins.

17.3 Benefits of Digital Twins in Power Generation

As depicted in Figure 17.4, benefits of digital twins in power generation include:

- **Better research and development**
  More efficient product research and design are made possible by the deployment of digital twins, which generate a wealth of data regarding probable performance outcomes. The insights derived from that data can assist businesses in making necessary product improvements prior to production.
- **Enhanced effectiveness**
  Digital twins are able to mirror and monitor production processes long after a new product has gone into production, with the aim of achieving and maintaining optimal efficiency throughout the manufacturing process.
- **Product lifecycle**
  Digital twins can also assist producers in determining what to do with products that need final processing, such as recycling, as their product lifespan is coming to a close. They can ascertain whether product materials are suitable for harvesting by employing digital twins.

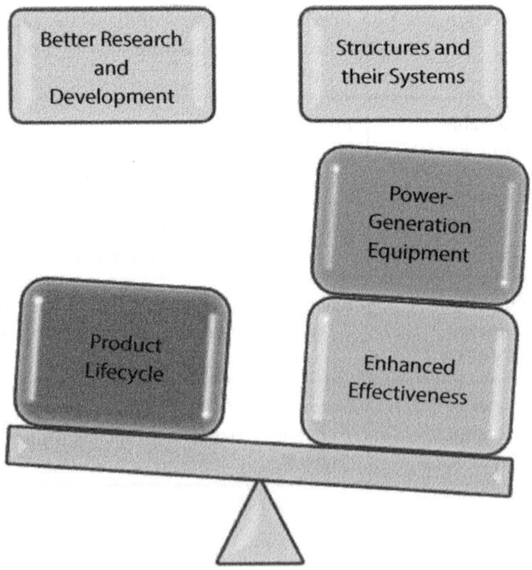

Figure 17.4 Benefits of digital twins in power generation.

- **Power-generation equipment**
  Digital twins provide substantial benefits for large engines—like those in jets, locomotives, and power generation turbines—particularly when it comes to creating optimized maintenance schedules.
- **Structures and their systems**
  Digital twins are useful, particularly in the design phase of large physical structures like skyscrapers or offshore drilling platforms. Building the HVAC systems and other systems that operate inside those structures is equally essential.

17.4 Challenges in Digital Twin Implementation

Several key challenges hinder the widespread adoption of digital twins:

- **Data Incompatibility:** Digital twins work on data collected from diverse sources with varying standards and protocols. This lack of standardization, compounded by low-quality data, hinders the creation of accurate virtual models and AI forecasts. Solutions include enforcing standardized data exchange formats, using data transformation techniques, and investing in data quality management.
- **Scalability Issues:** As the number of connected devices grows, digital twins must handle increasing data volumes. Poor scalability limits their effectiveness in large-scale applications. Addressing this requires optimizing system resources (storage, computing power, bandwidth) and leveraging scalable cloud infrastructure to handle fluctuating demands and expensive on-premise infrastructure.
- **Security and Privacy:** Digital twins are vulnerable to cyberattacks, potentially exposing sensitive data and compromising infrastructure. Compliance with privacy regulations (e.g., GDPR, CCPA) is crucial. Mitigation alternatives include strong firewalls, intrusion prevention systems, role-based access control, zero-trust policies, data encryption, and data anonymization techniques. It is essential to implement regular security audits.
- **High Implementation Costs:** Digital twin technology demands a considerable investment in sensors, 3D CAD applications, analytics tools, and potentially augmented/

extended reality technologies. These costs can be excessive, especially for smaller businesses and those with aging infrastructure. A phased implementation approach, starting with smaller pilot projects, and leveraging ready-made cloud solutions can mitigate these costs. Exploring funding opportunities and grants is also advisable.

- **Lack of Skilled Workforce:** A shortage of skilled personnel capable of effectively utilizing digital twin technology presents a significant barrier. Employee resistance to digital transformation may also exist. Tackling this issue calls for a mix of recruiting new talent, forming partnerships with educational organizations to create training initiatives, and working together with seasoned renewable energy software development companies. Providers of technology can enable in sharing the financial burden and reducing risks associated to initial investments.

17.5 Conclusion

This paper has presented a critical and systematic review of DT technology and research, with a specific focus on its application within the renewable energy sector. By examining various research studies related to power generation, this review has highlighted key applications of DTs in this domain. These applications span a range of areas, from optimizing energy production and predictive maintenance of renewable energy assets to improving grid stability and facilitating the integration of distributed energy resources. Furthermore, this work has also addressed the significant challenges currently hindering the widespread adoption of DTs in the renewable energy sector. These challenges include data acquisition and integration, model fidelity and validation, computational cost and scalability, and the need for standardized frameworks and interoperability. Addressing these challenges is crucial for realizing the full potential of DT technology in accelerating the transition to a sustainable and resilient energy future. Future research should focus on developing robust and scalable DT solutions that can effectively address the complexities of renewable energy systems and contribute to a more efficient and reliable energy landscape.

AI disclosure statement: The author confirms that no artificial intelligence (AI)-generated content or AI-assisted writing tools were used in the preparation of this chapter (including summaries and the abstract). All text, analysis, and conclusions are the result of the author's original work.

References

1. Liu, M., Fang, S., Dong, H., Xu, C., Review of digital twin about concepts, technologies, and industrial applications. *J. Manuf. Syst.*, 58, 346–361, 2021.
2. Blume, C., Blume, S., Thiede, S., Herrmann, C., Data-driven digital twins for technical building services operation in factories: A cooling tower case study. *J. Manuf. Mater. Process.*, 4, 4, 97, 2020.
3. Pimenta, F., Pacheco, J., Branco, C.M., Teixeira, C.M., Magalhães, F., Development of a digital twin of an onshore wind turbine using monitoring data. *J. Phys. Conf. Ser.*, 1618, 2, 022065, 2020, September, IOP Publishing.
4. Gao, J. and Huang, H., Stochastic optimization for energy economics and renewable sources management: A case study of solar energy in digital twin. *Sol. Energy*, 262, 111865, 2023.
5. Kavousi-Fard, A., Dabbaghjamanesh, M., Jafari, M., Fotuhi-Firuzabad, M., Dong, Z.Y., Jin, T., Digital Twin for mitigating solar energy resources challenges: A Perspective Review. *Sol. Energy*, 274, 112561, 2024.
6. Cioara, T., Anghel, I., Antal, M., Salomie, I., Digital Twin for Smart Energy Grid: A Comprehensive Survey. arXiv preprint arXiv:2104.07904, 2021.
7. Rasheed, A., Stadtmann, F., Fonn, E., Tabib, M., Tsiolakis, V., Panjwani, B., Johannessen, K.A., Kvamsdal, T., San, O., Tande, J.O.G., Barstad, I., Christiansen, T., Rishoff, E., Frøyd, L., Rasmussen, T., Digital Twin for Wind Energy: Latest Updates from the NorthWind Project. arXiv preprint arXiv:2403.14646, 2024.
8. Stadtmann, F., Rasheed, A., Kvamsdal, T., Johannessen, K.A., San, O., Kölle, K., Tande, J.O.G., Barstad, I., Benhamou, A., Brathaug, T., Firle, A.L., Fjeldly, A., Gleim, A., Høiberget, A., Meissner, C., Nygård, G., Olsen, J., Paulshus, H., Rasmussen, T., Rishoff, E., Scibilia, F., Skogås, J.O., Digital Twins in Wind Energy: Emerging Technologies and Industry-Informed Future Directions. arXiv preprint arXiv:2304.11405, 2023.
9. You, S., Zhang, H., Cai, H., Digital Twin-Based Day-Ahead Scheduling of Integrated Energy Systems Under Uncertainty. arXiv preprint arXiv:2109.14423, 2021.
10. Bassey, E. and Essien, E., Digital Twin Technology for Renewable Energy Microgrids: A Review. *Eur. Sci. J.*, 20, 3, 1857–7881, 2024.
11. Kamyabi, A. and Shaker, H.R., Digital Twin Applications in Power Systems: A Review. *Tecnol. Marcha*, 35, 2, 78–89, 2022.
12. Prodanovic, M. and Green, T.C., Data-Driven Digital Twins for Renewable Energy Grids, in: *Artificial Intelligence Applications in Energy Systems*, pp. 123–145, Springer, 2024.
13. Olatunji, O.O. and Akinlabi, E.T., Digital Twin Technology in Wind Turbine Fault Diagnosis and Condition Monitoring: A Review. *Sustainability*, 13, 6, 3259, 2021.

14. Xu, Y. and Li, J., Data-Driven Digital Twins for Renewable Energy Systems: Opportunities and Challenges. *Renewable Sustainable Energy Rev.*, 145, 111111, 2021.
15. Kim, J. and Park, S., Artificial Intelligence in Renewable Energy Systems: A Review. *Energies*, 13, 4, 789, 2020.

18

Enhancing Renewable Energy Efficiency with Digital Twin Technology: Real-Time Monitoring and Predictive Maintenance

Supriya[1] and Ashutosh Shukla[2*]

[1]*Department of AI & ML, School of Computing, COER University, Roorkee, Uttrakhand, India*
[2]*Electrical Cluster, School of Engineering, University of Petroleum and Energy Studies, Dehradun, Uttrakhand, India*

Abstract

Global sustainability depends on renewable energy, yet high maintenance costs and equipment breakdowns frequently prevent it from reaching its full potential. To monitor, evaluate, and improve energy systems, digital twin (DT) technology uses big data, artificial intelligence (AI), and Internet of Things (IoT) sensors to create a virtual version of a physical system. DTs contribute to decreased downtime and increased operational efficiency by providing real-time tracking and predictive maintenance. The functioning of DTs is the main subject of this study, which employs sensor data and machine learning techniques to identify early indications of equipment wear and failure. These prediction skills are especially useful in hydroelectric plants, wind farms, and solar farms since they guarantee efficient water resource management and sustainable energy production. Looking ahead, there are encouraging developments in store for DT technology in the field of renewable energy.

Keywords: Renewable energy, global sustainability, physical energy asset, IoT sensors

**Corresponding author*: ashutiet@gmail.com

Surajit Mondal, Paramjeet Singh Paliyal and Sachin Sharma (eds.) Digital Twin Technology for Solar Concentrators, (305–316) © 2026 Scrivener Publishing LLC

18.1 Introduction

Digital twins (DT) and industrial digitalization are becoming a potent tool for efficiently managing and streamlining site operations. By incorporating locally produced renewable energy sources, it promotes energy-efficient design, helps reduce particular energy consumption, advances the development of manufacturing processes, and helps create a green energy roadmap. With applications ranging from real-time control, production scheduling and planning, asset maintenance, and technology retrofitting and upgrades, DT technology offers a fundamental shift in the way sites function. The goal is to lower energy usage over a range of time periods and improve the incorporation of renewable energy.

A virtual version of a real-world item, procedure, system, or setting is known as a "digital twin". This computerized model, which was developed using data from sensors and other equipment, closely resembles its real-world counterpart, allowing for interactive application in a variety of industries.

DT technology stands apart by embodying three key attributes:

- ❖ Looks-like Attribute: Virtual modeling of the physical entity in 1D, 2D, or 3D forms.
- ❖ Behaves-like Attribute: Simulation and prediction of the entity's response to different inputs.
- ❖ Conncets-to Attribute: Real-time or automated data flows between physical and digital entities.

NASA's high-fidelity simulations from the Apollo 13 mission served as the inspiration for DT. Since then, it has developed to transform sectors like urban planning, energy management, manufacturing, and healthcare.

A DT is a digital thread that documents the progress of its physical counterpart over time, as well as a digital shadow that represents its activities and condition. DTs maximize decision-making, predictive maintenance, operational effectiveness, and product lifecycle management by utilizing AI, IoT, and advanced data technologies.

DT technology comprises three components:

- ❖ Physical Entity: The real-world object, system, or process being represented digitally.
- ❖ Virtual Representation: The digital counterpart replicating the structure, functions, and conditions of the physical entity.

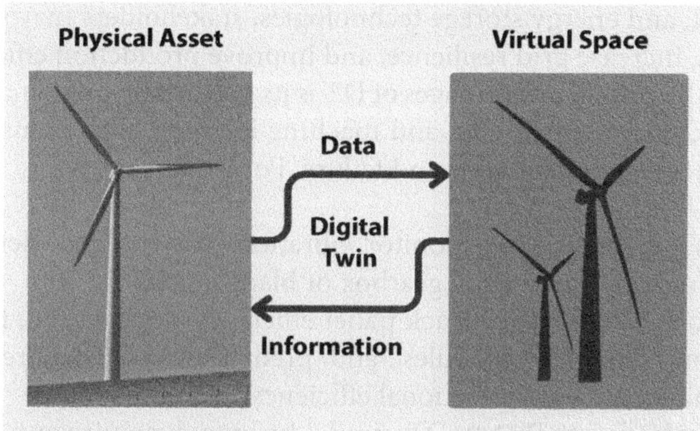

Figure 18.1 Potential of digital twins in renewable power sector.

- Data Connectivity: A bi-directional flow of real-time data that updates the digital model and provides actionable insights to the physical entity.

DTs play a key role in improving resource management and operational effectiveness in the context of renewable energy. Through sophisticated simulations and ongoing monitoring, they revolutionize industries like manufacturing, energy, and industrial operations by providing stakeholders with actionable information.

As depicted in Figure 18.1, above Digital Twin is a real-time, digital representation of a physical system, allowing engineers and researchers to simulate different scenarios, detect faults, and optimize performance. The Digital Twin concept consists of three primary components: the physical asset, the digital model, and the data exchange layer. The physical asset refers to the actual renewable energy system, such as a wind turbine, solar panel, or battery storage unit. The digital model is a virtual representation that mimics the behavior of the physical asset, helping to analyze and predict its performance. The data exchange layer connects the two spaces using IoT sensors and AI-driven analytics to process real-time data. This integration enables industries to make data-driven decisions, predict failures before they occur, and optimize the system for better efficiency and longevity.

18.1.1 Renewable Energy Generation with Digital Twin

Digital Twin (DT) technology, which provides sophisticated modeling, real-time monitoring, and optimization capabilities, is transforming the production of renewable energy. Through these applications, which include solar, wind, and energy storage technologies, stakeholders may save operating costs, increase grid resilience, and improve production efficiency.

One of the primary advantages of DT is its predictive maintenance capability, which uses sensor data and machine learning algorithms to detect early signs of equipment wear and failure. For instance:

- Wind Farms: DTs monitor vibration patterns and identify anomalies indicating gearbox or blade issues.
- Solar Farms: They track panel efficiency degradation, forecast cleaning schedules, and predict inverter failures to maintain peak operational efficiency.
- Hydropower Plants: DTs model turbine dynamics and flow rates, ensuring sustainable energy production while managing water resources.

Another important contribution of DTs is the effective management of energy storage. They aid in extending battery life, predicting system performance, and optimizing storage consumption by modeling battery charging and discharging cycles. This improves grid stability by guaranteeing stored energy is available during times of peak demand.

In the design phase, DTs enable virtual prototyping and simulations, allowing engineers to:

- Assess site configurations and evaluate energy production potential.
- Select optimal locations based on terrain characteristics and weather data.
- Simulate potential environmental impacts, aiding in regulatory compliance and strategic planning.

By leveraging real-time analytics, DTs assist in resource allocation and operational decision-making, helping operators optimize renewable energy yields and reduce inefficiencies.

18.1.2 Wind Energy

Wind energy is one of the most widely used renewable energy sources, but it faces operational challenges due to environmental conditions and mechanical wear and tear. Onshore wind turbines require continuous monitoring to prevent unexpected failures, and digital twins play a key role in predicting failures using AI-based algorithms. These models monitor fatigue life consumption, optimize maintenance strategies, and reduce repair costs. Offshore wind turbines operate in more extreme conditions, making maintenance even more challenging. Digital Twin models help by predicting the remaining useful life (RUL) of turbine components, optimizing maintenance schedules, and reducing overall repair costs by over 10%. By using digital twins, wind energy operators can increase efficiency and reduce downtime.

18.1.3 Solar Energy

Solar energy systems require precision in panel positioning and maintenance to maximize energy absorption. As shown in Figure 18.2 digital Twin technology is used in solar panel manufacturing to improve production quality and predict potential failures based on real-time weather and performance data. AI-powered digital twins help optimize solar panel angles to ensure maximum sunlight absorption, leading to higher efficiency and reduced maintenance costs. By integrating IoT sensors, digital twins

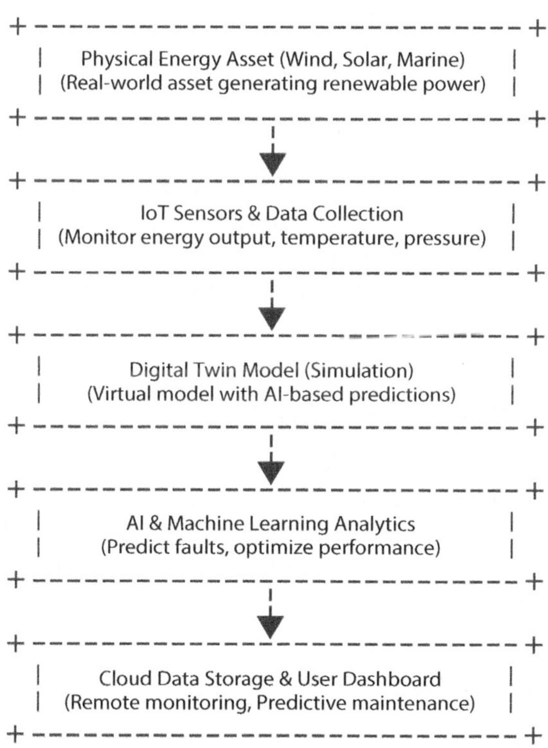

Figure 18.2 Diagram representation of digital twin in renewable energy systems.

continuously monitor panel conditions and send alerts when performance drops due to dirt accumulation, shading, or technical faults. This real-time monitoring ensures that solar farms operate at peak efficiency with minimal human intervention.

18.1.4 Marine Renewable Energy (MRE)

Marine energy, including wave and tidal power, has enormous potential but is still in the early stages of development. These systems operate in harsh ocean environments, making real-time monitoring essential. Digital twins help by tracking the performance of Wave Energy Converters (WECs) and analyzing wave patterns to optimize energy generation. AI-driven fault detection systems compare real-time data with expected performance values to identify anomalies and predict failures. This capability helps operators minimize maintenance costs and improve the reliability of marine renewable energy systems.

18.2 Digital Twin in Energy Transmission and Transformation

18.2.1 Power Transformers

Power transformers play a vital role in renewable energy transmission, but failures can lead to costly power outages. Digital Twin models simulate transformer operations, analyze real-time sensor data, and predict failures before they occur. This proactive approach helps reduce downtime, improve grid reliability, and extend the lifespan of transformers.

18.2.2 Gas-Insulated Switchgear (GIS)

Gas-insulated switchgear is widely used in high-voltage energy transmission systems. Digital twins enable real-time remote monitoring, allowing operators to detect potential failures early. AI-driven predictive maintenance models analyze operating conditions and recommend preventive actions, reducing the risk of system failures.

18.2.3 Power Cables

Power cables are critical for electricity transmission, and their failure can disrupt energy distribution. Digital Twin models track the condition of power cables using AI-driven analysis of thermal imaging, sensor data, and electrical signals. These models help detect insulation degradation, clamp defects, and overheating issues before they cause significant damage. By integrating Digital Twin technology, power companies can enhance the reliability and safety of their cable networks.

18.3 Digital Twin in Renewable Energy Storage Systems

18.3.1 Lithium-Ion Batteries (LIBs)

Lithium-ion batteries are widely used for storing renewable energy, but they degrade over time, reducing their efficiency. Digital twins track battery degradation, optimize charge-discharge cycles, and predict performance issues before they occur. This real-time monitoring helps extend battery life and improve the reliability of energy storage systems. AI-driven models analyze sensor data to ensure batteries operate within safe parameters, reducing the risk of overheating and failure.

18.3.2 Fuel Cells (PEMFC & SOFC)

Fuel cells are used in electric vehicles and power grids, and their efficiency depends on stable operating conditions. Digital Twin models enhance fuel cell performance by monitoring key parameters, predicting maintenance needs, and optimizing energy output. In proton exchange membrane fuel cells (PEMFCs), digital twins use AI-driven models to diagnose faults and improve overall efficiency. Similarly, in solid oxide fuel cells (SOFCs), digital twins provide real-time insights into operational conditions, helping operators make informed decisions to improve performance.

18.4 Advantages and Challenges of Digital Twin Technology

18.4.1 Advantages

Digital Twin technology offers several benefits to the renewable energy sector. It enables real-time monitoring, allowing operators to detect performance issues before they escalate. Predictive maintenance helps prevent unexpected failures, reducing maintenance costs and improving reliability. Digital twins also optimize energy systems, increasing efficiency and reducing operational expenses. Additionally, they enable remote monitoring, reducing the need for manual inspections and improving worker safety.

18.4.2 Challenges

Despite its advantages, Digital Twin technology faces some challenges. Processing vast amounts of sensor data requires high computational power, making it expensive for some organizations. Cybersecurity risks also pose a threat, as Digital Twin systems rely on cloud-based data sharing. Additionally, the lack of a standardized framework for Digital Twin implementation makes integration difficult across different industries. Addressing these challenges will be crucial for the widespread adoption of Digital Twin technology in renewable energy systems.

AI disclosure statement: The author confirms that no artificial intelligence (AI)-generated content or AI-assisted writing tools were used in the preparation of this chapter (including summaries and the abstract). All text, analysis, and conclusions are the result of the author's original work.

Bibliography

1. Lee, C.-H., Thanh, P.N., Yeh, C.-T., Cho, M.-Y., Three-Phase Load Prediction-Based Hybrid Convolution Neural Network Combined Bidirectional Long Short-Term Memory in Solar Power Plant. *Int. Trans. Electr. Energy Syst.*, 2022, Article ID 2870668, 15, 2022, https://doi.org/10.1155/2022/2870668.
2. Wu, L., Kong, C., Hao, X., Chen, W., A Short-Term Load Forecasting Method Based on GRU-CNN Hybrid Neural Network Model. *Math. Probl. Eng.*, 2020, Article ID 1428104, 10, 2020, https://doi.org/10.1155/2020/1428104.
3. de Freitas Viscondi, G. and Alves-Souza, S.N., A Systematic Literature Review on big data for solar photovoltaic electricity generation forecasting. *Sustainable Energy Technol. Assess.*, 31, 54–63, 2019. ISSN 2213-1388,https://doi.org/10.1016/j.seta.2018.11.008.
4. Ozbek, A., Yildirim, A., Bilgili, M., Deep learning approach for one-hour ahead forecasting of energy production in a solar-PV plant. *Energy Sources Part A*, 44, 4, 10465–10480, 2022. DOI: 10.1080/15567036.2021.1924316.
5. Prasad, S.S., Deo, R.C., Downs, N., Igoe, D., Parisi, A.V., Soar, J., Cloud Affected Solar UV Prediction with Three-Phase Wavelet Hybrid Convolutional Long Short-Term Memory Network Multi-Step Forecast System. *IEEE Access*, 10, 24704–24720, 2022, doi: 10.1109/ACCESS.2022.3153475.

6. Kalaiselvi, B., Karthik, B., Kumaravel, A., Variant Mode Data Analytics in Predicting the Radiation Effect on Solar Power Generation using Machine Learning Algorithms. *2022 IEEE International Conference on Data Science and Information System (ICDSIS)*, Hassan, India, pp. 1–6, 2022, doi: 10.1109/ICDSIS55133.2022.9915814.
7. Tang, L., Weiqi, H., Ashtine, M., Wallom, D., Distributed Photovoltaic System Capacity Estimation Using Feeder Load Data Based on Deep Learning. Available at SSRN: https://ssrn.com/abstract=4442265 or http://dx.doi.org/10.2139 /ssrn. 4442265.
8. Ciabattoni, L., Grisostomi, M., Ippoliti, G., Longhi, S., Fuzzy logic home energy consumption modeling for residential photovoltaic plant sizing in the new Italianscenario. *Energy*, 74, 359–367, 2014. ISSN0360-442 https://doi.org/10.1016/ j.energy.2014.06.100.
9. Ghimire, S., Nguyen-Huy, T., Prasad, R., *et al.*, Hybrid Convolutional Neural Network-Multilayer Perceptron Model for Solar Radiation Prediction. *Cognit. Comput.*, 15, 645–671, 2023, https://doi.org/10.1007/s12559-022-10070-y.
10. Pazikadin, A.R., Rifai, D., Ali, K., Zeesan Malik, M., Abdalla, A.N., Faraj, M.A., Solar irradiance measurement instrumentation and power solar generation forecasting based on Artificial Neural Networks (ANN): A review of five years research trend. *Sci. Total Environ.*, 715, 136848, 2020. ISSN:0048-9697,https://doi.org/10.1016/ j.scitotenv.2020.136848.
11. Das, S., Mandal, A., Saha, S., Soiling detection of solar panels using a transfer learning approach. *J. Renewable Energy*, 183, 1388–1397, 2023, doi: 10.1016/j.renene.2023.01.117.
12. Yadav, A., Singh, S., Kumar, P., A hybrid approach for soiling classification on solar PV panels in India. *J. Cleaner Prod.*, 348, 129827, 2023, doi: 10.1016/j.jclepro.2023.129827.
13. Mishra, A.K., Mishra, R.K., Mishra, S.K., A machine learning approach for soiling detection in solar photovoltaic systems. *Sol. Energy*, 211, 122251, 2023.
14. Singh, S., Srivastava, S., Kumar, P., A deep learning approach for soiling classification on solar PV panels in India. *Renewable Energy*, 186, 1425–1434, 2023, doi: 10.1016/j.renene.2023.02.059.
15. Zhang, W., Liu, S., Srinivasan, G., A deep learning-based probabilistic estimation of solar PV soiling loss. *Prog. Photovoltaics Res. Appl.*, 1–7, 2023.
16. Chen, Y., Zhang, C., Zhang, Y., A transformer-based approach for solar photovoltaic panel soiling classification. *Appl. Energy*, 267, 115287, 2022.
17. Li, Q., Zhang, C., Zhang, Y., A convolutional neural network with transfer learning for solar photovoltaic panel soiling classification. *Sol. Energy*, 228, 1308–1319, 2022.
18. Zhang, Y., Zhang, C., Li, J., A deep learning approach for solar photovoltaic panel soiling detection based on multi-scale features. *IEEE Access*, 10, 168289–168300, 2022.

19. Kim, J., Kim, H., Lee, S., Soiling classification of solar panel using deep learning. *Energy Rep.*, 7, 1015–1022, 2022, doi: 10.1016/j.egyr.2021.101510.
20. Mishra, A.K., Mishra, R.K., Mishra, S.K., A machine learning approach for soiling prediction in solar photovoltaic systems. *Sol. Energy*, 210, 122241, 2022.
21. Al-Ghamdi, N.M., Abdelfattah, A.M.A., Abdelkareem, M.A.M., A novel soiling mitigation technique using nanoparticles for solar photovoltaic systems in desert regions. *Sol. Energy Mater. Sol. Cells*, 230, 111297, 2022.
22. Liu, Y., Wang, W., Zhang, Y., Zhang, C., A convolutional neural network with attention mechanism for solar photovoltaic panel soiling classification. *IEEE Access*, 10, 154441–154450, 2022.
23. Yang, Y., Zhang, C., Zhang, Y., A generative adversarial network approach for solar photovoltaic panel soiling detection. *Appl. Energy*, 278, 115484, 2022.
24. Sharma, A., Singh, R.K., Kumar, A., A review of solar PV analyser tools and techniques. *Int. J. Renewable Energy Res.*, 12, 3, 2345–2354, 2022.
25. Li, H., Zhang, Y., Wang, J., Chen, Y., A hybrid forecasting model for renewable energy based on support vector machine and recurrent neural network. *Energy*, 249, 123732, 2022.
26. Sharma, V., Chaurasia, P., Sharma, G., Performance evaluation of support vector machine for photovoltaic power generation forecasting. *Mater. Today: Proc.*, 55, 41–46, 2022.
27. Li, Y., Chen, X., Wang, J., Application of random forest regression for short-term wind speed forecasting based on empirical mode decomposition and chaotic dynamic reconstruction. *Renewable Energy*, 189, 914–926, 2022, doi: 10.1016/j.renene.2022.05.187.
28. Zhao, Y., Zhang, J., Ren, Y., Wang, W., Guo, Z., A hybrid model based on random forest and convolutional neural network for short-term solar power forecasting. *Energy Convers. Manage.*, 267, 115944, 2022, doi: 10.1016/j.enconman.2022.115944.
29. Pachauri, R.K., Imperative role of optimization techniques to reconfigure solar photovoltaic array systems to diminish shading effects. *Int. J. Circuit Theory Appl.*, 50, 1, 317–353, 2022.
30. Pachauri, R.K., Pandey, J.K., Sharmu, A., Nautiyal, O.P., Ram, M. (Eds.), *Applied Soft Computing and Embedded System Applications in Solar Energy*, CRC Press, 2021.
31. Paliyal, P.S., Mondal, S., Layek, S., Kuchhal, P., Pandey, J.K., Automatic solar tracking system: a review pertaining to advancements and challenges in the current scenario. *Clean Energy*, 8, 6, 237–262, December 2024, https://doi.org/10.1093/ce/zkae085.
32. Paliyal, P.S., Mondal, S., Pandey, J.K., An Analysis of Springwater Parameter Status for Different Locations in the Rural Hilly Garhwal Region of Uttarakhand. *Environ. Claims J.*, *36*, 3, 243–277, 2024, https://doi.org/10.1080/10406026.2024.2423964.

33. Paliyal, P.S. and Mondal, S., An analysis of a cross-finned receiver for Scheffler-type solar collectors to optimize solar heating efficiency for direct water heating. *Int. J. Energy Water Resour.*, 2025, https://doi.org/10.1007/s42108-025-00393-5.
34. Paliyal, P.S., Mondal, S., Pathela, M., Kumar, A., Menon, S.K., Optimization of Solar Photovoltaic Array In-Depth Analysis of Perturb and Observe MPPT Algorithm. *2024 International Conference on Advances in Computing, Communication and Materials (ICACCM)*, Dehradun, India, pp. 1–6, 2024, doi: 10.1109/ICACCM61117.2024.11059143.
35. Paliyal, P.S., *et al.*, Location Analysis and Environmental Validation for Installation of Hybrid Solar-Wind Energy Generation System in Hilly Areas of Uttarakhand: Study Toward Forecasting, in: *Forecasting Methods for Renewable Power Generation*, pp. 21–47, 2025.
36. Menon, S.K., *et al.*, The Role of Hydrogen as a Sustainable Energy Source and its Integration with the Grid, in: *Advancements in Communication and Systems*, A.K. Tripathi and V. Shrivastava (Eds.), p. 397, Computing and Intelligent Systems, SCRS, India, 2023, (2025).
37. Kudapa, V.K., Paliyal, P.S., Mondal, A., Mondal, S., A critical review of fabrication strategies, separation techniques, challenges, and future prospects for the hydrogen separation membrane. *Fusion Sci. Technol.*, 80, 7, 803–825, 2024.
38. Mondal, A., Jangirh, R., Arya, R., Yadav, L., Ahlawat, S., Yadav, P., Paliyal, P.S., Bobde, P., Ghosh, P., Mondal, S., Rai, A., Analysing solid residential fuel usage patterns in rural and urban slums of Delhi: Implications for pollution reduction and sustainable practices. *Energy Sustainable Dev., 80,* 101460, 2024.
39. Paliyal, P.S., Kuchhal, P., Mondal, S., Nano Lubricants and their Applications, in: *Nanotechnology: A Quick Guide to Materials and Technologies*, pp. 425–456, Bentham Science Publishers, 2024.

19

Solar Concentrators: Decarbonizing Our Future, Securing Our Energy

Surya Prakash Chauhan[1]*, Sachin Sharma[2] and Rajesh Maithani[1]

[1]*Department of Mechanical Engineering, School of Advanced Engineering, UPES, Dehradun, Uttarakhand, India*
[2]*Mechanical Cluster, School of Advanced Engineering and Centre Head-BEST, UPES Dehradun, Uttarakhand, India*

Abstract

Climate change driven by anthropogenic greenhouse gas emissions has intensified the global urgency to transition toward low-carbon and sustainable energy systems. Concentrating solar power (CSP) technologies, including parabolic troughs, linear Fresnel reflectors, dishes, and heliostat-based central receiver systems, have emerged as promising solutions for large-scale decarbonization due to their ability to deliver high-temperature thermal energy with integrated long-duration storage. This work examines the role of solar concentrators in mitigating fossil-fuel dependency and reducing carbon emissions while enhancing energy security and grid reliability. Key technological advancements in molten salt thermal storage, high-temperature receivers, and supercritical CO_2 power cycles are reviewed alongside recent innovations in artificial intelligence, machine learning, and digitalization for performance optimization and predictive maintenance. The paper further analyzes major challenges hindering widespread deployment, including material degradation at elevated temperatures, water consumption, soiling losses, and high capital costs, and discusses viable cost-reduction strategies such as economies of scale, advanced storage media, and AI-driven operational optimization. Finally, future perspectives highlight the potential of next-generation CSP systems operating beyond 750°C, hybrid integration with thermochemical fuel production, and autonomous control architectures to position solar concentrators as a backbone technology in a fully decarbonized global energy system.

***Keywords*:** Solar concentrators, concentrating solar power, decarbonization, thermal energy storage, artificial intelligence

**Corresponding author*: csurya815@gmail.com

Surajit Mondal, Paramjeet Singh Paliyal and Sachin Sharma (eds.) Digital Twin Technology for Solar Concentrators, (317–328) © 2026 Scrivener Publishing LLC

19.1 Introduction

19.1.1 Overview of Climate Change

Human-driven greenhouse gas emissions-CO_2 released from coal, oil and natural gas combustion have pushed CO_2 levels above 420ppm as shown in Figure 19.1. This rapid rise has warmed the planet by roughly 1.2°C, Augmenting Extreme weather, increasing ice sheet melt and sea level rise. Energy generation accounts for 75% on the above emissions- meaningful DE carbonization. Solar concentrator technologies such as parabolic troughs, linear Fresnel reflectors, and heliostat-equipped central towers focus sunlight to produce high-temperature heat [1].

As the climate crisis intensifies and the urgency to shed fossilfuel carbon grows, power systems are steadily pivoting toward renewable energy boosting the share of hydropower, wind farms, and both photovoltaic and solarthermal technologies to create a cleaner and more sustainable energy [2].

Concentrating solar power (CSP) plants equipped with long-duration molten-salt storage are fundamentally transforming renewable energy systems by both extending storage times and enhancing delivery reliability. Central to CSP operation is the steamgeneration system (SGS), in which high-temperature molten salt transfers its thermal energy to water [3]. An optimally engineered SGS not only maximizes heattransfer efficiency but also preserves hydrodynamic stability, enabling rapid loadfollowing and precise response to fluctuations in grid demand [4].

Figure 19.1 Depicting climate change.

CSP is no longer a niche technology. Global CSP capacity grew by about 500 MW in 2025, lifting the cumulative total to roughly 8.2 GW by early 2025, a further 2plus GW of projects mostly moltensalt tower plants in China are already under construction and scheduled for completion within the next 18 months. Industry trackers therefore expect the fleet to edge past the 8 GW mark (and approach 9 GW if current timelines hold) before the end of 2026. Unlike photovoltaic (PV) modules, which turn sunlight straight into electricity, CSP plants harvest the sun's heat, store it in molten salt, and dispatch power whenever the grid needs it giving them a built-in long-duration thermal-energy-storage advantage [5].

19.1.2 Renewable Energy Transition

To keep the world Temperature near to 1.5°C trajectory, the energy transition must lean heavily on solar technologies both photovoltaic (PV) panels and concentrating solar power/thermal (CSP/CST) systems. Analysts project that annual global spending on PV will need to more than double, climbing from roughly USD 130 billion to USD 333 billion by 2050 [6]. CSP and CST require an even steeper scaleup yearly investment would have to surge from around USD 1 billion to roughly USD 89 billion over the same period. These figures underscore how pivotal large-scale solar deployment is to a climate-safe future and highlight the critical financing gap that must be closed in the coming decades [7]. By 2050 the solar energy technologies will contribute to 20% of the global energy supply in which CSP provides more than 1.3 PW h (petawatt hour), equal to 35% of the global electricity generation [8].

As the solar capacity scales up, so does the need for the raw materials to build and support these technologies. The rising demand could lead to resource shortages. Also, solar technologies aren't free from environmental impact. To analyze these approaches LCA (life cycle assessment is essential) [9].

19.2 Solar Concentrators

Solar concentrator system is built from mirrors(reflective) or lenses(refractive) that intercept sunlight over a large "aperture" area A_{ap} and redirect it onto smaller receiver area A_{rec}. The resulting concentration ratio $C = A_{ap} / A_{rec}$ amplifies the solar flux by tens to thousands of "Suns" enabling high temperature thermal cycles or the use of impact high efficiency photovoltaic cells.

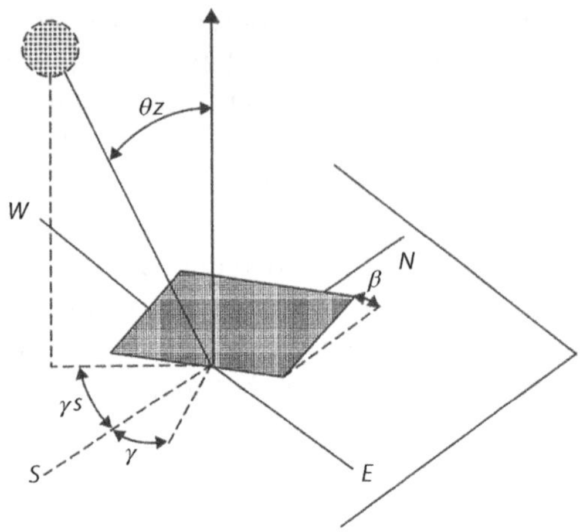

Figure 19.2 Radiation angles [10].

Solar concentrators are of different types such as heliostats, parabolic troughs, dishes or Fresnel lenses, that track the sun and focus a broad aperture o sunlight onto a much smaller receiver shown in Figure 19.2, this concentration multiplies the incident irradiance, heating a transfer fluid (oil, molten salt, steam or air) whose thermal energy then be used to drive a turbine generator set, power a Stirling or Brayton engine, with same optics equally adaptable to photovoltaic receivers in concentrator PV designs.

19.3 Role in Decarbonization

19.3.1 Fossil Fuel Dependency

As the climate crisis intensifies, we need energy options that do not rely on burning fossil fuels. Figure 19.3 depicts the clean energy transition converting sunlight into energy-dense "solar fuels" is especially attractive because, these fuels could move through much of the storage, transport, and end-use infrastructure for conventional fuels. Solar-fuel pathways are still in their infancy so current conversion efficiencies remain low, systems are difficult to scale beyond lab and pilot setups, and durability and cost hurdles persist (Figure 19.4 shows the artificial photosynthesis pathway, including water splitting and CO_2 hydrogenation). By contrast, concentrated solar energy (CSE) which captures and focuses sunlight to generate very high temperatures has progressed considerably in recent years, maturing in step with the rapid global build-out of large solar-thermal power plants and offering a technology platform that could ultimately help enable scalable solar fuel production [11].

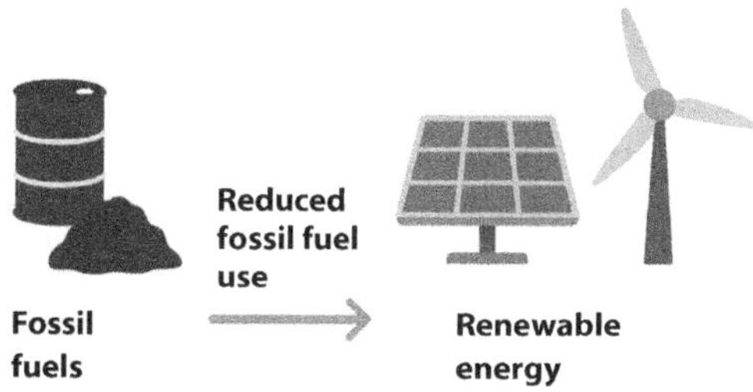

Figure 19.3 Clean energy transition.

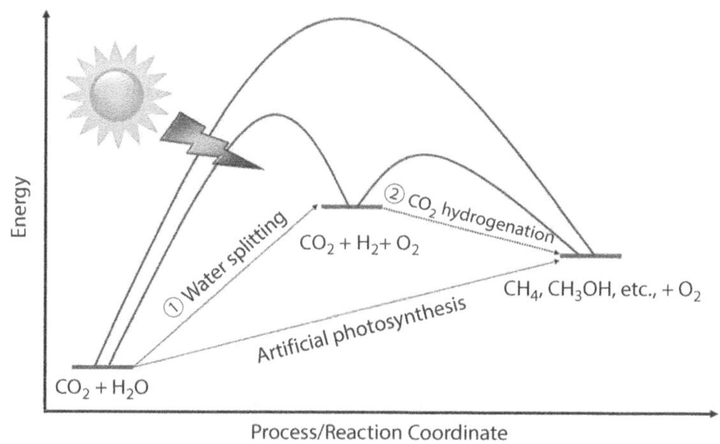

Figure 19.4 Artificial photosynthesis [12].

19.3.2 Impact on Carbon Emission

In recent years there has been a significant rise in the combustion of fuels leading to substantial emission of greenhouse gases, preferably CO_2. Apart from adverse impacts of these emissions on human health, they are main contributors to global warming [13]. Because coal, oil, and natural gas are ultimately exhaustible, finding dependable substitutes has become an urgent research priority. Today, renewable energy such as wind, geothermal, and solar still provides only a sliver of global energy, while fossil fuels continue to supply roughly four-fifths of our needs. To bridge this gap, scientists have spotlighted **chemicallooping combustion** as a promising avenue, an advanced process that yields useful heat while inherently separating CO_2, laying the groundwork for lower-carbon energy generation at scale [14].

19.3.3 Environmental and Economic Benefits

As a part of the energy transition and efforts to develop green ports, green hydrogen emerges as a promising and environmentally sound solution for achieving carbon neutrality. Cutting the carbon footprint of power generation and heavy industry demands a suite of cleanenergy technologies, and concentrating solar power (CSP) has emerged as a particularly compelling option. Unlike conventional photovoltaics, CSP couples its sunlightharvesting mirrors with low-cost thermal energy storage, letting plants bank heat for hours or even days and dispatch electricity whenever the grid needs it. This built-in storage, along with CSP's minimal greenhousegas emissions, positions the technology as a powerful tool for tackling global warming while keeping energy delivery both reliable and economical [15].

Concentrating solar power plants rely on specially blended moltensalt mixtures as both heattransfer fluids and thermalstorage media [16]. These salts soak up the Sun's heat, hold it with minimal loss, and later release it to run a steam or gas turbine cycle that generates electricity. In today's commercial setups parabolictrough (Generation-1) and tower (Generation-2) plants – nitrate formulations such as Solar Salt and Hitec XL work well at mid-range temperatures of roughly 400–550°C [17]. To squeeze costs down even further, the next wave of CSP (Generation-3) is being engineered to operate near 750°C, hot enough to feed a supercritical CO_2 Brayton cycle whose turbine inlet needs about 650°C or more [18].

19.4 Advancements and Innovations

19.4.1 Research and Development

Deep decarbonization is currently being accelerated by cutting-edge research in solar concentrators, which combine high-flux optics with solar-powered chemical reactions and next-generation thermal systems. Scientists are creating two-step thermochemical cycles that capture concentrated sunlight and split H_2O and CO_2 into green hydrogen, syngas, and liquid fuels producing carbon-neutral hydrocarbons without the use of fossil fuels by using metal-oxide redox pairings (such as ZnO/CeO_2, Fe_2O_3/Fe_3O_4, and SiO_2-based formulations). In order to increase solar-to-hydrogen efficiencies while utilizing inexpensive materials, luminescent solar concentrators (LSCs) combine carbon-dot and plasmonic nanostructures to direct broad-spectrum light into miniature electrolysis reactors [19].

Adopting advanced technical solutions to optimize energy management and curb exhaust emissions offers a powerful pathway to greener port operations. By examining both on-dock infrastructure and the interactions between vessels and shore facilities, the study highlights how integrating energy storage technologies and deploying intelligent port microgrids can unlock the flexible use of diverse power sources. Such systems not only streamline the supply and demand of electricity across the terminal but also dramatically cut greenhousegas outputs by shifting ships and equipment to cleaner, stored energy when docked [20].

19.4.2 AI and Machine Learning for Efficiency Optimization

The past few years have seen a surge in the adoption of blockchain and cloud-based platforms within port operations and supply chains. By providing secure, real-time data sharing and scalable computing resources, these technologies streamline communication, accelerate key workflows, and offer end-to-end visibility into every stage of port activity [21]. By giving data-driven control, calibration, and maintenance procedures that surpass conventional methods, artificial intelligence (AI) and machine learning (ML) are revolutionizing solar concentrator systems. Through adaptive control and model-predictive strategies, ML-based field-control algorithms learn and compensate for wind disturbances, thermal distortions, and mechanical misalignments, increasing overall solar-field efficiency by 2–10% and reducing tracking error by 10–50% [22].

In order to infer sub-millimeter surface deformations from a small number of calibration images, differentiable ray-tracing techniques combine physical optics models with gradient-based machine learning. This results in *in-situ* heliostat metrology that is as accurate as, if not more so than, stripe-pattern reflectometry [23]. Predictive maintenance systems driven by machine learning (AI) use historical operating data to forecast failures and schedule repairs, increasing component lifespans and reducing maintenance costs and downtime by roughly 10% to 20% [24].

Traditional controllers are unable to maximize the energy output of solar systems, artificial intelligence (AI) is essential for enhancing the energy generation of PV systems under a variety of climatic conditions [25]. These machine learning operations can function closer to the hardware by combining wireless networks and edge computing, which lowers latency and deployment costs and enables scalable, reliable control structures for next-generation concentrating solar power plants [24].

19.5 Challenges and Solutions

19.5.1 Technological Barriers

Some of the major technological obstacles preventing concentrated solar power (CSP) systems from reaching their full potential for decarbonization include thermal storage, material degradation at high temperatures, integrated with advanced power cycles and water use and soiling.

a. Thermal Storage Fluid Limitations
The cycle efficiency of traditional nitrate-salt mixes (such as Solar Salt and Hitec XL) is limited to 400–550°C. Higher temperatures are promised by advanced fluids (liquid metals, solid particles, and CO_2), but they also present unknown chemistry, sealing, and material compatibility issues [26].

b. Materials Degradation at Elevated Temperatures
The piping and receivers must be able to tolerate extreme heat cycling in molten salts or new heat-transfer fluids in order to increase thermodynamic efficiency (e.g., aiming for ≥750°C for Gen3 systems). Long-term dependability is compromised by creep, corrosion, and coating delamination in high-temperature alloys and selective coatings.

c. Integration with Advanced Power Cycles
Combining CSP with newer cycles (such as thermochemical fuel production and supercritical CO_2 Brayton) calls for customized reactor designs, heat exchangers, and turbo machinery that have not yet undergone long-duration field testing [26].

d. Water Use and Soiling
While dust accumulation on heliostats reduces optical performance by as much as 5–10% in between cleaning cycles, steam turbine mirror cleaning and cooling need a significant amount of water, which is frequently rare in ideal CSP sites [27].

19.5.2 Cost Reduction Strategies

a. Economies of Scale and Mass – Manufacturing
Steep learning curve effects allow for the scaling up of heliostat and receiver production: component costs per unit can be lowered by 20–30% for every doubling of cumulative capacity. By standardizing pipework, towers, and mirror modules into factory-built "plug-and-play" components, CAPEX and on-site installation time are further decreased.

b. Advanced Receiver and Storage Materials
Low-cost solid media (e.g., ARPA-E-funded demonstration of sand-based thermal storage) and next-generation receivers (e.g., the recent star-shaped tower receiver that reduces heat-receiver surface area while extending lifetime) promise to reduce material and maintenance costs by up to 15–25% compared to molten-nitrate systems.

c. Higher Temperature Operation
Raising operating temperatures from 550°C to 750°C boosts thermodynamic efficiency, shrinking the size (and cost) of both the solar field and thermalstorage tanks required per megawatt of output. NREL projects that such innovations could drive down CSP CAPEX from $7 900/kWh in 2022 to $5 200/kWh by 2030 a 35% reduction.

d. Digitalization and Predictive Maintenance
Real-time mirror alignment optimization, up to 5% optical loss reduction, and component deterioration detection prior to failures are all possible with AI-driven control and monitoring systems. In trial applications, these platforms have lowered maintenance costs by about 10% while reducing downtime and increasing annual capacity factors.

19.6 Conclusion and Future Perspective

In addition to producing low-carbon electricity, concentrating solar power has developed into a flexible clean energy technology that can also efficiently store thermal energy to mitigate the fluctuations in sunshine. Utilizing high-precision optics, dependable molten salt systems, and increasingly complex control algorithms, modern CSP plants are able to produce dispatchable, 24/7 output with low greenhouse gas emissions. Furthermore, the gap between solar photovoltaics and battery storage is closing as a result of material advancements, higher-temperature cycles, and hybridization arrangements. Combining CSP with new chemical-fuel and supercritical CO_2 power-cycle paths could decarbonize power grids and difficult-to-abate industrial heat sectors.

Future Perspective
Looking forward, the next wave of CSP will depend on a few big breakthroughs. First, we need corrosion-resistant alloys and new heattransfer fluids that can run reliably above 750°C pushing efficiency higher while shrinking plant size and cost. Second, rolling out AI-driven predictive

maintenance and real-time field control across entire solar fields can squeeze more energy from every ray and cut operating expenses. Third, pairing CSP with thermochemical fuel production or supercritical CO_2 Brayton cycles could deliver carbon-neutral fuels and ultra-compact power blocks but these hybrids still need full-scale demos to prove they work in the real world. Finally, modular, standardized designs and faster permitting will speed deployment, especially in sun-rich regions where CSPs builtin storage can anchor resilient, low-carbon grids. If these pieces come together, CSP can move from a niche option to a backbone technology in a fully decarbonized energy system.

AI disclosure statement: The author acknowledges the use of AI-based tools for minor language editing or grammatical correction. However, all intellectual contributions, analyses, and conclusions presented in this chapter are entirely the author's own.

References

1. Teixeira, B., Brito, M.C., Mateus, A., Raw materials for the Portuguese decarbonization roadmap: The case of solar photovoltaics and wind energy. *Resour. Policy*, 90, Mar. 2024, doi: 10.1016/j.resourpol.2024.104839.
2. Rangel, R., Arango-Manrique, A., Corredor, L., Sanjuan, M., Assessment of Colombian renewable energy auctions policy: Enabler or barrier for concentrating solar power plants. *Energy Policy*, 193, Oct. 2024, doi: 10.1016/j.enpol.2024.114300.
3. Barata, J., *et al.*, Experimental and theoretical study of luminescent solar concentrators based on vertically stacked arrays of optical fibers. *Sol. Energy Mater. Sol. Cells*, 292, Oct. 2025, doi: 10.1016/j.solmat.2025.113719.
4. Tian, J., Ren, B., Duan, Y., Li, B., Wang, Y., Thermal and hydraulic performance of molten salt steam generation system under varying operating conditions in concentrating solar power plants. *Case Stud. Therm. Eng.*, 72, Aug. 2025, doi: 10.1016/j.csite.2025.106340.
5. Lahlou, R., *et al.*, Pushing the envelope: Advanced 3D secondary concentrators for high-temperature solar power. *Renew. Sustain. Energy Rev.*, Oct. 01, 2025, Elsevier Ltd. doi: 10.1016/j.rser.2025.115941.
6. Soliman, M.S., Yassen, Y.E.S., El-Nahhas, K., Elminshawy, N.A.S., Performance investigation of solar still utilizing affordable thermal storage material and parabolic trough concentrator: An experimental investigation. *Process Saf. Environ. Prot.*, 201, Sep. 2025, doi: 10.1016/j.psep.2025.107473.

7. Cellura, M., Luu, L.Q., Guarino, F., Longo, S., A review on life cycle assessment of concentrating solar energy technologies. *Renewable Energy*, Aug. 15, 2025, Elsevier Ltd. doi: 10.1016/j.renene.2025.123203.
8. I. Energy Agency, Net Zero by 2050 - A Roadmap for the Global Energy Sector, 2050, [Online]. Available: www.iea.org/t&c/.
9. Araya, R., Bustos, F., Contreras, J., Fuentes, A., Life-cycle savings for a flat-plate solar water collector plant in Chile. *Renewable Energy*, 112, 365–377, 2017, doi: 10.1016/j.renene.2017.05.036.
10. Kumar Singh, A., Kumar, R., Chaturvedi, D.K., Naseerudin, I., Assessment of Self-Reliant Electric Vehicle Charging System Variables, in: *2024 International Conference on Advances in Computing, Communication and Materials (ICACCM)*, Nov. 2024, IEEE, pp. 1–6, doi: 10.1109/ICACCM61117.2024.11059046.
11. Fu, Y., Wang, Y., Huang, J., Lu, K., Liu, M., Solar fuel production through concentrating light irradiation. *Green Energy Environ.*, Oct. 01, 2024, KeAi Publishing Communications Ltd. doi: 10.1016/j.gee.2024.01.001.
12. Lin, H., Luo, S., Zhang, H., Ye, J., Toward solar-driven carbon recycling. *Joule*, Feb. 16, 2022, Cell Press. doi: 10.1016/j.joule.2022.01.001.
13. Saeedan, M. and Houshfar, E., Solar-driven chemical looping combustion: A pathway to low-impact carbon emission and sustainable hydrogen generation for a decarbonized energy sector. *Fuel Process. Technol.*, 273, Aug. 2025, doi: 10.1016/j.fuproc.2025.108230.
14. Tihanyi, L. and Szunyog, I., CO_2 emission trends in hungary, 2013.
15. Nithyanandam, K., Kant, K., Kondaiah, P., Pitchumani, R., Technoeconomics of a molten salt/supercritical carbon dioxide heat exchanger with fractal-textured corrosion resistant coatings for concentrating solar thermal systems. *Energy Convers. Manage.*, 341, Oct. 2025, doi: 10.1016/j.enconman.2025.120028.
16. Wang, Y., *et al.*, Radionuclide tracing based *in situ* corrosion and mass transport monitoring of 316L stainless steel in a molten salt closed loop. *Nat. Commun.*, 15, 1, Dec. 2024, doi: 10.1038/s41467-024-47259-8.
17. Boretti, A. and Castelletto, S., Techno-economic performances of future concentrating solar power plants in Australia. *Humanit. Soc. Sci. Commun.*, 8, 1, Dec. 2021, doi: 10.1057/s41599-021-01005-3.
18. Lee, W., Yoo, S., Park, D.K., Lee, K.Y., Design considerations of the supercritical carbon dioxide Brayton cycle of small modular molten salt reactor for ship propulsion. *Prog. Nucl. Energy*, 163, Sep. 2023, doi: 10.1016/j.pnucene.2023.104835.
19. Mandal, T., Mishra, S.R., Kumar, M., Singh, V., Emergence of carbon dots as luminescent solar concentrators for building integrated photovoltaics. *Sustainable Energy Fuels*, 8, 24, 5638–5671, 2024, doi: 10.1039/D4SE00806E.

20. Raihan, A., *et al.*, Nexus between carbon emissions, economic growth, renewable energy use, urbanization, industrialization, technological innovation, and forest area towards achieving environmental sustainability in Bangladesh. *Energy Clim. Change*, 3, Dec. 2022, doi: 10.1016/j.egycc.2022.100080.
21. Gerrero-Molina, M.-I., Vásquez-Suárez, Y.-A., Valdés-Mosquera, D.-M., Smart, Green, and Sustainable: Unveiling Technological Trajectories in Maritime Port Operations. *IEEE Access*, 12, 47713–47723, 2024, doi: 10.1109/ACCESS.2024.3376431.
22. Jimenez, V.J., Kim, H., Munim, Z.H., A review of ship energy efficiency research and directions towards emission reduction in the maritime industry. *J. Cleaner Prod.*, 366, Sep. 2022, doi: 10.1016/j.jclepro.2022.132888.
23. Pargmann, M., Ebert, J., Götz, M., Maldonado Quinto, D., Pitz-Paal, R., Kesselheim, S., Automatic heliostat learning for *in situ* concentrating solar power plant metrology with differentiable ray tracing. *Nat. Commun.*, 15, 1, Dec. 2024, doi: 10.1038/s41467-024-51019-z.
24. Liu, Q., Dai, Z., Wei, Y., Wang, D., Xie, Y., Transformative Impacts of AI and Wireless Communication in CSP Heliostat Control Systems. *Energies (Basel)*, 18, 5, 1069, Feb. 2025, doi: 10.3390/en18051069.
25. Singh, A.K., *et al.*, Application of Twisting Controller and Modified Pufferfish Optimization Algorithm for Power Management in a Solar PV System with Electric-Vehicle and Load-Demand Integration. *Energies (Basel)*, 18, 14, 3785, Jul. 2025, doi: 10.3390/en18143785.
26. Shahabuddin, M., Alim, M.A., Alam, T., Mofijur, M., Ahmed, S.F., Perkins, G., A critical review on the development and challenges of concentrated solar power technologies. *Sustainable Energy Technol. Assess.*, 47, 101434, Oct. 2021, doi: 10.1016/j.seta.2021.101434.
27. Alami, A.H., *et al.*, Concentrating solar power (CSP) technologies: Status and analysis. *Int. J. Thermofluids*, 18, 100340, May 2023, doi: 10.1016/j.ijft.2023.100340.

Index

Also of Interest

Check out these other related titles from Scrivener Publishing

Solar Energy Optimization Using Generative Artificial Intelligence, Edited by Abhishek Kumar, Pramod Singh Rathore, Arun Lal Srivastav, and Ashutosh Kumar Dubey, ISBN:9781394419463. Lead the sustainable energy revolution with this guide to mastering the AI-driven algorithms and smart material innovations that are revolutionizing solar energy.

Solar Energy Concentrators, Edited by Inamuddin, ISBN: 9781394204328. Discover the latest techniques and applications for solar energy concentrators in this essential guide for academics, researchers, environmentalists, and professionals seeking to harness the power of solar energy while reducing environmental impact and costs.

Optimization in Sustainable Energy: Methods and Applications, Edited Prasenjit Chatterjee, Anita Khosla, Ashwani Kumar and Gülay Demir, ISBN: 9781394242108. This state-of-the-art book offers cutting-edge optimization techniques and practical decision making frameworks essential for enhancing the efficiency and reliability of sustainable energy systems, making it an invaluable resource for researchers, policymakers, and energy professionals.

Secure Energy Optimization: Leveraging Internet of Things and Artificial Intelligence for Enhanced Efficiency, Edited by Abhishek Kumar, Surbhi Bhatia Khan, Narayan Vyas, Vishal Dutt, and Shakila Basheer, ISBN: 9781394271818. *Secure Energy Optimization: Leveraging Internet of Things and Artificial Intelligence for Enhanced Efficiency* is essential for anyone looking to navigate the transformative landscape of energy management, as it expertly combines the principles of IoT and AI with real-world case studies to provide actionable insights for achieving sustainable and efficient energy optimization.

Materials for Solar Energy Conversion: Materials, Methods and Applications, Edited by R. Rajasekar, C. Moganapriya and A. Mohankumar, ISBN: 9781119750604. This book provides professionals and students with a resource on the basic principles and applications of solar energy materials and processes, as well as practicing engineers who want to understand how functional materials operate in solar energy conversion systems.

Thermal Battery Management System for Hybrid and Electric Vehicles, Edited by Ashwani Kumar, Mukesh Kumar Awasthi, Nitesh Dutt, Yogesh Kumar Singla, and Sivasakthivel Thangavel, ISBN: 9781394289202. *Thermal Battery Management System for Hybrid and Electric Vehicles* is essential for anyone seeking to understand the cutting-edge advancements and challenges in battery thermal management, providing valuable insights that drive innovation and improve the performance of electric and hybrid vehicles.

Solar Electric, Water and Air Tribrid Auto Engineering, Edited by Chandan Deep Singh, Kanwaljit Singh, Davinder Singh, Talwinder Singh, Er. Jasvinder Singh, and Er. Rajdeep Singh, ISBN: 9781394166169. *Solar Electric, Water and Air Tribrid Auto Engineering* is a must-have for anyone in the automotive industry, as it offers a comprehensive analysis of cutting-edge technologies that could revolutionize vehicle design and fuel efficiency, paving the way for a more sustainable future.

Digital Convergence in Intelligent Mobility Systems, Edited by Rathishchandra R. Gatti & Chandra Singh, ISBN: 9781394275243. *Digital Convergence in Intelligent Mobility Systems* gives a comprehensive understanding of how digital technologies are revolutionizing transportation, equipping you with the insights needed to navigate the future of intelligent mobility systems.

AI for Autonomous Vehicles: The Future of Driverless Technology, Edited by Sathiyaraj Rajendran, Munish Sabharwal, Yu-Chen Hu, Rajesh Kumar Dhanaraj, and Balamurugan Balusamy, ISBN: 9781119847465. This title presents the research prospects and security challenges present in the exciting new field of autonomous vehicles by comprehensively introducing advanced concepts of artificial intelligence (AI) in driverless technology.

Introduction to Automotive Engineering, By R. Sakthivel, Faisal O. Mahroogi, S. Narayan, S. Abubakar, M. U. Kaisan, and Youssef Alammari, ISBN: 9781119479802. A brief introduction to automotive engineering, this volume is a useful reference as well, covering not just the basics, but also some of the latest innovations, such as electric and self-driving vehicles.

AUTONOMOUS VEHICLES VOLUME 1: Using Machine Intelligence, Edited by Romil Rawat, A. Mary Sowjanya, Syed Imran Patel, Varshali Jaiswal, Imran Khan, and Allam Balaram. ISBN: 9781119871958. Addressing the current challenges, approaches and applications relating to autonomous vehicles, this groundbreaking new volume presents the research and techniques in this growing area, using Internet of Things, Machine Learning, Deep Learning, and Artificial Intelligence.

AUTONOMOUS VEHICLES VOLUME 2: Smart Vehicles for Communication, Edited by Romil Rawat, Purvee Bhardwaj, Upinder Kaur, Shrikant Telang, Mukesh Chouhan, and K. Sakthidasan Sankaran, ISBN: 9781394152254. The companion to *Autonomous Vehicles Volume 1: Using Machine Intelligence,* this second volume in the two-volume set covers intelligent techniques utilized for designing, controlling and managing vehicular systems based on advanced algorithms of computing like machine learning, artificial Intelligence, data analytics, and Internet of Things with prediction approaches to avoid accidental damages, security threats, and theft.

Hydrogen Electrical Vehicles, Edited by Mehmet Sankir and Nurdan Demirci Sankir, ISBN: 9781394166381. Hydrogen electrical vehicles are an essential component of the "Green New Deal" and this book covers cutting-edge technologies designed for fuel-cell-powered cars.

Smart Charging Solutions for Hybrid and Electric Vehicles, Edited by Sulabh Sachan, Sanjeevikumar Padmanaban, and Sanchari Deb, ISBN: 9781119768951. Written and edited by a team of experts in the field, this is the most comprehensive and up to date study of smart charging solutions for hybrid and electric vehicles for engineers, scientists, students, and other professionals.

Printed and bound by CPI Group (UK) Ltd, Croydon, CR0 4YY
17/09/2026
14964282-0002